The Ending of the Shahnama

Mehdi Akhavan-e Sales
(translated by Sorour Soroudi)

This broken, out of tune harp
In the hands of the pale, old harpist, tamed,
At times it seems to dream
Of being Zoroaster's beloved
In the luminous court of the sun,
Or, a joyful fairy
In the pure and bright meadows of the moonlight.
False lights it sees -
The caravan of dead flames in the lagoon -
On the sacred face of the mosque.
It sings joyfully
The memory of the times of glory, pride and innocence
The sad song of exile:

"Say, where is
The metropolis of this century of false faith
and madness?
With its nights bright like day
Its rigid, dark days, like the night at the depth
of the legend
With its dreadful, firm, and hard castles
With the miserly smiling of its gates, cold
and strange

"Say, where is
The metropolis of this century of evil faith and terror?
The crooked-faced century
Which has passed the orbit of the Moon,
But is far from the pivot of the Sun.
The bloodthirsty century,
The century of the frightening message,
In which, by the fantastic dropping of a far flying bird
They rock the four pillars of God's seven climes
They demolish utterly
They sweep completely
Every existence, every height, every lowness

"Say, where is
The metropolis of this shameless and faithless century?
In which, without any respite
Every newly grown blossom is a plaything in the
hands of the wind
Just as the aged one, who has borne its fruit,
Whose respect is the victim of denial, blasphemy,
treachery and oppression.

Where is the metropolis of such a century?
Where?
On which traceless summit?
At which side?
Tell the watchmen not to fall asleep
On the top of their sentry, alert and cautious
Not to be deceived by the magic of the stars,
By the charm of the moonlight's silver city.
On the ships of rage, with sails of blood
We are coming to the century's metropolis, to conquer,
To lay bare
The wide, nine-folded nothingland of this heedless,
dusty place
By the dreadful clashing noise of our sharp swords,
The frightening thunder of our dread drums,
The stone splitting leap of our fleet arrows
To snatch quickly
The life bottle of the demons
From the amulet in the hidden fortress
Out of the hands of their magic guards
To dash it to the earth
And if the Earth - that weary cradle of the world,
Offers the soft hand of its verdure
To hide the stone from us,
We shall gash its face deeply.
We are
The conquerors of history's fortresses of glory
The witnesses of each century's cities of splendor.
We are
The survivors of the sad innocence of the epochs.
We are
The narrators of the cheerful and sweet tales,
The stories of the clear sky,
The flowing light, the water,
The cool breeze, the earth.
The stories of the most delightful message
From the limpidity of time's luminous brook.
The stories of the dense thicket, behind it the
mountain, at its foot the river
The stories of the friend's warm hand, in the cold
nights of the city
We are
The caravan of the wine cup and the harp,
Gypsies, our harp, singers of the fables of our lives,
Intoxicated and drunken cup bearers.
Say, where is
The metropolis of the century?
We are coming to conquer
To lay bare its nothingland...."

This broken harp, sad and absurd thinker,
The singer of the lonely sanctuary of imagination,
Covered with secrets eternally,
What stories it relates to itself day and night
O, helpless, delirious one! Change the tune.
Son of Dastan will not escape the pit of the
step-brother
Died, died, he died.
Begin the story of the Son of Farrokhzad.
He whose groan seems to come from the depth
of a deep well.
Moans and weeps,
Weeps and says:
"Oh, henceforth we are
Like hunchbacked, old conquerors,
On the ships of waves, sails of froth.
Our hearts bound by the memory of the lambs
of splendor, in the fields of empty days,
Our swords rusty, worn out, and weary,
Our drums, forever silent,
Our arrows, broken winged.
We are
The conquerors of the cities gone with the wind.
We relate the forgotten stories,
In a voice too weak to come out of the chest.
Nobody will pay attention or spare a copper for
our coins
As if they are of a foreign king,
Or, a prince whose dynasty is overthrown.
At times we hope to wake up from this spellbound sleep,
Like the cave companion's sleep,
We rub our eyes and say:
There it is, the golden rare palace of the charming morn
But, deathless is Daqyanus,
Woe, woe, alas."

In the

of

DAYS

The Intersection of Past and Present in Iranian Art

FIELDS

EMPTY

Linda Komaroff

With additional contributions by Sheila R. Canby, Sheida Dayani, Hamid Keshmirshekan, Hani Khafipour, Vali Mahlouji, Shabnam Rahimi-Golkhandan, Shadi Shafiei, and Sandra Williams

Los Angeles County Museum of Art
DelMonico Books • Prestel Munich, London, New York

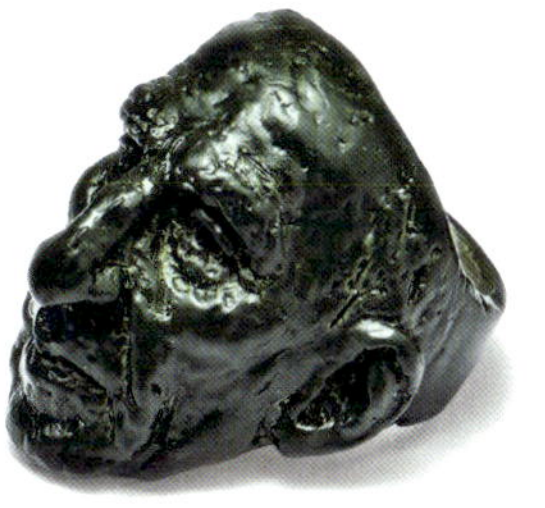

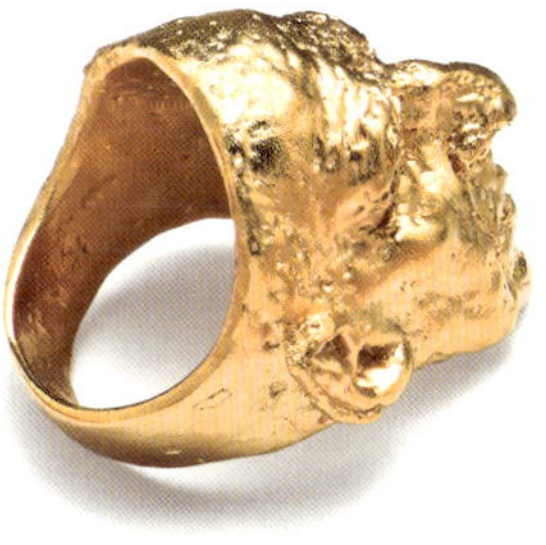

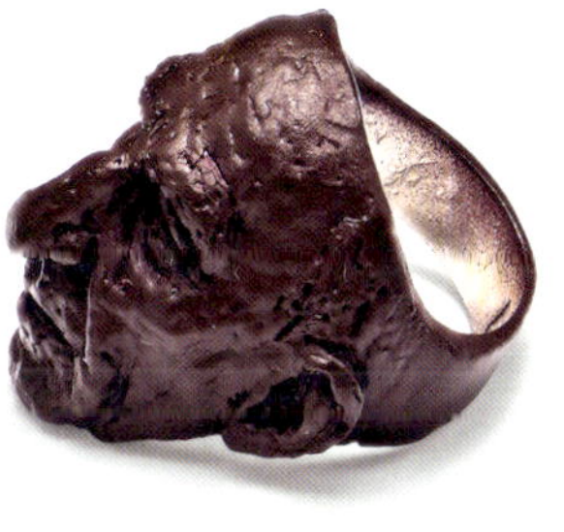

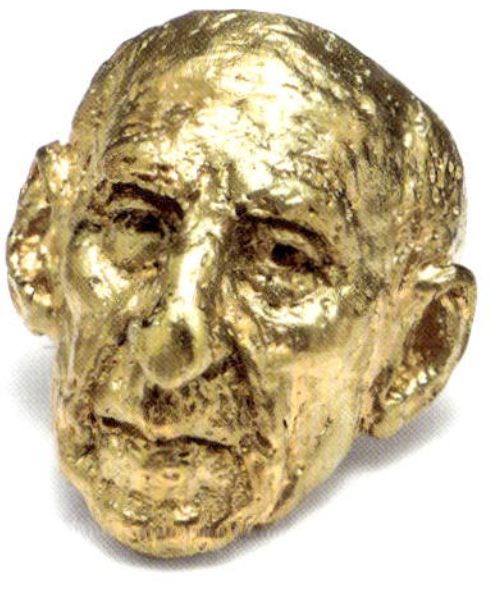

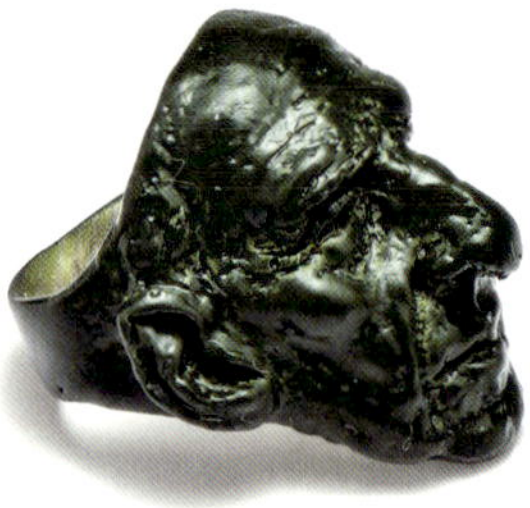

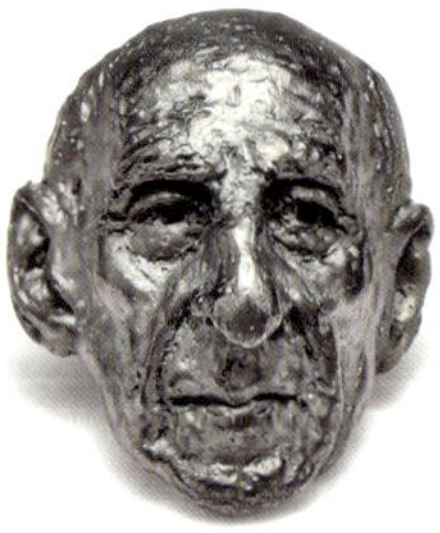

Sponsor Statement

We are proud to share in this revisioning of Iranian art and culture as seen through the paradox of time. As Nabokov said elsewhere about Proust, in the light of this study, Iranian art and culture emerge as "a treasure hunt where the treasure is time and the hiding place the past."

Houman M. Sarshar
and Sylvester Angel Cetina

Foreword

Past and present. These are the twin polarities that frame the museum. I have long thought that they should be inverted, that present ought to precede past. Exhibiting works of art as a presumably accurate reflection of what once was, for viewing by a distant audience, is often still assumed to be the true role of the museum, even though reconstructing remnants of a "real" past is scarcely possible. On the contrary, perceptions of art, like time itself, are changeable, and art, like an avowed birthdate, sometimes intentionally misleads. We wake each morning in the present and go about our daily lives, including visiting museums, in the present. So why not reposition the present ahead of the past? Ultimately, perhaps, it is our understanding of the present that will best inform us about art and artistic practice in the past.

The exhibition *In the Fields of Empty Days: The Intersection of Past and Present in Iranian Art* and its accompanying catalogue demonstrate this type of innovative approach, which seeks to move beyond the standard and often prescriptive linear narratives. The exhibition brings together historical and modern Iranian art, demonstrating that artists, present and past, meaningfully subvert the rules of time. Up until the modern era, at the instigation of their patrons, Iranian artists visualized the past in terms of the present, and by the twentieth century, as they were freed from the constraints of patronage, they began to camouflage the present in the past, as a means of social and political commentary. In keeping with the novel nature of its contents, this beautifully designed catalogue breaks new ground and brilliantly mirrors the nonlinear nature of its subject matter. It also perceptively captures the visual experience of the exhibition.

Almost half of the works in this exhibition are drawn from LACMA's own holdings, particularly our extensive collection of contemporary art of the Middle East. A little over ten years ago, I gave Linda Komaroff, the exhibition curator and LACMA's curator of Islamic art, an expanded mission: to provide a modern-day face for our historical Islamic art collection, to reveal the deep connection between present and past that is at the heart of an encyclopedic art museum. She did not disappoint. In many ways, *In the Fields of Empty Days* is the product of a decade of rethinking the parameters of her own specialized field as she built the collection. I would like to take this opportunity to thank her for her tireless efforts, and for sometimes including me in her travels in time.

This project has benefitted from the support of the National Endowment for the Arts. We are most grateful to Houman M. Sarshar and Sylvester Angel Cetina for their visionary and generous support of the catalogue. In addition, we recognize Romanov Investments Inc. for its contribution toward the catalogue.

Michael Govan

CEO AND WALLIS ANNENBERG DIRECTOR
LOS ANGELES COUNTY MUSEUM OF ART

Acknowledgments

In the Fields of Empty Days: The Intersection of Past and Present in Iranian Art is the result of several years of planning, research, and travel. An exhibition of this nature, with loans from the Middle East, Europe, and the United States, could not take place without the cooperation and generosity of numerous institutions and individuals. It is my enormous pleasure to be able to acknowledge them here.

We are deeply indebted to the lenders, who so graciously agreed to part temporarily with works from their collections for the purpose of this exhibition. I would like to gratefully acknowledge the following public and private institutions and collections, along with their directors, curators, and key administrative staff (in alphabetical order by city): Barbara Schneider-Kempf and Christoph Rauch at the Staatsbibliothek zu Berlin, Stiftung Preussischer Kulturbesitz, Berlin; collection of Azita Bina-Seibel and Elmar W. Seibel, Boston; Patti Gibbons at the University of Chicago Library; Farhad Farjam at The Farjam Foundation, Dubai; Mohammed Afkhami, Dubai, and the Mohammed Afkhami Foundation, Switzerland; Rami Farook and Nilo Pantig Jr. at The Farook Collection, Dubai; collection of Lamees Hamdan, Dubai; Joan ValaNejad, Laguna Niguel, CA; Philippe Vergne and Naomi Abe at the Museum of Contemporary Art, Los Angeles; collection of Emily and Teddy Greenspan, Los Angeles; Kimia Foundation, Los Angeles; Shulamit Nazarian, Los Angeles; collection of Houman M. Sarshar, Los Angeles; collection of Dr. Sep Sarshar, Los Angeles; collection of Babak Beheshti, Los Angeles; the Yale University Library, New Haven; Sheila R. Canby and Annick Des Roches, Department of Islamic Art, and Meredith Reiss, Department of Photographs, at the Metropolitan Museum of Art, New York; Lynn Gumpert and Michele Wong at the Grey Art Gallery, New York University; Leila Heller and Melanie Baer at Leila Heller Gallery, New York; Caroline Luce at Gladstone Gallery, New York and Brussels; Anne Pasternak and Joan Cummins at the Brooklyn Museum, New York; collection of Leila Taghinia-Milani Heller, New York; collection of Massoud

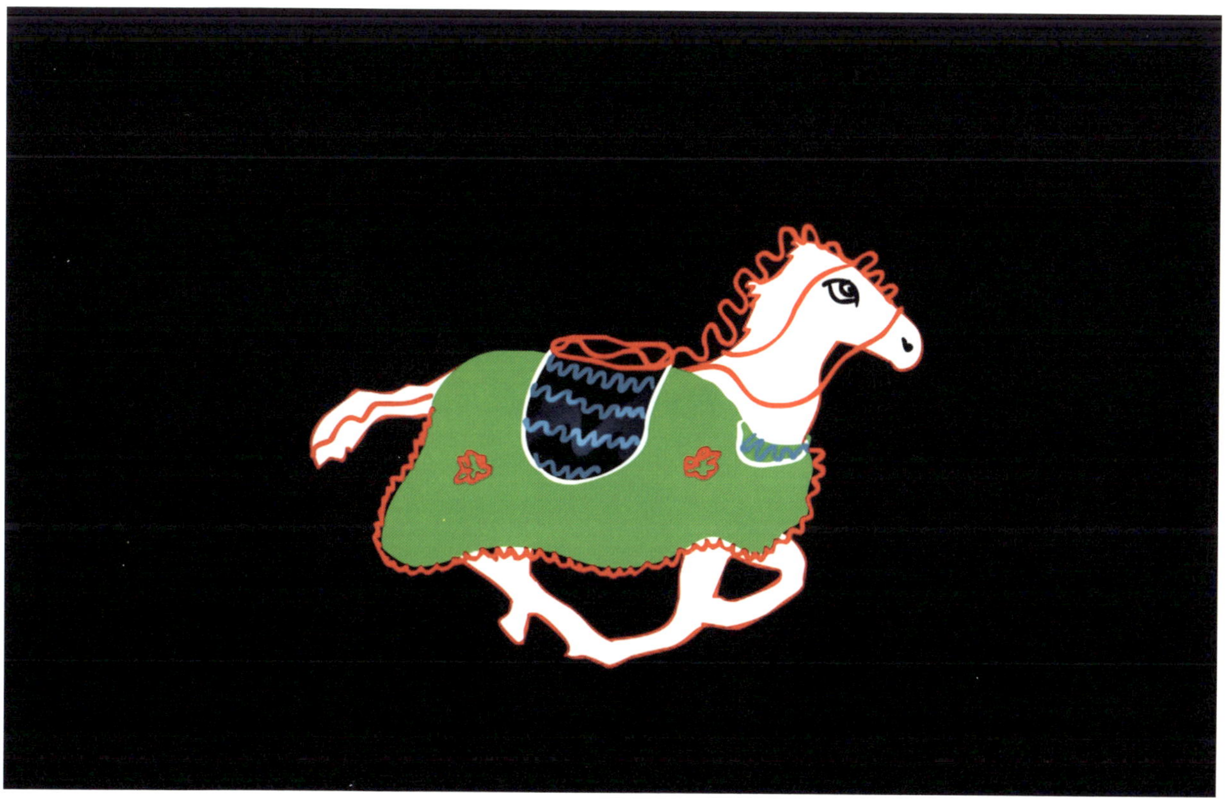

Nader, New York; collection of Bahman and Yasmin Mossavar-Rahmani, Riverside, CT; Ghassem Tirafkan at Tirafkan Cultural Foundation, Tehran; Julian Raby, Massumeh Farhad, and David Hogge at the Freer Gallery of Art and Arthur M. Sackler Gallery Archives, Smithsonian Institution, Washington, D.C.; and Carla Hayden and Rachel Waldron at the Library of Congress, Washington, D.C.

My sincere thanks to the catalogue contributors: Sheila R. Canby, Patti Cadby Birch Curator in Charge of the Department of Islamic Art, the Metropolitan Museum of Art; Sheida Dayani, preceptor in Persian, Near Eastern Languages and Civilizations, Harvard University, and PhD candidate in Middle Eastern and Islamic Studies, New York University; Hamid Keshmirshekan, associate professor at the Advanced Research Institute of Art, Iranian Academy of Arts, Tehran, and a research associate at the Middle East Institute (LMEI), SOAS University of London; Hani Khafipour, assistant professor in the Department of Middle East Studies at the University of Southern California; Vali Mahlouji, London-based curator and writer, and curatorial adviser to the British Museum on its modern and contemporary Iranian collection; Shabnam Rahimi-Golkhandan, PhD candidate in History of Art at Yale University; and in Art of the Middle East at LACMA, Assistant Curator Sandra Williams and Hagop Kevorkian Curatorial Fellow Shadi Shafiei. I am grateful to all of the authors, not only for their important contributions to the catalogue, but also for the generosity of their time and their good-natured collegiality. Special thanks to Fereydoun Ave, Shoja Azari, Siamak Filizadeh, Khosrow Hassanzadeh, Shirin Neshat, Nicky Nodjoumi, Yasmin Sinai, Parviz Tanavoli, and Newsha Tavakolian for their thoughtful artist's statements. I am also indebted to Wheeler Thackston for his sage advice, often at the drop of a hat, about transliterations and translations from Persian.

At LACMA, I am most grateful to CEO and Wallis Annenberg Director Michael Govan for his support of *In the Fields of Empty Days*, as well as for numerous conversations about nonlinear art history. I am indebted to the many colleagues whose efforts have borne fruit in the exhibition and its catalogue. I would like to express my gratitude to Deputy Director for Exhibitions and Planning Zoe Kahr for her unstinting support of the exhibition; to Carolyn Lifsey, for her assistance with exhibition planning; and, especially, to Victoria Behner, for her terrific exhibition design and unflagging good humor. In Art of the Middle East, I am pleased to recognize the hard work and commitment of Sandra Williams and Shadi Shafiei, as well as curatorial administrator Stephanie Rouinfar, UCLA Mellon Fellow Laura Horan, and intern Terri Morris. In the Conservation Center, I am grateful to Janice Schopfer, Soko Furuhata, Erin Jue, Margot Healey, Adriana Breisch, and Mellon Fellow Amanda Burr in Paper Conservation; John Hirx, Silviu Boariu, Elizabeth Homberger, and Abigail Duckor in Objects Conservation; Catherine McLean, Susan Schmalz, and Mellon Fellow Bermet Nishanova in Textile Conservation; and Virginia Rasmussen in Painting Conservation. Dale Daniel, David Armendariz, and Holly Rittenhouse skillfully handled framing and mount-making. Thanks to Errin Copple, Megan Smith, Jayne Manuel, and Katie Leavens in Registration and Collections. Special thanks to Patrick Heilman in Gallery Media. In Graphic Design I would like to acknowledge Katherine Go, Michael Pourmohsen, and David Karwan; in Communications, Miranda Carroll and Erin Yokomizo; in Insurance and Risk Management, Delfin Magpantay and Maia November. Alexis Curry, Tracy Kerr, Douglas Cordell, and Kristi Yuzuki provided valuable assistance in the research library, and I am grateful to Tomas Garcia, Sheida Koufigar, Nandi Dill Jordan, and Agnes Stauber in Web and Digital Media. In Development, my gratitude goes to Olympia Ammon, Katie Kennedy, Kris Lewis, and Caroline Maddox.

Peter Brenner, Jonathan Urban, Steve Oliver, and Laura Cherry in Photographic Services at LACMA are responsible for many of the beautiful images in this book. Special appreciation goes to Publisher Lisa Gabrielle Mark, who oversaw catalogue development and production; Erica Wrightson, who edited the book so skillfully; Claire Crighton, who provided editing assistance and meticulous proofreading; and Christina Zeek, who coordinated image rights. My sincere gratitude for the superb catalogue design to Lorraine Wild and Xiaoqing Wang of Green Dragon Office, who took my vague requests for something nonlinear, non-narrative, and non-Eurocentric and created a book unlike any in the museum's history.

My deepest gratitude goes to Houman M. Sarshar and Sylvester Angel Cetina for their generous support of this publication; thanks, too, to Romanov Investments Inc. and Georges Marci. I would like to acknowledge the members of LACMA's Art of the Middle East: CONTEMPORARY council, whose donations supported the acquisition of many of the works in the exhibition. I am greatly indebted to Leila Heller, Nazila Noebashari, and Shirin Partovi, not only for introducing me to some wonderful artists but also for their unflagging support and generosity. For sharing information and images and for random acts of kindness, all long distance, my thanks to Majid Abd-i Amin, Mansoureh Azadvari, Sheila Blair, Jonathan Bloom, Mehran Mafi Bordbar, Bahman Farmanara, Siamak Filizadeh, William Lawrie, Farshid Mesghali, Nahla Nassar, and Haleh Zarineh. Finally, I thank the Iranian artists both present and past whose work, as represented in these pages, continues to inspire and sustain me.

Linda Komaroff

CURATOR AND DEPARTMENT HEAD,
ART OF THE MIDDLE EAST
LOS ANGELES COUNTY MUSEUM OF ART

Our hearts bound by the memory of the lambs of splendor,
in the fields of empty days,
our swords rusty, worn out, and weary,
our drums, forever silent,
our arrows, broken winged.
We are the conquerors of the cities gone with the wind.[1]

TIME AND AGAIN

The Intersection of Past and Present in Iranian Art

Linda Komaroff

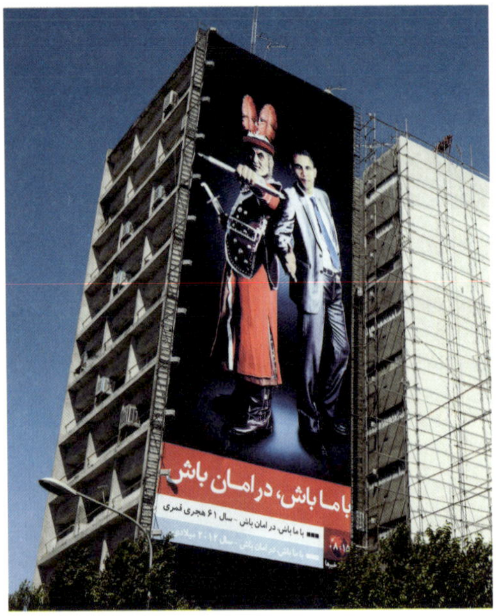

Billboard depicting President Barack Obama and Shimr, Vali'asr Square, Tehran

Predestination

In spring 2014, while driving past Vali'asr Square, one of Tehran's busiest intersections, I was startled to see on the side of a building a huge billboard of President Barack Obama standing beside a menacing-looking man clad in armor over a red robe and a helmet festooned with red feathers. As I later understood, the towering image appropriated and recontextualized a central event from the early history of the Shi'ite branch of Islam, the majority faith of Iran. It referenced an incident in 680 when the villainous Shimr offered refuge to and then murdered the Imam Husain at Karbala, in Iraq. Meant to convey a contemporary political message, it subtly linked Barack Obama with Shimr's odious duplicity.[2] Shimr's distinctive wardrobe, with its red accents, reflects not a seventh-century context, but rather the domain of *ta'ziya*, a Shi'ite passion play performed by costumed reenactors, something that would be recognizable to most passersby in Vali'asr, though not as yet to me.[3] But what struck me was the assured and authentic

---

1 From "The Ending of the Book of Kings" (*"Akhar-i Shahnama"*) by Mehdi Akhavan-e Sales. For the full poem and complete citation, see Sorour Soroudi, "Akhavan's 'The Ending of Shahnameh': A Critique," *Iranian Studies* 2, no. 2/3 (1969): 80–96; we have here largely relied on Soroudi's translation.

2 The billboard was put in place in January 2013, probably in connection with Obama's second inauguration on January 21, although other interpretations are possible. The image, which faded to pink and then gray at the times of my subsequent visits, was produced by Owj Arts and Media Organization. This organization was established in the spring of 2011 and is composed of a young, highly innovative team of graphic designers.

3 Nor was I as yet aware of the intended negative visual impact of pairing anyone with Shimr. The text, which serves as a caption, rendered in the manner of a BBC chyron, says: "Join us to be safe" (also in Persian a play on the name Obama) in large font, and on the bottom it repeats: "Join us to be safe, join us to be safe (61 AH [680 AD]) Join us to be safe, join us to be safe (2013)," perhaps linking Shimr's offer of friendship and safety to Husain and his followers to Obama's interest in beginning serious nuclear talks with Iran, something that would have become more realistic after his election to a second term. On the messaging of such imagery, see Houshang E. Chehabi and Fotini Christia, "The Art of State Persuasion: Iran's Post-Revolutionary Murals," *Persica* 22 (2008): 1–13; and Christiane Gruber, "The Message Is on the Wall: Mural Arts in Post-Revolutionary Iran," *Persica* 22 (2008): 1–13. For a general discussion of the history of this type of politically motivated "street art," see Talinn Grigor, *Contemporary Iranian Art: From the Street to the Studio* (London: Reaktion Books, 2014), 21–91.

manner in which this anachronistic pair of figures was presented, something familiar to me from my study of both historical and contemporary Iranian art.

The image of Obama and Shimr continued to intrigue me. This mixing of past and present for the purpose of political or social messaging is an important and longstanding characteristic of the art of Iran. It occurred to me that this visual manipulation of time and space might be a topic worth pursuing as an exhibition, especially as it would combine my twin interests in historical and contemporary art. Additionally, like for most of us, time and the possibility of time travel is something that fascinates me; this show would be about an art that willfully bends time and obscures place, rather than conforming to the sometimes forced linear narrative that we associate with traditional art history.

As part of my research for the project, I developed a small obsession with the previously noted ta'ziya, a traditional Persian theatrical genre in which the story is conveyed through music, recitation, and costumed reenactors. In ta'ziya, there is a dramatic device known as *guriz* or *guriz zadan* (meaning "digression"), which has allowed such performances to extend beyond the confines of time and space—to simultaneously exist, for example, in present-day Tehran and seventh-century Karbala.[4] I wondered if a similar concept existed in the visual arts of Iran, where past and present are often made to seamlessly merge. I have not yet answered that question, nor do I know where this interpretation of guriz might lead. But given the paucity of surviving texts on artistic theory and criticism from earlier periods in Iran, perhaps the present, in this case, may better inform us about art and artistic practice in the past.

4 See Peter Chelkowski, "Ta'ziyeh: Indigenous Avant-Garde Theatre of Iran," in *Ta'ziyeh: Ritual and Drama in Iran*, ed. Peter Chelkowski (New York: New York University Press / Soroush Press, 1979), 1–11, 8; Peter Chelkowski, "Time Out of Memory: Ta'ziyeh, the Total Drama," in *Eternal Performance: Ta'ziyeh and Other Shiite Rituals*, ed. Peter Chelkowski (London: Seagull Books, 2010), 13; also, see Iraj Anvar, "Peripheral Ta'ziyeh: The Transformation of Ta'zieyh from Muharram Mourning Ritual to Secular and Comical Theatre," in *Eternal Performance*, ed. Peter Chelkowski, 111–12. See also Babak Rahimi, "Takkiyeh Dowlat: The Qajar Theater State," in *Performing the Iranian State: Visual Culture and Representations of Iranian Identity*, ed. Staci Gem Scheiwiller (London: Anthem Press, 2014), 55–71, which although focused on the Qajar period provides a very good introduction to the topic of ta'ziya in general. For ta'ziya after the Iranian Revolution, see Ida Meftahi, "Sacred or Dissident: Islam, Embodiment, and Subjectivity on Post-Revolutionary Iranian Theatrical Stage," in *Islam and Popular Culture*, ed. Karin van Nieuwkerk, Mark LeVine, and Martin Stokes (Austin: University of Texas Press, 2016), 265–67. On ta'ziya in cinema, see Nacim Pak-Shiraz, *Shi'i Islam in Iranian Cinema: Religion and Spirituality in Film* (London: I. B. Taurus, 2011), 129–65. See Ali Akbar Dehkhoda, comp., and Mohammad Moin and Ja'far Shahidi, eds., *Lughat nama yi Dehkhoda*, vol. 16 (Tehran: Tehran University Publication, 1998), s.v. "Guriz Zadan," where it is defined as a means to connect one subject matter to another, or to join similar experiences; also, to connect random events to the ones of Karbala or one of the martyrs of Karbala; similarly, see Hasan Amid, *Farhang-i Farsi-yi Amid* (Tehran: Rah-i Rushd, 2010), 870. Hence, perhaps, the popular Persian expression *guriz zadan bi sahra-yi Karbala*, which means everything goes back to Karbala (mainly used in a secular context nowadays as a way of ironically noting when someone keeps reverting to the same subject regardless of the direction of the conversation). Here, as elsewhere, I am very grateful to Shadi Shafiei, for her insight into contemporary Iranian society and culture, and especially her translations from Persian.

About Time: Defining the Topic

The exhibition *In the Fields of Empty Days: The Intersection of Past and Present in Iranian Art* and this accompanying catalogue take as their theme the continuous and inescapable presence of the past in Iranian society, as reflected in both the previous anecdote and the poem excerpted at the head of this essay. This notion is revealed in art and literature in which long-ago kings and heroes are used in subsequent contexts as paradigms of grandeur and virtue, or as objects of derision and malevolence, while long-gone Shi'ite saints and martyrs are evoked as champions of the poor and the oppressed.

The connection between kingship past and present manifests most significantly in illustrated versions of the *Shahnama*, or Book of Kings, the Iranian national epic, which, though written in the Islamic era, tells of the pre-Islamic kings and heroes. From the first such royally commissioned manuscripts, from the period of Mongol rule in Iran (1256–1353), the ancient kings were recast as contemporary Islamic rulers.[5] The visual identification between the sovereign, often himself not a Persian, and earlier Iranian kings was deliberate and significant, used to validate the ruling elite. This type of politically motivated patronage helped ensure the cultural and aesthetic importance of the Book of Kings through the end of the nineteenth century; its kings and heroes are embedded still in Iranian culture.

PLATES 5–9, 34, AND 83

Iran's adoption of Shi'ite Islam as a state religion in the early sixteenth century also helped fix the past irrevocably in the present through the cycle of remembrance ceremonies for the martyred Shi'ite Imams, most notably Husain, grandson of the Prophet Muhammad. Murdered with his family and companions at Karbala, Husain is commemorated each year on the anniversary of his death (known as Ashura) through ta'ziya theater. Audience members become participants in this emotionally charged and graphic ritual in which they experience the killings and mourn the slain in present time.[6] The story was also pictured through large-scale paintings that survive only from the late nineteenth century; these in turn, along with ta'ziya performances, inspired artists to paint similarly sized images based on the *Shahnama*.[7]

PLATE 92

PLATES 19 AND 20

Both of these strands—ancient kings and heroes, and martyred Shi'ite Imams—carry forward, even sometimes overlapping, in contemporary Iranian art. While the past once was visualized in terms of the present, by the second half of the twentieth century the present began to be rendered anachronistically as a form of often barely disguised political and social commentary. *In the Fields of Empty Days* examines this appropriation and recontextualization of the past, largely in the context of the present. It covers a wide swath of Iranian art, including Safavid manuscript illustrations as well as Qajar-era photographs and other works, but it concentrates primarily on the art from the final years of the reign of Mohammad Reza Shah (r. 1941–79) in the 1970s, through the Islamic Revolution of 1979, and up to the present day. This is a novel and admittedly unusual approach to Iranian art that reveals that, by evoking the past, Iranian artists have created and continue to create new visual metaphors to describe their present day.

---

5 See Sheila R. Canby's essay in this volume.
6 See Chelkowski, "Time Out of Memory"; see also Sheida Dayani's essay in this volume.
7 For both types of paintings, see Peter Chelkowski, "Narrative Painting and Painting Recitation in Qajar Iran," *Muqarnas* 6 (1989): 98–111.

Somewhere in Time: The Confluence of Old and New

The nineteenth century, the era of the Qajar dynasty (1785–1925), represents a true juncture between historical and modern Iran, the perfect starting point for this nonlinear history of Iranian art. This transitional phase can be still further refined to the second half of the century during the long reign of Nasir al-Din Shah (r. 1848–96). Throughout this period, Iran faced the difficult challenge of escalating European interference, which helped precipitate an influx of technological and educational developments from Europe, all in the name of modernization. It was also an innovative era in the arts, perhaps best exemplified by the introduction of the newly conceived medium of photography sometime between 1839 and 1842.[8] Among the first Iranians to learn the art of photography was the young crown prince and future Nasir al-Din Shah, who had greater resources to pursue such interests after his accession. He not only commissioned photographs of his court

PLATES 54 AND 55 and palaces, as well as ancient Iranian sites, but he also became an accomplished photographer in his own right.[9] Dar al-Funun (established in 1851), Iran's first university with a secular curriculum, offered courses that explained the science and technology of photography, while others trained painters—some of whom went on to study in Europe—in the Western manner.[10] All of this helped transform visual culture in Iran, though not necessarily its impetus.[11] The last great royally sponsored Persian illustrated manuscript, a six-volume edition of *A Thousand and One Nights*, demonstrates this confluence of the old and the new.[12]

---

8 The invention of photography in France is generally dated to the beginning of 1839. In Iran, this was also a time of increased travel to Europe, including three visits by Nasir al-Din, who was thereby inspired to establish the first museum in Iran. On this private museum, known as the Talar-i Musée, which housed the shah's own collection, see Maryam Ekhtiar, "Nasir al-Din Shah and the Dar al-Funun. The Evolution of an Institution," *Iranian Studies* 34, no. 1/4 (2001): 161. The first photographic devices were presented as gifts to the Qajar ruler Muhammad Shah (r. 1834–48) sometime between 1839 and 1842 from the two European monarchs competing for influence in Iran: Queen Victoria of Great Britain and Czar Nicholas I of Russia. Although the photographic apparatuses came with instructions, it was only in 1844 that a Frenchman arrived at the royal court who was familiar with the complex equipment; among the first Iranians to learn the art of photography was Muhammad Shah's young son, the future Nasir al-Din Shah. See Ali Behdad, "The Power-Ful Art of Qajar Photography: Orientalism and (Self)-Orientalizing in Nineteenth-Century Iran," *Iranian Studies* 34, no. 1/4 (2001): 141–51, esp. 145; also see Shabnam Rahimi-Golkhandan's essay in this catalogue.

9 See Behdad, "The Power-Ful Art of Qajar Photography," 145.

10 On the Dar al-Funun in general, see Monica M. Ringer, *Education, Religion, and the Discourse of Cultural Reform in Qajar Iran* (Costa Mesa, CA: Mazda Publishers, 2001), 67–108. But specifically, in terms of the arts, see Ekhtiar, "Nasir al-Din Shah and the Dar al-Funun," 160–61.

11 See Layla S. Diba, ed., with Maryam Ekhtiar, *Royal Persian Paintings: The Qajar Epoch 1785–1925* (Brooklyn: Brooklyn Museum of Art; London: I. B. Tauris, 1998), 239–41, for a concise summary of the arts in this period.

12 The text of *A Thousand and One Nights* was translated from Arabic into Persian and subsequently was transformed into Persian verse; it is this version of the text along with illustrations that was commissioned for Nasir al-Din. On the presumed appeal of the text and images for the young king, see Abbas Amanat, *Pivot of the Universe: Nasir al-Din Shah Qajar and the Iranian Monarchy, 1831–1896* (Berkeley: University of California Press, 1997), 66. The first lithographed edition of the Persian version of the text was made in 1843–45. Interest in producing a Persian translation of the text and subsequently an illustrated version for the shah was probably based in part on British colonial attention to the text. See Ulrich Marzolph, "The Persian *Nights*: Links between the *Arabian Nights* and Iranian Culture," *Fabula* 45, no. 3/4 (2004): 275–93, esp. 282.

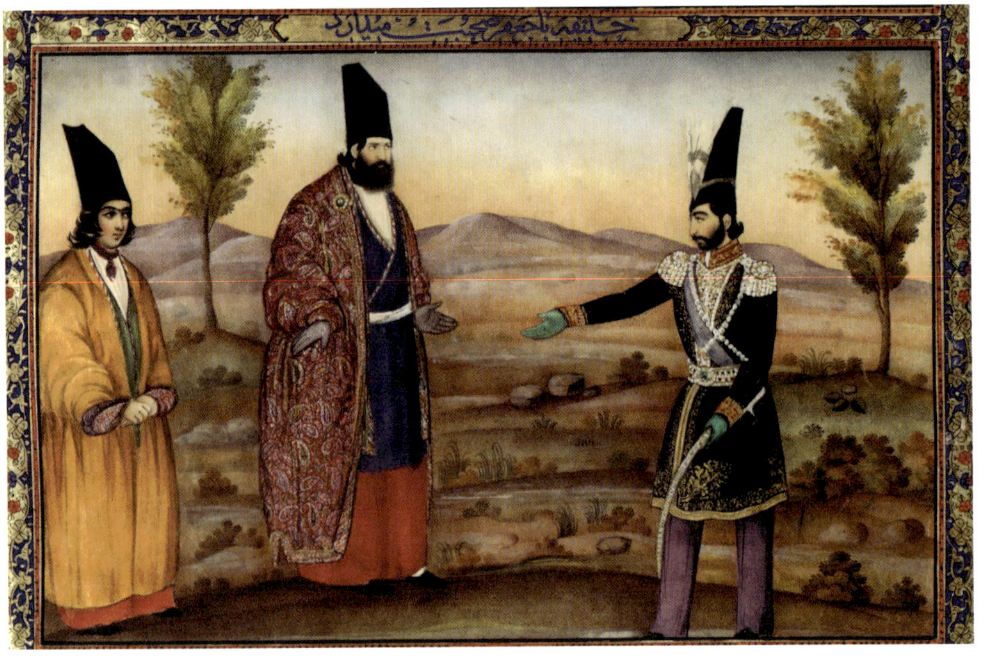

Abu'l-Hasan Ghaffari, scene from the story of Ghanim bin Ayyub in *A Thousand and One Nights*, vol. 1, 1852–59. Golestan Palace Library and Archive

Dating from 1852 to 1859, this monumental work comprises facing pages of text, alternating with illustrations (arranged in registers, generally three per page) that were painted by or under the supervision of the main court artist, Abu'l-Hasan Khan Ghaffari, later Sani al-Mulk, who had studied in Europe.[13] Western-style naturalism permeates the landscapes, in contrast to the more fanciful and idealized settings of earlier manuscript illustration, and most of the perspective evident in the palatial settings is based on a single point, rather than the multiple vantage points of classical Persian miniatures. But in keeping with the tradition of earlier manuscript illustration, these nineteenth-century book paintings are similarly unconcerned with historicism in terms of the characters and settings. Rather, they provide a detailed rendition of contemporary Qajar court life, palaces, costumes, and accoutrements, all of which are substantiated by contemporaneous photographs, including those made by and for Nasir al-Din. It is even possible to identify certain of the key figures in the illustrations with members of the Qajar court. For example, a scene from the story of Ghanim bin Ayyub depicts the Caliph (Harun al-Rashid) and his Vizier (Ja'far Barmaki), according to both the caption and text.[14] Here the Caliph is clearly recognizable as Nasir al-Din when compared with his youthful photographs and portraits.[15] The Vizier, PLATES 11–13 though traditionally assumed to be Amir Kabir (d. 1852), perhaps can be identified as Husain Ali Khan Mu'ayyir al-Mamalik (d. 1858), who held various high offices

13 The text was copied by the calligrapher Muhammad Husain Tihrani. See Yahya Zoka, *Life and Works of Sani' ol-Molk, 1814–1866*, ed. Cyrus Parham (Tehran: Iran University Press, 2003), 33–38; also see Mohammad Ali Rajabi, ed., *Iranian Masterpieces of Persian Painting* (Tehran: Museum of Contemporary Art, 2005), 385–403. See B. W. Robinson, "Abu'l-Hasan Khan Gaffari," in *Encyclopaedia Iranica* 1, fasc. 3 (London: Routledge & Kegan Paul, 1985), 306–8.

14 For an English version translated from an Arabic text that may have been comparable to the one used for the mid-nineteenth-century translation into Persian, I have relied on Sir Richard Burton's ten-volume work from the 1880s. For this section, see Richard Francis Burton, *The Book of the Thousand Nights and a Night*, vol. 2 (London: Kama Shastra Society, 1885–88), 45–76.

15 Abu'l-Hasan Ghaffari painted a portrait of Nasir al-Din seated in 1857, while the manuscript project was still in process. See Diba, ed., *Royal Persian Paintings*, 242.

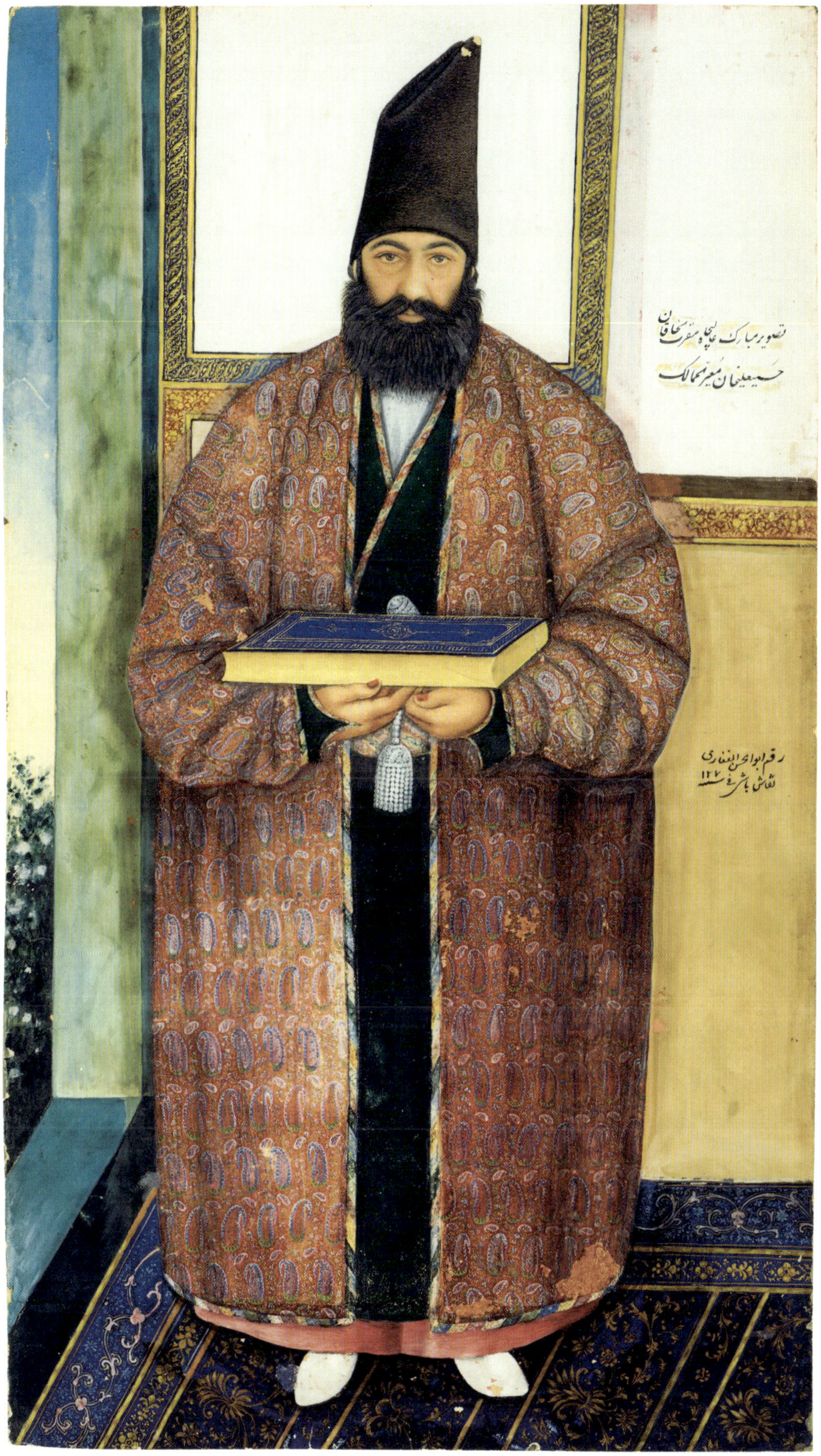

Abu'l-Hasan Ghaffari, *Husain Ali Khan Mu'ayyir al-Mamalik*. AH 1270/1853–54. Opaque watercolors and gold on heavy card. 13½×7¾ in. (34.1×19.5 cm). Nasser D. Khalili Collection of Islamic Art, MSS 825

in the early Nasiri period—and who is said to have supervised the manuscript project—based on close similarities with a portrait of this individual dated 1853–54 (AH 1270) and signed by Abu'l-Hasan Ghaffari.[16]

While Abu'l-Hasan Ghaffari made use of Western conventions in landscape and portraiture, his eliding of the then-present-day Qajar court with the largely fictionalized past of *A Thousand and One Nights* is typical of earlier manuscript illustrations, most notably of the *Shahnama*. Given the global settings of *A Thousand and One Nights*, including Persia, India, and China, the specifically Qajar context of the paintings universalizes Nasir al-Din's court in an intentionally flattering manner, in much the same way that the earlier royally sponsored manuscripts of the *Shahnama* enshrined their patrons within the history of Persian kingship. Because it is possible to connect certain literary figures in the

16 The portrait of Husain Ali Khan closely resembles the Ja'far figure in the manuscript in terms of the facial features of both subjects, especially the noses, which in each instance is distinctly inverted at the bridge. Husain Ali Khan evidently had frequent and close contact with the artist to the extent that Abu'l-Hasan Ghaffari might have used him as a model for Ja'far in recognition of their relationship. According to Zoka (*Life and Works of Sani' ol-Molk*, 39), Husain Ali Khan Mu'ayyir al-Mamalik supervised the manuscript project and presented a copy to the shah. The portrait (LEFT) was one of several Abu'l-Hasan Ghaffari made of Husain Ali Khan, suggesting that even beyond the manuscript project the two had a close connection; again, see Zoka (ibid., 26, 32, and 39) for the possibility that Husain Ali Khan may have underwritten the artist's trip to Europe around 1847; for two other portraits dated 1852; and for another portrait from 1852 with a young man, attributed to Abu'l-Hasan. One of these portraits, in the Moghaddam Museum, Tehran, further strengthens the connection between Husain Ali Khan and the Ja'far image; I am grateful to Haleh Zarineh for kindly providing an image of this painting, which includes a couplet at the bottom referencing the sitter's connection to an artist's workshop. Furthermore, Julian Raby (*Qajar Portraits* [London: Azimuth Editions in association with the Iran Heritage Foundation, 1999], 61) notes that part of the *A Thousand and One Nights* manuscript project was accomplished at Husain Ali Khan's home. It seems highly unlikely that Abu'l-Hasan Ghaffari would have depicted Amir Kabir posthumously standing beside the shah so soon after the vizier's disgrace and execution in January 1852. The tradition for associating the figure of Ja'far with Amir Kabir, Nasir al-Din Shah's ill-fated minister, is long-standing, perhaps going back to the late nineteenth century, but is without clear foundation. It is likely tied to the mythification of the vizier as well as the modern belief that the role of Ja'far, to Nasir al-Din's Harun al-Rashid, could only have been played by Amir Kabir. There is one confirmed portrait of Amir Kabir, commissioned by the shah and painted by Muhammed Ibrahim Naqqashbashi in 1848 (1265 AH), according to its inscription; it is now preserved in the Golestan Palace (https://en.wikipedia.org/wiki/Amir_Kabir#/media/File:AmirKabir_naghashbashi.jpg). The sitter's most striking feature is his nose, which is prominent and distinctly curved, and entirely unlike that of the Ja'far figure, who is not depicted wearing the vizier's insignia of office. It seems likely that Zoka, among the first art historians to insist on linking Amir Kabir with image of Ja'far (*Life and Works of Sani' ol-Molk*, 31, 36), was motivated by a work by Abu'l-Qasim ibn Nuri, active from the 1880s, incorporating a photograph of a painting alongside calligraphy of a poem eulogizing Amir Kabir, and identifying the painting as a portrait of Amir Kabir (in an album in the Golestan Library, and datable to around 1893, forty years after the death of Amir Kabir). The painting (in the photograph) is possibly a copy after the Ja'far figure from *A Thousand and One Nights*, with only the position of the hands altered; see Yahya Zoka, *Tarikh-i akkasi va akkasan-i pishgam dar Iran* [The History of Photography and Pioneer Photographers in Iran] (Tehran: Shirkat-i Intisharat-i Ilmi va Farhani, 1997), 117–18; also see Carmen Pérez González, *Local Portraiture: Through the Lens of the 19th-Century Iranian Photographers* (Leiden: Leiden University Press, 2012), 82–84, fig. 58. Perhaps as Amir Kabir's status was rehabilitated, the Ja'far figure came to be understood as Amir Kabir. The restoration of the vizier's reputation did not begin until well after the manuscript project was completed; see Amanat, *Pivot of the Universe*, 166, as well as pl. 9 for a posthumous image of Amir Kabir, based on a sketch by Nasir al-Din Shah, which closely resembles the portrait of 1848.

illustrations with actual members of the Qajar court, perhaps we can project backward to more sharply delineate the evidence of contemporaneity in earlier Persian illustrated manuscripts.[17]

Exposing the Present in the Past in *Shahnama* Illustration

Illustrated manuscripts like the *Shahnama* were the result of a collaborative effort, one that required wealthy, generally royal patrons who could afford the costly materials and large staff required. Such books were produced in the *kitabkhana* (literally "book house"), an atelier combining the functions of scriptorium, workshop, and library. Divided into fifty sections, each devoted to a mythical or historical king, the *Shahnama* allowed for a wide range of possible illustrations; over time, however, some sections of the text and certain scenes came to be repeated, while specific compositions were reused, but with subtle changes.[18] Existing scholarship on royally sponsored *Shahnama* manuscripts (only a few have survived intact) has sometimes categorized unusual or anomalous subjects and settings as reflections of their contemporary context, chosen because they mirrored events in the life of the patron or otherwise might have had special meaning for the intended audience.[19]

This interpretation can be extended to the inclusion of uncharacteristic figures, as in a *Shahnama* painting of a frequently depicted scene of combat between the Sasanian ruler Shah Khusrau Parviz (r. 590–628) and the would-be usurper
PLATE 7 Bahram Chubina, each of whom is identified by a crown. Bahram, the superior warrior, advances on foot toward a group of archers directed by Khusrau, who will lose the battle but win the war. But what are we to make of the tumbling figure, placed nearly at the center of the composition, just in front of Bahram, whose buttocks are exposed as he falls forward? No such incident is referenced in the text, but it might have to do with some contemporary event or individual associated with the court of Shah Isma'il II (r. 1576–77), for whom the now-dispersed manuscript was made.[20] The scraggly beard and gaunt face of the shamefully

---

17 On this topic, two specific manuscripts of the *Shahnama* can be cited: the Tahmasp *Shahnama* and the Berlin *Shahnama* dated 1605. For the first, see Sheila R. Canby, *The Shahnama of Shah Tahmasp: The Persian Book of Kings* (New York: Metropolitan Museum of Art, 2014), 20–60, esp. 20–22, where numerous and close comparisons are made between the objects of daily life depicted in the paintings and extant objects of the same period. At times the verisimilitude of the book paintings so closely reflects the actual objects that it must have been an intentional means of embedding the mythical stories within the present-day court of Tahmasp. For the second, see Kishwar Rizvi, "The Suggestive Portrait of Shah 'Abbas: Prayer and Likeness in a Safavid *Shahnama*," *Art Bulletin* 94, no. 2 (2012): 226–50, as well as Sheila R. Canby's essay in this volume.

18 See, for example, Ada Adamova, "Repetition of Compositions in Manuscripts: The *Khamsa* of Nizami in Leningrad," in *Timurid Art and Culture: Iran and Central Asia in the Fifteenth Century*, vol. 6, ed. Lisa Golombek and Maria Subtelny (Leiden: Brill, 1992), 67–75.

19 See for example, Oleg Grabar, "Why Was the Shahnama Illustrated?," *Iranian Studies* 43, no. 1 (2010): 91–96. But for more specific interpretations of particular manuscripts, see Robert Hillenbrand, "The Iconography of the Shah-nama-yi Shahi," in *Safavid Persia: The History and Politics of an Islamic Society*, ed. Charles Melville (London: I. B. Tauris, 1996), 53–78, and Abolala Soudavar, "The Saga of Abu-Sa'id Bahador Khan. The Abu-Sa'idname," in *The Court of the Il-Khans 1290–1340*, vol. 12, ed. Julian Raby and Teresa Fitzherbert (Oxford: Oxford University Press, 1996), 95–218. The illustrations also incorporate inscriptions that contemporize the paintings, especially in the *Shahnama of Shah Tahmasp*; see Massumeh Farhad, "Reading between the Lines: Word and Image in Sixteenth-Century Iran," in *By the Pen and What They Write: Writing in Islamic Art and Culture*, ed. Sheila Blair and Jonathan Bloom (New Haven: Yale University Press, 2017), 180–203.

20 B. W. Robinson, "Shah Isma'il II's Copy of the Shah-Nama" *Iran* 14 (1976): 1–8, and "Shah Isma'il II's Copy of the Shah-Nama: Additional Material," *Iran* 43 (2005): 291–99.

posed figure differs from the more generic countenances of the full-faced, beardless youths and mature warriors who populate the page. This is not to suggest an instance of portraiture, but rather a likeness that was intended to be recognizable in concert with the figure's undignified posture, perhaps referencing some out-of-favor courtier.[21]

Back to the Future

From the fourteenth to early seventeenth centuries, the heyday of book painting, the best artists were called upon to produce illustrated manuscripts of classical Persian poetry that portrayed the contemporary ruler and his court literally within the pages of history (or what was understood to be history).[22] Such royal tomes were meant to be viewed by an audience as select and as privileged as those who commissioned them. Even during the nineteenth century, when portraits of the king, leading courtiers, and other members of the elite had already supplanted commissions for book illustrations, artists were still largely dependent on patronage for their work. In looking forward (or backward) to the second half of the twentieth century, artists continued to mingle past and present but for different purposes and for a new and more expansive audience.

Beginning in the 1960s, the artists of the modernist movement known as Saqqakhana (literally "house of the water-bearer," after Shi'ite-themed public drinking fountains) were inspired by traditional art and architectural decoration, both religious and secular, but focused more on color, form, and the repetition of designs rather than on subject matter and meaning.[23] Their art, nevertheless, achieved a level of popular success precisely because its themes and materials were easily recognized by a broad Iranian audience.[24] Parviz Tanavoli, one of the founders of the Saqqakhana school, employed a typically Persian medium for his "lion and sword" carpets from the 1970s. His work highlights a time-honored emblem of kingship and the Iranian state—a lion with sun rising from its back (*Shir u Khurshid*)—which became linked to Shi'ism in the Safavid period (1501-1722).[25] The

PLATES 25 AND 26

21 Although portraiture in Persian painting is a large topic, for a very succinct description, see David J. Roxburgh, *The Persian Album, 1400–1600: From Dispersal to Collection* (New Haven: Yale University Press, 2005), 301.

22 In terms of the periodization of Persian manuscript illustration, the fourteenth century is generally considered to be the formative period, the fifteenth and sixteenth centuries the Classical period, and from about the second quarter of the seventeenth century on a period of decline. There are many books on Persian manuscript illustration; among the most accessible for the general reader is Sheila R. Canby, *Persian Painting* (London: British Museum Press, 1993).

23 This artistic movement is discussed more fully elsewhere in this volume; see the essays by Hamid Keshmirshekan and also Sheida Dayani. For a very succinct summary, also see Karim Emami, "Saqqakhaneh School Revisited," and Peter Lamborn Wilson, "The Saqqa-Khaneh," in *Iran Modern*, ed. Fereshteh Daftari and Layla S. Diba (New York: Asia Society, 2013), 230–31 and 231–33, respectively.

24 See Emami, "Saqqakhaneh School Revisited," 230–31.

25 On Tanavoli, see most recently Lisa Fischman and Shiva Balaghi, *Parviz Tanavoli* (Wellesley, MA: Davis Museum, 2015), esp. 146–53 for his lion imagery. The combination of lion and sword (beginning in the nineteenth century as a symbol of the Qajar state) also has strong Shi'ite connotations as they are each associated with Imam Ali. See Fahmida Suleman, "Ali as the Lion of God," in *The Art and Material Culture of Iranian Shi'ism: Iconography and Religious Devotion in Shi'i Islam*, ed. Pedram Khosronejad (London: I. B. Tauris, 2012), 217–20. See Afsaneh Najmabadi, *Women with Mustaches and Men without Beards: Gender and Sexual Anxieties of Iranian Modernity* (Berkeley: University of California Press, 2005), 63–96, for an insightful, feminist approach to the subject.

lion and sun with sword was the symbol of Pahlavi Iran (1925–79), and appeared most conspicuously on the national flag. Tanavoli's use of it in the carpets, includ-
PLATE 25 ing with what appears to be an antique lock on the animal's hind leg, suggests a subtle form of political commentary. It also reinforces the inherent Shi'ism of the image and the artist's ties to the Saqqakhana movement.[26]

Other artists working in the 1970s looked to the past to create a visual commentary on the Pahlavi state, one that often eschewed subtlety. These artists focused on the Qajar period, perhaps for a variety of factors. Most obviously, the Qajars were the dynasts who immediately preceded the Pahlavis and as such would have been better known than more distant rulers, while the remnants of Qajar visual culture would have been more accessible.[27] Popular culture, such as the 1974 film classic *Shazdeh Ehtejab*, or "Prince Ehtejab," from Houshang Golshiri's
PLATE 61 acclaimed novel, also may have played a role in disseminating Qajar imagery.[28] Like the book, the film focuses on a Qajar prince and is nominally set in the mid-1920s, but is equally and intentionally suggestive of contemporary Pahlavi Iran. The prince's crumbling mansion is filled with the relics of his royal ancestors whose actions haunt him. Among the household mementos included for the purposes of the film were photographs made from actual glass-plate negatives of Qajar royalty, which the director, Bahman Farmanara, employed for the sake of creating an authentic ambience.[29] This gesture may have helped introduce Qajar photography as something artistically valid and potentially inspirational rather than purely documentary.[30]

---

26 For Tanavoli's collection of old Iranian locks, which he had at the time the carpets were made, see Parviz Tanavoli and John T. Wertime, *Locks from Iran: Pre-Islamic to Twentieth Century* (Washington, D.C.: Smithsonian Institution, 1976), 20–29, for a discussion of locks in a Shi'ite context, including the *saqqakhana*.

27 See James Buchan's introduction to his translation of Houshang Golshiri's *The Prince* (*Shazdeh Ehtejab*), first published in Persian in 1968–69, where he notes that the types of Qajar-era objects Golshiri described as part of the setting for the ruined mansion of Prince Khusrau were being sold in the Isfahan bazaar, along with old portrait photographs, in the late 1960s, so that the author would not have had to go far afield for suitable inspiration. See Houshang Golshiri, *The Prince*, trans. James Buchan (London: Harvill Secker, 2006), 15; also, see below. Qajar painting began to attract the attention of collectors and scholars in the 1960s and 1970s, first in Europe and then Iran. The Negaristan Museum of eighteenth- and nineteenth-century art was founded in Tehran in 1975 and the year before sixty-three Qajar paintings were acquired to initiate the new museum's collection. See Diba, ed., *Royal Persian Paintings*, 8, 12–13. An exhibition of Zand and Qajar paintings from private collections was held at the Iran America Society in spring 1974, which included some of the works acquired for the Negaristan. See *Zand & Qajar Paintings from Private Collections* (Tehran: Iran America Society, 1974).

28 See Farzaneh Taheri and Abdolali Azimi, eds., *Hamrah ba Shazdeh Ehtejab* [Along with Shazdeh Ehtejab] (Tehran: Nashr-i Digar, 2001), esp. 19, which quotes an interview conducted by Kaveh Golestan in 1993, in which Golshiri spoke about how past and present intersected for Prince Khusrau; also, see 53, for an interview from 1969, in which Golshiri discusses the stream of consciousness in his work as a form of guriz.

29 In an interview with Bahman Farmanara, he told Shadi Shafiei that prints from the glass plate negatives along with vintage prints were obtained from Tahami Photo Studio in Baharistan Square, Tehran. Shadi Shafiei (research assistant, Art of the Middle East, LACMA), in conversation with the director, February 12, 2017.

30 Qajar photography was little known at that time; see Maria Francesca Bonetti, Khadijeh Mohammadi Nameghi, and Alberto Prandi, "The First Hundred Years of Iranian Photography: A Bibliography," *History of Photography* 37, no. 1 (2013): 126–33, for an extensive bibliography that demonstrates the paucity of publications on Iranian photography, in any language, prior to the 1990s.

Qajar photographs played a key role in a unique group of photographs produced in 1976 by Kaveh Golestan, who remains better known as a photojournalist.[31] His innovative and striking images were shot on Polaroid film by moving collaged fragments in front of an open shutter of a single-lens reflex camera.[32] The process produced surrealistic and fanciful pictures that mix gruesomely fantastical images with historical ones by appropriating Qajar photographs. The collages create potent visions of reptile-headed kings and leonine army officers, set against natural and architectural backgrounds referencing both the 1970s and the late Qajar era. Golestan's father-in-law had given him a royal Qajar photographic album, which he used for some of the collages captured on Polaroid, but it is hard to imagine that his work was not inspired in some way by *Shazdeh Ehtejab*, one of the most popular films of the day.[33]

PLATES 28 A–H

The contemporaneous artist and satirist Ardeshir Mohassess was distinguished for his illustrations that blended often-macabre humor with biting social commentary. Though he left Iran in 1976, settling in New York, he closely followed the events leading up to the Islamic Revolution and its aftermath, as in his sharply observed series Life in Iran. Many of these drawings refer to and reflect incidents that took place in the time leading up to and during the 1979 revolution, but are set in the late Qajar period as the very specific costumes and headdresses demonstrate.[34] Mohassess had made use of Qajar imagery even before he left Iran; these earlier works rendered in dark, thick ink are reminiscent of Qajar paintings and photographs.[35]

PLATES 73 A–F

PLATE 72

---

31 Of the fifty images in this series, LACMA has ten; as far as I am aware, the other forty images are largely unpublished. For a black-and-white image of one of the Polaroids, see Daftari and Diba, eds., *Iran Modern*, 101. This is similar, if not identical, to LACMA's M.2015.188.6. I am grateful to Vali Mahlouji for first bringing these remarkable photographs to my attention and especially to Nina Ansari for her generosity in helping LACMA acquire our group of ten. For Golestan's documentary photographs, see Malu Halasa and Hengameh Golestan, eds., *Kaveh Golestan: Recording the Truth in Iran* (Ostfildern, Germany: Hatje Cantz Verlag, 2007).

32 He used the Polaroid SX-70. See Vali Mahlouji's essay in this catalogue.

33 On the means by which the Qajar photo album came into Golestan's possession, and some of its related history, see Jadid Online (in Persian), http://www.jadidonline.com/story/25022013/frnk/nasseruddin_shah_personal_album. For a consideration of the film, including the manner in which it distorts time, see Hamid Naficy, *A Social History of Iranian Cinema*, vol. 2 (Durham, NC: Duke University Press, 2011), 368. Certainly, the period in which the collaged Polaroids were made represents the confluence of a variety of art forms connected in some way to the Qajar period. The enormously popular Qajar costume-drama television series *Sultan-i Sahib Gharan* also aired between 1975 and 1977. Another likely source of influence was the 1969 Soviet cult classic *The Color of Pomegranates*, which incorporates Qajar imagery inspired by nineteenth-century paintings that the director, Sergei Parajanov, saw at the Georgian Art Museum in Tbilisi, his hometown. See James Steffen, *The Cinema of Sergei Parajanov* (Madison: University of Wisconsin, 2013), 144, 250. *The Color of Pomegranates* was screened in Tehran in 1972. See Shahla Mirbakhtyar, *Iranian Cinema and the Islamic Revolution* (Jefferson, NC: McFarland, 2006), 172n35. It appears to have first been shown in Iran at the Shiraz Arts Festival. See Mahasti Afshar, "Festival of Arts, Shiraz-Persepolis 1976–1977" (2015), 38, https://www.academia.edu/12568899/Festival_of_Arts_Shiraz-Persepolis_1967–1977_updated_May_2015_.

34 See Ardeshir Mohassess, *Life in Iran: The Library of Congress Drawings* (Washington, D.C.: Mage, 1994).

35 Many of these early works have been lost. See Ardeshir Mohassess, *A Retrospective* (Tehran: Iran America Society, 1972). Also, see Hamid Dabashi, "Ardeshir Mohassess, Etcetera," in *Ardeshir Mohassess: Art and Satire in Iran*, ed. Shirin Neshat and Nicky Nodjoumi (New York: Asia Society, 2008), 17–29, for an essay that focuses on the artist largely in the context of his life in Iran; see as well an interview with the artist in that same volume, 34–37, where he notes an interest in Qajar *parda* (coffeehouse painting) and photography. Also, see Ardeshir Mohassess, *Puppets: 101 Drawings and Collages* (San Francisco: C. Bean Associates, 1977), 10, 18, 23, 27, 30, 40, 50, 61, for drawings that seem to have been influenced by Qajar photographs.

A Wrinkle in Time

Iran's 1979 revolution had an incalculable impact on nearly all of its citizens, many of whom lost their lives or homes. The period from October 1977, when demonstrations against and for the shah began, culminating in the shah's resignation and departure in January 1979 and Ayatollah Khomeini's return from exile soon after, was extensively recorded by Iranian photographers creating, in some instances, photographic memoirs documenting the progression of the revolution and its immediate aftermath. A trio of photographs, abridged from the larger group included in the exhibition, serves here as a striking visual summary of certain key moments that chronicle the demise of twenty-five centuries of kingship in Iran.

PLATE 62 The first, from 1978, captures a group of men burning a portrait of the shah; it was shot by the most renowned photographer of the Iranian Revolution, known PLATE 70 by the single name Abbas.[36] The next image, from January 16, 1979, marks the celebrations following the departure of the shah from Iran, as underscored by the sign held up in the foreground with two simple words: *shah raft* ("the shah left"), echoing the Persian newspaper headlines of the day.[37] Photographed by Maryam Zandi, one of the few women photojournalists to cover the revolution, it is typical of her carefully framed and often provocative compositions.[38] Also from 1979 is PLATE 68 a remarkable image that perfectly encapsulates the shattering transfer of power, although it is devoid of any outward violence. Shot by Ahmad Aali, one of Iran's most productive and artistically versatile photographers, it shows the Shahyad monument in Tehran, a huge tower completed in 1971 to commemorate the 2,500th anniversary of Persian Kingship, on which was stenciled the ominously stern face of Khomeini.[39]

---

36 See Abbas, *Iran Diary, 1971–2002* (Paris: Autrement, 2002), and Shiva Balaghi, "Writing with Light: Abbas's Photographs of the Iranian Revolution of 1979," in *Picturing Iran: Art, Society and Revolution*, ed. Shiva Balaghi and Lynn Gumpert (London: I. B. Tauris, 2002), 103–25.

37 Also see plate 69, for Kaveh Golestan's iconic image of men holding a newspaper aloft. This imagery was re-created and parodied three decades later in a collage by Ramin Haerizadeh, *He Came, He Left, He Left, He Came* (SEE PLATE 38).

38 For her work from this period, see Maryam Zandi, *The Revolution of Iran '79: Photographs* (Tehran: Nazar Art Publication, 2014).

39 The monument was renamed Burj-i Azadi (or "Freedom Tower") after the revolution. For visual documentation of Ahmad Aali's long career, see *Ahmad Aali Selection of Paintings and Photographs 1953–2014* (Tehran: Nazar Art Publication, 2016), and *Ahmad Aali Selection of Works 1961–2009* (Tehran: Nazar Art Publication, 2009).

Time after Time

The aftermath of the 1979 revolution, especially the period from the 1990s onward, has been a prolific one for Iranian artists, both those in Iran and those living in diaspora, many of whom have turned to using imagery from the past as a way of addressing the present. Some of them incorporate or re-create Qajar-era photographs, while others look to the *Shahnama*, which has an appeal and an elasticity that has allowed successive generations to discover or invent new meanings.

As a documentary photographer and as an artist, historian, and teacher, Bahman Jalali was among the first to appropriate Qajar photographs as a means of visually investigating contemporary Iranian culture, using the image as evidence that can be re-experienced over time.[40] His student Shadi Ghadirian also explores the complex relationship between past and present, but in a different manner and from a female perspective.[41] Inspired by the studio portraiture of the late nineteenth century, Ghadirian re-created the earlier settings in a set of thirty-three photographs known as the Qajar series. She employed painted backdrops and dressed her models in vintage clothes to emulate the fashion of the day, adding modern-day elements such as a Pepsi can, a single-lens reflex camera, and a pair of sunglasses to create ironic images reflecting the tension between tradition and modernity in Iranian society.[42]

PLATE 45 A–B

PLATES 35 A–D

Rustam, the great but flawed hero of the *Shahnama*, is frequently portrayed in contemporary Iranian art as either the redeeming champion or the superhero who has turned to the dark side. He is more of the latter in Rustam 2—The Return, an ingenious mixed-media series in which the artist Siamak Filizadeh transports the mythical hero into the twenty-first century. In the most iconic image of the series, Rustam 2 is represented as a bazooka-carrying, bare-chested bodybuilder, clothed in the type of short pants worn by members of the *zurkhana* (literally meaning "house of strength" and somewhat akin to a gymnasium).[43] Despite his exaggerated Qajar-style mustache, the colorful pseudo-Safavid arch that frames the hero, and the archaizing rocky outcroppings in the background that reference Persian miniature painting, the setting is clearly present-day Tehran; visible over Rustam 2's left shoulder is the now-familiar Shahyad monument renamed Burj-i Azadi (or "Freedom Tower").[44]

PLATES 4 AND 48

PLATE 2

40 See Catherine David, Bahman Jalali, and Hamid Dabashi, eds., *Bahman Jalali* (Barcelona: Fundació Antoni Tàpies, 2007), esp. 276–96, for his series Image of Imagination.

41 On Ghadirian, see for example Rose Issa, ed., *Shadi Ghadirian: Iranian Photographer* (London: Saqi, 2008).

42 For the full series, which LACMA owns, see https://collections.lacma.org/node/580927.

43 The zurkhana can be defined as the location where a traditional system of athletics originally used to train warriors in Iran, which combines martial arts, calisthenics, and strength training with music and religious chanting, takes place. Also, see Sandra Williams's essay in this volume.

44 The series is more fully discussed in Linda Komaroff, "The Return Engagement of Rostam," in *Ferdowsi, the Mongols and the History of Iran: Art, Literature and Culture from Early Islam to Qajar Persia*, ed. Robert Hillenbrand, A. C. S. Peacock, and Firuza Abdullaeva (London: I. B. Tauris, 2013), 381–90. Also see my short essay in this volume on Filizadeh's later series Underground.

The Paris-based artist Malekeh Nayiny also draws upon the hero Rustam in a group of works that addresses the universal notion of confronting one's personal demons, as well as the specifically regional theme of the Iranian Book of Kings. In terms of the latter, the demons are those defeated by Rustam, as depicted in PLATES 5 AND 48 two prints. In one, the classic illustration of Rustam slaying the White Div—a diabolical monster who captured the Iranian king—is re-created as a wall mural and announced in the Persian caption beneath the hero's raised dagger. In the PLATE 49 other, the embattled pair of Rustam and the White Div is repeated and applied like wallpaper behind the unsettling image of a child disguised as a pink demon.[45]

In her 2012 photographic series The Book of Kings, Shirin Neshat, the best-known artist of the Iranian diaspora, returned to the process of inscribing directly on the print, as she did in her groundbreaking Women of Allah series more than two decades earlier. In the more recent photographs, the storyline derives from the *Shahnama*, but was inspired by the protests and demonstrations that defined the Green Movement in Iran in 2009 and the Arab Spring from 2010 to 2011.[46] Neshat brings the inherent nationalism of the Iranian national epic into the present by using portraits of friends and acquaintances with their hands crossed diagonally PLATES 21 A–B over their hearts to depict patriots and a smaller group of villains represented by full-length male portraits with tattoo-like battle scenes from the *Shahnama* (including Rustam) covering their bare upper torsos.[47]

Sculptor Yasmin Sinai, working in her characteristic medium of paper and cardboard, reinterprets the mythological story of a great woman warrior in the PLATES 33 AND 34 *Shahnama*, indeed the only woman combatant in the text. Gurdafarid is the daughter of a petty ruler whose fortress guards the border between Iran and Turan. When her father's chief champion is captured by the invading Turanian army, she dons armor and rides out to challenge the enemy's leader.[48] Sinai extracts and dramatically visualizes her story for a contemporary audience, in part as a reminder of the significant role women have played and continue to play in Iran. The two faces of Gurdafarid—the puppet head and the mounted warrior—are self-portraits of the artist.[49]

---

45 Relatively little so far has been written about this artist. For general biographical details and images of some of her other works, see Saeb Eigner, *Art of the Middle East: Modern and Contemporary Art of the Arab World and Iran* (London: Merrell, 2010), 372–73.

46 See Melissa Chiu and Melissa Ho, eds., *Shirin Neshat: Facing History* (Washington, D.C.: Smithsonian Books, 2015), see 162–83 for the Book of Kings series.

47 The tattoo-like images are derived from a lithograph edition of the text, *Shahnama-yi Bahaduri*, Tehran, 1901–8, belonging to the artist. See Ulrich Marzolph, "The Last Qajar *Shahnama*: The *Shahnama-yi Bahaduri* (1319–26/1901–8)," *Pembroke Papers* 5 (2006): 259–76. Such tattoos may also link the figures with members of the zurkhana (SEE PLATE 24). See Shadi Shafiei's essay in this volume.

48 She is opposed by the Turanian hero Suhrab, whom she does not defeat in single combat, but her bravery delays the invasion of Iran. She also plays a key role in presaging the greatest tragedy of the *Shahnama*—the death of Suhrab at the hands of his father, Rustam, as from the safety of her father's fortress, she taunts the now-smitten Suhrab by predicting his downfall.

49 This sculptural group is part of a larger installation piece, including video components, and is divided into discrete sections, first shown at the Courtyard Gallery, Dubai, in 2015.

Out of Time

In this essay, as in the exhibition itself, the goal has been to portray the ideas of identity, politics, faith, history, and culture that help define the remarkably diverse artistic heritage of Iran as viewed through the lens of time. The recurrent themes highlighted here are those that Iranian artists have rediscovered, reinterpreted, and repurposed with the passage of time, in each instance creating something artistically novel and culturally, socially, and politically relevant. Rather than look toward the future for the possibility of time travel, perhaps we should look to the past; time and again, by invoking the past as a means of describing the present, Iranian art (like ta'ziya theater) allows us to transcend the traditional constraints of time and space. It is perhaps inherent to our nature to look not only ahead but behind us.

Behind us no bird sings
Behind us no wind blows
Behind us the green window of the poplar is shut
Behind us the dust has settled over every pinwheel
Behind us lies the weariness of history

پشت سر مرغ نمی خواند
پشت سر باد نمی آید
پشت سر پنجره ی سبز صنوبر بسته است
پشت سر روی همه فرفره ها خاک نشسته است
پشت سر خستگی تاریخ است

Sohrab Sepehri,
from "The Sound of Water's Footsteps," 1964

Sheida Dayani on

The Theatrical Roots of Contemporary Visual Arts in Iran

It is alleged that shortly before his untimely death, renowned modernist poet and painter Sohrab Sepehri (1928–1980) was asked about his profession by a friendly, religious hajji: "What job do you do?" "Just what you see here, painting." "Painting doors and walls?" "No, just what you see here." "What? Trees?" "Yes." "Why don't you paint icons?" "Icons?! I'm an icon myself." Years later, the bewildered hajji was still asking why the painter called himself an icon.[1]

Beyond its humor, this anecdote succinctly captures a spectrum of visual arts that existed in Iran during the 1970s. At one end was the pious act of painting in the pictorial traditions; at the other was Sepehri's minimalist yet mystical modernism, void of any religious or national inflection. Between them lay the Saqqakhana school, which revolved around mixing the traditional past with the modern contemporary to create a "national" artistic identity.[2] Among its pioneers were Charles Hossein Zenderoudi, Faramarz Pilaram, and Parviz Tanavoli, whose works—including those in this catalogue—have left their mark of neo-traditionalism on the visual and graphic arts of contemporary Iran. The Saqqakhana school has been studied as both an art form and a social phenomenon; its theatrical subtext, however, remains largely unexplored. The theatrical quality found in the works of the Saqqakhana school is a common thread that binds contemporary artworks, religious murals, and miniatures of epic-heroic poetry books, like the *Shahnama*. It also accounts for the humorous comparison Sepehri made between himself as a mystical icon of modernism and the religious icons that he was urged to revive from the past.

The Saqqakhana school is named after the public water fountains built in memory of Imam Husain and the Shi'ite martyrs who endured extreme thirst in the Battle of Karbala on the day of Ashura in the month of Muharram of 680.[3] According to popular Shi'ite belief, participating in annual mourning ceremonies and reenacting the suffering of the Karbala martyrs paves the way to salvation and guarantees intercession by Imam Husain on the Day of Judgment. Over centuries, Muharram ceremonies have taken various forms; none, however, inculcates the reliving of the past as efficiently as *ta'ziya*, the passion play of Shi'ite Islam in which performers reenact the martyrdom of Karbala. Ta'ziya evolved in the mid-eighteenth century out of public lamentations (*rauzakhani*).[4] It spread as the main form of Iranian drama under Nasir al-Din Shah Qajar (r. 1848–96) because it assisted him in maintaining an alternative form of popular Shi'ism in contrast to its official practice, thus counterbalancing the monopoly on religion by the ulama (the Muslim clerical class with authority on

1 Massoud Behnoud, "Timsal-i Sohrab," YouTube video, 3:43, from the video series *Hizar Dastan ba Massoud Behnoud*, May 31, 2017, https://www.youtube.com/watch?v=j18mQe42dXA.

2 The term "Saqqakhana" was coined in 1962 by Karim Emami and developed by him in 1977 to refer to paintings, sculptures, and decorative arts that use Shi'ite and Iranian motifs, Perso-Islamic iconography, Persian calligraphy, and geometric compositions in modern Western forms with recurrent colors inspired by mourning traditions (green, red, black, brass yellow, and soft blue). The school is typified by Parviz Tanavoli's *Lion and Sword* carpets (SEE PLATES 25 AND 26). See Karim Emami, "Saqqakhaneh School Revisited" in *Saqqakhaneh*, ed. Karim Emami and Peter Lamborn Wilson (Tehran: Tehran Museum of Contemporary Art, 1977), republished in *Iran Modern*, ed. Fereshteh Daftari and Layla S. Diba (New York: Asia Society, 2013), 230–31. See also Hamid Keshmirshekan, "Neo-Traditionalism and Modern Iranian Painting: The *Saqqa-khaneh* School in the 1960s," *Iranian Studies* 38, no. 4 (December 2005): 607–30.

3 Imam Husain, grandson of the prophet Muhammad, and his family and followers were brutally murdered in battle against the army of the Sunni caliph Yazid on the day of Ashura, the tenth day of the month of Muharram. For an actual *saqqakhana*, formerly in Hamadan, see Daftari and Diba, eds., *Iran Modern*, 31, fig. 12.

4 Some scholars, such as Bahram Beyzai, date ta'ziya to the seventeenth century. See Peter Chelkowski, ed., *Ta'ziyeh: Ritual and Drama in Iran* (New York: New York University Press/Soroush Press, 1979), and "Ta'zia," in *Encyclopaedia Iranica*, July 15, 2009, http://www.iranicaonline.org/articles/tazia.

religion and law).[5] The ubiquity and amusing aspects of ta'ziya pushed this theatrical tradition beyond its function as a mourning ritual and normalized it as a form of entertainment, however tragic. The Qur'anic, mythological, and literary plots that entered its repertoire in the second half of the nineteenth century included stories with romantic, comic, and melodramatic dimensions. Some ta'ziya began with humorous preludes from the indigenous Iranian comedic form known as *taqlid* (parody); the integration of the two forms with subject matters other than the Karbala tragedy helped create "comic ta'ziya" (*shabih-i muzhik*). This hybrid genre has left its imprint on contemporary Iranian visual art—even on works that appear void of discernible comedic effects.

The "mixed spirit of mournfulness and fanfare" in which ta'ziya was performed influenced the Saqqakhana school's avant-garde combination of Western abstraction and Perso-Islamic motifs, as reflected in the works of Malekeh Nayiny

PLATES 1 A–J, 2, 48, AND 49

(2007) and Siamak Filizadeh (2009 and 2014).[6] It is also the spirit of Sepehri's joke about religious icons. Ta'ziya and the Saqqakhana school both draw on the symbols of Karbala and share popular Shi'ite motifs such as hands, amulets, talismanic seals, tents, armors, and animals. Zenderoudi's

PLATE 79

The Hand (c. 1960) is an example *par excellence*: the holy khamsa (Shi'ite palm symbol)[7] rises from a basin of water, which, in ta'ziya decor, represents the Euphrates River. The margins of Zenderoudi's collage are embellished with disparate sentences about lack of water and withering trees, signifying the arid Karbala.

A performance of ta'ziya surrounds its viewers physically and relies on the emotional response of its audience. Often the viewers sit around the stage while the actors and the animals move from the stage to the back of the seating area, then back to the stage. Animals usually include doves, sometimes with their wings painted red for blood, and horses of the battlefield. More elaborate performances may include other animals like deer at the ta'ziya of Imam Riza, camels at the ta'ziya of the Levant Captives, and lions—or, recently, lion mascot costumes—at the ta'ziya of Imam Husain. Physically and emotionally, the viewers are participants in the drama. Pouya Afshar's video installation *Mourn Baby Mourn* (2017) encom-

PLATES 93 A–B

passes its viewers in a tent in the same way ta'ziya would engulf its audience, although Afshar enhances the experience with a nonlinear narrative and an unusual mix of an "Ave Maria" recording and *damam-zani*, the mourning music of southern Iran. The actors hold their middle and index fingers around their eyes to signal that the audience is being watched and evaluated for its loyalty. Through the transparent face of Ali Asghar, Imam Husain's crying baby, a viewer is seen rising. As the baby's role subsides, the image of the viewer grows. This is a significant reference to the dramatic structure of ta'ziya: the further the plot develops, the closer the actors and the audience become and the more the audience participates. Afshar has also chosen the colors of the work mindfully, to either represent or rearrange the conventional colors of ta'ziya: green for saints, red for villains, yellow for the doubtful, and white for jinns and soon-to-be martyrs.

These digital references to ta'ziya are not without precedent; the indigenous theatrical form has been incorporated into the visual arts for two centuries. In the mid- to late nineteenth century, ta'ziya inspired narrative paintings of Karbala, primarily on large portable canvases and then on walls and tiles. The paintings on canvas, known as *parda* or *shamayel*, depicted a central scene surrounded by related vignettes. Pardas were also referred to as "coffeehouse paintings" because the canvases were commissioned by coffeehouses for their *naqqali* (storytelling) custom; this practice carried into the 1960s, when the Saqqakhana school was thriving.[8] Parda paintings were originally based on the events of Karbala, but the Qur'anic and mythological stories that entered ta'ziya also appeared in parda painting. Ta'ziya similarly influenced Karbala imagery on walls and tiles; Rana Javadi's *Never Ending Chaos 2* and *Never Ending Chaos 7* (both

PLATES 81 AND 82

2013) incorporate images of Karbala tilework in

5 Abbas Amanat, *Pivot of the Universe: Nasir al-Din Shah Qajar and the Iranian Monarchy, 1831–1896* (Berkeley: University of California Press, 1997), 434–35.

6 Ibid., 434.

7 *Khamsa* (the holy hand) here signifies the martyrdom of Abbas, Imam Husain's younger brother, whose hands were amputated in Karbala while he was taking water to his family. In other Shi'ite contexts, *khamsa* is known as the hand of Fatima, and symbolizes the five holy Shi'ites (Muhammad, Ali, Fatima, Hasan, and Husain). In both Shi'ism and Sunnism, *khamsa* is also emblematic of the five pillars of Islam, which vary in each branch.

8 Peter Chelkowski, "Narrative Painting and Painting Recitation in Qajar Iran," *Muqarnas* 6 (1989): 109.

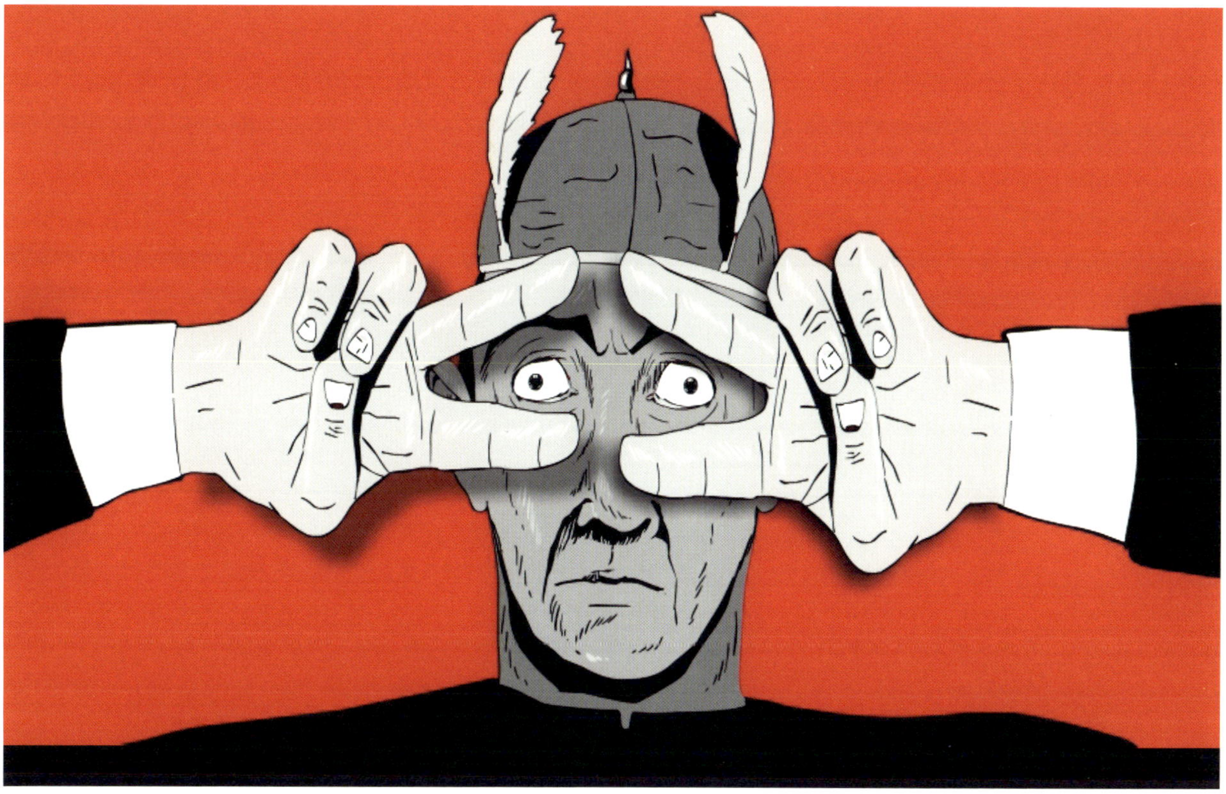

Pouya Afshar, detail from *Mourn Baby Mourn*, 2017 (SEE PLATES 93 A–B)

Kermanshah's Mu'avin al-Mulk *takiyya* (edifices built for mourning rituals).[9]

Regardless of the medium or subject matter, the productions reflected the ta'ziya theatrical praxis. For example, women were often depicted as faceless, covered in black garments. These representations were not based on piety, but resulted from a stage device designed to disguise the masculinity of the male actors playing women's roles in ta'ziya. In an 1851 lithograph by Mirza Ali Qoli Khu'i (SEE IMAGE AT RIGHT), Imam Husain's sister Zainab appears in a tent, covered in black. Next to her is a jinn dressed in white with a half-human body and an aura of light around its head, similar to the celestial aura around Imam Husain's decapitated head. In ta'ziya, jinns' faces are also covered with thin fabric or, more recently, with masks as a result of the integration of ta'ziya with improvisational comedy. Women's facelessness survived in iconography until 1979.[10] In this catalogue, the works of Afshar, Javadi, and Mohsen Yazdipour reflect the faceless portrayal of women in ta'ziya and parda paintings.

PLATES 88 A–E In his series Icons (2010) Shoja Azari reverses this convention by surpassing gender boundaries in his portraits of male Shi'ite saints. Siamak
PLATE 1J Tilizadeh's *Execution* (2014) shows women with veiled and unveiled faces and men in Qajar hats taking cell phone images of a Christlike Mirza Riza Kirmani being publically hung, not crucified, and put on display as an object of art. Such fusions of periods and identities recall the chaotic sequencing of events in vertical divisions in parda painting. As depicted in the late nineteenth- or early twentieth-century painting *Battle of*
PLATE 92 *Karbala* by Abdallah Musavar, the right side of every parda displays the hereafter, with saints in the serene paradise above and enemies tortured in hell below.[11] Similarly, one of Mohsen Yazdipour's
PLATE 80 B untitled 2008 photographs shows Imam Husain's daughter Sakina in front of his wounded horse

9 The takiyya of Mu'avin al-Mulk is covered entirely in underglaze painted tiles, which presumably were made after 1894–97, as some of the secular-themed tiles were derived from a lithographed book published at that time, see Jennifer Scarce, "Ancestral Themes in the Art of Qajar Iran," in *Islamic Art in the 19th Century: Tradition, Innovation, and Eclecticism*, ed. Doris Berens-Abouseif and Stephen Vernoit (Leiden: Brill, 2006), 231–56, 243–44.

10 Chelkowski, "Ta'zia."

11 Chelkowski, "Narrative Painting and Painting Recitation in Qajar Iran," 103.

after his murder, while in ta'ziya she pleads with him beforehand to beg him not to go to the battlefield. In contemporary works, artists not only rearrange the sounds, chronologies, and identities, but also redefine the sanctity of the past.
PLATES 80A–B Yazdipour's photographs equalize the Shi'ites and Yazid's army by blending the colors that traditionally represent good and evil in ta'ziya: Imam Husain holds a red flag and both sides are dressed in a mixture of green and red. Kazem Chalipa's
PLATE 89 *Every Day is Ashura* (1980s) predates this turnabout of colors. The archetypal Shi'ite figure with the green waist shawl and flag, who could be Imam Husain's brother Abbas, wears red armor on his head and red footwear, and is faceless like a woman, a jinn, or Shimr (Imam Husain's killer).[12] This amalgamation of good and evil colors is possible because blood, symbolized by red, is visible on both the killers and the killed. The inscription, a motto from mourning rituals, encapsulates the prevalent penchant for fusion: "Every day is Ashura, every land is Karbala."[13]

The anachronism of contemporary Iranian visual art, which is rooted in ta'ziya, depicted in parda, and resuscitated by the Saqqakhana school, allows artists to combine, reverse, and distort not only time periods, but also places, identities, and beliefs. This anachronism has enabled artists to revisit the past and revise its melodramatic frame of all-good versus all-evil. Regardless of the form, the past is revived and relived, either tragically, humorously, or in mixed spirit. And theater, with its inward eye, continues to provide the means for this self-assessment.

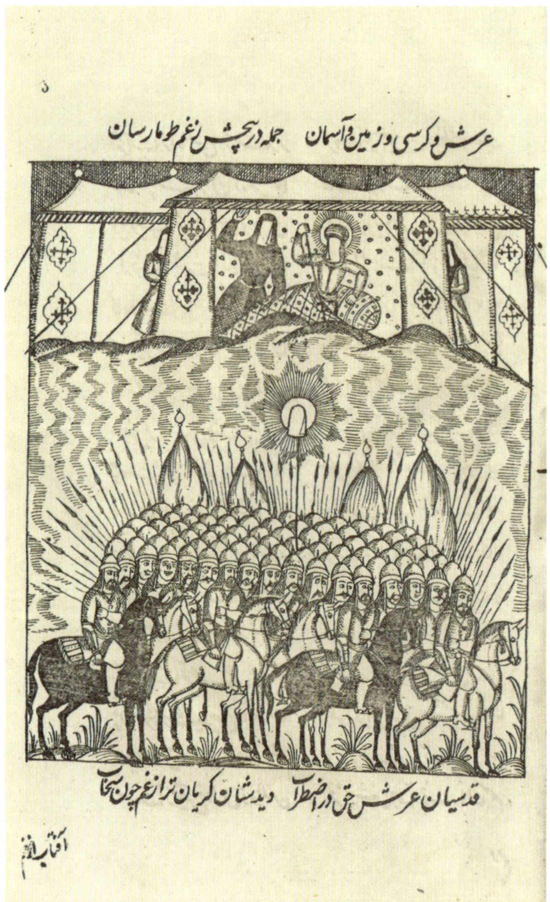

Ali Quli Khu'i, *Husain's head being paraded by the enemy forces at Karbala* from the *Asrar al-shahada*, AH 1268/1851, ZV 2222. fol. 148a (FOR MANUSCRIPT, SEE PLATE 94)

12 Sometimes the face of Shimr is also covered, suggesting that even the force of evil is shameful of this act.

13 This motto, which was famously used by Ayatollah Khomeini during the 1979 revolution, also appears in Habibollah Sadeghi's poster with the same title from the early 1980s.

Shabnam Rahimi-Golkhandan on

Ideology and Photography in Nineteenth-Century Iran

In September 1889, when Mishkat al-Mulk concluded his treatise on photography—*Risala-yi Aksiyya-yi Hashriyya*—the medium was already embedded in daily life in the Qajar state.[1] Taught at Tehran's institution of higher education, Dar al-Funun, and used as an instrument of both art education and military formation and survey, the practice of photography was also popularized by commercial studios and camera-wielding travelers. In such a viable market for photographic manuals, evidenced by many of the kind in circulation, Mishkat al-Mulk wrote a treatise on photography that only tangentially conforms to the genre. In it, he weaves a cursory review of the technical demands of the art and the trade, drawing connections between photography and life, death, and the afterlife. The author sums up his intentions in a Qur'anic verse: "Soon we will show them Our Signs in all the earth." He contends that he is producing "a treatise in photography with a higher purpose," summing it all up in a verse reminiscent of *The Conference of Birds*:[2]

دیده می‌خواهم که باشد شه شناس
تا شناسد شاه را در هر لباس

I need an eye that can recognize kings
So that it will know the king in any garb.[3]

Mishkat al-Mulk analogizes the recording of an image on photographic surfaces, negative and positive, with the divine documentation of a man's every deed on earth as explicated in this Qur'anic verse: "So, he who has done an atom's weight of good shall see it. And he who has done an atom's weight of evil shall see it."[4] He preaches the necessity of constant self-awareness—people ought to live their lives in unerring consciousness of the divine camera that captures their every move, thought, and indiscretion only to reveal them for review on the Day of Judgment. But rather than emphasizing the evidentiary and archival possibility the analogy affords, Mishkat al-Mulk ponders the implications of this sacred documentation as an instrument of self-regulation and self-fashioning. If a person is presented with photographs of their transgressions in a community of their peers, Mishkat al-Mulk says, they can neither deny the events nor alleviate the shame of their past actions. He asks the reader to imagine, on the other hand, the shame of being presented with the record of not just every indiscreet action, but also every impure thought and temptation in front of one's creator: a photographic record of both the material and the immaterial. In the ever-recording eye of this divine camera, the most virtuous is comparable only to the most self-aware sitter in front of the photographer or the painter who "tries his utmost to present himself as dignified and graceful...so that whoever sees the resultant image (*timsal*) doesn't ridicule and reproach him."[5]

The perpetual self-fashioning at the core of much of Mishkat al-Mulk's theological interpretation is on display in the four photographs of
PLATES 12–14 AND 16 Nasir al-Din Shah in this exhibition. From the earliest example of a young Nasir al-Din leaning
PLATE 13 on a chair in his palace courtyard to the now-iconic image of the seasoned monarch
PLATE 14 sitting on the footsteps of his Peacock Throne, Nasir al-Din embodies Mishkat al-Mulk's ideal portrait model. Self-aware and in control of his image, Nasir al-Din prided himself on his taste for and knowledge of photography.[6] He is credited with supporting all photographic endeavors in the court and with becoming one of the earliest royal practitioners and collectors of the new medium.[7]

1 The many albums in the collection of the Golestan Palace Museum of constructions and renovations of historic (mostly religious) sites around the country attest to the extensive surveys undertaken by Nasir al-Din Shah's court photographers. Likewise, the many photographers who accompanied military envoys to the country and photographed its different sites and peoples have also left behind albums of photographs in the Golestan as well as elsewhere in the world. Muhammad Hasan Khan I'timad al-Saltana, *Al-Ma'athir wa'l-Athar*, vol. 1, ed. Iraj Afshar (Tehran: Intisharat-i Asatir, 1984), 131.

2 Muhammad ibn Ali Mishkat al-Mulk, *Risala-yi Aksiyya-yi Hashriyya*, 1889, Majles Library (call number 17630/208795).

3 For the actual verse, see Attar's *Mantiq al-Tair*, Turbat-i Jam's Social, Cultural, News Website, http://www.iqbalcyberlibrary.net/pdf/MT.pdf. I am grateful to Professor Wheeler Thackston for his assistance with the translation.

4 Qur'an 99:7–8.

5 *Risala-yi Aksiyya-yi Hashriyya*, 1889, Majles Library.

6 On his first trip to Europe in 1873, when Nadar visits him to take his photo, the shah mentions only the photographer's past as balloon-rider and not much of the photograph.

7 Reza Sheikh and Carmen Pérez González, "Editorial," *History of Photography* 37, no. 1 (2013): 1–6.

Historians are quick to credit Nasir al-Din Shah with the rise of photography in Iran, but the evolution of his engagement with the medium has gone unnoticed. The withering theatricality of the earlier, more private portraits of the king—mostly captured in his own palace and courtyard—allows a glimpse of that evolution. In the latter years of Nasir al-Din's reign, he became increasingly occupied with photographic enactments of royal stature rather than records of self-expression. This gradual shift of focus in the court is concurrent with another, perhaps more widespread, phenomenon: photographs rapidly became commonplace keepers and markers of time rather than reminders of celebrated events or playful experiments in image making. Of course there are exceptions. Antoin Sevruguin's image of Nasir al-Din on the footsteps of his throne stages the exclusive connection between the king and the cherished photographer and echoes the earlier visual vocabulary of meticulously staged royal portraits. The image appears contemporaneous with another in the exhibition: Herbert Rose Barraud's portrait of a rather apprehensive Nasir al-Din Shah. In it, Nasir al-Din Shah gazes into the distance and leans forward in his seat, his glove tucked under his right hand. The photograph marked the occasion of his third and final trip abroad and the all-important British royal reception.[8] Both photographs of the king present him in full regalia, seemingly dressed for an event. In the Sevruguin photo, the out-of-focus textures in the background, the intricate filigree (*zari* or *serme*) of the king's coat, and his reclining pose embed Nasir al-Din in the image of his court's opulence. It contrasts sharply with Barraud's photograph—a spare background and tight crop tilt the whole composition slightly forward toward the viewer, magnifying the king's impatient posture and the ephemerality of the occasion: he doesn't belong there and is eager to leave.

PLATES 12 AND 13

PLATE 14

PLATE 16

In the conclusion of his manuscript, Mishkat al-Mulk notes that he has written his treatise at the behest of a Mirza Muhammad Khan, *Muqarrab al-Khaqan*, the most special servant of the king (پیشخدمت خاصه).[9] Only one such Muhammad—granted both the title of Khan and the position of special servant before being promoted to that of Naqqashbashi and later Kamal al-Mulk—a one Mirza Muhammad Khan Ghaffari Kashani, appears in the archives and diaries of the time. Could the renowned painter of the Qajar period be the one who requested the treatise?[10] The answer is unclear, but it seems that by the 1890s in Iran, the normalized symbiosis between portrait photography and painting implied that a reassessment of the former's practices had an unfiltered reflection on the latter's. Mishkat al-Mulk's ideal portrait model was as self-conscious in front of the photographer as he was in front of the painter, so that the two might produce identical timsals of the thing in front of them. The painter with his canvas and brushes should function the same as the photographer with his camera; they aimed to produce the same idealized image. And Mishkat al-Mulk isn't the only one unfazed by such close ties. In his diaries, the king's confidant and historian I'timad al-Saltana writes about the effect of teaching painting from photographs on his contemporaries' depiction of portrait (and landscape), making them "life-like."[11] Mishkat al-Mulk's treatise offers an explanation of precisely what such life-likeness entails or connotes. His attempt at defamiliarizing the camera as an analogy for theological mystery, on the other hand, should read as another ode to that ubiquity and the varied modes of self-fashioning it ushered in.[12]

8 The significance of the Nasir al-Din Shah's royal reception in London remained a contentious part of his planning for the trip. Upon his second visit in 1878, the king was not invited to London and his only contact with British royalty was a brief encounter with "the crown prince" in his hotel room in Paris. Nasir al-Din Shah, *Ruznama-yi Khatirat-i Nasir al-Din Shah dar Safar-i Duvvum-i Farangistan* (1295) [The Diary of Nasir al-Din Shah in His Second Trip Abroad (1878)] (Tehran: Intisharat-i Sazman-i Asnad-i Milli-yi Iran, 2000), 162.

9 *Risala-yi Aksiyya-yi Hashriyya*, 1889, Majles Library.

10 Archival evidence of the life and career of Mishkat al-Mulk is scarce. I have yet to come across any indication of a connection between him and Kamal al-Mulk.

11 I'timad al-Saltana, *Al-Ma'athir wa'l-Athar*, vol. 1, 168.

12 For more on the relationship between painting and photography, see David J. Roxburgh, "Troubles with Perspective: Case Studies in Picture-Making from Qajar Iran," in *Art History in the Wake of the Global Turn*, ed. Jill H. Casid and Aruna D'Souza (New Haven: Yale University Press, 2014), 107–25, and Layla S. Diba, "Qajar Photography and Its Relationship to Iranian Art: A Reassessment," *History of Photography* 37, no. 1 (2013): 85–98; on Kamal al-Mulk Muhammad Ghaffari, see A. Ashraf with Layla S. Diba, "Kamal-al-Molk, Mohammad Ghaffari Kashani," in *Encyclopaedia Iranica* 15 (New York: Encyclopaedia Iranica Foundation, 2010), 417–33.

The Anachronistic Role of SAFAVID MANUSCRIPT ILLUSTRATIONS

Sheila R. Canby

In Iranian art, whether contemporary or premodern, the historical past is entwined with the present. Whereas today an artist might revive a figure from a well-known story or historical episode in order to encrypt a message about current events, manuscript illustrations from the sixteenth and seventeenth centuries often do the opposite. During the Safavid dynasty (1501–1722), manuscripts embellished with illuminated decoration and highly complex and colorful paintings illustrating fictional tales, historic events, or scientific information were as highly prized as large oil paintings were in Europe. In these manuscripts, artists depicted historical characters from the relevant stories in the guise of modern men and women. This form of anachronism extended to pictures of historical settings containing objects and architecture, which artists portrayed as the accoutrements and settings of Safavid court life. As early as the fourteenth century under the Ilkhanid rulers of Iran, artists inserted contemporary meanings into representations of historical figures by choosing unusual episodes that could give pictorial form to a poet's words and subtly suggest comparisons with known figures in the circle of the manuscript's royal patron.[1] The Safavid illustrations discussed here encompass several approaches and invite multiple interpretations.

While many poetic manuscripts were illustrated, the text that includes the greatest number of references to historical figures is the *Shahnama* (Book of Kings) of Abu'l-Qasim Firdausi (d. c. 1020).[2] Royal social gatherings depicted in the *Shahnama* produced for Shah Tahmasp (r. 1524–76) reflect practices mentioned in contemporary sixteenth-century accounts, despite the fact that the king and his circle described in the manuscript are the stuff of legend. One unusual illustration that shows Firdausi on the ship of Shi'ism with the Prophet Muhammad, Ali, and Ali's sons conflates historical periods, delivering an undeniable religious message of relevance to the Safavids. In another illustration, from a seventeenth-century manuscript, an ancient king is depicted with a mustache in the style of Shah Abbas I and is shown kneeling in prayer, details not seen in any single-page portrait of the king. All of the paintings discussed in this essay present ambiguous references, enabling both the manuscripts' patrons and contemporary viewers to examine them at face value as illustrations of the text, or as metaphors exploring the practices and mores of their own societies.

In the illustration *Manuchihr Welcomes Sam but Orders War upon Mihrab*, the king, crowned and enthroned in a pavilion, has just proclaimed a festival upon hearing his paladin Sam recount his successes in battle. Whereas most fifteenth-century depictions of this scene include a minimal number of courtiers and concentrate on the encounter between Manuchihr and Sam, this scene portrays a festive occasion. Not only does a servant stand ready to proffer a cup of wine to the king or Sam, but musicians play and grandees tipple on carpets arrayed before the throne. PLATE 8

1 Abolala Soudavar states in regard to the dispersed Mongol *Shahnama*, "every painting was designed to have a dual representation: to reflect a story of the *Shāhnāmé*, and to evoke an episode of Mongol history." Abolala Soudavar, "The Saga of Abu-Sa'id Bahador Khan. The Abu-Sa'idname," in *The Court of the Il-Khans 1290–1340*, vol. 12, ed. Julian Raby and Teresa Fitzherbert (Oxford: Oxford University Press, 1996), 95.

2 Considered the national epic of Iran, the *Shahnama* consists of between 50,000 and 60,000 rhyming couplets, depending on the recension. It was completed in 1010 and its patron was Mahmud of Ghazna.

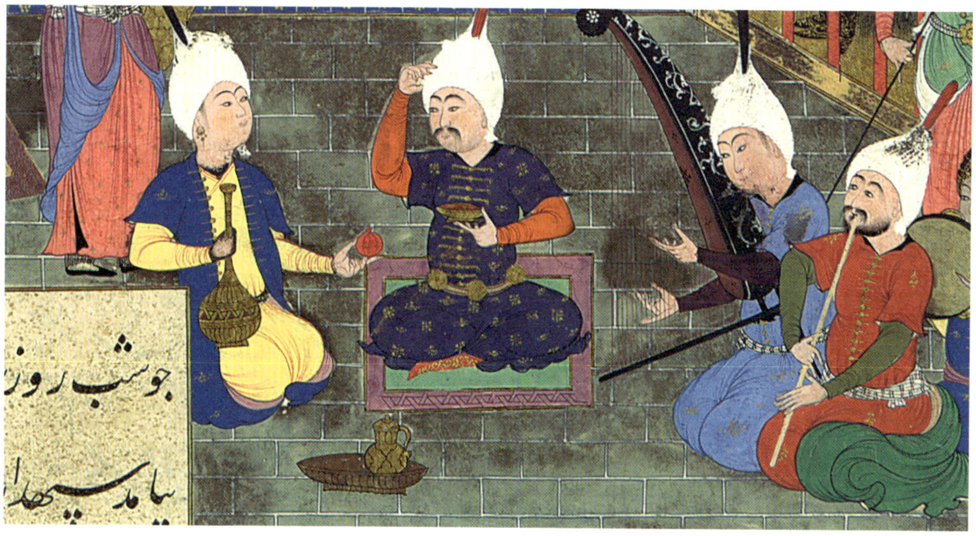

Young women peer down at the scene from the upper story of the palace. All of the male figures wear the distinctive Safavid headgear: a turban wrapped around a tall, baton-like *kulah*, or cap, called a *taj*. Since Manuchihr appears early in the *Shahnama*—in Iran's prehistoric, mythologized past—the painter of the illustration, Abdul-Aziz, can be forgiven for not trying to reproduce the dress, musical instruments, and tableware of that bygone era. Instead, he has pictured a gathering that could have taken place in the late 1520s at the Safavid court. From the gold throne with high sides to the long-necked wine bottles and royal belt with gold medallions, the details of material culture in this image are consistent with the few extant counterparts in modern collections, suggesting that Abdul-Aziz chose to portray the world of his patron, Shah Tahmasp, as accurately as possible.[3]

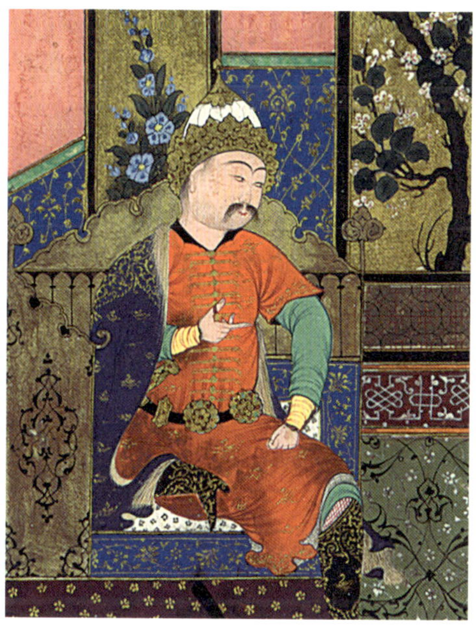

Painting attributed to Abdul-Aziz, details from *Manuchihr Welcomes Sam but Orders War upon Mihrab*, from the *Shahnama* of Firdausi, c. 1525 (SEE PLATE 8)

3 A seventeenth-century gold throne set with gems is comparable in type but is square. See Sheila R. Canby, *The Shahnama of Shah Tahmasp: The Persian Book of Kings* (New York: Metropolitan Museum of Art, 2014), fig. 56. For the bottle and belt see Jon Thompson and Sheila R. Canby, eds., *Hunt for Paradise: Court Arts of Safavid Iran, 1501–1576* (Milan: Skira, 2003), figs. 8.3, 8.5.

Why would this Safavid artist represent historical and legendary figures as if they were contemporaries of his patron, in a modern setting and with up-to-date accoutrements? By populating the scene with familiar-looking figures, did Abdul-Aziz embed a coded message equating Shah Tahmasp, who acceded to the Safavid throne in 1524, at age ten, with Manuchihr, who had also come to the throne as a boy? While such an interpretation is plausible for some illustrations in Shah Tahmasp's *Shahnama*, the attire and architecture appearing throughout the manuscript are consistently Safavid in style, whereas only some images resonate with actual events and individuals from the reign of Shah Tahmasp or that of his father, Shah Isma'il. By visually linking the past with the present in Shah Tahmasp's *Shahnama*, the artist legitimizes the Safavid dynasty and the continuum of kingship from Iran's dimmest past to the present. With the past "dressed" as the present, the current relevance of this historical moment would have been obvious but unstated to Safavid viewers. Similarly, but in reverse, Iranian works of the twentieth and twenty-first centuries employ figures sporting historical costumes to draw parallels between events and personalities of the past and those of the present day.

Since the *Shahnama* recounts the history of Iran's kings before the Arab conquest and the adoption of Islam, Safavid artists faced challenges of another sort when making explicit references to Islam and, in particular, to Shi'ism, the sect followed by the Safavids and established in Iran as what might be termed "the state religion." Firdausi's *Parable of the Ship of Shi'ism* from the *Shahnama of Shah Tahmasp* PLATE 83 presents an explicitly sectarian interpretation of a section of Firdausi's prologue to his epic. The parable itself concerns seventy ships on a stormy sea, including one "in the shape of a bride" carrying Muhammad and his son-in-law and successor, Ali. All the ships are doomed to sink, but the "clever one" will find salvation in death if he chooses to ride on the ship carrying the Prophet, Ali, and the *ahl-i bait-i nabi*, the Prophet's descendants.[4] Although the illustration and the section on which it is based are from the earliest part of the manuscript written by Firdausi, they are preceded by a foreword written in 1426 for the Timurid prince Baysunghur that includes two additional paintings depicting Firdausi. In this prologue, Firdausi states, "I am the slave of the *ahl-i bait-i nabi*, the praiser of the dust under the feet of the inheritor [Ali],"[5] thus identifying with the "clever one" who joins the ship and confirming his devotion to the Shi'ite hierarchy.

Although illustrations of this scene appear in several *Shahnama* manuscripts from the fourteenth and fifteenth centuries,[6] the painting in Shah Tahmasp's *Shahnama* stands apart for the complexity of its composition and the numerous details that emphasize the new Shi'ite orthodoxy established under the Safavids. On a sea, once silver and now tarnished to black, a large ship with a red-and-white sail and a duck-headed bowsprit moves toward the right side of the page, while two smaller craft float nearby. In the bow is a pavilion in which two veiled, haloed

4 Raya Y. Shani, "Illustrations of the Parable of the Ship of Faith in Firdausi's Prologue to the *Shahnama*," in *Shahnama Studies I*, ed. Charles Melville (Cambridge: University of Cambridge, 2006), 3.

5 Ibid., 34.

6 Ibid., 2–28.

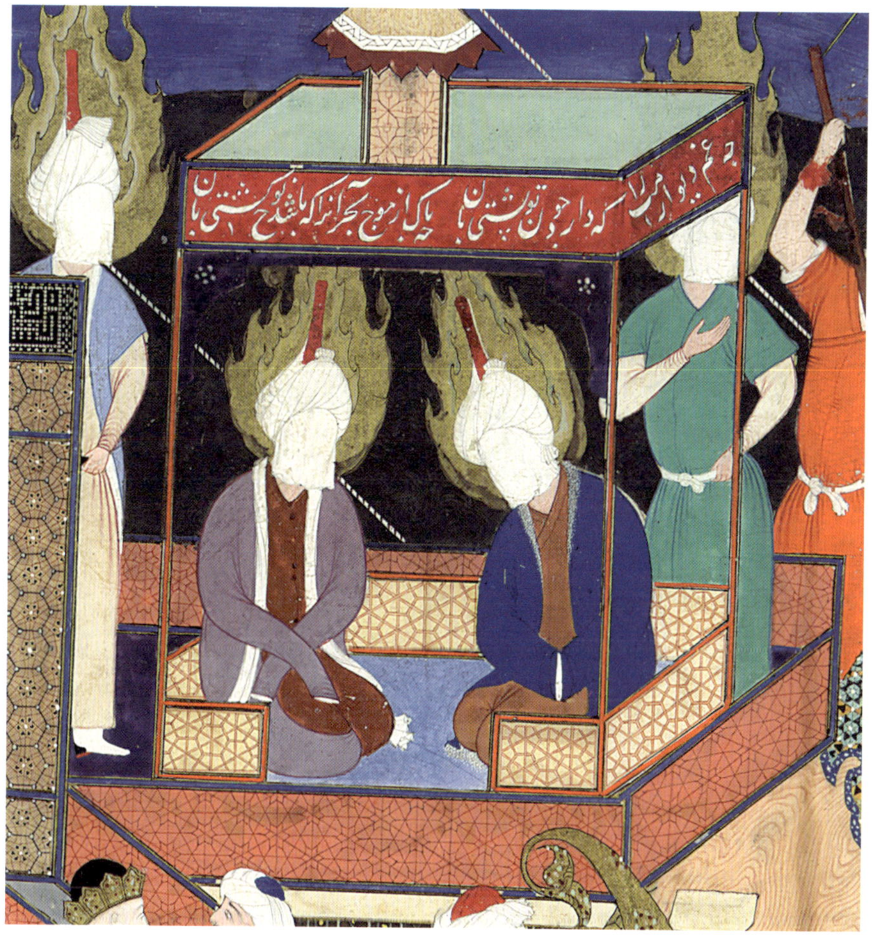

Painting attributed to Mirza Ali, detail from *Parable of the Ship of Sh'ism*, from the *Shahnama* of Firdausi, c. 1530–35 (SEE PLATE 83)

figures kneel. Behind them to the left and right are two standing figures, also veiled with heads surrounded by flaming aureoles. These are the four members of the *ahl-i bait-i nabi*, the family of the house of the Prophet: Muhammad and Ali (kneeling), and Ali's sons Hasan and Husain (standing). None of these figures holds an attribute, but several details suggest that the kneeling figure in the blue robe is Muhammad. Not only is his cloak lined with fur, possibly an indication of his status, but he is also placed beneath the name "Muhammad" in the hemistich of text set above the pavilion, while the name "Ali" appears to the left on the same line. The poetry that runs along the roof of the pavilion is addressed to Muhammad, referred to as "you": "What fear need be for the ramparts of a people whose mainstay is you."[7] The word "you" appears directly above the head of the blue-robed kneeling figure, reinforcing the identification of this figure as Muhammad. The inscription over the gate to the pavilion reads, "May the portals of this threshold forever open upon opportunity!"[8] These words and their placement may allude to Ali, as on the preceding page Firdausi quotes Muhammad as saying, "For I am the city of knowledge, Ali is my door."[9]

7 Martin B. Dickson and Stuart Cary Welch, eds., *The Houghton Shahnameh*, vol. 2 (Cambridge, MA: Harvard University Press, 1981), no. 6.
8 Ibid.
9 Shani, "Illustrations of the Parable," 34.

The turbans wrapped around kulahs with the taj imply that the figures are as relevant to the era of the Safavids as to that of the parable. Even more specific to Safavid belief is the veiling of Muhammad and his relatives, a pictorial innovation under the first Safavid shah, Isma'il I (r. 1501–24).[10] The result of garbing Muhammad, Ali, Hasan, and Husain in Safavid clothing is an elision of time whereby the Shi'ite past and present are one. Their veils amplify the mystery of their corporeal identities so the viewer can merge the first four Imams with the latter-day sayyids or shahs, including Shah Tahmasp, all of whom claimed descent from Muhammad through Ali's wife, Fatima.

Two other figures on the ship deserve scrutiny. A seated man, seen from the back, wears a crown and is presumably a king. His white beard indicates that he cannot be the manuscript patron, Shah Tahmasp, who would have been around fifteen years old at the time this painting was produced. Rather, the artist may have intended to portray Shah Isma'il (1487–1524) or his father, Haidar (1459–1488), the charismatic shaikh of the Sufi shrine at Ardabil. In a dream, Ali came to Haidar and described the *taj-i haidari*, a skullcap with a long, baton-like vertical extension, which Haidar and his Turkmen devotees subsequently adopted. Although Haidar's adherence to Shi'ism is not confirmed by this story, by the reign of his son Isma'il, both the taj and twelver Shi'ism—which accepts twelve historical descendants of Muhammad, called Imams, as spiritual leaders—were defining signifiers of the Safavid dynasty and its followers. The final figure of note on the large ship, the white-bearded standing figure who wears a fur-lined red cloak and

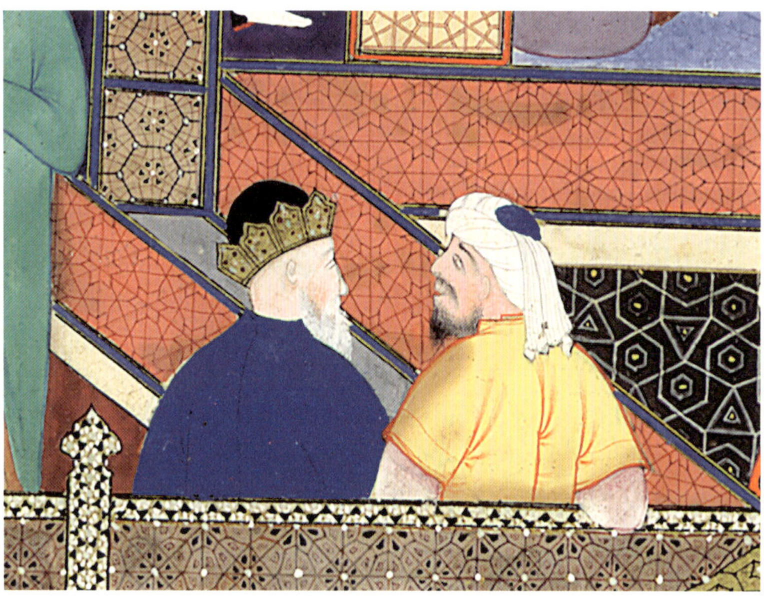

Painting attributed to Mirza Ali, detail from *Parable of the Ship of Sh'ism*, from the *Shahnama* of Firdausi, c. 1530–35 (SEE PLATE 83)

10 Christiane Gruber, "Between Logos (*Kalima*) and Light (*Nūr*): Representations of the Prophet Muhammad in Islamic Painting," *Muqarnas* 26 (2009): 254n5. According to Gruber, the facial veil "was used as a purposeful means of associating the ruler's persona with that of the Prophet [in the period of Shah Isma'il]." However, Gruber states that under Shah Tahmasp the veil "lost its initial religio-political associations with" Shah Isma'il and was used "to inhibit a viewer's full witnessing of the Prophet."

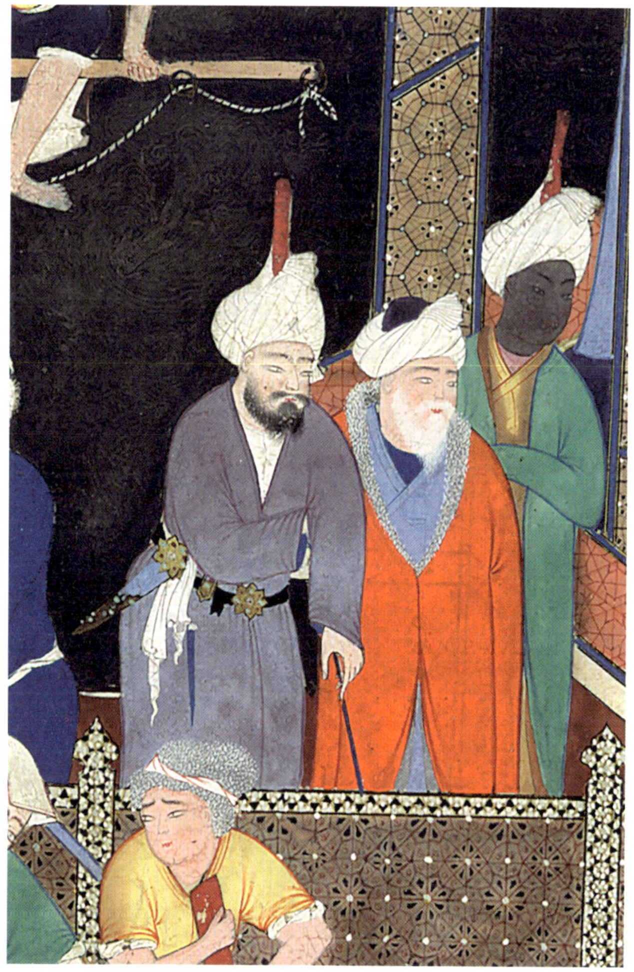

Detail from *Parable of the Ship of Sh'ism*, from the *Shahnama* of Firdausi, c. 1530–35 (SEE PLATE 83)

a turban with a low kulah, may be Firdausi. In his first appearance in the manuscript, *Firdausi Encounters Three Poets of Ghazna*,[11] he sports a turban with a similarly shaped kulah. In *The Houghton Shahnameh*, Martin B. Dickson and Stuart Cary Welch have suggested that the figure next to him, who holds a walking stick and has a dagger in his belt, is Firdausi. However, the fur-lined cloak and white beard accord better with the idealized image of the revered poet, through whose words the centrality of religion to all the exploits described in the *Shahnama*, and thus all the events of Iranian history, is expressed.

By the second century of the Safavid dynasty, Shi'ite religious practices were well established in Iran. Two illustrations in a *Shahnama* of 1605 depict their protagonists praying: in one instance asking for God's forgiveness, and in the other thanking Him. As art historian Kishwar Rizvi has explained, the praying figures, Kai Kavus and Gushtasp, kneel on prayer rugs. Placed on the rugs are prayer beads (*tasbih*) and round clay disks known as *muhrs*, which the praying person would

PLATE 9

11 Canby, *The Shahnama of Shah Tahmasp*, 64. The image is on folio 7 recto.

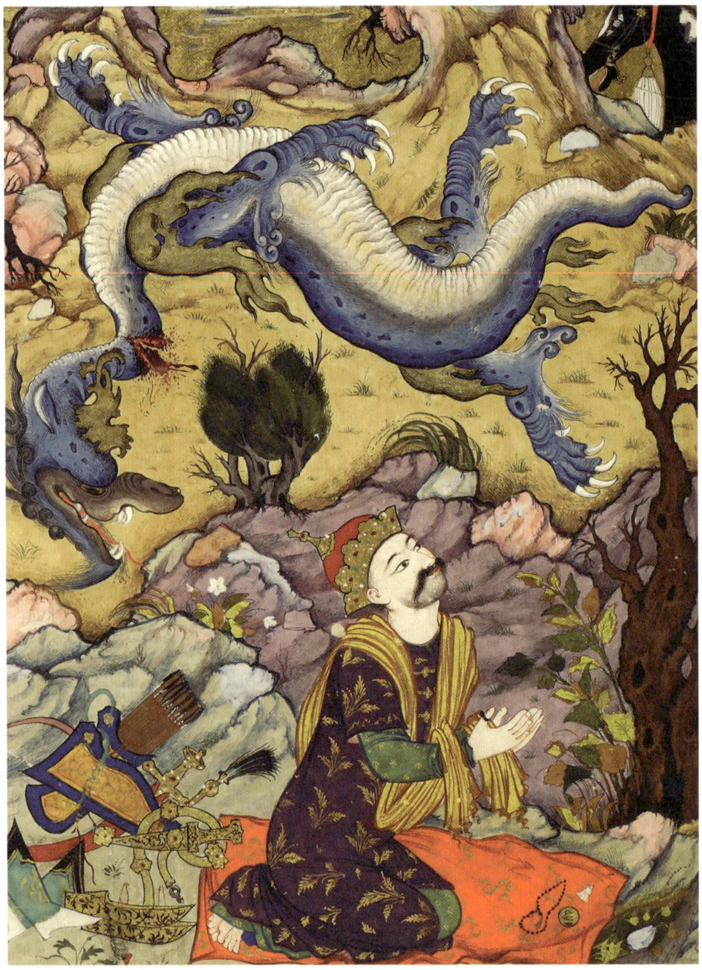

Detail from *Gushtasp and the Dragon of Mount Sakila*, from the *Shahnama* of Firdausi, AH 1014/1605 (SEE PLATE 9)

touch with his forehead.[12] Not only are these objects specific to Muslim prayer, but they are especially relevant in the context of Shiʿite Islam, the branch of the religion practiced by the Safavids. Muhrs are made from earth found in Shiʿite holy sites such as Karbala and Najaf, as well as Mashhad, home to the Shrine of Imam Riza. By 1605, the fifth Safavid shah, Abbas I, had been in power for eighteen years. During this time he had sought to normalize the observance of Shiʿite Islam, rooting out Sufis and others whose rituals he considered heterodox, and defeating the Uzbeks, a Sunni Turkic dynasty based mostly in Central Asia that had sacked and occupied the Shrine of Imam Riza in 1590. In the interest of religion, Shah Abbas commissioned the construction of congregational mosques such as the Masjid-i Shah in Isfahan, his capital, and reinstated Friday prayers and the sermons that accompanied them. Shah Abbas chose to project himself as a pious leader through both charitable acts and demonstrations of religious devotion, including a 1,000-kilometer pilgrimage on foot from Isfahan to the Shrine of Imam Riza in 1601.

12 Kishwar Rizvi, "The Suggestive Portrait of Shah ʿAbbas: Prayer and Likeness in a Safavid *Shahnama*," *Art Bulletin* 94, no. 2 (June 2012): 230–31.

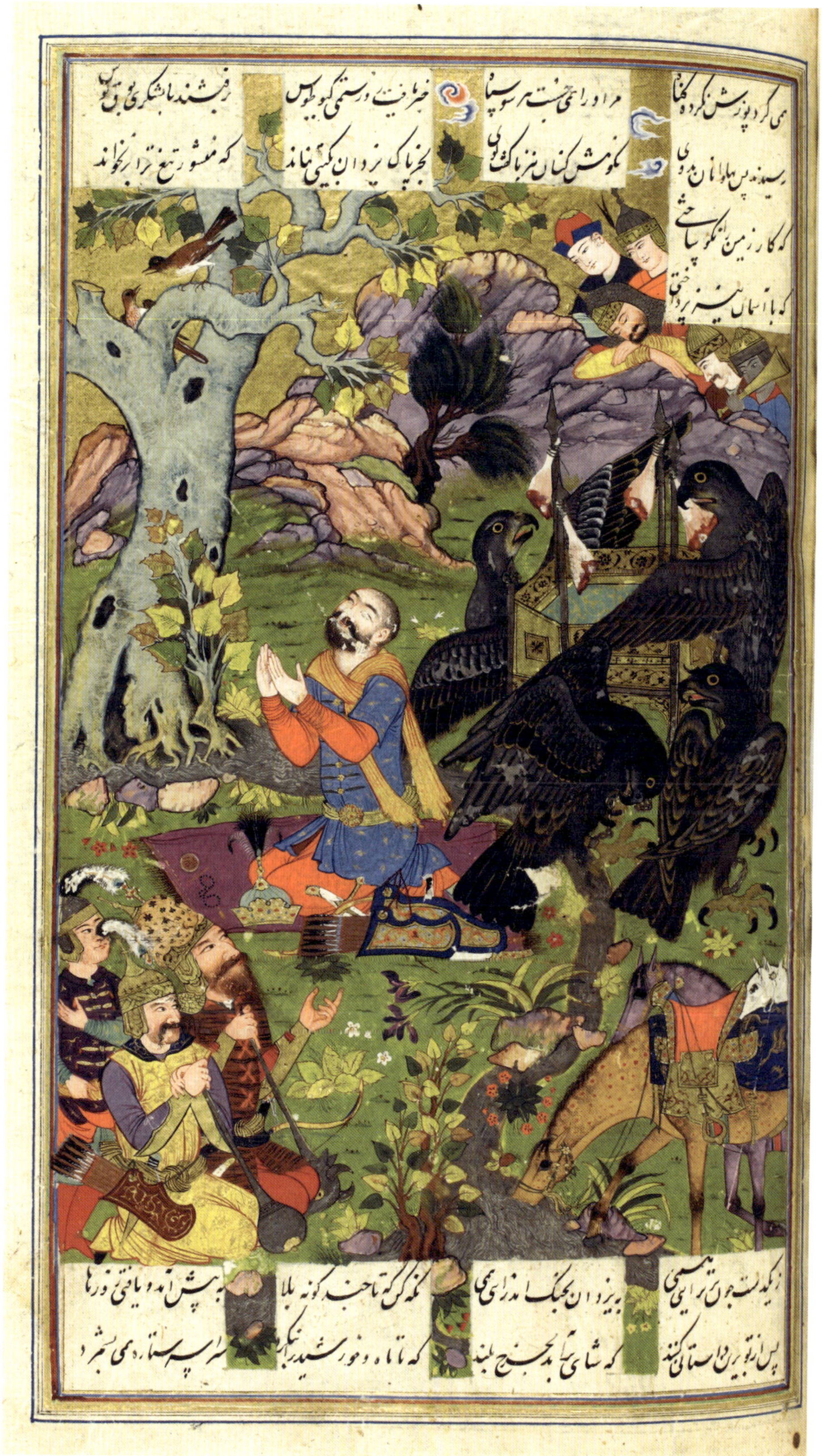

The Story of Kai Kavus and His Deception by Iblis, from the *Shahnama* of Firdausi, 1605. MS or. Fol. 4251, fol. 219r (FOR MANUSCRIPT, SEE PLATE 9)

Depictions of Kai Kavus and Gushtasp engaged in Shi'ite Muslim prayer are exceedingly rare in Safavid illustrated *Shahnama* manuscripts.[13] Yet while they appear to reference Shah Abbas's emphasis on the readoption of conventional Islamic practices, they do not necessarily portray Abbas in the guise of the repentant shah Kai Kavus or the victorious prince Gushtasp. The figures both sport long mustaches and short beards (or stubble, in the case of Gushtasp). Portraits of Shah Abbas from the second and third decades of the seventeenth century include this distinctive long mustache, invariably without a beard.[14] Yet throughout the 1605 *Shahnama* the same mustache appears on a range of figures, from Garshasp to Sam and Kai Khusrau to unnamed personages.[15] While the mustache suggests a likeness of Shah Abbas, it also reflects the desirability of looking like the shah and of adopting his "style" as a sign of respect and devotion to the king. In addition, the male facial hair depicted in drawings and paintings in the period of Shah Abbas signified age, with youths and young men represented with smooth cheeks, middle-aged men with mustaches, and older men with beards.[16] The figures of Kai Kavus and Gushtasp praying as well as the hairstyles, turban types, and horse trappings depicted throughout the 1605 *Shahnama* reflect the world of the artists and their patrons, possibly communicating messages of relevance to seventeenth-century viewers or simply drawing a parallel with the values and meaning of the *Shahnama* and the present day.

In the context of Iran's unbroken tradition of visual imagery and sophisticated poetic devices, artists and poets were masters of suggestion. Sufi ideas of the unreality of the physical world versus the hidden reality of spiritual fulfillment reinforced the acceptability of layering and hiding meanings; artists thus incorporated a rich matrix of references to the past and present into individual paintings rather than merely providing visual analogues to literary passages. Where a Safavid writer might avoid mentioning practices such as drinking alcohol, ostensibly prohibited by Shah Tahmasp and at times by Shah Abbas, a painter could, with impunity, depict a Safavid soiree complete with wine, as long as it illustrated the *Shahnama*. Such strategies changed depending on the era, but the power of evoking the present through representing the past remained constant.

13 Ibid., 232n34.

14 In this I disagree with Rizvi, who states that Gushtasp's "face stands out in particular, recognizable as that of Shah 'Abbas" (Rizvi, "The Suggestive Portrait of Shah 'Abbas," 244). See Ernst J. Grube and Eleanor Sims, "The Representations of Shāh 'Abbās I," in *L'Arco di fango che rubò la luce alle stelle: Studi in onore di Eugenio Galdieri per il suo settantesimo compleanno*, ed. Michele Bernardini et al. (Lugano: Edizioni Arte e Moneta, 1995), pls. 1–11. In none of the portraits illustrated by Grube and Sims does Shah Abbas sport a beard.

15 Volkmar Enderlein and Werner Sundermann, *Schāhnāme: Das persische Königsbuch, Miniaturen und Texte der Berliner Handschrift von 1605* (Leipzig, Germany: Kiepenheuer, 1988), 68, 74, 76, 79, 80, 85, 92, 95, 117, 127, 130, 134, 149, 155, 158, 161, 163, 177, 178, 182, 187, 190, 193.

16 Sheila R. Canby, "Age and Time in the Work of Riza," in *Persian Masters: Five Centuries of Painting*, ed. Sheila R. Canby (Bombay: Marg Publications, 1990), 71–84.

Sandra Williams on

Heroism in Contemporary Iranian Art

The hero's exceptionalism destines him to a life in which the very same qualities that set him apart also dictate his eventual demise. As Joseph Campbell wrote in his seminal work on the hero's journey, "The hero, the waker of his own soul, is himself but the convenient means of his own dissolution."[1] In Iran this dissolution is magnified and often characterized by a tragic end, as with the country's best-known heroes, Rustam and Imam Husain, who are discussed below. The tragedy of the hero is a significant and prolific subject in contemporary Iranian art, particularly as a vehicle for social and political commentary. This essay looks at two types of Iranian heroes, the *pahlavan* (champion)[2] and *shahid* (martyr), and how artists employ the hero and his end as a critical model. These two types of heroes often overlap in a manner that seems unique to Iran.[3]

The preeminent champion in the eleventh-century national epic the *Shahnama* (Book of Kings), Rustam is known for his superior battle skills and repeated defense of Iran's kings. He is also known for mistakenly killing his son Suhrab and later dying by the treachery of his stepbrother.[4] Rustam was frequently illustrated in manuscripts and paintings and remains a popular subject for contemporary artists.

PLATES 5, 19, AND 20

For example, Fereydoun Ave looks to Rustam, in the guise of Olympic silver medalist wrestler Abbas Jadidi, as a symbol of masculinity and virtue in his collage works *Rostam in Late Summer—Revisited* and *Rostam in the Dead of Winter*.

PLATES 3 AND 4

In the former, against a background of blooming roses, the hero's image is repeated several times to create an intimidating army of Rustams, whose effect is magnified by an image of the wrestler defeating an opponent. The triumphal moment, however, gives way in the second work, where the vibrancy of summer is replaced with the pale white wash of winter, marred by splatters of red, blood-like paint, and Rustam is shown alone, beleaguered by hyenas and vultures. The jarring decline of the warrior's environment unsettles his power and calls into question the effectiveness of the hero in modern times. In a more lighthearted but no less critical manner, Pouya Afshar and Soroush Rezaee's five-episode video work *Rostam in Wonderland* also considers Rustam in modern Iran.

PLATE 77

The hero comically stumbles over the perils of contemporary society, from falling victim to con men to accidentally purchasing knockoffs of pharmaceuticals. Here Rustam is more hapless than heroic. The work is a biting and witty criticism of contemporary Iranian society where even the most renowned hero struggles. Both the collages and videos diminish the epic hero, suggesting that his skill set is no longer suited to the conditions of this world.

---

1 Joseph Campbell, *The Hero with a Thousand Faces* (New York: Pantheon Books, 1953), 260.

2 The term has several related meanings, including hero, athlete, champion, and courageous. Philippe Rochard, "The Identities of the Iranian Zūrkhānah," *Iranian Studies* 35, no. 4 (2002): 331.

3 It is common for secular and religious heroes to share attributes. For example, in the *Khavarannama* (Book of the East), Imam Ali, the martyred son-in-law of the Prophet, embarks on a series of adventures and is depicted in a manner similar to the nationalist hero Rustam in the *Shahnama*. For more on the *Khavarannama*, see Maryam Ekhtiar, Sheila R. Canby, Navina Najat Haidar, and Priscilla P. Soucek, eds., *Masterpieces from the Department of Islamic Art in The Metropolitan Museum of Art* (New York: Metropolitan Museum of Art, 2011), 185–86, and Mohammed Ali Rajabi, ed., *Iranian Masterpieces of Persian Painting* (Tehran: Museum of Contemporary Art, 2005), 77–83.

4 Beyond these tragedies, Rustam's lineage and character also make him a conflicted hero; he is a descendent of the evil demon-king Zahhak and was known for getting drunk, acting belligerently toward others, and relying on trickery to overcome his opponents. See Dick Davis, "Rustam-i Dastan," *Iranian Studies* 32, no. 2 (Spring 1999): 231–32, and Olga M. Davidson, *Poet and Hero in the Persian Book of Kings* (Costa Mesa, CA: Mazda Publishers, 2006), 124–25.

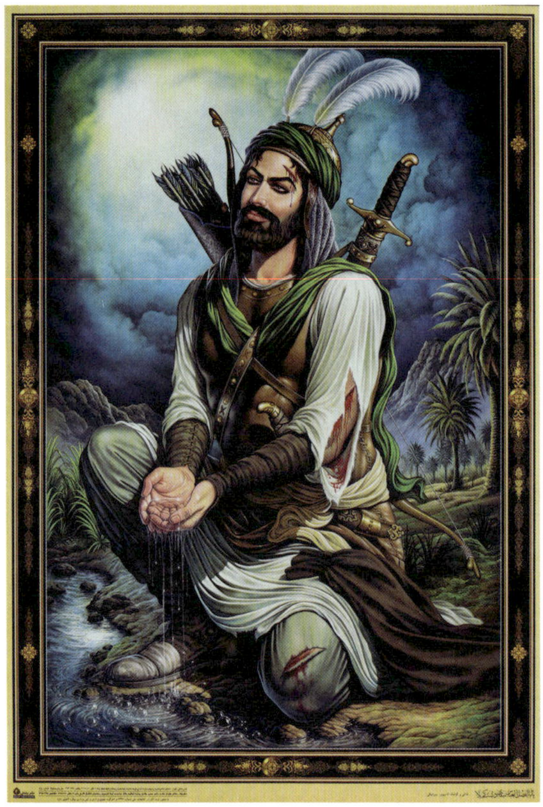

Poster of Abbas at the Euphrates River

The hero's decline is similarly explored in works by Khosrow Hassanzadeh that center on another form of pahlavan: the populist athlete who practices the ritualized exercises of *varzish-i bastani* (ancient sport).[5] Hassanzadeh's nostalgia for the dwindling pahlavan class—once admired as local heroes[6]—has inspired several types of artwork. These works all combine nineteenth-century photographs of the athletes with references to their training, such as exercise equipment, and depictions of the Shi'ite Imams and the wrestler and cult hero Gholamreza Takhti.[7] Drawing on Iran's traditional architectural decoration, Hassanzadeh created a large-scale tile wall panel onto which he printed images of the athletes against a dazzling blue background covered in religious inscriptions. The grand scale monumentalizes the anonymous men while the title, *Remember*, implores viewers to recall a fading tradition and the heroes that once were.

PLATES 43 AND 44

PLATE 41

Perhaps the most tragic of Iran's heroes is the martyr, the most revered of whom is Husain, the grandson of the Prophet Muhammad who was killed at Karbala in 680. He is venerated for his self-sacrifice and adherence to his eschatological

5 *Varzish-i bastani* is a series of gymnastic and bodybuilding exercises performed to music and chanting, often including religious invocations to the Shi'ite Imams. The exercises are closely linked to Iranian heroes, including Rustam and Husain, and the traditional gymnasium (*zurkhana*) in which the athletes typically meet is often decorated with images of both. See Lloyd Ridgeon, "The Zūrkhāna between Tradition and Change," *Iran* 45 (2007): 243–65; Rochard, "The Identities of the Iranian Zūrkhānah," 313–40.

6 The reason for the decline of the pahlavans is debated, but is perhaps due in part to their conflicted status within Iranian society. Although revered by some, the pahlavans are also associated with the *luti*, a type of street-thug-cum-hero. See Ridgeon, "The Zūrkhāna between Tradition and Change," 255, and Rochard, "The Identities of the Iranian Zūrkhāna," 323.

7 Shiva Balaghi, "Khosrow Hassanzadeh's Haft Khan," in *Khosrow Hassanzadeh, Haft Khan: The Seven Labors of Rostam* (New York: Leila Heller Gallery, 2012), n.p. Gholamreza Takhti was the wildly popular pahlavan who won an Olympic gold medal for wrestling in 1956. He is remembered for his chivalry and sportsmanship, as well as the mysterious circumstances of his death.

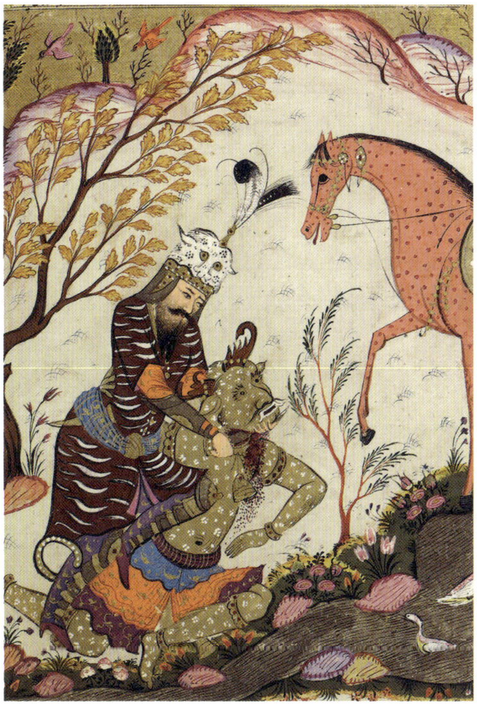

Rustam Cuts the Throat of the Div Akvan, from the *Shahnama* of Firdausi, c. 1670. MS or. Fol. 3380 [fol. 212v] (FOR MANUSCRIPT, SEE PLATE 5)

destiny despite options to escape.[8] His death is remembered in *ta'ziya*, a passion play that reenacts the events at Karbala, evoking the tragedy in real time and often collapsing the divide between past and present.[9] Pouya Afshar's recent video work *Mourn Baby Mourn*, which grew out of the artist's coping with the death of a mentor, explores this collapse of time. In videos projected inside of a tent (within and around which the audience is meant to move), a young boy leads the viewer through both a ta'ziya performance and the historical martyrdom, with the delineation between the two blurred. Like ta'ziya, Afshar closes the temporal gap, bringing viewers into contact with the moment of Husain's heroism and the visceral experience of mourning.

PLATES 93 A–B

The enlivening of religious martyrs in the present moment takes on a new form in Shoja Azari's Icon series. Closely based on popular posters that depict the Shi'ite holy men (SEE POSTER OF ABBAS), Azari's videos replace the static male faces with those of women who are animated to subtly move and even cry. The works were inspired by mothers who lost children during Iran's 2009 Green Movement, and Azari's desire to, like Renaissance painters, depict saints as ordinary people.[10] By changing the saints' gender and elevating ordinary people to the role of icons, Azari challenges traditional Shi'ite iconography and offers a more egalitarian view of heroes. This sort of transformation is also achieved, in a subtler and more tragic manner, in Newsha Tavakolian's Mothers of Martyrs series. Tavakolian photographed women posed with portraits of their sons who died in the Iran-Iraq War (1980–88), memorializing the aged women alongside their perpetually youthful children. Tavakolian draws a corollary between the martyred sons, who are highly respected in Iran, and their grieving mothers. This visual parallel suggests that the mothers themselves are heroes. In Tavakolian's works, the reverence is not only for those who have died, but also for those who survive.

PLATES 88 A–E

PLATE 85

The heroes' exalted as well as tragic status makes them fruitful material for contemporary Iranian artists who reframe and rethink their position under modern conditions. By using heroes as a conduit for social and political commentary, the artists destabilize the role models they employ and invite us to look more critically at whom we consider a hero. In doing so they show that the hero's status is not constant but mutable, ultimately dissolving established notions of heroism in the present day.

8 Numerous times Husain is tempted to avoid his fate, either by staying with his family members or through the intercession of a powerful being. Each time he resists and chooses martyrdom. See Rebecca Ansary Pettys, "The Ta'ziyeh of the Martyrdom of Hussein," in *Eternal Performance: Ta'ziyeh and Other Shiite Rituals*, ed. Peter Chelkowski, (London: Seagull Books, 2010), 19–41.

9 Peter Chelkowski describes this collapse, called *guriz*, as follows: "Through the guriz, all ta'ziyeh drama expands beyond spatial and time constraints to merge the past and present into one unifying moment of intensity that allows the spectators to be simultaneously in the performance space and at Karbala." Peter Chelkowski, "Time Out of Memory: Ta'ziyeh, The Total Drama," in *Eternal Performance: Ta'ziyeh and Other Shiite Rituals*, ed. Peter Chelkowski (London: Seagull Books, 2010), 13. For more information on ta'ziya see Sheida Dayani's essay, and for more on guriz see Linda Komaroff's essay, both in this volume.

10 Carol Kino, "Putting New Faces on Islamic History," *New York Times*, May 19, 2010, http://www.nytimes.com/2010/05/23/arts/design/23azari.html?mcubz=2. The Green Movement comprised large-scale protests that erupted in Iran following the contested results of the 2009 presidential election.

Vali Mahlouji on

The Fantastical Polaroids of Kaveh Golestan

The history of photography, especially between the 1960s and 1980s, is testament to the fact that the instantaneous nature of the Polaroid as a medium afforded many artists a new spontaneity and encouraged new, radically experimental results in image making. In 1976, two years before the pioneering Iranian photographer Kaveh Golestan[1] began to document the overthrow of the monarchy, he produced a hitherto underexposed, intensely personal, and profoundly experimental series of photographic collages using a Polaroid camera. He titled this unique body of work Az Div o Dad (Of Demon and Beast), referencing an oft-cited verse of the classical Persian poet Rumi,[2] in which the poet yearns for humanity in the face of the ever-present brutalities of real life—hypocrisy, demons (*div*), and beasts (*dad*).

PLATES 28 A–H

This mysterious series of Polaroids may be comfortably accommodated within the socially engaged modus operandi of Golestan's broader oeuvre (primarily consisting of black-and-white, ostensibly straight-documentary photography);[3] it clearly displays explicit overtones of political subversion and engagement. However, the Az Div o Dad Polaroids, produced feverishly during a single year, stand out as a distinct and independent series. The work is distinguished by a very potent paradigm of artistic licence and fantasy, which, by all accounts, unleashed a relentless and powerful period of aesthetic and creative freedom unmatched in the rest of Golestan's work. The result was a riotous, surrealistic collage aesthetic that remains complex, nuanced, defiant, and ambiguous.

To produce these images, Golestan used the newly released SX-70 Polaroid camera, the first of its kind that allowed for manual control of exposure time. My close analysis has revealed that Golestan essentially employed two methods. Sometimes, he first created the desired collage using found photographs and cutouts, and then photographed the final artwork using the Polaroid camera. In other instances, and these created the most haunting effects, Golestan devised a time-based process through which he meticulously layered and constructed the image in front of an open shutter. He set up the camera in a darkened, light-controlled environment; positioned his chosen background, found photograph, or collage in front of the open shutter; and manually animated various fragmentary cutout elements in front of it. To do this, he attached discreet sticks to these cutouts, which functioned as handles and allowed for the necessary control. In the artist's archives, we have the artworks and the individual fragmentary elements that were used in creating many of these works, which shed light on the process.

Golestan often produced sequences of the same composite images with varying time lengths of superimpositions. His sequential superimpositions produced a gradual transformation of one element into another (creating incremental serial montages like a series of film stills). The controlled and incremental exposure of interjected

1 For Kaveh Golestan's photographs of the revolution see Kaveh Golestan and Mohammad Sayyad, *Shouresh (Rebellion)* (Tehran: 1980); Malu Halasa and Hengameh Golestan, eds., *Kaveh Golestan: Recording the Truth in Iran* (Ostfildern, Germany: Hatje Cantz Verlag, 2007), 80–113.

2 The original verse is, "کز دیو و دد ملولم و انسانم آرزوست," which translates loosely to "...Weary of the demonic and beastly, I yearn for the human...."

3 See Kaveh Golestan, "The Citadel: An Alternative View (1)—And So They Build A Cage," *Ayandegan Newspaper*, September 11, 1977, 5; Kaveh Golestan, "The Citadel: An Alternative View (2)—Prostitutes, Victims of Traders," *Ayandegan Newspaper*, September 12, 1977, 5; Kaveh Golestan, "The Citadel: An Alternative View (3)—Prostitution: Is It an Inevitable Phenomenon?," *Ayandegan Newspaper*, September 12, 1977, 5; Kaveh Pedram, "Golestan's Camera Investigates the Truth in Kayhan," *Ayandegan Newspaper*, May 10, 1978; Kaveh Golestan, *Three Reports: Prostitute, Worker, Asylum* (Tehran: Tehran University, 1978); Kim Knoppers, "Kaveh Golestan: The Citadel: A Conversation between Guest Curator Vali Mahlouji and Foam curator Kim Knoppers," (Amsterdam: Foam Fotografiemuseum Amsterdam, 2014); Vali Mahlouji, "Recréer Shahr-e No: La politique intime du marginal," in *Unedited History: Séquences du moderne en Iran des années 1960 à nos jours* (Paris: Musee d'Art Moderne de la Ville de Paris, 2014), 60–71.

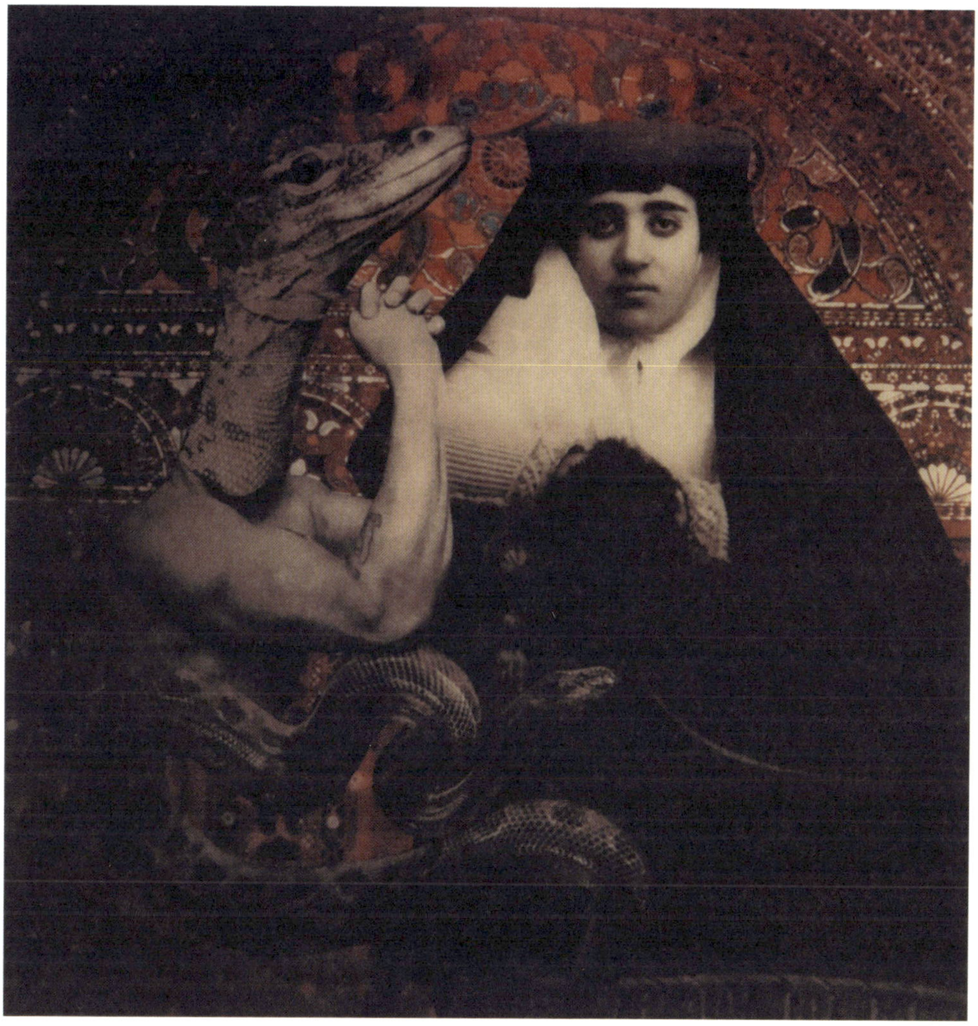

Kaveh Golestan,
Untitled from the series
Az Div o Dad, 1976
(SEE PLATE 28 F)

and superimposed components enabled an aesthetic of metamorphosis more potent than one relying solely on juxtaposition. The macabre and fluid, sometimes visceral, horror of these particular images evokes a sense of the Bataillian *l'informe*.[4] Georges Bataille's *l'informe* ("the formless") referred to the world's inherent irrelevance, which renders our thinking about it utterly pointless, a visual metaphor that strongly resonates with Dadaism and Surrealism.[5]

This aspect of the images' materiality also gives a sense of physical compression—both of images within images, as well as the flickering of figure-ground reversals—which produces a material potency alongside the attraction and repulsion we feel toward the strange, mystical hybrids displayed. The sense of a shifting, intangible representation abides by the logic of dreams, like the compression of time and memory in dreamlike fiction. Golestan further

4 Georges Bataille, *Visions of Excess: Selected Writings, 1927–1939*, ed. Allan Stoekl (Minneapolis: University of Minnesota Press, 1985), 31. Bataille wrote, "...a term that serves to bring things down in the world, generally requiring that each thing have its form. What it designates has no rights in any sense and gets itself squashed everywhere, like a spider or an earthworm. In fact, for academic men to be happy, the universe would have to take shape. All of philosophy has no other goal: it is a matter of giving a frock coat to what is, a mathematical frock coat. On the other hand, affirming that the universe resembles nothing and is only formless amounts to saying that the universe is something like a spider or spit."

5 The exhibition *L'Informe: mode d'emploi*, at the Centre Pompidou in Paris in 1966, curated by Yve-Alain Bois and Rosalind Krauss, returned to Bataille's formulation of *l'informe* in a critical and provocative reading of modernism in order to dismantle the dominant narrative of high modernism and its hegemony.

embellished the photographs and their various iterations by applying a range of hues through the use of different filters, flooding the images with various shifting levels of color, brightness, and shadow.

Peering into these compact Polaroid squares, the viewer enters a wonderfully textured world that is suffocated by an airless intensity of visual iconographies in which the binary oppositions of fact and fantasy collapse onto each other. Golestan repossessed found images (mainly from the Qajar era) and thrust them into a complex visual network of mannerisms, grotesques, and ornamentations, loaded with references, associations, and meanings that are actual and symbolic as well as political and archetypal. The Qajar photographs he used came from several sources, including a photograph dealer in Tehran and a Nasir al-Din Shah album that was given to him by his father-in-law, Fathollah Jalali, previously a gift from Mostowfi al-Mamalek (prime minister from 1910 to 1927).[6]

Golestan repeatedly spliced those found official portraits of Qajar royalty, military dignitaries, political personalities, ordinary citizens, and female nude figures with snake tails, vulture and bat heads, unidentifiable reptile fragments, and mechanistic elements, like screws. These appear and reappear in various compositions and, as a result, a fantastically diverse array of images is tied together by an element of repetition. His physical introjections visually occupy spaces of power and flip agency and power. We might discover the ghostly partial transformation and eerie slippage of a regal bust into that of a bat or a lion, as seen, for example, in the hybrid image of the young Qajar prince, probably Nusrat al-Din Mirza Salar
PLATE 28 A al-Saltana, Nasir al-Din's son. This photograph belongs to a sequential montage in which the young monarch gains a pair of butterfly wings that appear to flutter as his face flickers between human and leonine. Displacement onto the found images of nineteenth- and early-twentieth-century Qajar figureheads and political men safely relocates a contemporary subversive gesture toward loci of power—regal or military—onto the historical. These subversive defacements do not leave a simple void; instead we are presented with an array of anthropomorphic figures that resist overtly specific or contextual exegesis.

The viewer is compelled to read into and through the multifaceted and macabre maze of political, mythological, allegorical, and personal virtualities of hybridization and bizarrerie. On one hand, it is vital to view the works critically and art historically against long cross-cultural trajectories of the hybrid and the grotesque. These trajectories have produced scenes that are mythologically anthropomorphic, ritualistically magical, and supernatural and shamanic, as well as satirical and politically, socially, or sexually subversive. The human-animal hybrid yokes the context to still greater expanses of time and history, given its intercultural and temporal ubiquity. On the other hand, these frequently dark, obscure, small-format Polaroids suggest the secretive or, rather, private individual of Golestan's interior world. The images are anchored within a personal artistic lexicon of tropes. Ultimately, any reading of the works ought to allow for the private mystery to prevail and must refrain from reductive interpretations aimed at fixing meaning. What is certain is that Golestan delighted in creating grotesquely theatrical happenings in the Bakhtinian *carnivalesque* sense, where hierarchies are dissolved and inverted, the sacred and the profane are mixed, and riot and disorder prevail over certainty and stability.[7]

---

6 Golestan purchased Qajar photographs at Tahami Photo Studio on Baharistan Square in Tehran, as did other members of the arts community. The studio still exists in the same location.

7 Mikhail Bakhtin, *Rabelais and His World* (Bloomington: Indiana University Press, 1941).

REFLECTING THE PAST INTO THE PRESENT versus CONSTRUCTIVE SPECIFICITY

in Modern and Contemporary Art in Iran

Hamid Keshmirshekan

This essay explores encounters with the question of cultural identity and specificity as reflected in the art of twentieth- and twenty-first-century Iran. It examines the variety of approaches, arguing that a paradigm shift can be traced when examining this history, and tackles the question of artistic specificity within an Iranian context and its transformation during this period. The first approach concerns particularly the period in Iranian art when there was a growing preference for confronting conflicts between past and present, and when the quest for a national artistic identity coincided with forces of modernization—an approach toward prevailing traditional heritage that I call neo-traditionalism.[1] The neo-traditionalists concentrated on articulating a synthesis between a pictorial heritage of the past and methodologies of Western modern art, aiming to visualize history in terms of the present. This first paradigm signifies how negotiations between traditional forms and modernist aesthetics, intersections between internationalism and national identity, and questions of authenticity versus derivativeness informed artists' engagement with art of the 1960s and 1970s.

A second paradigm emerged in more recent times, when the past began to be practiced as a form of often barely masked political and social commentary. Globalization and its attendant cultural transformations contributed to an increase in the international mobility of works of art and artists, the rise of new media, and the reconfiguration of older aesthetic essentials. Alternative visions of cultural specificity and collective identity have emerged as new themes for contemporary artists. Since the turn of the century, a number of young Iranian artists have developed their work as an important facet of the kaleidoscope of contemporary cultural life, contributing a diverse yet distinct vocabulary formed by their artistic, cultural, and social commentary. This essay addresses key questions about how contemporaneity and specificity apply to Iranian visual culture, and explores several factors that have contributed to the formation of these two paradigms of Iranian art.

1 For a full examination of this concept and its affiliation to Iranian art in the 1960s, see Hamid Keshmirshekan, "Neo-Traditionalism and Modern Iranian Painting: The *Saqqa-khaneh* School in the 1960s," *Iranian Studies* 38, no. 4 (December 2005): 607–30; and "Saqqâ-kâna School of Art," in *Encyclopaedia Iranica*, August 15, 2009, http://www.iranicaonline.org/articles/saqqa-kana-ii-school-of-art.

Altermodernism: "Reflecting" the Past into the Present

Understanding contemporary Iran requires an appreciation of the legacy of the experience of modernity itself. It is said that modernism, as a universal form, originated in Western Europe and resulted in a binary between the assumed universality of modernism as an inclusive language on the one hand and a quest for certain locally specific content with which to displace it on the other. In this vein, non-Western modernization discourse became entangled with a need to present modernism as compatible with local traditions and culture. This led to a deep concern with the "authentic" and "indigenous" constructions of the notion of an alternative modernity.[2]

To better understand the possibility of an alternative modernity and the resultant altermodernism, we need to survey the foundation of this subject. According to social scientist Ali Mirsepassi, the more archetypal version of modernity "considers Western culture an essential part of modernization, viewing non-Western cultures and traditions as fundamentally hostile to modernity and incompatible with modernization."[3] American philosopher Marshall Berman suggests that the various experiences of modernity become meaningful only in the reflexiveness of their context and, therefore, the culture of modernity is not and should not be necessarily based on Western experience or cultural beliefs.[4] This also supports the idea of a multiple modernities paradigm—an alternative to mainstream views within modernization studies that emerged in the 1990s and 2000s. Unlike its competitors, this model refrains from offering an exclusionary definition of modernity based on characteristics of Western experiences. Instead, the theory defines modernization as the erratic progression of change undergone by society.[5] Its main premise is that modernity takes so many different forms based on history and culture that it cannot be characterized as singular or unique.[6] The hypothesis envisages a kind of fusion stemming from the asymmetrical development of diverse traits on the local level instead of the more standard notion of the conflict between modernity and tradition.[7] In light of this assumption, an alternative Iranian modernism can be acknowledged.[8]

With regard to the earlier course of modernization promoted by the Pahlavi state (1925–79), Mirsepassi maintains that "during the 1960s and 1970s, Iranian society underwent a state-sponsored modernization program that affected

2 Monica M. Ringer, review of *Intellectual Discourse and the Politics of Modernization: Negotiating Modernity in Iran*, by Ali Mirsepassi, *Iranian Studies* 40, no. 4, (2007): 555–57.

3 Ali Mirsepassi, *Intellectual Discourse and the Politics of Modernization: Negotiating Modernity in Iran* (Cambridge: Cambridge University Press, 2000), 2.

4 Marshall Berman, *All That Is Solid Melts into Air: The Experience of Modernity* (New York: Penguin, 1988).

5 See Shmuel Noah Eisenstadt, "Multiple Modernities," *Daedalus* 129 (2000): 1–29. See also Peter Wagner, "Modernity—One or Many?," in *The Blackwell Companion to Sociology*, ed. Judith R. Blaue (Oxford: Blackwell, 2000), 30–42.

6 See Elsje Fourie, "A Future for the Theory of Multiple Modernities: Insights from the New Modernization Theory," *Social Science Information* 51, no. 1 (2012): 52. Social scientist Ibrahim Kaya argues that this concept suggests that there have been multiple paths to modernity and that those multiple ways give rise to multiple consequences that do not come to a meeting point. Ibrahim Kaya, *Social Theory and Later Modernities: The Turkish Experience* (Liverpool: Liverpool University Press, 2004).

7 Eisenstadt, "Multiple Modernities," 5–6.

8 See Ernest Gellner, "Foreword," in *From Nationalism to Revolutionary Islam*, ed. Saïd Amir Arjomand (Albany: State University of New York Press, 1984), viii.

the economic relations, social institutions, and cultural patterns of the country."[9] At the same time, among Iranian intellectuals, the concept of *Gharbzadigi* (Westoxication) came to symbolize anti-Western nostalgia, which rejected borrowing from and imitating the West, and instead substituted a notion of modernity that could only be achieved within the context of Iran itself.[10]

The most important advocate of this concept was Jalal Al-i Ahmad, who articulated a formidable critique of the hegemonic power of the West based on the concept of Gharbzadigi. Mirsepassi argues that this critique attacked Iranian secular intellectuals as complicit in Western power, and incapable of effectively constructing an authentically Iranian modernity.[11] He suggests that a return to an authentic Islamic culture is necessary if Iran is to avoid the homogenizing and alienating forces of socio-technological modernization. Yet Mirsepassi believes that "Al-e Ahmad's populist Islam would not reject modernization as such, but would seek to reimagine modernity in accordance with Iranian-Islamic tradition, symbolism, and identities."[12] Ali Shariati (1933–1977, active during the 1960s and 1970s), one of the most significant Iranian intellectuals of the twentieth century, also embraced the notion of Gharbzadigi; he likewise endeavored to reconcile Shi'ite Islam with modernization. Shariati contended that a nation must regain its cultural and religious traditions as a precursor to modernizing on its own terms.[13]

At this juncture, the authenticity discourse was offered as a means of reconciling the universal idea of modernity with the Iranians' indigenous cultural context.[14] The main similarity between the movements affiliated with this discourse was an encouragement of Iranians to discover their identity, traditions, and national roots. These tendencies, which originated among the intelligentsia in the 1940s and 1950s, manifested in criticism of the insatiable desire among the majority to imitate and emulate the West and its products in various aspects of life, literature, and art. At the same time, the intellectual quest for artistic identity intensified too. New impulses from inside the country were assimilated, while Iranian artists aimed to contribute to the process of modernization and its alternative formulation—the notion of collective cultural and national identity—within Iran. In this context, many artists of the 1960s were committed to creating a synthesis of indigenous, historical, and folkloristic materials and contemporary Western trends to record their country's intellectual discussions and encourage a newly confident national integrity through their art. Visual expressions of such ideals were complex and individualistic, but the challenge of realizing those ideals through the use of both local materials and universal modes of expression was immediately evident in the work of these artists. Their output from this period

---

9 Mirsepassi, *Intellectual Discourse and the Politics of Modernization*, 73.

10 Mirsepassi maintains that "The romanticism of the Islamic and Iranian traditions induced a very hostile reaction against modernization and a Western-centered project. The romanticism of the *Gharb-zadegi* discourse embodied an image of modernity that could only be realized in the context of Iranian national settings." Ibid., 77.

11 Mirsepassi argues that this critique attacked Iranian secular intellectuals as complicit in Western power, and incapable of effectively constructing an authentically Iranian modernity. Ibid.

12 Ibid., 96.

13 Ibid., 13.

14 Ibid., 97.

signifies that "modernity in the Iranian context was a complex field of negotiation and accommodation—and not a simple act of imitation and mimicry."[15]

Along with this growing self-awareness was a newfound sense of their own otherness. The Saqqakhana movement was the perfect representation of this discourse.[16] The artists affiliated with this movement drew seminal inspiration from traditional art and revisited it in the context of the present. Their myriad approaches to and interpretations of the transition of tradition and its creative depiction as an image of aesthetic appreciation aimed to enrich a purely synthesized style of modern art. For example, artists employed motifs and patterns found on earlier objects made using traditional materials, such as textiles and metalwork,
PLATE 79 as well as in popular folk art, which they incorporated into their practices at will. Here the question of cultural transfer and reception seems to be a key concern.[17]

Euro-American styles were a required but not necessarily adequate element in the shaping of modern art discourse in Iran. This process ultimately involved recontextualization of the different forms and sources from the original culture and traditional materials from the artists' own culture. As a result, we encounter the establishment of an art discourse perhaps best termed neo-traditionalism, a concept based on the idea that there is a possible constructed quality of all modern traditions, unlike the haphazardness of customs legitimated in part by their isolation and independence.[18] Neo-traditional art should be positioned within modern discourse because it is mainly the product of a modern situation[19]—fractional accommodations, often misunderstood, in which the dominant artistic conversation is "seen as integral, with its own values and assimilations from outside given a precarious status for types of art practice, or at best acknowledged as a parallel discourse for the expression of culturally ephemeral but now socially constant modern values."[20]

While artists were deeply affected by the intellectual developments of the time, they compromised with the cultural officials of the country who had become the advocates of this kind of art. Although it is true that this pioneering approach depended on individual initiative, these enterprises were largely backed by the state. At this juncture, the official body of the Pahlavi government—in particular

15 Shiva Balaghi, "Iranian Visual Arts in 'The Century of Machinery, Speed, and the Atom': Rethinking Modernity," in *Picturing Iran: Art, Society and Revolution*, ed. Shiva Balaghi and Lynn Gumpert (London: I. B. Tauris, 2002), 25.

16 Saqqakhana was termed by Karim Emami (1930–2005), an art critic and journalist at the *Kayhan International* newspaper. The term was in fact mainly applied to the works of artists—both painters and sculptors—who used specific elements and material culture, drawn from votive Shi'ite pictorial tradition, in their modernist practices. It later came to be used for various forms of modern Iranian art practices that referenced all kinds of traditional decorative material from the Iranian old material culture.

17 With regard to the designation of the process of cultural "transfer" and "reception," see the proposed argument of art historian John Clark; John Clark, *Modern Asian Art* (North Ryde, NSW: Craftsman House in association with G+B Arts International, 1998), 49.

18 Ibid., 73.

19 Ibid., 75.

20 Ibid. Eric Hobsbawm has already classified what he called "invented traditions" by function into three overlapping types: those that established social cohesion; those legitimizing institutions, status, or relations of authority; and those whose purpose was socialization, inculcation of beliefs, value systems, and conventions of behavior. It can indeed be said that Iranian neo-traditional art was an incorporation of the first two categories. Eric Hobsbawm and Terence Ranger, eds., *The Invention of Tradition* (Cambridge: Cambridge University Press, 1992), 9.

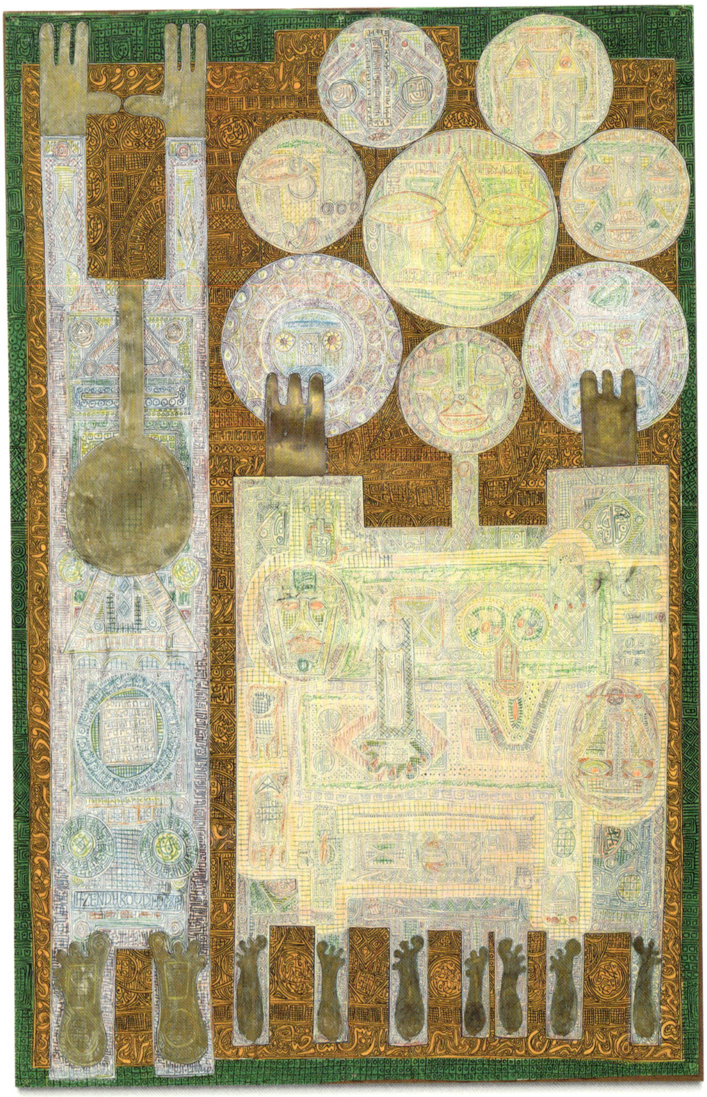

Charles Hossein Zenderoudi, *K+L+32+H+4. Mon père et moi (My Father and I)*, 1962. Felt-tip pen and colored ink on paper on board. 89×58⅝ in. (225.9×148.7 cm). Museum of Modern Art, New York, Philip Johnson Fund, 317.1962

the Ministry of Culture and Art, later joined by administrations affiliated with the office of Queen Farah[21]—provided support in the form of scholarships, grand national exhibitions, the creation of new institutions, and mechanisms intended to promote Iranian modern art as part of the international art scene (particularly in Europe and America). Although such packages were initiated in the preceding decade, they were realized on a much more outstanding scale during the 1960s and 1970s, mainly because of the economic boom caused by increasing oil revenues.[22]

21 It became the Shahbanou Farah Foundation in 1977.

22 See Karim Emami, "Art in Iran XI Post-Qajar," in *Encyclopaedia Iranica* 2, fasc. 6 (London: Routledge & Kegan Paul, 1987), 640–46. See also Hamid Keshmirshekan, "Neo-Traditionalism and Modern Iranian Painting." The economic boom was a strong factor in the state's patronage of art, which the government cultural department now intended to support especially after the mid-1950s and particularly in the 1960s. This period also coincided with a time when state economic growth was pronounced. See Julian Bharier, *Economic Development in Iran, 1900–1970* (London: Oxford University Press, 1971), 91. Bharier argues that although the overall effect of the White Revolution (launched in 1963) is hard to determine, since the real annual growth of the economy was running at about 10 per cent from 1964 to 1969, it is possible that, directly or indirectly, they helped to instill the type of confidence that would encourage the profit expectations of industrialists to rise. Ibid., 96, 98.

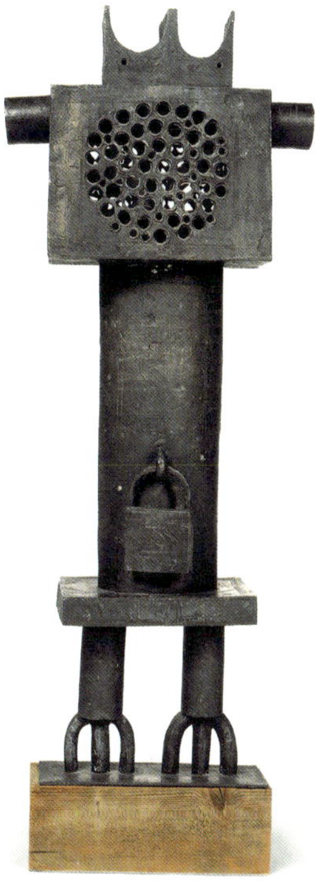

Parviz Tanavoli,
Bronze Prophet, 1963.
Bronze. 39½×15×7½ in.
(100.3×38.1×19.05 cm).
Walker Art Center,
gift of Ben and Abby Grey
Foundation, 1963.20

In the 1960s Iran saw a compromise between accepting the legitimacy of art forms and techniques and attempting to remake the origins of that legitimacy.[23] This compromise applied to both works of art and the codified ideas from which the artists had drawn their inspiration. In terms of the artworks, traditional forms could be used to produce new variations and novel expansions of the formal relationships as well as questions that artists of the earlier generation had left mostly unanswered.[24] As for ideas, the fundamental aesthetic or religious (here Shi'ite iconography, presented in a secular manner) viewpoint was often made explicit in ways to be representative of Iranianness. Legitimation, then, could also be established by referencing artistic forms and styles drawn from Western modernism within an intellectual space developed in Iran.

PLATES 78 AND 79

As art historian John Clark maintains, "neo-traditional art has seen several positions develop from which to assert its quest for legitimacy. One is that of nationalism, the claim to represent in a modern form the aesthetic values of a past but in a way suited to modern conditions."[25] In this process the use of certain pictorial signs helps reorganize what is accepted as Iranian rather than merely looking for something that indicates Iranianness via their placement. It suggests the types of political change that neo-traditionalism as a contested discourse can

23 See also Clark, *Modern Asian Art*, 73–74.

24 It should, however, be mentioned that there were attempts by the artists of the earlier generation to adopt Western modernism in their work by localizing the contents vividly. For example, Jalil Ziapour, one of the pioneers of the Iranian modern art movement in the 1940s, "devised his version of an Iranian Cubism: local in content, Western in form." See Fereshteh Daftari, "Another Modernism: An Iranian Perspective," in *Picturing Iran: Art, Society and Revolution*, ed. Shiva Balaghi and Lynn Gumpert (London: I. B. Tauris, 2002), 47. The most typical approach during the 1940s and 1950s involved a combination of Iranian subject matter and stylistic drawing from the Western modern art movements in line with the prototypes suggested by the Pahlavi cultural policy. See Hamid Keshmirshekan, *Contemporary Iranian Art: New Perspectives* (London: Saqi, 2013).

25 Clark, *Modern Asian Art*, 75.

carry in certain circumstances. For example, traditional values were displayed by artists as a sign of cultural authenticity in the midst of growing nationalist and nativist sentiments in 1960s Iran.[26] The artist became a mediator of what was Iranian; his or her audience was to accept references from inside and outside the country. This artistic process exemplified the function of visual images that signified belonging to the past, as well as typified models for accurate deportment in the present (SEE TANAVOLI'S *Bronze Prophet*, OPPOSITE). Such codification of visual images and variation required that the interpretations of the artists were readable by both Iranian and foreign audiences. Their works were based on a universal validity that balanced inherited specifics and pragmatic modernism, which marked the Iranian art of their time. At this point the artists "sought to reconcile the nation-state identity with internationalism."[27] Through their tributes to the past, the artists of the very popular Saqqakhana movement and other allied styles, such as the calligraphic trend, termed *Naqqashi-khatt*,[28] discovered visual symbols in religious rituals in the form of prayers, incantations, old manuscripts, and traditional calligraphy. They approached them, however, through a formalistic scheme, PLATE 32 using preexisting materials and appropriating symbols from traditional Iranian culture and interpreting them with modernist (mainly abstract) conventions.[29]

Through this contextual framework (although it was dramatically changed after the 1979 Islamic Revolution based on radical aspirations and the concept of Islamic ideals) one can track the reemergence of neo-traditionalism in the art of the 1990s as the major artistic discourse within the sociocultural context of postrevolutionary Iran. Driven by political urgency and revolutionary sentiments, Islamicism influenced art and artistic practice during the first decade after the revolution. It proved how political subjectivity affects the way art is produced. This anti-modernist sentiment was a direct and indirect response to the policies of positivist modernity implemented by the Pahlavi regime. Much of modern culture and modernity was suddenly viewed as essentially decadent, founded upon existential and materialistic values. The earlier modernist discourse, however, was not entirely forsaken and can be seen as the motivation behind a new quest

26 Art historian Layla S. Diba believes that "global politics played an increasingly important role in Iran. The Cold War and the emergence of nationalism across the globe from Africa to India and Japan also would influence art and cultural development in Iran." See Layla S. Diba, "The Formation of Modern Iranian Art: From Kamal-al-Molk to Zenderoudi," in *Iran Modern*, ed. Fereshteh Daftari and Layla S. Diba (New York: Asia Society, 2013), 52–53.

27 Daftari, "Another Modernism," 47. Daftari also argues, "They reflected a national dilemma: how to preserve an Iranian identity, termed 'authentic' that was threatened by near-abdication to the omnipresent West, without retreating into xenophobic parochialism or renouncing the aspiration to be modern." Ibid., 65.

28 See Hamid Keshmirshekan, "Neo-Calligraphism and Its Different Varieties in Modern and Contemporary Iranian Art," in *Metalwork and Material Culture in the Islamic World: Art, Craft and Text*, ed. Mariam Rosser-Owen and Venetia Porter (London: I. B. Tauris, 2012), 441–60. There were other parallel movements of Muslim calligraphic modernism, particularly the *Huruffiya* movement of the Arab and North African world and the art of Muslim South Asia. For more elaboration on this movement, see Venetia Porter, *Word into Art: Artists of the Modern Middle East* (London: British Museum Press, 2006), and for a comparative study of modern calligraphy, see Iftikhar Dadi, "Rethinking Calligraphic Modernism," in *Discrepant Abstraction*, ed. Kobena Mercer (London: Institute of International Visual Arts; Cambridge, MA: MIT Press, 2006), 94–115.

29 This "modernism...provided an answer to the problem critics had been debating: this was the hoped-for Iranian voice." Daftari, "Another Modernism," 72.

for modernity under the Islamic Republic.[30] A synthesis of the traditional and the modern inherent in the revolution gradually emerged in Iranian culture and art. It can therefore be argued that prerevolutionary art to a certain extent contributed to subsequent Iranian visual culture. Although revolutionary art first condemned or repudiated all kinds of prerevolutionary art, a careful consideration of certain works by the group of revolutionary artists[31] reveals a measure of affiliation with the 1960s works by artists of the Saqqakhana movement.[32] This applies at least to their use of popular religious pictorial elements and motifs even in formalist structures. In the varied forms of revolutionary art (especially posters, stamps, and murals), calligraphic forms and Shi'ite iconography, and themes and notions such as martyrdom and the cosmic battle between good and evil were dominant features (particularly during the Iran-Iraq War, 1980–88).[33]

PLATES 89 AND 90

In this period the ontological and political underpinnings of Gharbzadigi, which, as mentioned, had been addressed through a critical interpretation of works by Iranian intellectuals of the 1960s and 1970s, were still influential. In official cultural and artistic events, clear encouragement was given to taking refuge in cultural authenticity, historical specificities, and traditional values, especially of Islam or the Irano-Islamic Shi'ite traditions.[34] Here again, the prevailing question of the postrevolutionary artists[35] was what could constitute the specificity of their art; the essence of neo-rationalism could be traced in their endless quest. The majority of the national exhibitions in the early 1990s consisted of works in which one could discern an inclination toward traditional Islamic and folkloric arts as references to Iranian-Islamic heritage. Within this context, formalistic agendas such as decorative motifs, traditional calligraphy, and religious traditions and rituals were set up (SEE MEMARZADEH'S *Heritage*, OPPOSITE). Persian painting also provided inspiration despite its apparent celebration of Iran's old kingship, but was perhaps justified with reference to the Iranian "self" and by its stronger affiliation with Islamic Iranian heritage. Through a modernist lens, artists drew from the conceptual and pictorial aspects of the art of the past. Experimenting with

PLATE 8

30 See Farzin Vahdat, *God and Juggernaut: Iran's Intellectual Encounter with Modernity* (Syracuse: Syracuse University Press, 2002), xiii. Mirsepassi likewise argues, "the Islamic Republic of Iran is not inherently antithetical of modernity, but an attempt at creative synthesis, well within the discourse of modernity itself." In Ringer, review of *Intellectual Discourse and the Politics of Modernization*, 556.

31 The main bodies of revolutionary artists were affiliated with the Art Bureau of Islamic Propaganda Organization (*Hauza-yi hunari-yi sazman-i tablighat-i islami*).

32 For further details see Hamid Keshmirshekan, "Discourses on Postrevolutionary Iranian Art: Neotraditionalism during the 1990s," *Muqarnas* 23, no. 1 (2006): 131–57, and *Contemporary Iranian Art*.

33 See Christiane Gruber, "Media/ting Conflict: Iranian Posters of the Iran-Iraq War (1980–88)," in *Crossing Cultures: Conflict, Migration, Convergence, Proceedings of the 32nd Congress of the International Committee of the History of Art*, ed. Jaynie Anderson (Melbourne: University of Melbourne, 2009), 685. For thoughtful considerations of Iranian revolutionary posters, see also Michael M. J. Fischer and Mehdi Abedi, *Debating Muslims: Cultural Dialogues in Postmodernity and Tradition* (Madison: University of Wisconsin Press, 1990), 339, and Haggai Ram, "Multiple Iconographies: Political Posters in the Iranian Revolution," in *Picturing Iran: Art, Society and Revolution*, ed. Shiva Balaghi and Lynn Gumpert (London: I. B. Tauris, 2002), 95.

34 See Keshmirshekan, "Discourses on Postrevolutionary Iranian Art."

35 After the revolution, the population largely increased. Despite the war and the turbulent conditions, a great many of the younger generation gravitated toward different forms of arts, especially visual arts. During the late 1980s and 1990s, the number of artists, art practitioners, and applicants to study art increased. Many young people studied fine art and music, and this resulted in significant production.

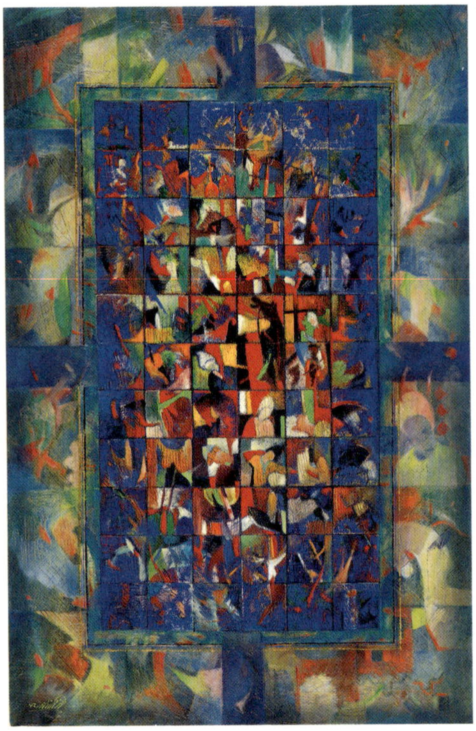

Mohammad Memarzadeh, *Heritage*, 1995. Oil on canvas. 47⅜×31½ in. (120×80 cm). Tehran Museum of Contemporary Art

different branded modernist styles, particularly Expressionism, Symbolism, and Surrealism, helped them express their objectives. They tried to adapt these styles to subjects like Iranian mythology and mysticism. A large body of artworks created in the late 1980s and 1990s, however, showed the characteristic hesitation of a transitional episode between revolutionary radicalism and the upcoming contemporary concerns. This period still saw the maintenance of the ever-present concern for legitimacy mixed with tributes to the past in the name of the future.

Contemporaneity vis-à-vis "Constructive" Specificity in the New Millennium

The question of cultural identity and specificity, even with the aim of interacting with the global contemporary art scene—now the main interest of artists and official art institutions[36]—is a key concern that continues to be discussed in the new millennium in Iran. At this juncture, artists have had to confront the dominant binary or dichotomy in cultural and artistic notions.[37] One is the idea of contemporaneity being infused with the spirit of the time, signifying global contemporary value systems, the prevailing preoccupation of the new generation, born after the revolution. On the other hand, there is the idea of specificity, mainly as it relates to the issue of cultural specificities, which are a rather compelling force, as well as other accepted particularities, such as traditional values and forms, social issues, and political concerns. The second refers to the inescapable obsession with the cultural and, frequently, social concerns with which Iranian artists have been

36 After about two decades in the postrevolutionary period, the Tehran Museum of Contemporary Art and the Ministry of Culture and Islamic Guidance increased their participation in biennials and exhibitions worldwide. Artists were sponsored to attend major art events in North America and Europe.

37 For full exploration of this discourse, see Hamid Keshmirshekan, "Contemporary or Specific: The Dichotomous Desires in the Art of Early Twenty-First Century Iran," *Middle East Journal of Culture and Communication* 4, no. 1 (2011): 44–71.

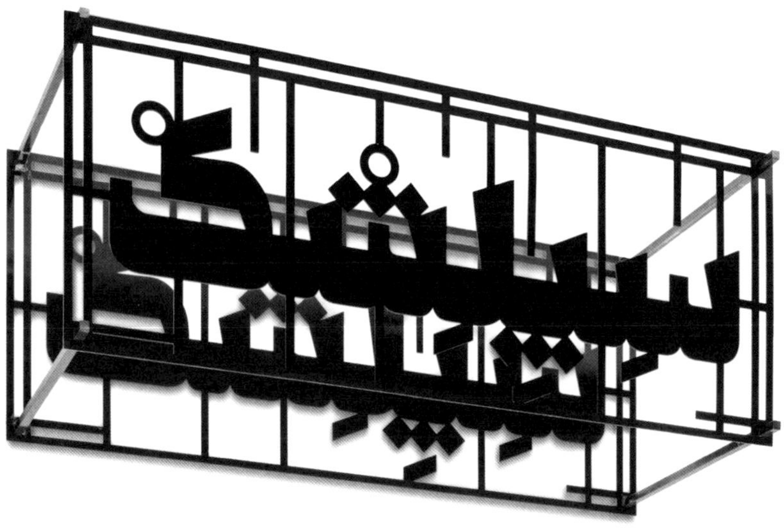

Iman Safaei, *Sepeleshk* from the series Popular, 2014. Iron. 18⅞×46¼×20¼ in. (48×117.5×51.5 cm). LACMA, purchased with funds provided by the HAND Foundation with additional funds provided by Clare Wagner, M.2015.181

engaged, both within the country and across the diaspora. This is still an intense debate that touches on inherent anxieties about national and cultural identity.

At the same time, the formulated interest of the Iranian state clearly promotes particular values as resistance against the secular norms of cultural globalization. Iranian artists and art activists concerned with the new dialectics of global culture in contemporary Iran were therefore compelled to employ novel strategies to appear to conform to the prescribed ideology. A gradual paradigm shift in cultural ideas away from the earlier vision of identity—characterized as a preexisting and essential entity—has revealed deep-rooted anxieties that relate to the issue of cultural belonging and its possible relationship with international concerns. This also exposes the dilemma of how contemporary Iranian artists should respond to the social and cultural complexities inherent to Iran. In this new paradigm, represented in works of art and practiced by different means and techniques in new media, traditions and cultural standards are referenced in a critical way signifying confrontations and questioning of any kind of predefined or preexisting collective identity.[38]

This position is partly affected by the social and political agendas in the postrevolutionary period and the reaction to the government's programs of standardization of culture and essentialization of collective Islamic identity. Nonetheless, this formulated collective has received less of a response than the more prominent notion of the subjective voice. Practice for the most committed artists of this period seems to be an intellectual and enlightened project that serves as a fitting site for the possibility of a responsible and sociopolitical art; it is a response to the long-standing concerns of art and activism in Iranian literature

38 This idea reaches agreement with what social anthropologists John Campbell and Alan Rew argue, noting that "because of the subjective, experiential dimension of identity, effective identity narratives such as those deployed by (ethnic) nationalism are exercises in the mobilization of emotion through a selective drawing upon affective elements, for example a contextually defined sense of exclusion, fear and anxiety vis-à-vis significant Others." John R. Campbell and Alan Rew, eds., *Identity and Affect: Experiences of Identity in a Globalising World* (London: Pluto Press, 1999), 13.

and art. This set of critical practices showcases the possibilities of an activist art that operates in what has been characterized as a sort of contemporary art. In their own ways, these artists seek to challenge questions of identity and how to reconcile these issues in the present. They thus refuse a paradigm that associates a vernacular formal language or particular sociopolitical stereotypes based on neo-Orientalist or ethnogeographical clichés with identity. Instead, they insist on distinguishing between an art produced for and engaged with the immediate local context and one that claims authenticity in the process. When these artists produce and circulate work within local and international art circles, they also negotiate global concepts vis-à-vis local values, mainly by appropriating them. Although a large number of artists in this group deny any references to a predefined collective, their work coheres around an ironic[39] and, on other occasions, humorous approach to the purportedly documentary desires of the recent past. PLATES 1 E, 80 A–B, AND 91 Through the deconstruction of the essential collective values, they recreate a variety of individual identities. They dispute the Orientalist construct of the Other and resist self-exoticism. This means that they challenge the injection of culturally coded motifs and stereotypes that serve the needs of the political agenda defined by official culture, or the market,[40] or as a means to win the sympathy of outsiders.[41] Artists themselves question the validity of art that reinforces this objectification and exoticism.

As political scientist Fatemeh Sadeghi correctly argues, the younger generation in Iran is constructed of individuals who are affected by the failures of a revolutionary Islamic utopia. This experience has led them to a uniquely critical view of the collective.[42] The paradigm shift occurred through interpretation and deconstruction of the past; it was no longer merely based on its romanticization and a return to the glorified traditions, but now seen collectively as a constructive reality. Many of the works created by contemporary artists address present-day themes informed by the complexities of the artists' lives within a specifically Iranian context (SEE SAFAEI'S *Sepeleshk*, OPPOSITE). To many of them, contemporary art cannot simply be translated or interpreted formulaically, since that would contradict the artists' perceptions of their own autonomy. This position has enabled them to depict social reactions to an internal and external stimulus and its subsequent consequences for the political and social trajectory of contemporary Iranian culture.

---

39 A similar approach could be seen in the works of a few artists from the earlier generation such as Ardeshir Mohassess and Kaveh Golestan whose works are included in this exhibition. (SEE PLATES 28 A–H AND 73 B).

40 Given the recent development in the market, both regionally and locally, for modern and contemporary Iranian art, a substantial role is played by the market in the formation of trend-oriented art productions in Iran. This has created a problem: this market-oriented agenda has become very rarefied. The question of exclusivity is the important subject for criticism. The art market has provided to some extent a local, regional, and international channel of possibility for only particular genres of art to be developed. In effect, it has caused the concealment of other kinds of contemporary art, in particular the alternative art production in this scene.

41 See Hamid Keshmirshekan, "The Question of Identity vis-à-vis Exoticism in Contemporary Iranian Art," *Iranian Studies* 43, no. 4 (2010): 489–512.

42 See Fatemeh Sadeghi, "Negotiating with Modernity: Young Women and Sexuality in Iran," *Comparative Studies of South Asia, Africa, and the Middle East* 28, no. 2 (2008): 259.

Shadi Shafiei on

Tattoo Culture of the *Zurkhana*

For her photographic series The Book of Kings, Shirin Neshat marked her subjects with dense figural scenes of combat (and Persian text) applied like tattoos to bare chests, legs, faces, and arms.[1] She adopted the imagery from an early twentieth-century lithograph edition of the Iranian national epic, the *Shahnama* (Book of Kings), which she owns. In Siamak Filizadeh's series devoted to a modern-day version of the *Shahnama* hero Rustam, the artist rendered his champion as a bare-chested member of the *zurkhana* (a gymnasium), and appropriately gave him a tattoo on his upper arm.[2] In their work, both Neshat and Filizadeh are referencing a tradition in Iran extending back to ancient times of marking the body with permanent and temporary designs. Tattoo culture continued to be practiced in Iran after the advent of Islam in the mid-seventh century, although Islamic canonical law (Sharia) forbids tattooing. Shi'ite Islam, the state religion of Iran from the sixteenth century onward, takes a somewhat more ambiguous view.[3] The numerous references to tattooing in Persian literature (*kabudzani* or *khalkubi*) suggest that it was common among both rural and urban dwellers, male and female.[4] Tattooing continued into the early modern era and through the mid-twentieth century among various ethnic groups, especially in southern Iran and in the *pahlavan* class of urban athletes.

PLATES 21A–B AND 23

Pahlavans were a unique group of male athletes, mostly wrestlers, known for their acts of chivalry, courage, and generosity as well as occasional banditry—they often acted independently, sometimes siding with or against the established authority. Pahlavans began to incorporate tattoo art into their tradition as a form of affiliation and recognition of their brotherhood. Their use of the lion as a symbol of bravery is attested in Persian poetry of the twelfth and thirteenth centuries.[5] Accounts of seventeenth- and eighteenth-century foreign travelers and photographs of the nineteenth century provide a better understanding of pahlavan culture as that of low-class wrestlers, perhaps more entertainers than athletes, and later on within the traditional Persian gymnasium, or zurkhana, where they were admired but not respected. Nineteenth-century photographs of pahlavans suggest that tattooing was not standard; the ancient practice experienced a revival in modern Iran. In the mid-1930s the zurkhana institution and its wrestlers enjoyed a newfound popularity through government support. Under Reza Shah (r. 1925–41), the zurkhana was given a contrived pre-Islamic, anti-Arab lineage and the name of the sport was changed to *varzish-i bastani* (literally "ancient sport") to give it a more ancient patina.[6] Scholars and literati of the period praised the pahlavans'

PLATE 42

1 See Melissa Chiu and Melissa Ho, eds., *Shirin Neshat: Facing History* (Washington, D.C.: Smithsonian Books, 2015), 162–81, and *Shirin Neshat: The Book of Kings* (Paris: Galerie Jerome de Noirmont, 2012).

2 See Linda Komaroff, "The Return Engagement of Rostam," in *Ferdowsi, the Mongols and the History of Iran: Art, Literature and Culture from Early Islam to Qajar Persia*, ed. Robert Hillenbrand, A. C. S. Peacock, and Firuza Abdullaeva (London: I. B. Tauris), 2013, 381–90; in this same series, Suhrab, his son and rival, is also depicted as having a tattoo, pl. 51.

3 See Mahmoud Katiraie, *Az Khisht ta Khisht* (Tehran: Intisharat-i Mu'asisi-yi Mutali'ati Ijtima'i, 1969), 408.

4 Willem Floor, "Ḵālkubi," in *Encyclopaedia Iranica*, last modified October 7, 2011, http://www.iranicaonline.org/articles/kalkubi.

5 As demonstrated in the verses of the twelfth-century poem by Sharaf al-Din Shafraveh, the image of the lion, as a symbol of bravery, was one of the pahlavans' favorite tattoo designs. Moreover, there is another reference to the popularity of the design of lion in Rumi's *Mathnavi*, narrating the story of a pahlavan whose cowardly fear of needles resulted in the lion on his back being tattooed without tail or mane. Ibid.

6 See Houchang E. Chehabi, "Zur-Ḵāna," in *Encyclopaedia Iranica*, August 15, 2006, http://www.iranicaonline.org/articles/zur-kana.

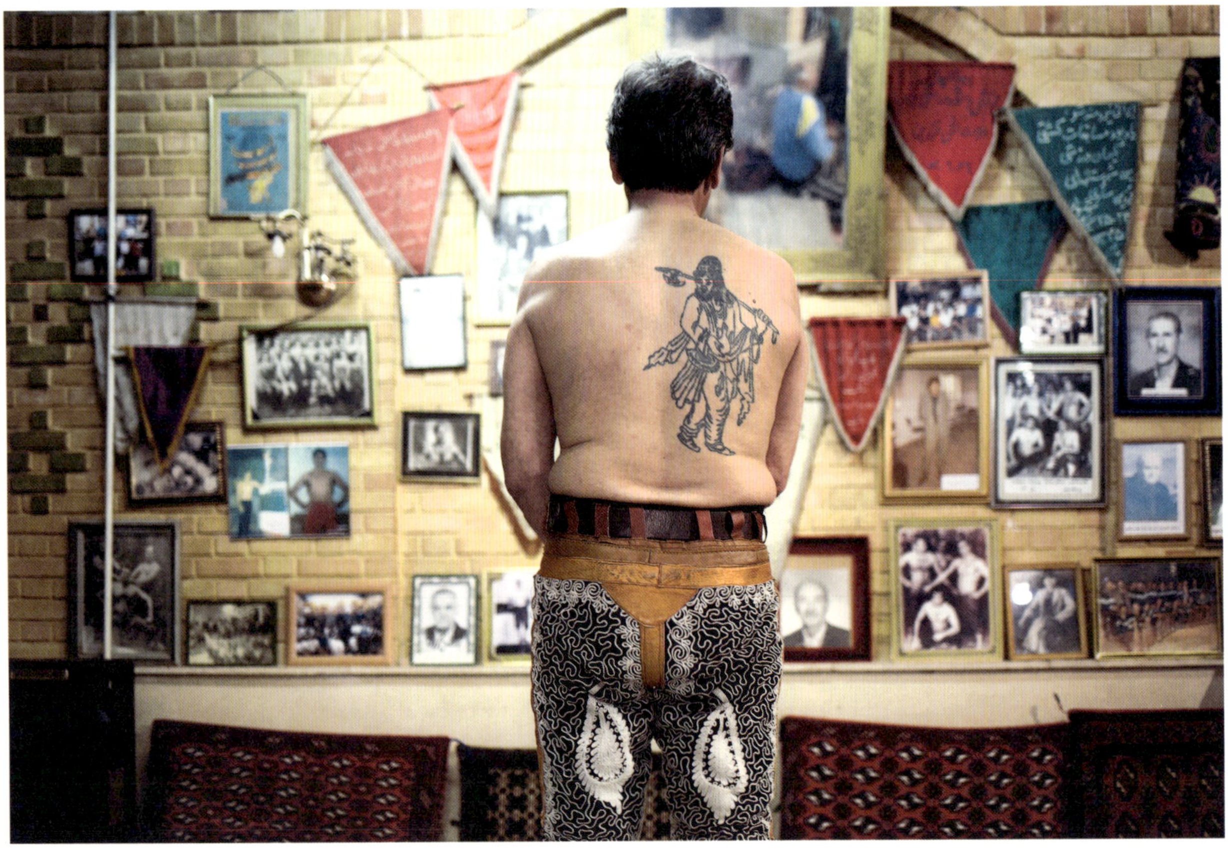

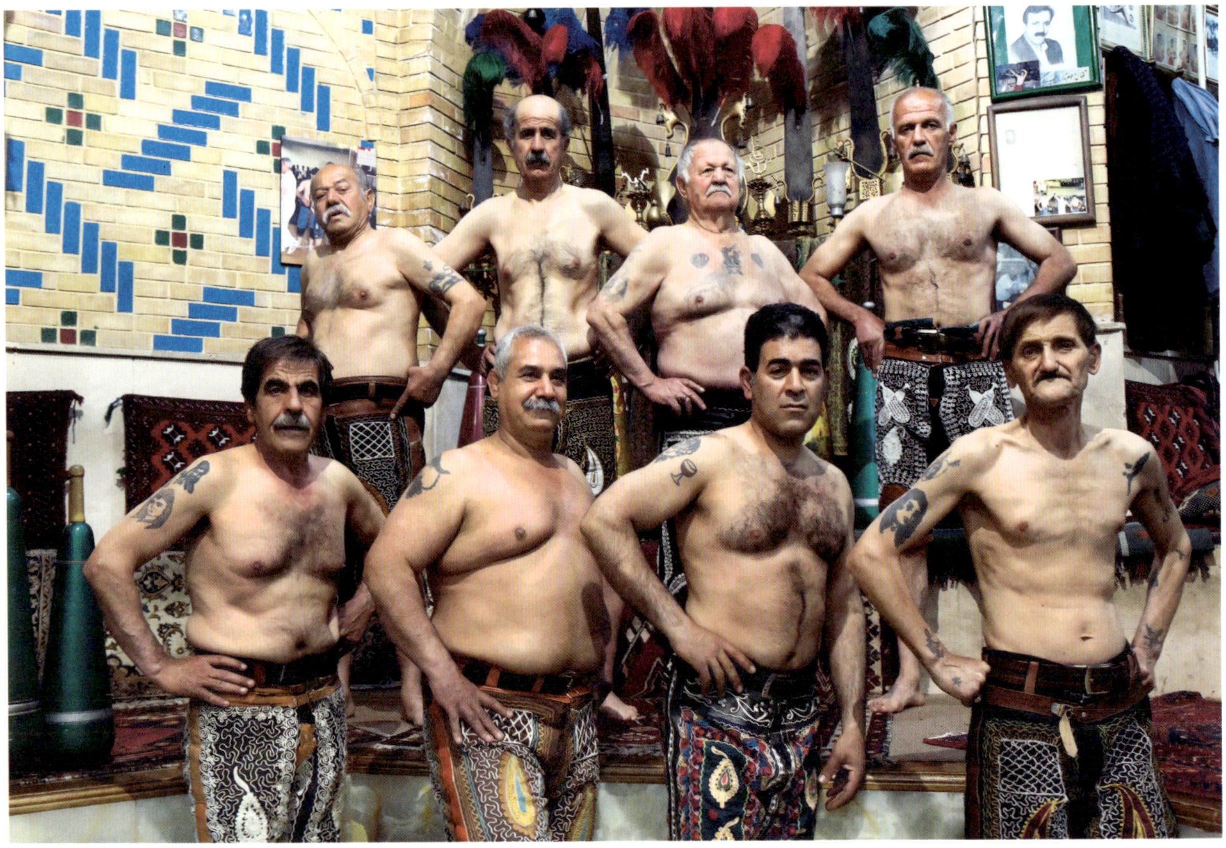

Mehran Mafi Bordbar's tattoo project, 2016–17

patriotic influence as preservers of Persian culture.[7] Subsequently, tattooing became more fashionable among the pahlavans (perhaps related to their new status) and the designs mirrored their system of belief and way of life. In a photograph from 1971 by Abbas, two heavily tattooed pahlavans are presented bare chested and barefoot, as is the custom of the zurkhana, clothed in traditional short pants (*tunban*) while
PLATE 24 wrestling. The high level of secrecy surrounding the pahlavans' tattoos and their association with urban gangs (the *luti* branch of the pahlavan) gave them a mysterious appeal. The tattoos were usually done either by the *dallak*, the barbers and washers in the public bathhouses, or sometimes in prison by a fellow prisoner. Although the tattoos were created in a traditional Persian style reminiscent of lithography, just as today, the specific content of the design was a matter of personal choice.

Pahlavans who claimed descent from Iran's ancient heroes showed enthusiasm for designs depicting Rustam. Religious imagery was just as popular, given that Ali, the first Shi'ite Imam, was the guardian of the zurkhana, and a symbol of chivalry and bravery (*futuvva*). Aside from Imam Ali's portrait, he was represented abstractly in the form of his famous bifurcated sword (*zulfiqar*), or through the image of a lion connoting Ali as the lion of God (*shir-i khuda*).[8] The theme of Karbala in which Imam Husain, the third Shi'ite Imam, was martyred in 680, was equally significant. Tattoos of Imam Husain, his half-brother Abbas (depicted in the 1971 photograph—
PLATE 24 the bust of a warrior with helmet and feather), or Husain's infant son Ali Asghar were used, respectively, as a symbols of sacrifice, loyalty, or, most tragic and unjust, the death of an innocent. Designs of dervishes and Sufis and their attributes were also common subjects, in particular the image of Puriya Vali, a fourteenth-century pahlavan, who first made mysticism an intimate part of the art of wrestling, as depicted in a tattoo on the back of a contemporary wrestler probably from the 1950s.[9] The practice of tattooing was largely abandoned after the mid-twentieth century because of its unsavory association with *lutis*, mainly gang members and prisoners, who represented the lower end of the pahlavan class. At this same time, medal-winning Olympic wrestlers, most notably the great Takhti, who were popularly hailed as Iran's new heroes, did not mark their bodies with tattoos.[10] Many legitimate pahlavans either tried to remove their tattoos or hide them. The Islamic Revolution of 1979 brought restrictions against the pahlavans appearing bare-chested in public, further obscuring their tattoos. But today, due to the popularity of tattooing among younger Iranians, both male and female, older pahlavans are once more willing to display their body art, as demonstrated in a series of photographs by Mehran Mafi Bordbar commissioned by the Los Angeles County Museum of Art in 2016, two of which are reproduced here.

---

7 These scholars and literati included Mohammad Taqi Bahar and Mehrdad Bahar. For further information on this subject, see ibid.

8 I am grateful for the information on zurkhana tattoo culture provided by Seyed Ghasim, who is himself a pahlavan. Seyed Ghasim, in conversation with author, December 2016.

9 Other tattoo designs include the old national emblem of lion and sun as the symbol of the pahlavan's sense of nationalism; tattoos of the Pahlavis' crown and the images of Reza Shah and Mohammad Reza Shah also were popular. In addition, romantic designs like Shahrazad as the symbol of female beauty and quotations from texts about mothers were likewise common. Ghasim, conversation.

10 See Siah Armajani's *Night Letter #1* (SEE PLATE 31). The text includes Takhti's name in gold and the bust of a winged angel that resembles the tattoo of one of the pahlavan wrestlers photographed by Abbas (SEE PLATE 24).

Linda Komaroff on

Siamak Filizadeh's Underground

PLATES 1A–J In his 2014 print series Underground Siamak Filizadeh takes as his theme the long reign of Nasir al-Din Shah (r. 1848-96), who was assassinated just short of his fiftieth jubilee (his golden jubilee, as calculated in lunar years).[1] Filizadeh's king rules an underground city for fifty-year intervals: he dies, is resurrected, and governs again exactly as before. The nature of the storyline was inspired by an alleged quote attributed to the dying Nasir al-Din: "I will rule you in a different manner, if I live…." As the lessons of history have shown, part of the great tragedy of Nasir al-Din Shah's reign is that the types of mistakes he made were repeated under the Qajar ruler's successors, royal and otherwise.

A martyred king, Nasir al-Din Shah is a semi-tragic figure with much the same appeal as a literary character or even a modern-day politician. He was the first shah to visit Europe, coming of age as photography, printed newspapers, and telegraphic communication all coalesced to enhance and disseminate his celebrity status while also preserving a full record of his deeds and misdeeds. Details of his family life and loves are preserved in a variety sources, including his own photographs of the royal harem.[2] All of this makes Nasir al-Din Shah fascinating subject matter for Filizadeh. But whether Filizadeh's visual inspiration is derived from historical or contemporary sources, the venue for his narrative and its meaning are always anchored in today's Iran.

Rather than beginning the series with the untried, seventeen-year-old king, Filizadeh has chosen throughout to portray Nasir al-Din Shah in his middle years: an iconic image of a thick-set, mustachioed man prematurely aged, debauched, and greedy—a likeness familiar from PLATES 11–14 AND 16 Nasir al-Din's many photographs and portraits, as well as his depictions on stamps and currency. The first of Filizadeh's prints is a celebratory court scene with the enthroned ruler at center wearing a careful reproduction of the famous Kayanid PLATE 1A Crown, a twenty-four-pound jewel-encrusted creation. This image serves to introduce the principle characters much like a theatrical ensemble—a musical one, perhaps, as some of the enactors are recast here as a rock band, with the king's future assassin as lead singer.

Nasir al-Din Shah learned photography as a thirteen-year-old prince and pursued this interest once he ascended the throne, becoming an accomplished photographer.[3] His most intriguing images are those he made of his intimates at court, including his wives and children. Among them is a photograph of his wife, Anis al-Daula, shown semi-reclining on a European-style settee, clothed in a short, flounced skirt, white socks, and black slippers; while this is typical royal female attire from the time of Nasir al-Din, the ensemble gives the sitter an oddly childlike PLATE 1B quality. Filizadeh reproduces this scene, emphasizing its disquieting nature, which he conflates with another picture of Anis al-Daula holding a European doll.[4]

As already noted, Nasir al-Din was the first Iranian ruler to tour Europe. In Filizadeh's PLATE 1G rendition of the return trip, the shah and his family are shown in a darkened courtyard, womenfolk and son bent forward under the burden of their Gucci, Cartier, and Givenchy bags. At the center, lit by a spotlight, the king is clothed and posed like Michael Jackson doing his signature moonwalk. The irony of this gently derisive scene is that it is preceded in the series (and the

1 A longer version of this essay first appeared in *Underground* (Tehran: Nazar Art Publication, 2016,), n.p. On Nasir al-Din Shah, see Abbas Amanat, *Pivot of the Universe: Nasir al-Din Shah Qajar and the Iranian Monarchy, 1831–1896* (Berkeley: University of California Press, 1997).

2 Women, not only his domineering mother, Mahd Ulya, but also several of his wives, left their marks on Nasir al-Din's reign and on the public imagination. Exceptionally for her time, one of his daughters wrote her memoires, much of which focused on her life in the harem. See Taj al-Saltana, *Crowning Anguish, Memoirs of a Persian Princess from the Harem to Modernity 1884–1914*, ed. with introduction and notes by Abbas Amanat (Washington, D.C.: Mage, 1993).

3 See Ali Behdad, "The Power-ful Art of Qajar Photography: Orientalism and (Self)-Orientalizing in Nineteenth-Century Iran," *Iranian Studies* 34, no. 1/4 (2001): 141–51, 145.

4 See Behdad, "The Power-ful Art of Qajar Photography," pl. 3, for the first photograph of Anis al-Daula, and for the second see Mohammad Hassan Semsar and Fatameh Sarian, comps., *Kakh-i Golestan (Album Khana) Fihrist-i aksha-yi barzugida-yi asr-i Qajar* [Golestan Palace (Photo Archive) Catalogue of Selected Qajar Photographs] (Tehran: Kitabkhana-yi Saltanati, 2003), 159. In Filizadeh's version, the reclining Anis al-Daula holds a doll and is surrounded by chickens (a possible reference to Sergei Parajanov's film *The Color of Pomegranates* or else an allusion to Anis al-Daula's non-royal lineage), in a room evocative of the French-inspired interiors preserved in Nasir al-Din–era photographs and paintings of the Golestan Palace—see for example the painting by Muhammad Ghaffari, Kamal al-Mulk, "Hall of Mirrors," in Layla S. Diba, ed., with Maryam Ekhtiar, *Royal Persian Paintings: The Qajar Epoch, 1785–1925* (Brooklyn: Brooklyn Museum of Art; London: I. B. Tauris, 1998), fig. xxvi.

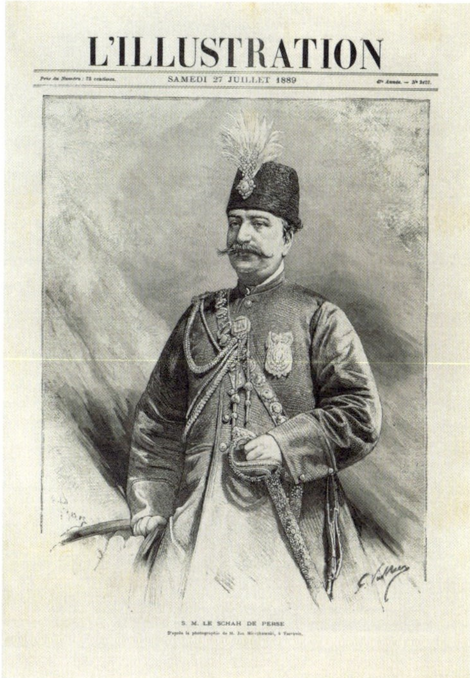
L'ILLUSTRATION

SAMEDI 27 JUILLET 1889

S. M. LE SCHAH DE PERSE

Cover of *L'Illustration* featuring Nasir al-Din Shah, July 27, 1889

actual European tours were bracketed historically) by bread riots, social and religious unrest, and armed government retaliation.

Popular agitation against the shah eventually led to his assassination. In 1896, while visiting a shrine to give thanks for his long rule, Nasir al-Din was shot at point-blank range by Mirza Riza Kirmani, an impoverished petty merchant who had been jailed and tortured for his pan-Islamist
PLATE 1I views.[5] Filizadeh makes Mirza Riza the sympathetic subject of several prints—the first of which echoes the familiar poster image for the 1976 movie *Taxi Driver* with the would-be assassin in the guise of Travis Bickle (Robert De Niro), the
PLATE 1H film's lonely and depressed antihero. Set at night in Tehran, the image shows the rumpled and slightly deranged Mirza Riza standing outside a cinema advertising *Taxi Driver*; an antique Paykan taxi is parked behind him.

The series concludes with Mirza Riza's public hanging, conceived as a grand triptych (also, SEE
PLATE 1J PLATE 18 for a contemporaneous photograph of the execution). The work recalls a Baroque altarpiece, with the bloody, Christlike figure of Mirza Riza hanging limply at the center; a velvet-roped stanchion below helps keep back groups of onlookers, who crowd the two side panels. Segregated by gender and clothed in nineteenth-century outerwear, the mob experiences the execution in an entirely contemporary manner—through their cell phone cameras—all except for a single blind man who seems unaware of the fateful event.

These prints clearly have a sinister side that is only partially mitigated by the artist's frequent touches of humor and irony.[6] His flawless blending of past and present, an integral part of his artistic vision, lends the fictionalized depictions an aura of authenticity that is further enhanced by the digitally manipulated photographic medium. The storyline of these (re-)imagined events dictates that they take place over and over again, giving the series an added darkness and evoking Edmund Burke's oft-quoted dictum, "Those who don't know history are doomed to repeat it."

5 Amanat, *Pivot of the Universe*, 440–44.

6 As in earlier work by Filizadeh, see Komaroff, "The Return Engagement of Rostam," in *Ferdowsi, the Mongols and the History of Iran: Art, Literature and Culture from Early Islam to Qajar Persia*, ed. Robert Hillenbrand, A. C. S. Peacock, and Firuza Abdullaeva (London: I. B. Tauris, 2013), 381–90.

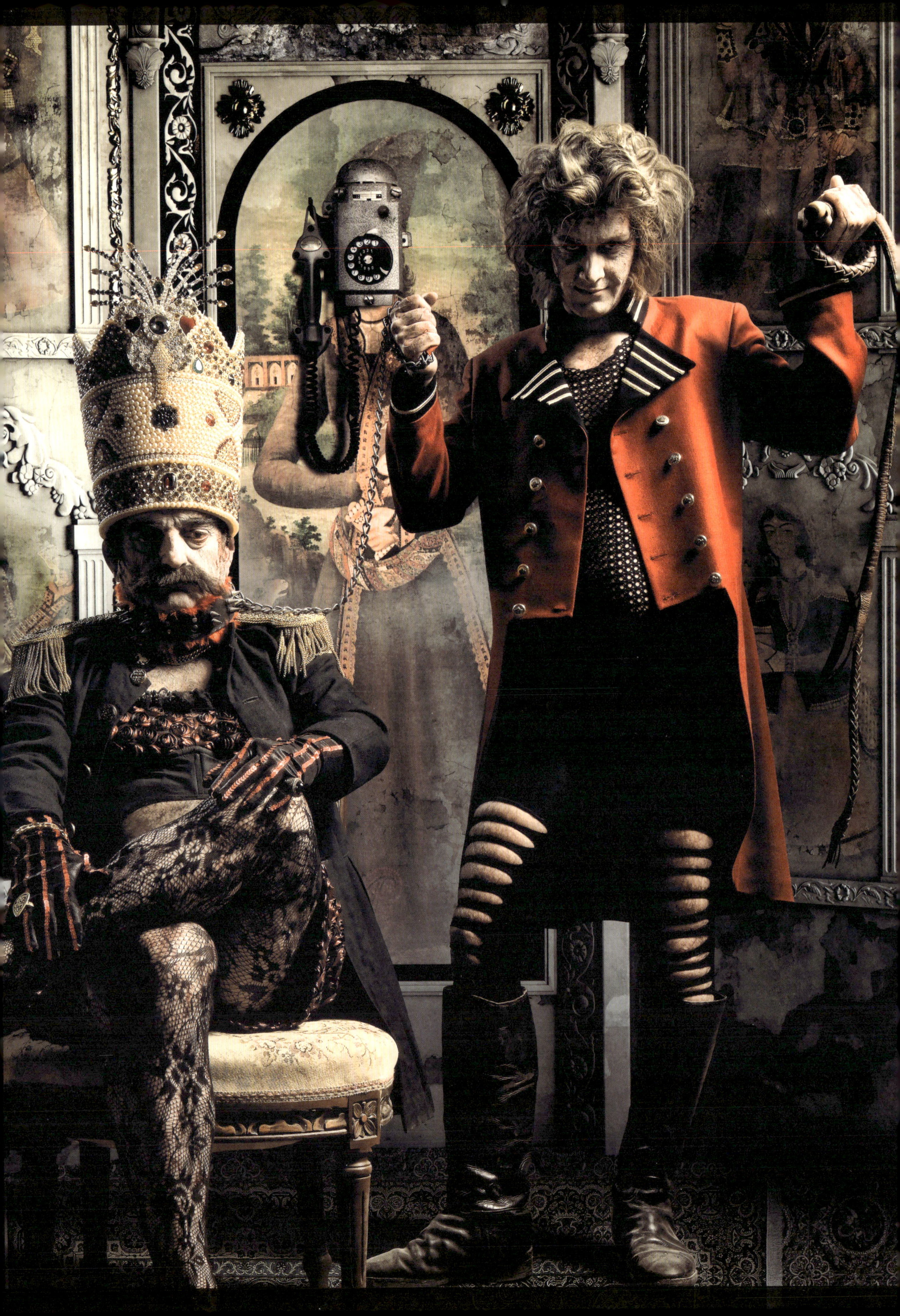

ECHOES OF THE SAFAVID PAST

Hani Khafipour

I offer two personal anecdotes to underscore my emphasis on the Safavid dynasty (1501–1722) in this essay on Iranian history from the sixteenth century to the present. A few years ago, I was riding a bus in Shiraz, Iran, next to an elderly man who, after the usual greeting that is exchanged between two strangers, casually asked what I did for living, apparently intrigued by a facsimile of a part of a manuscript that I had in my hand. "I write about history," I responded. "What region—Europe, America?" he asked. "No," I responded, "mostly Iran of the Safavid era." He then fully turned to face me and woefully said, "*Har chi mikashim az dast-i hamin Safaviyanast*" (All that we suffer is from the hands of these Safavids), pointing out the window to an oversized poster of Iran's supreme leader, Ayatollah Ali Khamenei, on the side of a government building. What could one say to such a verdict? Where does one begin?

On another occasion, thousands of miles away, in Chicago at a weekly gathering of expat literati, I was asked by a nice gentleman seated next to me a similar question, to which I offered an analogous thorny response. He replied with a faint smile, "*Chih ali, hamay-i badbakhtihamun az hamin asr shuru shud, vahdat-i dunya-yi Islam ru shikastand*" (How great; all of our misfortune began from this age, [when] they broke the unity of the Islamic world), perhaps in hopes that I could offer an explanation as to what exactly went wrong since I was the expert and clearly privy to the secrets of political decay or, better yet, civilizational decline.

My compatriots' opinions were not formed without justification. The man on the bus had rightly connected the theocratic rule of contemporary Iran and its regulation of morality in the public sphere, the paramount ideology of governance by a *faqih* (jurist), and all of the sociopolitical and economic woes that have befallen Iran today—as some believe happens when mullahs become politicians and politicians become mullahs—to theocracy's Safavid origins, and had decided what that meant to him. The second gentleman's verdict had a more specific rationale behind it and referenced the widespread assumption that the establishment of the Safavid Shi'ite state in the sixteenth century caused a major schism in an otherwise unified Muslim world. This rupture is widely believed among non-academics and certain religious conservatives to have cut off Iran from the rest of the Islamic world, then thriving behind the shield of the Sunni Ottoman Empire, the self-proclaimed "defenders of faith." Influential Iranian thinkers like Ahmad Kasravi (d. 1946) had scorned the Safavids decades before, and others who read his work closely, such as Jalal Al-i Ahmad (d. 1969), whose writings were quite popular among the literati, developed similar views:

> When our clergy were incorporated into the ruling body to become agents of oppression, when Mir Damad and Majlisi [high-ranking theologians] served the Safavid court, at least with their silence, in order to have a free hand in promulgating Shi'ism, we were transformed from

> travelers in the universal caravan of Islam into guardians of tombs, into beggars picking crumbs from the tables of departed martyrs. When we gave up the chance for martyrdom to content ourselves with glorifying the martyrs of the past, we became the gatekeepers of graveyards.[1]

This interpretation, however unforgiving and imprecise, had from a sociohistorical perspective one oft-shared and overriding feature: the golden-age syndrome, namely, the notion that Iran was fantastically great at some point in the past and now was in shambles.[2] Other eras that evoke the same syndrome, depending on the context, include the epochs before the Arab conquest (which some believe imposed Islam on Iranians) and before the Mongols (who brought the apocalypse in the thirteenth century), as well as the period before the Qajars (who milked the country dry and handed it over to the imperialist powers on a silver platter). The Pahlavi period (1925–79), the latest casualty, has been a setting for the exchange of multiple discourses on topics including the intersection of history and contemporary art.

The strong judgments levied against the Safavids partly stem from the fact that this dynasty had achieved the unimaginable: the establishment of a powerful Shi'ite state in the heart of the Islamic world, a feat that had not been realized since the Fatimid's takeover of most of North Africa and Egypt (909–1171). The Shi'ite order closest to ascending to their level in Iran was the Buyid dynasty (945–1055).[3] The Buyids, however, did not endure long enough to alter the religiopolitical alignment of Iran's governance, nor did they embody the ideological substance to radically reshape the mode of spirituality of the Iranian people. The Safavid community (i.e., the diverse and overlapping marginal groups that initially supported the Safavid house's claim to sovereignty) represented a salvational movement, one whose followers intended to right centuries of oppression and injustice. The characteristic quietism of Shi'ite leadership did not appeal to this group. They were bent on altering the course of their history by blood and blade. Isma'il Safavi's assumption of power in Tabriz in 1501 as the new shah was a defining moment in the long history of this land.[4]

The Safavids' hard-won ascendency in the early sixteenth century was the outcome of the complex sociopolitical and religious processes of the preceding three centuries (to draw an intentional line on the historical spectrum of this land so as to limit our *longue durée* gaze). The Safavid political culture had inherited a treasure trove of traditions: the Persianate patrimonialism with its ideals of kingship, the vitality of a politically conditioned Sufi order, and the powerful blending of antinomian Sufi-Shi'ite religiopolitical ethos. Added to this synthesis was the

---

1 Jalal Al-i Ahmad, *Occidentosis: A Plague from the West*, trans. R. Campbell (Berkeley: Mizan Press, 1984), 45.

2 Observers of contemporary American politics can readily recognize this outlook, which was encapsulated in the winning slogan, "Make America great again," which Donald Trump's campaign team borrowed from Ronald Reagan.

3 See Ali Asghar Faqihi, *Shahanshah-yi Azud-al-Daula* (Tehran: Matbuati-yi Isma'iliya, 1968); Saeed Hasan, *The Early History of the Buwaihids* (Allahabad, India: Senate House, 1948); and Roy Mottahedeh, *Loyalty and Leadership in an Early Islamic Society* (London: I. B. Tauris, 1980).

4 See Rasul Ja'fariyan, *Safaviyya dar Arsah-yi Din, Farhang va Siyasat* (Qum, Iran: Pizhuhishkadah-yi Hauzah va Danishgah, 2000); Mansur Sifatgul, *Sakhtar-i Nahad va Andishah-yi Dini dar Iran-i Asr-i Safavi* (Tehran: Mu'assasah-yi Khadamat-i Farhangi-yi Rasa, 2002).

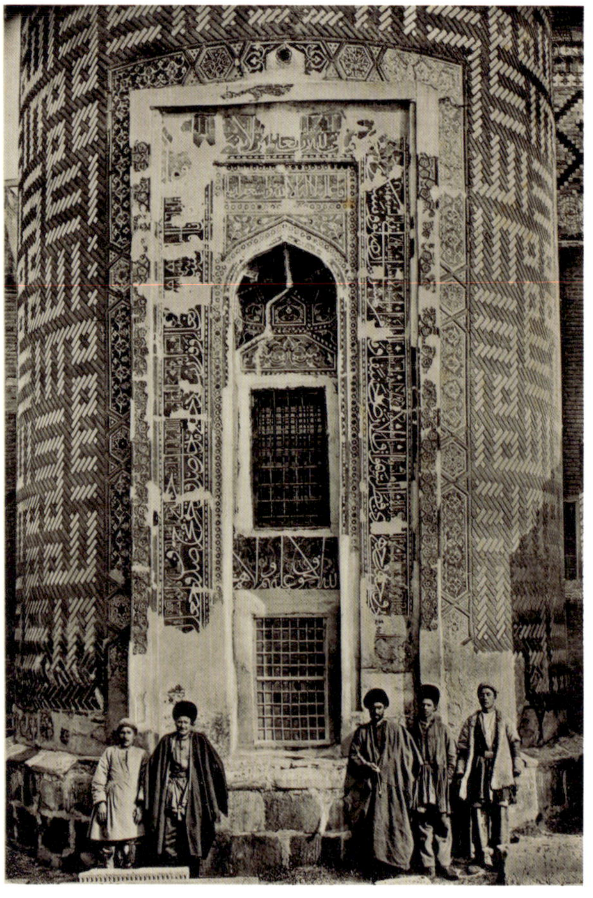

Antoin Sevruguin, *Tomb of Shaykh Safi* (progenitor of Safavid dynasty), Ardabil, 1880s–1924

Turco-Mongol warrior culture of their military, later known as the Qizilbash (the "red heads," referring to their red turbans), without whose support they could not have achieved much in the way of territorial conquest. Above all, the Safavid house had managed to tap into the Shiʿite historical narrative of suffering, martyrdom, and self-sacrifice, and to monopolize the community's paramount claim to sovereignty by maintaining that they were descendants of the Prophet—through his daughter Fatima and his cousin and son-in-law Ali, the first of the Shiʿite Imams—and therefore the rightful claimants to the leadership of the Muslim community.[5]

Over the course of the sixteenth century, with the help of native and émigré Shiʿite ulama (scholars of Islamic law and theology), the Safavids promoted Shiʿite learning, marginalized and persecuted religious dissenters (who included the Sunni elites and other Sufi orders), and projected onto the larger society their vision of the long-awaited just state. One can gain a glimpse of this vision by reading the extant Safavid royal public proclamations inscribed on stone slabs and mounted in mosques across the country.[6] As a result of such policies, the Shiʿite ulama under the court's patronage gained ground in the political arena on an unprecedented scale.

5 See Hani Khafipour, "The Safavid Claim to Sovereignty According to a Court Bureaucrat," in *Empires of the Near East and India: Source Studies of the Safavid, Ottoman, and Mughal Literate Communities*, ed. Hani Khafipour (New York: Columbia University Press, forthcoming); Michel M. Mazzaoui, "Shiism and the Rise of the Safavids" (PhD diss., Princeton University, 1965); and Ahmad Tajbakhsh, *Tarikh-i Safaviyyah* (Shiraz: Intisharat-i Nuvid, 1994).

6 See Hani Khafipour, "Beyond Charismatic Authority: The Crafting of a Sovereign's Image in the Public Sphere," in *The World of the Safavids*, ed. Rudi Matthee (London: Routledge, forthcoming).

The Safavids with their cadre of devoted literati (such as Abdi Beg Shirazi, Muhtasham Kashani, and Sa'ib Tabrizi), dedicated Shi'ite ulama, and zealous troops promoted Shi'ite culture and orthodoxy in their territory as well as in other communities in Ottoman-held regions. This process was not a disingenuous political stratagem to inculcate the masses with artificial religious sentiments and bring them into line with state ideology, but it seems to have been a dyadic practice, developing gradually between the religiopolitical orientation of the Safavid order and the general population's deep veneration for Shi'ite Imams.[7] As mentioned earlier, however, this process of "Shi'itization" has had its critics.

Kasravi and Al-i Ahmad were not alone in their punitive reappraisal of the Safavid legacy. The sociologist Ali Shariati claimed that Safavid Shi'ism (*tashayyu'-i Safavi*) created a distorted version of the Shi'ite doctrinal narrative of salvation that appealed to the sentiment of oppression with the hollow adoration of saviors, instead of producing a historical reawakening shaped by the intimate knowledge of the Prophet's household and the deeds of the Imams and their companions, which he distinguished as a true Alid Shi'ism (*tashayyu'-i Alavi*).[8] Safavid Shi'ism had betrayed the martyrdom of Imam Ali and later his son Husain at Karbala by
PLATES 80 A–B, 89, AND 92
divesting them of their revolutionary messages. He indicted the Shi'ite ulama for carrying out the task, thereby forfeiting their role as guides of the contemporary community. The responsibility, he asserted, now lay on the shoulders of the intelligentsia, who—armed with new humanistic and socio-scientific methodologies—could revive the true historical revolutionary Shi'ism and educate the masses.

Whether the ulama betrayed the Shi'ite Imams' true legacy or not, an archetype such as Husain, the "prince of martyrs," would offer the newly established Islamic Republic a major ideological source to harness during the war with Iraq (1980–88). The ulama equated the Iraqi government with modern-day Umayyads (661–750), who ruthlessly killed the Prophet's grandson Husain and enchained
PLATE 85
his family. Iranian soldiers carrying "*Ya Husain*" banners, wearing red headbands with the words "*labayk ya Husain*" and walking into minefields in hopes that the Occulted Imam Mahdi was waiting on the other side to escort them to paradise became popular images during the war. Today, one needs only to listen to Lebanon's Hezbollah's *nashids* to discern the potent connection between this type of historical narrative and political survival.

While the power of the Safavids waned and the dynasty crumbled in 1722, the ulama's social power remained intact throughout the dark eighteenth century. When the Qajars were finally able to assert their dominance over the other tribes, some of the ulama offered their assistance to the new rulers of the land. Of course, the Qajar dynasty (1794–1925) did not enjoy the level of religiopolitical legitimacy that the Safavids had achieved, and they were eager to receive ideological support, however unpersuasive.[9]

---

7 See Rasul Ja'fariyan, *Siyasat va Farhang-i Ruzgar-i Safavi* (Tehran: Nashr-i Ilm, 2009).

8 See Ali Shariati, *Tashayyu Alavi va Tashayyu Safavi* (Tehran: Intisharat-i Chapakhsh, 1998); and Ali Rahnema, *An Islamic Utopian. A Political Biography of Ali Shari'ati* (London: I. B. Tauris, 1998).

9 Abbas Amanat, *Pivot of the Universe: Nasir al-Din Shah Qajar and the Iranian Monarchy, 1831–1896* (Berkeley: University of California Press, 1997), 199; and Nikki R. Keddie, *Qajar Iran and the Rise of Reza Khan, 1796–1925* (Costa Mesa, CA: Mazda Publishers, 1999).

The Qajars, one of the first tribes that gave its allegiance to the Safavid cause, has had a difficult time generating a positive image in the contemporary public imagination, with little hope of rehabilitation in sight. After all, this was the dynasty that could not repel European imperialism, lost enormous territory to Britain and Russia, including the fertile lands of southern Caucasus, and repeatedly granted disastrous concessions to European firms in exchange for loans and negligible proceeds.

The Qajar officials, like their neighboring statesmen in the dissolving Ottoman Empire, had very few sources of power and political preparedness with which to outflank European imperialist objectives. The European military advantage had set the terms of engagement as it still does today, and there was no denying that the Qajar administration knew the damage it was exacting on society by submitting to the demands of Britain and Russia.[10] What remained for the Qajars after they signed the humiliating Turkmenchay Treaty in 1828 were a paper army, an empty treasury, and a fragile claim to sovereignty. Nevertheless, it is difficult to overemphasize their collective incompetence as rulers, especially Nasir al-Din Shah (r. 1848–96), whose reign lasted forty-eight long years. When, on May 1, 1896, Mirza Riza Kirmani, a disciple of opposition leader Jamal al-Din Afghani, put a bullet in the shah's chest, many must have breathed a sigh of relief. Considering Nasir al-Din's close association with political stagnancy and pitiful decadence in contemporary perceptions, it is not surprising that he occupies, derisively, center stage in the work of Iranian artists such as Siamak Filizadeh.

PLATES 1C–D

PLATES 11 AND 73A

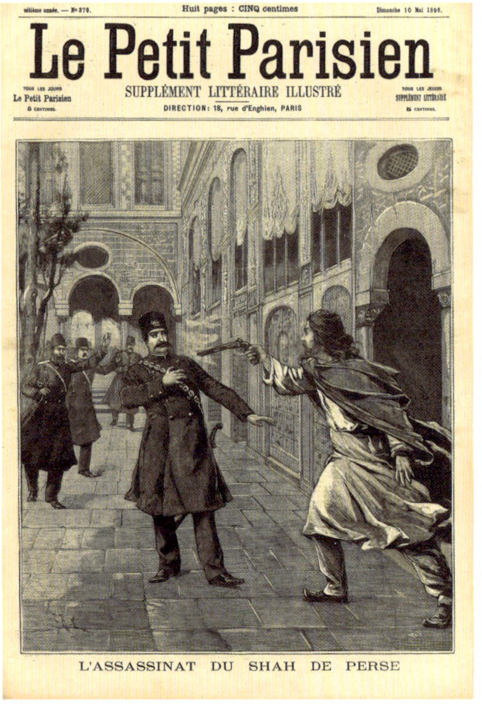

Assasination of Nasir-al Din, cover of *Le Petit Parisien*, May 10, 1896

10 See Touraj Atabaki, *Iran and the First World War: Battleground of the Great Powers* (London: I. B. Tauris, 2006); and Daniel R. Headrick, *The Tools of Empire: Technology and European Imperialism in the Nineteenth Century* (Oxford: Oxford University Press, 1981).

Prominent members of the ulama who had managed to remain largely independent of the Qajar court exhibited their sources of social power when they called for holy war in response to the Russian invasion of 1826, demanded repeal of the Reuter concession of 1873 (which Lord Curzon had described as "the most complete surrender of the entire resources of a kingdom into foreign hands that has ever been dreamed of, much less accomplished in history"),[11] and called for the boycott of tobacco in 1891 to compel Nasir al-Din Shah to cancel the British concession. These sporadic calls for action notwithstanding, their organizational capabilities during the Constitutional Revolution (1905–11) secured for these members of the ulama a central place within the political sphere.[12] The Constitutionalists failed but not without important gains, the least of which was the legacy its leaders left behind.

When Reza Shah Pahlavi (r. 1925–41) finally settled the questions of monarchy and constitutionalism with his coup d'état in 1921, and, four years later, placed the crown on his head with his own hands, the tumultuous events of the previous decades had already produced a cautious group of ulama hardened by decades of politicking. Reza Shah immediately recognized and dreaded their power. This was a group with great social cohesion with deep roots in the communities they served. Reza Shah and later his son Mohammad Reza Shah (r. 1941–79), as part of their domestic policy, tried to undermine the clerical establishment through institutional reforms and modernization measures by targeting precisely the

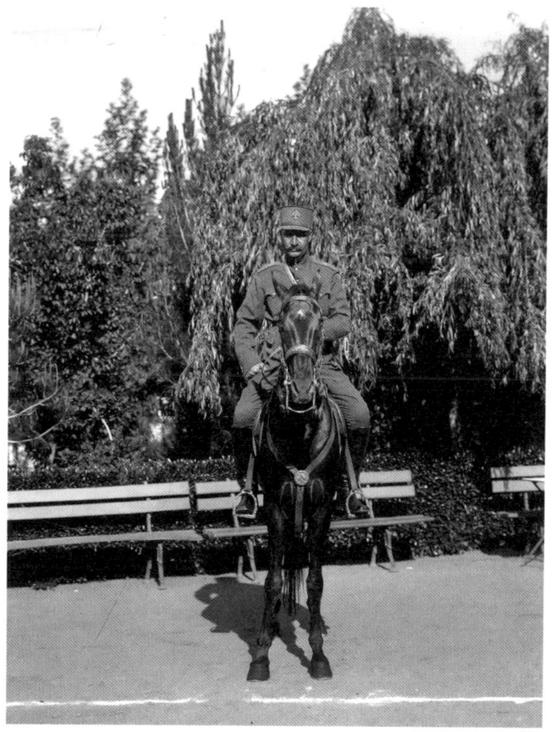

Antoin Sevruguin, *Portrait of Reza Shah Pahlavi (Reza Khan) on a Horse while Minister of War*, 1923–25. Glass plate negative. 9½×7 in. (23.8×17.8 cm). Myron Bement Smith Collection: Antoin Sevruguin Photographs. Freer Gallery of Art and Arthur M. Sackler Gallery Archives. Smithsonian Institution, Washington D.C. Gift of Katherine Dennis Smith, 1973–1985

11 George Nathaniel Curzon, *Persia and the Persian Question*, vol. 1 (London: Longmans, Green & Company, 1892), 480.

12 Ahmad Kasravi, *Tarikh-i Mashrutah-i Iran* (Tehran: Amir Kabir, 1968; Tehran: Negah Publications, 2003). I refer to the Negah edition.

sources of their power in the fields of education, law, and supervision of pious endowments. Yet they could do little to sever the intricate bond that connected them with the intelligentsia and the urban middle class—the *bazaris*—who cooperatively financed many of their undertakings. Some of the intelligentsia, such as Ali Shariati, were deeply troubled by the growing cleric-bazari alliance.[13]

It is hard to deny that the Pahlavi state's assault on the ulama created a profound sense of resentment in the hearts of the masses. When, for example, the state-controlled paper *Ittila'at* ran an editorial in January 1978 defaming Ayatollah Khomeini (d. 1989), one of its prominent members, as a lewd British collaborator, thousands took to the street in protest. The severe crackdown on any political dissent carried out by Iran's intelligence service, SAVAK, trained by the United States' and Israel's intelligence agencies, only further demonized the monarchy in the eyes of the people and reinforced what Khomeini had decried, that the Pahlavis were deeply beholden to the imperialist powers and their ruthless ally, Israel.[14] This is not to say that the monarchy did not have supporters. They tended to be members of the elite and mostly from the upper middle class in urban centers—a small percentage of the population.

PLATE 62

PLATE 65

During the 1970s, the Pahlavi house's legitimacy became a target for the opposition. When the future first president of the Islamic Republic, Abolhasan Banisadr, published in exile his article "Fifty Years of Treason" in 1976, he pointed out that Reza Shah's reign, established by a coup d'état, lacked legitimacy.[15] Banisadr continued that his successor was also kept in power by the U.S.-British-Pahlavi coup of 1953. This was the infamous overthrow that ruined Prime Minister Mossadeq (d. 1967) who had tried to nationalize Iran's oil industry along with many others, coming so close to bringing about a major political breakthrough—a tragic turning point in Iran-U.S. relations.

PLATE 40

Aside from the issue of legitimacy, the fact that the state had become unabashedly secular in its approach to modernity and reform against the national sentiment, and the fact that, beyond its modern Western facade, the monarchy had become an authoritarian police state with thousands of tortured political prisoners, was, as the saying goes, the cherry on top. When *60 Minutes* reporter Mike Wallace interviewed Mohammad Reza Shah on October 24, 1976, he asked him if he was aware that the CIA had a psychological profile on him and whether His Majesty would be interested in his reading it:

---

13 In his last work, *Islam's Class Bias*, Shariati severely criticized the ulama for their compromised social position and ineffective political involvement. Ali Shariati, *Jahatgiri-yi Tabaqati dar Islam* (Tehran: Intisharat-i Qalam, 2001).

14 Ruhollah Khomeini, *Islam and Revolution: Writings and Declarations of Imam Khomeini (1941–1980)*, ed. and trans. Hamid Algar (Berkeley: Mizan Press, 1981), 197–98; see also Jahangir Amuzegar, *The Dynamics of the Iranian Revolution: The Pahlavis' Triumph and Tragedy* (Albany: State University of New York Press, 1991).

15 Abolhassan Banisadr, "Fifty Years of Treason," *Khabarnama*, April 1976.

"Do I have your permission?" Wallace asks, to which the shah responds, "Yes, sure."

"You won't send me to the SAVAK, if I ask?" Wallace asks with a smirk. After a short, awkward pause, the shah smiles and responds, "No, I will spare you this terrible ordeal of going through torture."[16]

The state's brutal suppression of political dissent and the recurring issue of torture had become common knowledge, while Amnesty International on more than one occasion had labeled the shah as one of the worst violators of human rights. Beyond its three sources of power (the military, the bureaucracy, and the elite patronage system) that crumpled in the aftermath of the revolution, the Pahlavi house had only the United States and its European allies to preserve it, which by the winter of 1979, many analysts realized, was a lost cause.

Like most revolutions, Iran's in 1979 brought sweeping changes that touched every sector of the society with mixed results irrespective of political orientation, for it penetrated family law and education and regulated morality. Moreover, its vehement opposition to Western hegemonic aims in the Middle East and its ideological assaults on the neighboring monarchies by questioning their claims to legitimacy invited harsh criticism, distrust, and fear of Iran's new government. The revolution also provoked war as the new and ambitious Iraqi president Saddam Hussein (1979–2003), with U.S.-European blessing, launched a massive invasion of Iran.[17] The ensuing war (or "holy defense," as it is known in Iran) that lasted eight years mobilized the nation, entrenched the ulama in high government positions, and with its revolutionary tribunals and executions created an atmosphere of terror reminiscent of the system it had recently overthrown. Again, those in power felt justified in their brutality for they were convinced that they were the ones in possession of the knowledge and methodology to transform the society and set it on the right path. This tension soon became apparent in the debates regarding the fundamental laws of the land.

In drafting the constitution, the vision of Mehdi Bazargan, the first prime minister of the new republic for a "Democratic Islamic Republic," was met by Khomeini's fundamental opposition. In an interview with the *New York Times*, Khomeini clearly articulated how divergent their ideas were:

> What the nation needs is an Islamic Republic—not a Democratic Republic or a Democratic Islamic Republic. Don't use the Western term "democratic." Those who call for such a thing don't know anything about Islam.... Islam does not need adjectives such as democratic. Precisely because Islam is everything, it means everything. It is sad for us to add another word near the word Islam, which is perfect.[18]

16 Mike Wallace, "The Shah of Iran," *60 Minutes*, CBS, October 24, 1976.

17 See Farhang Rajaee, ed., *Iranian Perspectives on the Iran-Iraq War* (Gainesville: University Press of Florida, 1997); Pierre Razoux and Nicholas Elliott, *The Iran-Iraq War* (Cambridge, MA: Belknap Press of Harvard University Press, 2015); and Williamson Murray and Kevin Woods, *The Iran-Iraq War: A Military and Strategic History* (Cambridge: Cambridge University Press, 2014).

18 Oriana Fallaci, "An Interview with Khomeini," *New York Times*, October 7, 1979; see also Ervand Abrahamian, *A History of Modern Iran* (Cambridge: Cambridge University Press, 2008), 163.

Bazargan warned that the drafted constitution created a ruling class out of ulama, and might in fact undercut Islam since later generations could blame the state's flaws on religion. Was it this loss of Islam observed all around him that the stranger on the bus seated next to me lamented?

Today, when Western observers of Iranian politics are puzzled by Khamenei's discourse on the country's domestic and foreign policy, it helps to know that, ideologically, Khamenei views himself as the custodian of the revolution's agenda—centering on resistance to Western domination of the Middle East and propulsion toward the ever-elusive economic independence (or self-sufficiency) through national unity and domestic ingenuity. The politics of UN sanctions and international monopolies, however, have shown the difficulties of the path toward independence, or, its reduced version, independence through equal partnerships. Was it the promise of economic prosperity after the revolution that never materialized, thus leaving many impoverished, for which my compatriot on the bus now blamed the state? Perhaps both, for Imam Ali's adage, "when poverty comes through the door, faith and religion go out the other" had certainly rung true for some.

There is an uninterrupted friction in Iran between acceptance and rejection of the past. Were the martyrs of Karbala unfairly resurrected to give the Safavids their rise and, by extension, the Islamic Republic's ideological affluence? Was it the constitutionalists who had failed to produce a new paradigm, which ultimately caused the Pahlavi crown to be replaced by a black turban? Each new generation deals with this uncontainable, overpowering past that they are forced to disentangle from and orient themselves to. This very notion of struggling with the living past is brilliantly captured in Ramin Haerizadeh's *He Came, He Left, He Left, He Came*, in which a heart-shaped sticker with the Republic's flag emblem is placed on the former Queen Farah Diba's face, and the shah's head is replaced by an elephant whose trunk is cut off, its tusk glued to its forehead, producing a creature no one can recognize. The disfigured elephant is undoubtedly the central character in the political satire *The Town of Tales* (Shahr-i Qissah) by Bijan Mofid; after taking advice from everyone in the village in order to cure his ailment, the character becomes, as Mofid puts it, "*hashalhaf*," something useless, confused, and debased.[19]

PLATE 38

Collapsing the multiple pasts onto an ever-shifting present at various historical crossings is one way for a new generation of Iranians, especially as expressed by contemporary artists, to reclaim and revive that history and weave into its tapestry their own thread of ideals, disenchantments, and critiques.

19 Bijan Mofid, *Shahr-i Qissah* (Tehran: Intisharat-i Sazman-i Jashn-i Hunar Takht-i Jamshid, 1968).

Works in the Exhibition

Works are listed in order of their appearance in the plate section of the book, from right to left. The country of birth, when known, is provided for each artist. Checklist is accurate as of November 2017.

Siamak Filizadeh (IRAN, B. 1970)

PLATE 1A (PAGE 92)
Coronation FROM THE SERIES Underground, 2014
Inkjet print
70⅞ × 55⅛ in. (180 × 140 cm)
LACMA, purchased with funds provided by Kitzia and Richard Goodman through the 2016 Collectors Committee, M.2016.138.1

PLATE 1B (PAGE 93)
Anis al-Daula FROM THE SERIES Underground, 2014
Inkjet print
59 × 39⅜ in. (150 × 100 cm)
LACMA, purchased with funds provided by Kitzia and Richard Goodman through the 2016 Collectors Committee, M.2016.138.2

PLATE 1C (PAGE 94)
Shah and the British Ambassador FROM THE SERIES Underground, 2014
Inkjet print
59 × 39⅜ in. (150 × 100 cm)
LACMA, purchased with funds provided by Kitzia and Richard Goodman through the 2016 Collectors Committee, M.2016.138.5

PLATE 1D (PAGE 94)
Shah and the Russian Ambassador FROM THE SERIES Underground, 2014
Inkjet print
59 × 39⅜ in. (150 × 100 cm)
LACMA, purchased with funds provided by Kitzia and Richard Goodman through the 2016 Collectors Committee, M.2016.138.6

PLATE 1E (PAGE 96)
Vigor FROM THE SERIES Underground, 2014
Inkjet print
59 × 39⅜ in. (150 × 100 cm)
LACMA, purchased with funds provided by Kitzia and Richard Goodman through the 2016 Collectors Committee, M.2016.138.12

PLATE 1F (PAGE 97)
Harem FROM THE SERIES Underground, 2014
Inkjet print
59 × 39⅜ in. (150 × 100 cm)
LACMA, purchased with funds provided by Kitzia and Richard Goodman through the 2016 Collectors Committee, M.2016.138.13

PLATE 1G (PAGE 98)
Return from Europe FROM THE SERIES Underground, 2014
Inkjet print
51¼ × 51¼ in. (130 × 130 cm)
LACMA, purchased with funds provided by Kitzia and Richard Goodman through the 2016 Collectors Committee, M.2016.138.14

PLATE 1H (PAGE 99)
Mirza Riza Kirmani FROM THE SERIES Underground, 2014
Inkjet print
59 × 39⅜ in. (150 × 100 cm)
LACMA, purchased with funds provided by Kitzia and Richard Goodman through the 2016 Collectors Committee, M.2016.138.16

Siamak Filizadeh (CONT.)

PLATE 1I (PAGE 100)
Assassination FROM THE SERIES Underground, 2014
Inkjet print
55⅛ × 84⅝ in. (140 × 215 cm)
LACMA, purchased with funds provided by Kitzia and Richard Goodman through the 2016 Collectors Committee, M.2016.138.17

PLATE 1J (PAGE 101)
Execution FROM THE SERIES Underground, 2014
Inkjet prints
48⅜ × 38⅞ in. (122.9 × 98.7 cm); 84⅜ × 53⅜ in. (214.3 × 135.6 cm); 48⅜ × 38⅞ in. (122.9 × 98.7 cm)
LACMA, purchased with funds provided by Kitzia and Richard Goodman through the 2016 Collectors Committee, M.2016.138.21a–c

PLATE 2 (PAGE 102)
Rostam II returns at age of 30 having been brought up abroad, 2009
Digital print on canvas
55 × 42 in. (139.7 × 106.5 cm)
LACMA, purchased with funds provided by the Karl Loring Trust and Art of the Middle East: CONTEMPORARY, M.2011.45.2

Fereydoun Ave (IRAN, B. 1945, ACTIVE IRAN AND FRANCE)

PLATE 3 (PAGE 103)
Rostam in the Dead of Winter, 2009
Inkjet print and mixed media on handmade paper
22½ × 30 in. (57.1 × 76.2 cm)
LACMA, purchased with funds provided by Shidan Taslimi, M.2015.189

PLATE 4 (PAGE 104)
Untitled FROM THE SERIES Rostam in Late Summer—Revisited, 2009
Inkjet print on canvas
59½ × 39½ in. (150 × 100 cm)
Mohammed Afkhami Foundation, Switzerland

PLATE 5 (PAGE 106)
Rustam's Seventh Labor: He Kills the White Div FROM THE *Shahnama* of Firdausi, c. 1670
Ink and opaque watercolor on paper
14⅜ × 9¼ in. (36.5 × 23.5 cm)
Staatsbibliothek zu Berlin, Preussischer Kulturbesitz, Berlin (MS or. fol. 3380, fol. 78r)

PAINTING BY **Mu'in Musavvir** (ACTIVE C. 1630–97)

PLATE 6 (PAGE 106)
The Div Akvan Carries Rustam to the Sea FROM THE *Shahnama* of Firdausi, 1660s
Opaque watercolor and ink on paper
Painting: 10 × 5⅝ in. (25.2 × 14.3 cm)
Metropolitan Museum of Art, New York, Bequest of Monroe C. Gutman, 1974 (1974.290.43, fol. 158v)

ATTRIBUTED TO **Ali Asghar**

PLATE 7 (PAGE 107)
The Combat of Khusrau Parviz and Bahram Chubina FROM THE *Shahnama* of Firdausi for Shah Isma'il II (r. 1576–77), c. 1577
Ink, opaque watercolor, and gold and silver on paper
18 × 12½ in. (45.7 × 31.8 cm)
LACMA, purchased with funds provided by H. Tony and Marti Oppenheimer, Christopher V. Walker, Carolyn and Bill Powers, Lynda and Stewart Resnick, Kathrine and Frank Baxter, Caron and Steven D. Broidy, John and Leslie Dorman, the Kayne Foundation, Ric and Suzanne Kayne, Jerry D. Kayne, Myron Laskin, Camilla Chandler Frost, and Ellen and Michael Korney through the 2006 Collectors Committee, M.2006.114

PAINTING ATTRIBUTED TO **Abdul-Aziz** (ACTIVE FIRST HALF OF THE 16TH CENTURY)

PLATE 8 (PAGE 108)
Manuchihr Welcomes Sam but Orders War upon Mihrab FROM THE *Shahnama* of Firdausi, c. 1525
Opaque watercolor, ink, and gold and silver on paper
18⅝ × 12½ in. (47.1 × 31.8 cm)
Metropolitan Museum of Art, New York, gift of Arthur A. Houghton Jr., 1970 (1970.301.9, fol. 80v)

PLATE 9 (PAGE 109)
Gushtasp and the Dragon of Mount Sakila FROM THE *Shahnama* of Firdausi, AH 1014/1605
Opaque watercolor, ink, and gold on paper
14⅛ × 9½ in. (36 × 24 cm)
Staatsbibliothek zu Berlin, Preussischer Kulturbesitz, Berlin (MS or. fol. 4251, fol. 460r)

Fataneh Dadkhah (IRAN, B. 1952)

PLATE 10 (PAGE 110)
Untitled FROM THE SERIES Destruction, 2006
Chromogenic print
44¼ × 30 in. (112.4 × 76.2 cm)
LACMA, purchased with funds provided by Art of the Middle East: CONTEMPORARY, M.2016.241.1

PLATE 11 (PAGE 111)
Early Portrait of Nasir al-Din Shah (r. 1848–96), c. 1850
Ink, opaque watercolor, and gold on paper
24 × 16 in. (61 × 40.6 cm)
LACMA, purchased with funds provided by the Nasli M. Heeramaneck Collection, gift of Joan Palevsky, AC1992.211.1

POSSIBLY **Luigi Pesce** (ITALY, 1818–1891)

PLATE 12 (PAGE 112)
Nasir al-Din Shah, c. 1855–58
Salted paper print from paper negative
7¾ × 5⅜ in. (19.6 × 13.5 cm)
Metropolitan Museum of Art, New York, gift of Charles K. and Irma B. Wilkinson, 1977, 1977.683.24

PLATE 13 (PAGE 112)
Nasir al-Din Shah, c. 1852–55
Salted paper print from glass negative
13¼ × 8⅜ in. (33.7 × 21.2 cm)
Metropolitan Museum of Art, New York, gift of Charles K. and Irma B. Wilkinson, 1977, 1977.683.22

PLATE 14 (PAGE 113)
Antoin Sevruguin (IRAN, D. 1933)
Nasir al-Din Shah Sitting on the Lower Step of Takht-i Tavus or the Peacock Throne, late 19th century
Glass negative
7⅛ × 9⅜ in. (18 × 23.9 cm)
Freer Gallery of Art and Arthur M. Sackler Gallery Archives, Smithsonian Institution, Washington, D.C., Myron Bement Smith Collection, gift of Katherine Dennis Smith, 1973–1985, FSA A.4 2.12. GN.31.01 (exhibition copy)

PLATE 15 (PAGE 114)
Parviz Tanavoli (IRAN, B. 1937, ACTIVE CANADA AND IRAN)
Nassereddin Shah FROM THE SERIES Universal Icons, 2016
Acrylic on canvas
63 × 43⅜ in. (160 × 110 cm)
Courtesy of the artist

PLATE 16 (PAGE 116)
Herbert Rose Barraud (UNITED KINGDOM, 1845–1896)
Portrait of Nasir al-Din Shah Wearing Formal Attire, 1889
Woodburytype
14 × 10¼ in. (35.6 × 26 cm)
Collection of Azita Bina-Seibel and Elmar W. Seibel, Boston

PLATE 17 (PAGE 116)
Antoin Sevruguin (IRAN, D. 1933)
Mirza Riza Kirmani, Nasir al-Din Shah's Assassin, 1896
Albumen print
8⅜ × 6 in. (21.1 × 15.2 cm)
Collection of Azita Bina-Seibel and Elmar W. Seibel, Boston

PLATE 18 (PAGE 117)
Execution of Mirza Riza Kirmani, Nasir al-Din Shah's Assassin, 1896
Albumen print
9⅞ × 7⅞ in. (25 × 20 cm)
Collection of Azita Bina-Seibel and Elmar W. Seibel, Boston

PLATE 19 (PAGE 118)
PROBABLY **Hussein Qular Aqasi** (IRAN, D. 1966)
Rustam with Suhrab, mid-20th century
Oil on canvas
48½ × 75 in. (123.1 × 190.5 cm)
Collection of Dr. Sep Sarshar, Los Angeles

PLATE 20 (PAGE 119)
Rustam Battling Ashkbus, mid-20th century
Oil on canvas
48.5 × 75 in. (123.2 × 190.5 cm)
Collection of Dr. Sep Sarshar, Los Angeles

PLATE 21A (PAGE 120)
Shirin Neshat (IRAN, B. 1957, ACTIVE UNITED STATES)
Bahram (Villains) FROM THE SERIES The Book of Kings, 2012
Gelatin silver print with ink
99 × 49½ in. (251.5 × 125.7 cm)
Courtesy of Shulamit Nazarian, Los Angeles

PLATE 21B (PAGE 120)
Amir (Villains) FROM THE SERIES The Book of Kings, 2012
Gelatin silver print with acrylic
99 × 49½ in. (251.5 × 125.7 cm)
LACMA, gift of Lynda and Stewart Resnick through the 2017 Collectors Committee, M.2017.77

PLATE 22 (PAGE 122)
Ardeshir Mohassess (IRAN, 1938–2008)
Untitled, 1972
Ink on paper
Framed: 19 × 19 in. (48.3 × 48.3 cm)
Collection of Massoud Nader, New York

PLATE 23 (PAGE 123)
Shirin Neshat (IRAN, B. 1957, ACTIVE UNITED STATES)
Divine Rebellion FROM THE SERIES The Book of Kings, 2012
Gelatin silver print with acrylic
62 × 49 in. (157.5 × 124.5 cm)
Courtesy of the artist and Gladstone Gallery, New York and Brussels (exhibition copy)

PLATE 24 (PAGE 123)
Abbas (IRAN, B. 1944, ACTIVE FRANCE)
Wrestlers at training, wearing old traditional trousers, 1971, printed 2016
Gelatin silver print
16 × 12 in. (40.6 × 30.5 cm)
LACMA, purchased with funds provided by Shidan Taslimi, M.2016.199.2

PLATE 25 (PAGE 124)
Parviz Tanavoli (IRAN, B. 1937, ACTIVE CANADA AND IRAN)
Lion and Sword III, 1976
Bijar weave
62¼ × 91 in. (158 × 231 cm)
Courtesy of the artist

PLATE 26 (PAGE 125)
Lion and Sword II, 1975
Bijar weave
52¾ × 78¾ in. (134 × 200 cm)
Courtesy of the artist

PLATE 27 (PAGE 126)
Shoja Azari (IRAN, B. 1958, ACTIVE UNITED STATES)
Idyllic Life, 2012
High-definition color video with sound
Duration: 10 minutes, 11 seconds
LACMA, purchased with funds provided by Anousheh and Ali Razi, Shirine Reza, Wahideh Khaleeli, Darioush and Shahpar Khaledi, Chala Aryana, Hormoz and Fariba Ameri, and Angela and Isaac Larian, M.2015.104.1

PLATES 28A–H (PAGES 128–29)
Kaveh Golestan (IRAN, 1950–2003)
Untitled FROM THE SERIES Az Div o Dad, 1976
Diffusion transfer prints
Images: 4 × 4 in. (10 × 10 cm) each
LACMA, purchased with funds provided by Nina Ansary, M.2015.188.10, M.2015.188.3, M.2015.188.5, M.2015.188.4, M.2015.188.2, M.2015.188.1, M.2015.188.8, M.2015.188.6

PLATE 29 (PAGE 130)
Taravat Talepasand (UNITED STATES, B. 1979)
Why So Worried King?, 2009
Graphite and glair on paper
40 × 30 in. (101.6 × 76.2 cm)
Private collection

PLATE 30 (PAGE 131)
Ali Akbar Sadeghi (IRAN, B. 1937)
Boasting XVIII, 1973
Animation celluloid with drawn background (plastic and paper)
35 × 30 in. (88.9 × 76.2 cm)
LACMA, purchased with funds provided by Navabeh Borman in memory of Darius Nourafchan, with additional funds provided by Houman Nikbakht, and Harvey and Beth Plotnick, M.2017.248

PLATE 31 (PAGE 132)
Siah Armajani (IRAN, B. 1939, ACTIVE UNITED STATES)
Night Letter #1, 1957
Watercolor, ink, and seal on paper
17¼ × 20½ in. (43.8 × 52 cm)
Collection of Bahman and Yasmin Mossavar-Rahmani, Riverside, Connecticut

PLATE 32 (PAGE 133)
Reza Mafi (IRAN, 1943–1982)
Siyah mashq, 1971
Ink on paper
7½ × 11½ in. (19.1 × 29.2 cm)
Collection of Houman M. Sarshar, Los Angeles

PLATE 33 (PAGES 134–35)
Yasmin Sinai (IRAN, B. 1969, ACTIVE UNITED ARAB EMIRATES)
The Act of Gurdafarid, the Female Warrior, 2015
Cardboard, paper, and glue
72 × 46 × 21⅝ in. (183 × 117 × 55 cm)
LACMA, gift of Lynda and Stewart Resnick through the 2017 Collectors Committee, M.2017.116a-u

PLATE 34 (PAGE 136)
Suhrab Fights Gurdafarid FROM the *Shahnama* of Firdausi, AH 1014/1605–7
Ink, opaque watercolor, and gold and silver on paper; lacquer binding
14¾ × 9¾ in. (37.5 × 24.8 cm)
Metropolitan Museum of Art, New York, gift of Alexander Smith Cochran, 1913 (13.228.16, fol. 095r)

PLATES 35A–D (PAGES 138–39)
Shadi Ghadirian (IRAN, B. 1974)
Untitled FROM THE SERIES Qajar, 1998
Gelatin silver bromide prints
10 × 8 in. (25.4 × 20.3 cm); 10 × 8 in. (25.2 × 20.3 cm); 10 × 8 in. (25.2 × 20.2 cm); 8 × 10 in. (20.3 × 25.2 cm)
LACMA, purchased with funds provided by the Art of the Middle East Acquisition Fund, Art of the Middle East Deaccession Fund, the Ralph M. Parsons Fund, the Joan Palevsky Bequest by exchange, and Catherine Benkaim, with additional funds provided by Angella and David Nazarian, M.2008.35.1, M.2008.35.9, M.2008.35.27, M.2008.35.14

PLATE 36 (PAGE 140)
Sadegh Tirafkan (IRAN, 1965–2013)
The Loss of Our Identity #1 (Boy) FROM THE SERIES The Loss of Our Identity, 2007
Chromogenic print
43 × 35 in. (109.2 × 88.9 cm)
Brooklyn Museum, Museum Expedition 1913–1914, Museum Collection Fund, by exchange, 2008.51

PLATE 37 (PAGE 141)
Afsoon (IRAN, B. 1961, ACTIVE UNITED KINGDOM)
Shah and His Three Queens FROM THE SERIES Fairytale Icons, 2009
Chromogenic prints
16⅝ × 23¼ in. (42 × 59 cm) each
Collection of Leila Taghinia-Milani Heller, New York

PLATE 38 (PAGE 142)
Ramin Haerizadeh (IRAN, B. 1975, ACTIVE UNITED ARAB EMIRATES)
He Came, He Left, He Left, He Came, 2010
Mixed media and collage on canvas
78.7 × 118.1 in. (200 × 300 cm)
The Farook Collection, Dubai

PLATE 39 (PAGE 143)
Asad Faulwell (UNITED STATES, B. 1982)
Pillars—Iran (1882–1989), 2009
Acrylic and paper on canvas
48 × 24 in. (122 × 61 cm)
LACMA, gift of Guy and Ann Roberts, New York, courtesy Kravets Wehby Gallery, New York, M.2017.224

PLATE 40 (PAGES 144–45)
Koushna Navabi (IRAN, B. 1962, ACTIVE UNITED KINGDOM)
Mussy Duck, 2016
Sterling silver with various coatings (gold plated, oxidized silver, and powder coated)
25 rings, each: 1½ × 1½ × 1 in. (3 × 3 × 2.5 cm)
LACMA, purchased with funds provided by Homeira Goldstein, M.2017.246.1–.5; courtesy of the artist

PLATE 41 (PAGES 146–47)
Khosrow Hassanzadeh (IRAN, B. 1963)
Remember, 2010
Mixed media on ceramic tile
79 × 189 in. (200 × 480 cm)
The Farjam Foundation, Dubai

PLATE 42 (PAGE 148)
Antoin Sevruguin (IRAN, D. 1933)
Studio Portrait: Three Wrestlers Taking the Pose, late 19th century
Glass negative
7 × 5 in. (17.7 × 12.7 cm)
Freer Gallery of Art and Arthur M. Sackler Gallery Archives, Smithsonian Institution, Washington, D.C., Myron Bement Smith Collection, gift of Katherine Dennis Smith, 1973–1985, FSA A.4 2.12. GN.26.06 (exhibition copy)

PLATE 43 (PAGE 149)
Khosrow Hassanzadeh (IRAN, B. 1963)
Untitled III FROM THE SERIES Remember, 2010
Silkscreen and gold leaf on paper
83 × 48 in. (210 × 122 cm)
The Farjam Foundation, Dubai

PLATE 44 (PAGE 150)
Pahlavan II, Ready to Order, 2008
Mixed-media box
76 × 52 × 10 in. (193 × 132.1 × 25.4 cm)
LACMA, gift of Lynda and Stewart Resnick through the 2017 Collectors Committee, M.2017.68

PLATE 45A (PAGE 152)
Bahman Jalali (IRAN, 1945–2010)
Untitled FROM THE SERIES Image of Imagination, 2003
Chromogenic print
Framed: 27⅝ × 27⅝ in. (70 × 70 cm)
Collection of Azita Bina-Seibel and Elmar W. Seibel, Boston

PLATE 45B (PAGE 152)
Untitled FROM THE SERIES Image of Imagination, 2003–5
Chromogenic print
20¼ × 20 in. (51.4 × 50.8 cm)
LACMA, purchased with funds provided by Karl Loring, M.2009.124.2

PLATE 46 (PAGE 153)
Nicky Nodjoumi (IRAN, B. 1942, ACTIVE UNITED STATES)
Untitled, 2015
Ink on paper
28¾ × 22 in. (73 × 55.9 cm)
LACMA, purchased with funds provided by Homa and Nejat Sarshar, M.2017.244

PLATE 47 (PAGE 154)
Study for Inspector's Scrutiny, 2012
Ink on paper
28½ × 22½ in. (72.4 × 57.2 cm)
Metropolitan Museum of Art, New York, 2011 NoRuz at The Met Benefit, 2014, 2014.153

PLATE 48 (PAGE 156)
Malekeh Nayiny (IRAN, B. 1955, ACTIVE FRANCE)
A Ruin from the Past, 2007
Dye coupler print
47¼ × 31½ in. (120 × 80 cm)
LACMA, purchased with funds provided by Nina Ansary, M.2017.13.1

PLATE 49 (PAGE 157)
All in Pink, 2007
Dye coupler print
47¼ × 35⅜ in. (120 × 89.9 cm)
LACMA, purchased with funds provided by Nina Ansary, M.2017.13.2

PLATE 50 (PAGE 158)
Kourosh Golnari (IRAN, B. 1964)
The Renowned Sovereign, 2017
Brass and feather
11½ × 23⅝ × 56¾ in. (30 × 60 × 144 cm)
LACMA, purchased with funds provided by Dr. Homa Mahmoudi with Dr. Jason and Mrs. Yaas Snibbe, May and Samuel Rudin Family Foundation, Inc., Roshi Rahnama and Kayhan Shakib, and an anonymous donor, M.2017.243a-b

PLATE 51 (PAGE 159)
Shahpour Pouyan (IRAN, B. 1979, ACTIVE UNITED STATES)
Projectile 8, 2012
Iron and brass
72⅞ × 32½ in. (185.1 × 82.6 cm)
Collection of Emily and Teddy Greenspan, Los Angeles

PLATE 52 (PAGE 160)
Antoin Sevruguin (IRAN, D. 1933)
Portrait of Ahmad Shah, c. 1909
Albumen print
7⅞ × 5⅝ in. (20 × 14.2 cm)
The Kimia Foundation, Los Angeles

PLATE 53 (PAGE 161)
Salam Ceremony in front of Ahmad Shah's Portrait, early 20th century
Albumen print
Image: 3½ × 5 in. (8.9 × 12.7 cm)
The Kimia Foundation, Los Angeles

PLATE 54 (PAGE 162)
Antoin Sevruguin (IRAN, D. 1933)
Qajar Rock Relief Depicting Fath Ali Shah near Rayy, late 19th century
Gelatin silver print
9½ × 7 in. (24 × 18 cm)
Freer Gallery of Art and Arthur M. Sackler Gallery Archives, Smithsonian Institution, Washington, D.C., Myron Bement Smith Collection, gift of Katherine Dennis Smith, 1973–1985, FSA A.4 2.12.Sm.41

PLATE 55 (PAGE 163)
Luigi Pesce (ITALY, 1818–1891)
Bas Relief at Nakshi Rustam, 1858
Salted paper print from paper negative
7¾ × 9½ in. (19.6 × 24.2 cm)
Metropolitan Museum of Art, New York, gift of Kay Gregory, 1967, 67.606.15

PLATE 56A (PAGE 164)
Kimon Evan Marengo (EGYPT, 1904–1988)
Ahriman-Goebbels, disguised as Zahhak-Hitler's cook, causes serpents with the faces of Mussolini and Tojo to grow out of his shoulders, 1942
Offset lithograph on paper
13½ × 9 in. (34.3 × 22.9 cm)
LACMA, purchased with funds provided by Shidan Taslimi, M.2016.180.1

PLATE 56B (PAGE 164)
Zahhak-Hitler's dream about the three warriors who will cause his demise—here depicted as Churchill, Stalin, and Roosevelt, 1942
Offset lithograph on paper
13½ × 9 in. (34.3 × 22.9 cm)
LACMA, purchased with funds provided by Shidan Taslimi, M.2016.180.3

Kimon Evan Marengo (CONT.)

PLATE 56C (PAGE 164)
The arrival of the promised warriors, Churchill, Stalin, and Roosevelt, led by the symbol of Iranian national liberation, Kava, 1942
Offset lithograph on paper
13½ × 9 in. (34.3 × 22.9 cm)
LACMA, purchased with funds provided by Shidan Taslimi, M.2016.180.5

PLATE 56D (PAGE 164)
Zahhak-Hitler is nailed to Mt. Damavand by the liberated Iranian people, 1942
Offset lithograph on paper
13½ × 9 in. (34.3 × 22.9 cm)
Yale University Library, New Haven, World War II Collection, MS 668 (exhibition copy)

Abbas (IRAN, B. 1944, ACTIVE FRANCE)

PLATE 57 (PAGE 165)
At the tomb of Cyrus the Great, celebrations of the 2500th anniversary of the monarchy, 1971, printed 2016
Gelatin silver print
12 × 16 in. (30.5 × 40.6 cm)
LACMA, purchased with funds provided by Art of the Middle East: CONTEMPORARY, M.2016.199.4

PLATE 58 (PAGE 165)
The shah with Hoveyda's cabinet, 1977, printed 2016
Gelatin silver print
12 × 16 in. (30.5 × 40.6 cm)
LACMA, purchased with funds provided by Art of the Middle East: CONTEMPORARY, M.2016.199.3

Nicky Nodjoumi (IRAN, B. 1942, ACTIVE UNITED STATES)

PLATE 59 (PAGE 166)
The Trash Can of History, c. 1979
Offset lithograph on paper
18½ × 12½ in. (47 × 31.8 cm)
Courtesy of the artist

PLATE 60 (PAGE 166)
Forward to Establish a People's Revolutionary Court, c. 1979
Offset lithograph on paper
18½ × 12½ in. (47 × 31.8 cm)
Courtesy of the artist

Farshid Mesghali (IRAN, B. 1943)

PLATE 61 (PAGE 167)
Shazdeh Ehtejab, 1974
Offset print on paper
27⅝ × 19¾ in. (70 × 50 cm)
LACMA, purchased with funds provided by Akhtar Ellen Motamedi, M.2017.241

Abbas (IRAN, B. 1944, ACTIVE FRANCE)

PLATE 62 (PAGE 168)
Men burning a portrait of the shah, 1978, printed 2016
Gelatin silver print
12 × 16 in. (30.5 × 40.6 cm)
LACMA, purchased with funds provided by Art of the Middle East: CONTEMPORARY, M.2017.15

Maryam Zandi (IRAN, B. 1947)

PLATE 63 (PAGE 168)
Mural News / Streets of Tehran, 1979, printed 2016
Gelatin silver print
24 × 29¼ in. (61.1 × 74.3 cm)
LACMA, purchased with funds provided by Art of the Middle East: CONTEMPORARY, M.2016.240.1

Maryam Zandi (CONT.)

PLATE 64 (PAGE 169)
Untitled, 1979, printed 2016
Gelatin silver print
24 × 28⅛ in. (61.1 × 71.4 cm)
LACMA, purchased with funds provided by Art of the Middle East: CONTEMPORARY, M.2016.240.2

Abbas (IRAN, B. 1944, ACTIVE FRANCE)

PLATE 65 (PAGE 170)
Woman at a pro-shah demonstration, 1979, printed 2016
Gelatin silver print
12 × 16 in. (30.5 × 40.6 cm)
LACMA, purchased with funds provided by Harvey and Beth Plotnick, with additional funds provided by Art of the Middle East: CONTEMPORARY, M.2016.199.1

PLATE 66 (PAGE 170)
Ayatollah Ruhollah Khomeini's portrait is exhibited by the crowd attending the opening of the Tehran University, 1979, printed 2016
Gelatin silver print
12 × 16 in. (30.5 × 40.6 cm)
LACMA, purchased with funds provided by Art of the Middle East: CONTEMPORARY, M.2016.199.5

Maryam Zandi (IRAN, B. 1947)

PLATE 67 (PAGE 171)
Untitled, 1979, printed 2016
Gelatin silver print
28⅛ × 21⅛ in. (71.4 × 53.7 cm)
LACMA, purchased with funds provided by JoAnn Busuttil, M.2016.240.3

Ahmad Aali (IRAN, B. 1935)

PLATE 68 (PAGE 171)
Tehran, 1979, 1979, printed 2017
Inkjet print
40¼ × 29⅛ in. (102.2 × 74 cm)
LACMA, purchased with funds provided by JoAnn Busuttil, M.2017.247

Kaveh Golestan (IRAN, 1950–2003)

PLATE 69 (PAGE 172)
The Shah Left, 1979, printed 2015
Gelatin silver print
24 × 30 in. (61 × 76.2 cm)
LACMA, gift of the Estate of Kaveh Golestan, M.2016.97

Maryam Zandi (IRAN, B. 1947)

PLATE 70 (PAGE 172)
Happiness of People on the Day the Shah Left Iran, Enghelab and Other Streets, January 16, 1979, printed 2016
Gelatin silver print
21⅜ × 28⅛ in. (54.3 × 71.4 cm)
LACMA, purchased with funds provided by Art of the Middle East: CONTEMPORARY, M.2016.240.5

PLATE 71 (PAGE 173)
Untitled, 1979, printed 2016
Gelatin silver print
28¼ × 21 in. (71.8 × 53.3 cm)
LACMA, purchased with funds provided by Art of the Middle East: CONTEMPORARY, M.2016.240.4

Ardeshir Mohassess (IRAN, 1938–2008)

PLATE 72 (PAGE 174)
Religious Prohibition of the Caviar Fish and an untitled drawing, REPRODUCED IN *A Retrospective*, PUBLISHED BY THE IRAN-AMERICA SOCIETY, TEHRAN, 1972
Exhibition catalogue
10½ × 8¼ in. (26.7 × 21 cm)
Courtesy of Joan ValaNejad, Laguna Niguel, California

Ardeshir Mohassess (CONT.)

PLATE 73A (PAGE 175)
King and I FROM THE SERIES Life in Iran, 1978
Ink on paper
17⅜ × 23¼ in. (44.2 × 59 cm)
Prints & Photographs Division, Library of Congress, Washington, D.C., LC-DIG-ppmsca-17423

PLATE 73B (PAGE 175)
That huge fire which took place suddenly, burned and over turned everything FROM THE SERIES Life in Iran, 1978
Ink on paper
18 × 23¾ in. (45.7 × 60.3 cm)
Prints & Photographs Division, Library of Congress, Washington, D.C., LC-DIG-ppmsca-17433

PLATE 73C (PAGE 176)
The grand father citing an along [sic] *epical poem, the son is citing a love poem and the grand son citing a short poem* FROM THE SERIES Life in Iran, 1978
Ink on paper
17⅞ × 23¾ in. (45.7 × 60.2 cm)
Prints & Photographs Division, Library of Congress, Washington, D.C., LC-DIG-ppmsca-17431

PLATE 73D (PAGE 176)
The body of martyr Imam is also supposed to be arrived [sic] *tonight by the airplane* FROM THE SERIES Life in Iran, 1977
Ink on paper
18 × 23¾ in. (45.7 × 60.4 cm)
Prints & Photographs Division, Library of Congress, Washington, D.C., LC-DIG-ppmsca-17426

PLATE 73E (PAGE 177)
The king is always above the people FROM THE SERIES Life in Iran, 1978
Ink on paper
18 × 23¾ in. (45.7 × 60.2 cm)
Prints & Photographs Division, Library of Congress, Washington, D.C., LC-DIG-ppmsca-17435

PLATE 73F (PAGE 177)
The governmental airplanes got there which [sic] *the prayers were bending in front of God* FROM THE SERIES Life in Iran, 1977
Ink on paper
18 × 23¾ in. (45.7 × 60.4 cm)
Prints & Photographs Division, Library of Congress, Washington, D.C., LC-DIG-ppmsca-17430

Noureddin Zarrinkelk (IRAN, B. 1937, ACTIVE UNITED STATES)

PLATE 74 (PAGE 178)
Amir Hamza the Lover and the Dancing Zebra, 1977
Single-channel video
Duration: 22 minutes, 21 seconds
LACMA, gift of the artist, M.2017.240

Ali Akbar Sadeghi (IRAN, B. 1937)

PLATE 75 (PAGE 179)
Flower Storm, 1972
Single-channel video
Duration: 8 minutes, 19 seconds
Courtesy of the artist and Shirin Gallery, Tehran

Ali Akbar Sadeghi (CONT.)

PLATE 76 (PAGE 180)
The Rook, 1974
Single-channel video
Duration: 9 minutes, 42 seconds
Courtesy of the artist and Shirin Gallery, Tehran

Pouya Afshar (IRAN, B. 1984, ACTIVE UNITED STATES) and **Soroush Rezaee** (IRAN, B. 1983)

PLATE 77 (PAGE 181)
Rostam in Wonderland, 2012–14
Single-channel video
Duration: 33 minutes, 7 seconds
LACMA, gift of the artist, M.2015.68.1

Faramarz Pilaram (IRAN, 1937–1983)

PLATE 78 (PAGE 184)
Imam, c. 1962
Watercolor on paper
78 × 52¼ in. (198.1 × 132.7 cm)
Collection of Houman M. Sarshar, Los Angeles

Charles Hossein Zenderoudi (IRAN, B. 1937, ACTIVE FRANCE)

PLATE 79 (PAGE 185)
The Hand, 1960–61
Paper collage with ink, watercolor, and gold and silver paint
27½ × 18¼ in. (69.9 × 46.4 cm)
Grey Art Gallery, New York University Art Collection, gift of Abby Weed Grey, G1975.38

Mohsen Yazdipour (IRAN, B. 1980)

PLATE 80A (PAGE 186)
Untitled FROM THE SERIES A Play with Feelings, 2008
Chromogenic print
29¼ × 41¼ in. (74.3 × 104.8 cm)
LACMA, purchased with funds provided by Art of the Middle East: CONTEMPORARY, M.2017.55.1

PLATE 80B (PAGE 187)
Untitled FROM THE SERIES A Play with Feelings, 2008
Chromogenic print
29½ × 41¼ in. (74.9 × 104.8 cm)
LACMA, purchased with funds provided by Art of the Middle East: CONTEMPORARY, M.2017.55.2

Rana Javadi (IRAN, B. 1953)

PLATE 81 (PAGE 188)
Never Ending Chaos 7, 2013
Inkjet print on canvas
36¼ × 34⅝ in. (92 × 88 cm)
Collection of Azita Bina-Seibel and Elmar W. Seibel, Boston

PLATE 82 (PAGE 189)
Never Ending Chaos 2, 2013
Inkjet print on canvas
36¼ × 34⅝ in. (92 × 88 cm)
Collection of Azita Bina-Seibel and Elmar W. Seibel, Boston

Painting attributed to Mirza Ali (ACTIVE C. 1525–75)

PLATE 83 (PAGE 190)
Parable of the Ship of Shi'ism FROM THE *Shahnama* of Firdausi, c. 1530–35
Opaque watercolor, ink, and gold and silver on paper
18½ × 12½ in. (47 × 31.8 cm)
Metropolitan Museum of Art, New York, gift of Arthur A. Houghton Jr., 1970 (1970.301.1, fol. 18v)

Khosrow Hassanzadeh (IRAN, B. 1963)

PLATE 84 (PAGE 191)
Untitled, 2001
Silkscreen and acrylic on paper
Framed: 94⅞ × 46⅝ in. (241 × 118.4 cm)
Collection of Lamees Hamdan, Dubai

Newsha Tavakolian (IRAN, B. 1981)

PLATE 85 (PAGE 192)
Mothers of Martyrs FROM THE SERIES Mothers of Martyrs, 2006
Chromogenic print
Image: 27⅝ × 41⅞ in. (70.2 × 106.4 cm)
LACMA, purchased with funds provided by Nina Ansary, M.2017.9

Sadegh Tirafkan (IRAN, 1965–2013)

PLATE 86 (PAGE 194)
Multitude #5 FROM THE SERIES Multitude, 2008
Chromogenic print
29½ × 44 in. (75 × 112 cm)
Courtesy of Tirafkan Cultural Foundation, Tehran (exhibition copy)

Tahmineh Monzavi (IRAN, B. 1988)

PLATE 87 (PAGE 195)
Tina FROM THE SERIES Tina, 2010–12
Pigment print
17¼ × 25 in. (43.8 × 63.5 cm)
LACMA, Purchased with funds provided by Catherine Benkaim and Barbara Timmer, M.2017.245.1

Shoja Azari (IRAN, B. 1958, ACTIVE UNITED STATES)

PLATE 88A (PAGE 196)
Icon #1 FROM THE SERIES Icons, 2010
Video portrait
Courtesy of the artist and Leila Heller Gallery, New York

PLATE 88B (PAGE 197)
Icon #2 FROM THE SERIES Icons, 2010
Video portrait
Courtesy of the artist and Leila Heller Gallery, New York

PLATE 88C (PAGE 197)
Icon #3 FROM THE SERIES Icons, 2010
Video portrait
Courtesy of the artist and Leila Heller Gallery, New York

PLATE 88D (PAGE 198)
Icon #4 FROM THE SERIES Icons, 2010
Video portrait
Courtesy of the artist and Leila Heller Gallery, New York

PLATE 88E (PAGE 199)
Icon #5 FROM THE SERIES Icons, 2010
Video portrait
Courtesy of the artist and Leila Heller Gallery, New York

Kazem Chalipa (IRAN, B. 1957)

PLATE 89 (PAGE 200)
Every Day Is Ashura and Every Land Is Karbala, 1980s
Offset lithograph on paper
13½ × 9⅜ in. (34.3 × 23.8 cm)
Special Collections Research Center, University of Chicago Library

Habibollah Sadeghi (IRAN, B. 1957)

PLATE 90 (PAGE 201)
Every Day Is Ashura and Every Land Is Karbala, early 1980s, printed 2017
Lithograph
27⅝ × 19¾ in. (70 × 50 cm)
LACMA, gift of the artist, M.2017.239.1

Shoja Azari (IRAN, B. 1958, ACTIVE UNITED STATES)

PLATE 91 (PAGES 202–3)
The Day of the Last Judgment (Coffee House Painting), 2009
Video projection
Duration: 5 minutes, 30 seconds
The Museum of Contemporary Art, Los Angeles, gift of Leila Heller, 2012.50

Abdallah Musavar (IRAN, D. 1931)

PLATE 92 (PAGES 204–5)
Battle of Karbala, late 19th–early 20th century
Oil on canvas
66½ × 112 in. (169 × 285 cm)
Collection of Leila Taghinia-Milani Heller, New York

Pouya Afshar (IRAN, B. 1984, ACTIVE UNITED STATES)

PLATES 93A–B (PAGE 206)
Mourn Baby Mourn, 2017
Video installation
Duration: 6 minutes, 37 seconds
Courtesy of the artist

Ali Quli Khu'i (IRAN, ACTIVE 1846–1855)

PLATE 94 (PAGE 207)
Shimr Kills Husain (right-hand page from a double-page composition) FROM THE *Asrar al-shahada*, AH 1268/1851
Lithograph
10½ × 6⅜ in. (26.5 × 16 cm)
Staatsbibliothek zu Berlin, Preussischer Kulturbesitz, Berlin (Zv 2222, fol. 139b)

Selected Bibliography

Abbas. *Iran Diary, 1971–2002.* Paris: Autrement, 2002.

Abrahamian, Ervand. *A History of Modern Iran.* Cambridge: Cambridge University Press, 2008.

Adamova, Ada. "Repetition of Compositions in Manuscripts: The *Khamsa* of Nizami in Leningrad." In *Timurid Art and Culture: Iran and Central Asia in the Fifteenth Century,* vol. 2, edited by Lisa Golombek and Maria Subtelny, 67–75. Leiden: Brill, 1992.

Afshar, Mahasti. "Festival of Arts, Shiraz-Persepolis 1967-1977." Last modified May 2015. https://www.academia.edu/12568899/Festival_of_Arts_Shiraz-Persepolis_1967-1977_updated_May_2015_.

Ahmad Aali Selection of Paintings and Photographs 1953–2014. Tehran: Nazar Art Publication, 2016.

Ahmad Aali Selection of Works 1961–2009. Tehran: Nazar Art Publication, 2009.

Al-i Ahmad, Jalal. *Occidentosis: A Plague from the West.* Translated by R. Campbell. Berkeley: Mizan Press, 1984.

Amanat, Abbas. *Pivot of the Universe: Nasir al-Din Shah Qajar and the Iranian Monarchy, 1831–1896.* Berkeley: University of California Press, 1997.

Amid, Hasan. *Farhang-i Farsi-yi Amid.* Tehran: Rah-i Rushd, 2010.

Amirsadeghi, Hossein, ed. *Different Sames: New Perspectives in Contemporary Iranian Art.* London: TransGlobe Publishing, 2009.

Amuzegar, Jahangir. *The Dynamics of the Iranian Revolution: The Pahlavis' Triumph and Tragedy.* Albany: State University of New York Press, 1991.

Anvar, Iraj. "Peripheral Ta'ziyeh: The Transformation of Ta'ziyeh from Muharram Mourning Ritual to Secular and Comical Theatre." In *Eternal Performance: Ta'ziyeh and Other Shiite Rituals,* edited by Peter Chelkowski, 110–21. London: Seagull Books, 2010.

Ashraf, A., with Layla S. Diba. "Kamal-al-Molk, Mohammad Ghaffari Kashani." In *Encyclopaedia Iranica* 15, 417–33. New York: Encyclopaedia Iranica Foundation, 2010.

Atabaki, Touraj. *Iran and the First World War: Battleground of the Great Powers.* London: I. B. Tauris, 2006.

Bakhtin, Mikhail. *Rabelais and His World.* Bloomington: Indiana University Press, 1941.

Balaghi, Shiva. "Iranian Visual Arts in 'The Century of Machinery, Speed, and the Atom': Rethinking Modernity." In *Picturing Iran: Art, Society and Revolution,* edited by Shiva Balaghi and Lynn Gumpert, 21–38. London: I. B. Tauris, 2002. Exhibition catalogue.

———. "Khosrow Hassanzadeh's Haft Khan." In *Khosrow Hassanzadeh, Haft Khan: The Seven Labors of Rostam,* np. New York: Leila Heller Gallery, 2012. Exhibition catalogue.

———. "Writing with Light: Abbas's Photographs of the Iranian Revolution of 1979." In *Picturing Iran: Art, Society and Revolution,* edited by Shiva Balaghi and Lynn Gumpert, 103–25. London: I. B. Tauris, 2002. Exhibition catalogue.

Balaghi, Shiva, and Lynn Gumpert, eds. *Picturing Iran: Art, Society, and Revolution.* London: I. B. Tauris, 2002. Exhibition catalogue.

Bataille, Georges. *Visions of Excess: Selected Writings, 1927–1939.* Edited by Allan Stoekl. Translated by Allan Stoekl, with Carl R. Lovitt and Donald M. Leslie, Jr. Minneapolis: University of Minneapolis Press, 1985.

Behdad, Ali. "The Power-Ful Art of Qajar Photography: Orientalism and (Self)-Orientalizing in Nineteenth-Century Iran." *Iranian Studies* 34, no. 1/4 (2001): 141–51.

Behnoud, Masoud. "Timsal-i Sohrab." YouTube video, 3:43. May 31, 2017. https://www.youtube.com/watch?v=j18mQe42dXA.

Berman, Marshall. *All That Is Solid Melts into Air: The Experience of Modernity.* New York: Penguin, 1988.

Bharier, Julian. *Economic Development in Iran, 1900–1970.* London: Oxford University Press, 1971.

Bonetti, Maria Francesca, Khadijeh Mohammadi Nameghi, and Alberto Prandi. "The First Hundred Years of Iranian Photography: A Bibliography." *History of Photography* 37, no. 1 (2013): 126–33.

Boozari, Ali. "Hazar u Yakshab-i Sani al-Mulk: Puli bain-i Shargh va Gharb" [Sani al-Mulk's One Thousand and One Nights: A Bridge Between East and West]. *Faslnama-yi Farhangi-yi Mardum* 11–12 (2004): 49–60.

Burton, Richard Francis. *The Book of the Thousand Nights and a Night.* London: Kama Shastra Society, 1885–88.

Campbell, John R., and Alan Rew, eds. *Identity and Affect: Experiences of Identity in a Globalising World.* London: Pluto Press, 1999.

Campbell, Joseph. *The Hero with a Thousand Faces.* New York: Pantheon Books, 1953.

Canby, Sheila R. "Age and Time in the Work of Riza." In *Persian Masters: Five Centuries of Painting,* edited by Sheila R. Canby, 71–84. Bombay: Marg Publications, 1990.

———. *Persian Painting.* London: British Museum Press, 1993.

———. *The Shahnama of Shah Tahmasp: The Persian Book of Kings.* New York: Metropolitan Museum of Art, 2014.

Chehabi Houchang E. "Zur-Ḵāna." In *Encyclopaedia Iranica.* Published August 15, 2006. http://www.iranicaonline.org/articles/zur-kana.

Chehabi, Houchang E., and Fotini Christia. "The Art of State Persuasion: Iran's Post-Revolutionary Murals." *Persica* 22 (2008): 1–13.

Chelkowski, Peter. "Narrative Painting and Painting Recitation in Qajar Iran." *Muqarnas* 6 (1989): 98–111.

———. "Ta'zia." In *Encyclopaedia Iranica.* Published July 15, 2009. http://www.iranicaonline.org/articles/tazia.

———. "Ta'ziyeh: Indigenous Avant-Garde Theatre of Iran." In *Ta'ziyeh: Ritual and Drama in Iran,* edited by Peter Chelkowski, 1–11. New York: New York University Press / Soroush Press, 1979.

———. "Time Out of Memory: Ta'ziyeh, the Total Drama." In *Eternal Performance: Ta'ziyeh and Other Shiite Rituals,* edited by Peter Chelkowski, 1–18. London: Seagull Books, 2010.

———, ed. *Eternal Performance: Ta'ziyeh and Other Shiite Rituals.* London: Seagull Books, 2010.

———, ed. *Ta'ziyeh: Ritual and Drama in Iran.* New York: New York University Press / Soroush Press, 1979.

Chelkowski, Peter, and Hamid Dabashi. *Staging a Revolution: The Art of Persuasion in the Islamic Republic of Iran.* London: Booth-Clibborn Editions, 2000.

Chiu, Melissa, and Melissa Ho, eds. *Shirin Neshat: Facing History.* Washington, D.C.: Smithsonian Books, 2015. Exhibition catalogue.

Clark, John. *Modern Asian Art.* North Ryde, NSW: Craftsman House in association with G+B Arts International, 1998.

Curzon, George Nathaniel. *Persia and the Persian Question.* Vol. 1. London: Longmans, Green & Company, 1892.

Dabashi, Hamid. "Ardeshir Mohassess, Etcetera." In *Ardeshir Mohassess: Art and Satire in Iran,* edited by Shirin Neshat and Nicky Nodjoumi, 17–29. New York: Asia Society, 2008. Exhibition catalogue.

Dadi, Iftikhar. "Rethinking Calligraphic Modernism." In *Discrepant Abstraction,* edited by Kobena Mercer, 94–115. London: Institute of International Visual Arts; Cambridge, MA: MIT Press, 2006.

Daftari, Fereshteh. "Another Modernism: An Iranian Perspective." In *Picturing Iran: Art, Society and Revolution,* edited by Shiva Balaghi and Lynn Gumpert, 39–88. London: I. B. Tauris, 2002. Exhibition catalogue.

Daftari, Fereshteh, and Layla S. Diba, eds. *Iran Modern.* New York: Asia Society, 2013. Exhibition catalogue.

David, Catherine, Bahman Jalali, and Hamid Dabashi, eds. *Bahman Jalali.* Barcelona: Fundació Antoni Tàpies, 2007. Exhibition catalogue.

Davidson, Olga M. *Poet and Hero in the Persian Book of Kings.* Costa Mesa, CA: Mazda Publishers, 2006.

Davis, Dick. "Rustam-i Dastan." *Iranian Studies* 32, no. 2 (Spring 1999): 231–41.

Diba, Layla S. "The Formation of Modern Iranian Art: From Kamal-al-Molk to Zenderoudi." In *Iran Modern,* edited by Fereshteh Daftari and Layla S. Diba, 45–65. New York: Asia Society, 2013. Exhibition catalogue.

———. "Qajar Photography and Its Relationship to Iranian Art: A Reassessment." *History of Photography* 37, no. 1 (2013): 85–98.

Diba, Layla S., ed., with Maryam Ekhtiar, *Royal Persian Paintings: The Qajar Epoch, 1785–1925.* Brooklyn: Brooklyn Museum of Art; London: I. B. Tauris, 1998. Exhibition catalogue.

Dickson, Martin B., and Stuart Cary Welch, eds., *The Houghton Shahnameh.* Vol. 2. Cambridge, MA: Harvard University Press, 1981.

Eigner, Saeb. *Art of the Middle East: Modern and Contemporary Art of the Arab World and Iran.* London: Merrell, 2010.

Eisenstadt, Shmuel Noah. "Multiple Modernities." *Daedalus* 129 (2000): 1–29.

Ekhtiar, Maryam. "Nasir al-Din Shah and the Dar al-Funun: The Evolution of an Institution." *Iranian Studies* 34, no. 1/4 (2001): 153–63.

Ekhtiar, Maryam, Sheila R. Canby, Navina Najat Haidar, and Priscilla P. Soucek, eds. *Masterpieces from the Department of Islamic Art in The Metropolitan Museum of Art*. New York: Metropolitan Museum of Art, 2011.
Emami, Karim. "Art in Iran XI Post-Qajar." In *Encyclopaedia Iranica* 2, fasc. 6, 640–46. London: Routledge & Kegan Paul, 1986.
——. "Negahi dobreh beh maktab-e Saqqa-Khaneh." In *Saqqakhaneh*, edited by Karim Emami and Peter Lamborn Wilson, n.p. Tehran: Tehran Museum of Contemporary Art, 1977. Exhibition catalogue.
——. "Saqqakhaneh School Revisited." In *Iran Modern*, edited by Fereshteh Daftari and Layla S. Diba, 230–31. New York: Asia Society, 2013. Exhibition catalogue.
Enderlein, Volkmar, and Werner Sundermann. *Schāhnāme: Das persische Königsbuch, Miniaturen und Texte der Berliner Handschrift von 1605*. Leipzig, Germany: Kiepenheuer, 1988.
Fallaci, Oriana. "An Interview with Khomeini." *New York Times*, October 7, 1979.
Faqihi, Ali Asghar. *Shahanshah-yi Azud-al-Daula*. Tehran: Matbuati-yi Isma'iliya, 1968.
Farhad, Massumeh. "Reading Between the Lines: Word and Image in Sixteenth-Century Iran." In *By the Pen and What They Write: Writing in Islamic Art and Culture*, edited by Sheila Blair and Jonathan Bloom, 108–203. New Haven: Yale University Press, 2017.
Filizadeh, Siamak. *Underground*. Tehran: Nazar Art Publication, 2016.
Fischer, Michael M. J., and Mehdi Abedi. *Debating Muslims: Cultural Dialogues in Postmodernity and Tradition*. Madison: University of Wisconsin Press, 1990.
Fischman, Lisa, and Shiva Balaghi. *Parviz Tanavoli*. Wellesley, MA: Davis Museum, 2015. Exhibition catalogue.
Floor, Willem. "Ḳālkubi." In *Encyclopaedia Iranica*. Last modified October 7, 2011. http://www.iranicaonline.org/articles/kalkubi.
Fortenberry, Diane, ed. *Honar: The Afkhami Collection of Modern and Contemporary Iranian Art*. London: Phaidon Press, 2017.
Fourie, Elsje. "A Future for the Theory of Multiple Modernities: Insights from the New Modernization Theory." *Social Science Information* 51, no. 1 (2012): 52–69.
Gellner, Ernest. "Foreword." In *From Nationalism to Revolutionary Islam*, edited by Saïd Amir Arjomand, vii–xi. Albany: State University of New York Press, 1984.
Golshiri, Houshang. *The Prince*. Translated by James Buchan. London: Harvill Secker, 2006.
González, Carmen Pérez. *Local Portraiture: Through the Lens of the 19th-Century Iranian Photographers*. Leiden: Leiden University Press, 2012.
Grabar, Oleg. "Why Was the Shahnama Illustrated?" *Iranian Studies* 43, no. 1 (2010): 91–96.
Grigor, Talinn. *Contemporary Iranian Art: From the Street to the Studio*. London: Reaktion Books, 2014.
Grube, Ernst J., and Eleanor Sims. "The Representations of Shāh 'Abbās I." In *L'arco di fango che rubò la luce alle stelle: Studi in onore di Eugenio Galdieri per il suo settantesimo compleanno*, edited by Michele Bernardini et al., 177–208. Lugano: Edizioni Arte e Moneta, 1995.
Gruber, Christiane. "Between Logos (*Kalima*) and Light (*Nūr*): Representations of the Prophet Muhammad in Islamic Painting." *Muqarnas* 26 (2009): 229–62.
——. "Media/ting Conflict: Iranian Posters of the Iran-Iraq War (1980–88)." In *Crossing Cultures: Conflict, Migration, Convergence, Proceedings of the 32nd Congress of the International Committee of the History of Art*, edited by Jaynie Anderson, 684–89. Melbourne: University of Melbourne, 2009.
——. "The Message Is on the Wall: Mural Arts in Post-Revolutionary Iran." *Persica* 22 (2008): 15–46.
Halasa, Malu, and Hengameh Golestan, eds. *Kaveh Golestan: Recording the Truth in Iran*. Ostfildern, Germany: Hatje Cantz Verlag, 2007.
Hasan, Saeed. *The Early History of the Buwaihids*. Allahabad, India: Senate House, 1948.
Headrick, Daniel R. *The Tools of Empire: Technology and European Imperialism in the Nineteenth Century*. Oxford: Oxford University Press, 1981.
Hillenbrand, Robert. "The Iconography of the Shah-nama-yi Shahi." In *Safavid Persia: The History and Politics of an Islamic Society*, edited by Charles Melville, 53–78. London: I. B. Tauris, 1996.
Hobsbawm, Eric, and Terence Ranger, eds. *The Invention of Tradition*. Cambridge: Cambridge University Press, 1992.
Hoseini, Mehdi, and Natasha Moharramzadeh. "Barrasi-yi Nagara: Vaghti kah Khalifa ba Ja'far Suhbat Midarad, az Majmu'a-yi Hazar u Yakshab Mussavar-i Sani al-Mulk" [A Study of the Illustration of the Conversation of the Caliph with Ja'far: From the Collection of One Thousand and One Night by Sani al-Mulk]. *Majala Nagarina Hunar-i Islami* 2 (2014): 25–38.
Issa, Rose, ed. *Shadi Ghadirian: Iranian Photographer*. London: Saqi, 2008. Exhibition catalogue.
I'timad al-Saltana, Muhammad Hasan Khan. *Al-Ma'athir wa'l-Athar*. Edited by Iraj Afshar. 3 vols. Tehran: Intisharat-i Asatir, 1984.
Ja'fariyan, Rasul. *Ṣafaviyya dar Arsah-yi Din, Farhang va Siyasat*. Qum, Iran: Pazhuhishkada-yi Hauzah va Danishgah, 2000.
———. *Siyasat va Farhang-i Ruzgar-i Ṣafavi*. Tehran: Nashr-i Ilm, 2009.
Kasravi, Ahmad. *Tarikh-i Mashrutah-i Iran*. Tehran: Negah Publications, 2003. First published 1968 by Amir Kabir.
Katiraie, Mahmoud. *Az Khisht ta Khisht*. Tehran: Intisharat-i Mu'asisi-yi Mutali'ati Ijtima'i, 1969.
Kaya, Ibrahim. *Social Theory and Later Modernities: The Turkish Experience*. Liverpool: Liverpool University Press, 2004.
Keddie, Nikki R. *Qajar Iran and the Rise of Reza Khan, 1796–1925*. Costa Mesa, CA: Mazda Publishers, 1999.
Keshmirshekan, Hamid. *Contemporary Iranian Art: New Perspectives*. London: Saqi, 2013.
——. "Contemporary or Specific: The Dichotomous Desires in Art of Early Twenty-First Century Iran." *Middle East Journal of Culture and Communication* 4, no. 1 (2011): 44–71.
——. "Discourses on Postrevolutionary Iranian Art: Neotraditionalism during the 1990s." *Muqarnas* 23, no. 1 (2006): 131–57.
——. "Neo-Calligraphism and Its Different Varieties in Modern and Contemporary Iranian Art." In *Metalwork and Material Culture in the Islamic World: Art, Craft and Text*, edited by Mariam Rosser-Owen and Venetia Porter, 441–60. London: I. B. Tauris, 2012.
——. "Neo-Traditionalism and Modern Iranian Painting: The *Saqqa-khaneh* School in the 1960s." *Iranian Studies* 38, no. 4 (December 2005): 607–30.
——. "The Question of Identity vis-à-vis Exoticism in Contemporary Iranian Art." *Iranian Studies* 43, no. 4 (2010): 489–512.
——. "Saqqā-kāna School of Art." In *Encyclopaedia Iranica*. August 15, 2009. http://www.iranicaonline.org/articles/saqqa-kana-ii-school-of-art.
Khafipour, Hani. "Beyond Charismatic Authority: The Crafting of a Sovereign's Image in the Public Sphere." In *The World of the Safavids*, edited by Rudi Matthee. London: Routledge (forthcoming).
——. "The Safavid Claim to Sovereignty According to a Court Bureaucrat." In *Empires of the Near East and India: Source Studies of the Safavid, Ottoman, and Mughal Literate Communities*, edited by Hani Khafipour. New York: Columbia University Press (forthcoming).
Khomeini, Ruhollah. *Islam and Revolution: Writings and Declarations of Imam Khomeini (1941–1980)*. Edited and translated by Hamid Algar. Berkeley: Mizan Press, 1981.
Knoppers, Kim. "Kaveh Golestan: The Citadel: A Conversation between Guest Curator Vali Mahlouji and Foam Curator Kim Knoppers." Amsterdam: Foam Fotografiemuseum, 2014. Exhibition brochure.
Komaroff, Linda. "The Return Engagement of Rostam." In *Ferdowsi, the Mongols and the History of Iran: Art, Literature and Culture from Early Islam to Qajar Persia*, edited by Robert Hillenbrand, A. C. S. Peacock, and Firuza Abdullaeva, 381–90. London: I. B. Tauris, 2013.
Mahlouji, Vali. "Recréer Shahr-e No: La politique intime du marginal." *Unedited History: Séquences du moderne en Iran des années 1960 à nos jours*. Paris: Musée d'Art Moderne de la Ville de Paris, 2014.
Marzolph, Ulrich. "The Last Qajar *Shahnama*: The *Shahnama-yi Bahaduri* (1319–26/1901–8)." *Pembroke Papers* 5 (2006): 259–76.
——. *Narrative Illustration in Persian Lithographed Books*. Leiden: Brill, 2001.
——. "The Persian *Nights*: Links between the *Arabian Nights* and Iranian Culture." *Fabula* 45, no. 3/4 (2004): 275–93.
Mazzaoui, Michel M. "Shiism and the Rise of the Safavids." PhD diss., Princeton University, 1965.
Meftahi, Ida. "Sacred or Dissident: Islam, Embodiment, and Subjectivity on Post-Revolutionary Iranian Theatrical Stage." In *Islam and Popular Culture*, edited by Karin van Nieuwkerk, Mark LeVine, and Martin Stokes, 258–77. Austin: University of Texas Press, 2016.
Mirbakhtyar, Shahla. *Iranian Cinema and the Islamic Revolution*. Jefferson, NC: McFarland, 2006.

Mirsepassi, Ali. *Intellectual Discourse and the Politics of Modernization: Negotiating Modernity in Iran.* Cambridge: Cambridge University Press, 2000.
Mofid, Bijan. *Shahr-i Qissah.* Tehran: Intisharat-i Sazman-i Jashn-i Hunar Takht-i Jamshid, 1968.
Mohassess, Ardeshir. *Life in Iran: The Library of Congress Drawings.* Washington, D.C.: Mage, 1994. Exhibition catalogue.
——. *Puppets: 101 Drawings and Collages.* San Francisco: C. Bean Associates, 1977.
——. *A Retrospective.* Tehran: Iran America Society, 1972. Exhibition catalogue.
Mottahedeh, Roy. *Loyalty and Leadership in an Early Islamic Society.* London: I. B. Tauris, 1980.
Murray, Williamson, and Kevin Woods. *The Iran-Iraq War: A Military and Strategic History.* Cambridge: Cambridge University Press, 2014.
Musée d'Art Moderne de la Ville de Paris. *Unedited History: Séquences du moderne en Iran des années 1960 à nos jours.* Paris: Musée d'Art Moderne de la Ville de Paris, 2014. Exhibition catalogue.
Naficy, Hamid. *A Social History of Iranian Cinema.* Vol. 2. Durham, NC: Duke University Press, 2011.
Najmabadi, Afsaneh. *Women with Mustaches and Men without Beards: Gender and Sexual Anxieties of Iranian Modernity.* Berkeley: University of California Press, 2005.
Nasir al-Din Shah. *Ruznama-yi Khatirat-i Nasir al-Din Shah dar Safar-i Duvvum-i Farangistan (1295)* [The Diary of Nasir al-Din Shah in His Second Trip Abroad (1878)]. Tehran: Intisharat-i Sazman-i Asnad-i Milli-yi Iran, 2000.
Neshat, Shirin, and Nicky Nodjoumi, eds. *Ardeshir Mohassess: Art and Satire in Iran.* New York: Asia Society, 2008. Exhibition catalogue.
Pak-Shiraz, Nacim. *Shi'i Islam in Iranian Cinema: Religion and Spirituality in Film.* London: I. B. Taurus, 2011.
Pettys, Rebecca Ansary. "The Ta'ziyeh of the Martyrdom of Hussein." In *Eternal Performance: Ta'ziyeh and Other Shiite Rituals,* edited by Peter Chelkowski, 19–41. London: Seagull Books, 2010.
Porter, Venetia. *Word into Art: Artists of the Modern Middle East.* London: British Museum Press, 2006. Exhibition catalogue.
Raby, Julian. *Qajar Portraits.* London: Azimuth Editions in association with the Iran Heritage Foundation, 1999. Exhibition catalogue.
Rahimi, Babak. "Takkiyeh Dowlat: The Qajar Theater State." In *Performing the Iranian State: Visual Culture and Representations of Iranian Identity,* edited by Staci Gem Scheiwiller, 55–71. London: Anthem Press, 2014.
Rahnema, Ali. *An Islamic Utopian: A Political Biography of Ali Shari'ati.* London: I. B. Tauris, 1998.
Rajabi, Mohammed Ali, ed. *Iranian Masterpieces of Persian Painting.* Tehran: Museum of Contemporary Art, 2005. Exhibition catalogue.
Rajaee, Farhang, ed. *Iranian Perspectives on the Iran-Iraq War.* Gainesville: University Press of Florida, 1997.
Ram, Haggai. "Multiple Iconographies: Political Posters in the Iranian Revolution." In *Picturing Iran: Art, Society and Revolution,* edited by Shiva Balaghi and Lynn Gumpert, 89–102. London: I. B. Tauris, 2002.
Razoux, Pierre, and Nicholas Elliott. *The Iran-Iraq War.* Cambridge, MA: Belknap Press of Harvard University Press, 2015.
Ridgeon, Lloyd. "The Zūrkhāna Between Tradition and Change." *Iran* 45 (2007): 243–65.
Ringer, Monica M. *Education, Religion, and the Discourse of Cultural Reform in Qajar Iran.* Costa Mesa, CA: Mazda Publishers, 2001.
——. Review of *Intellectual Discourse and the Politics of Modernization: Negotiating Modernity in Iran,* by Ali Mirsepassi. *Iranian Studies* 40, no. 4 (2007): 555–57.
Rizvi, Kishwar. "The Suggestive Portrait of Shah 'Abbas: Prayer and Likeness in a Safavid *Shahnama.*" *Art Bulletin* 94, no. 2 (June 2012): 226–50.
Robinson, B. W. "Abu'l-Hasan Khan Gaffari." In *Encyclopaedia Iranica* 1, fasc. 3, 306–8. London: Routledge & Kegan Paul, 1985.
——. "Shah Isma'il II's Copy of the Shah-Nama," *Iran* 14 (1976): 1–8.
——. "Shah Isma'il II's Copy of the Shah-Nama: Additional Material," *Iran* 43 (2005): 291–99.
Rochard, Philippe. "The Identities of the Iranian Zūrkhānah." *Iranian Studies* 35, no. 4 (Autumn 2002): 313–40.
Roxburgh, David J. *The Persian Album, 1400–1600: From Dispersal to Collection.* New Haven: Yale University Press, 2005.
——. "Troubles with Perspective: Case Studies in Picture-Making from Qajar Iran." In *Art History in the Wake of the Global Turn,* edited by Jill H. Casid and Aruna D'Souza, 107–25. New Haven: Yale University Press, 2014.
Sadeghi, Fatemeh. "Negotiating with Modernity: Young Women and Sexuality in Iran." *Comparative Studies of South Asia, Africa, and the Middle East* 28, no. 2 (2008): 250–59.
Scarce, Jennifer. "Ancestral Themes in the Art of Qajar Iran." In *Islamic Art in the 19th Century: Tradition, Innovation, and Eclecticism,* edited by Doris Behrens-Abouseif and Stephen Vernoit, 231–56. Leiden: Brill, 2015.
Semsar, Mohammad Hassan, and Fatemeh Sarian, comps. *Kakh-i Golestan (Album Khana) Fihrist-i aksha-yi barguzida-yi asr-i Qajar* [Golestan Palace (Photo Archive) Catalogue of Selected Qajar Photographs]. Tehran: Kitabkhana-yi Saltanati, 2003.
Shani, Raya Y. "Illustrations of the Parable of the Ship of Faith in Firdausi's Prologue to the *Shahnama.*" In *Shahnama Studies I,* edited by Charles Melville, 1–39. Cambridge: University of Cambridge, 2006.
Shariati, Ali. *Jahatgiri-yi Tabaqati dar Islam.* Tehran: Intisharat-i Qalam, 2001.
Sheikh, Reza, and Carmen Pérez González. "Editorial." *History of Photography* 37, no. 1 (2013): 1–6.
Shirin Neshat: The Book of Kings. Paris: Galerie Jerome de Noirmont, 2012. Exhibition catalogue.
Sifatgul, Mansur. *Sakhtar-i Nahad va Andishah-yi Dini dar Iran-i Asr-i Safavi.* Tehran: Mu'assasah-yi Khadamat-i Farhangi-yi Rasa, 2002.
Soroudi, Sorour. "Akhavan's 'The Ending of Shahnameh': A Critique." *Iranian Studies* 2, no. 2/3 (1969): 80–96.
Soudavar, Abolala. "The Saga of Abu-Sa'id Bahador Khan. The Abu-Sa'idname." In *The Court of the Il-Khans 1290–1340,* vol. 12, edited by Julian Raby and Teresa Fitzherbert, 95–218. Oxford: Oxford University Press, 1996.
Steffen, James. *The Cinema of Sergei Parajanov.* Madison: University of Wisconsin, 2013.
Suleman, Fahmida. "Ali as the Lion of God." In *The Art and Material Culture of Iranian Shi'ism: Iconography and Religious Devotion in Shi'i Islam,* edited by Pedram Khosronejad, 215–32. London: I. B. Tauris, 2012.
Taheri, Farzaneh, and Abdolali Azimi, eds. *Hamrah ba Shazdeh Ehtejab* [Along with Shazdeh Ehtejab]. Tehran: Nashr-i Digar, 2001.
Taj al-Saltana. *Crowning Anguish, Memoirs of a Persian Princess from the Harem to Modernity 1884–1914.* Edited with introduction and notes by Abbas Amanat. Washington, D.C.: Mage, 1993.
Tajbakhsh, Ahmad. *Tarikh-i Safaviyyah.* Shiraz: Intisharat-i Nuvid, 1994.
Tanavoli, Parviz, and John T. Wertime. *Locks from Iran: Pre-Islamic to Twentieth Century.* Washington, D.C.: Smithsonian Institution, 1976. Exhibition catalogue.
Thompson, Jon, and Sheila R. Canby, eds. *Hunt for Paradise: Court Arts of Safavid Iran, 1501–1576.* Milan: Skira, 2003.
Vahdat, Farzin. *God and Juggernaut: Iran's Intellectual Encounter with Modernity.* Syracuse: Syracuse University Press, 2002.
Wagner, Peter. "Modernity—One or Many?" In *The Blackwell Companion to Sociology,* edited by Judith R. Blau, 30–42. Oxford: Blackwell, 2000.
Wallace, Mike. "The Shah of Iran." *60 Minutes,* CBS, October 24, 1976.
Wilson, Peter Lamborn. "The Saqqa-Khaneh." In *Iran Modern,* edited by Fereshteh Daftari and Layla S. Diba, 231–33. New York: Asia Society, 2013. Exhibition catalogue.
Zand and Qajar Paintings from Private Collections. Tehran: Iran America Society, 1974. Exhibition catalogue.
Zandi, Maryam. *The Revolution of Iran '79: Photographs.* Tehran: Nazar Art Publication, 2014.
Zoka, Yahya. *Life and Works of Sani' ol-Molk, 1814–1866.* Edited by Cyrus Parham. Tehran: Iran University Press, 2003.
——. *Tarikh-i akkasi va akkasan-i pishgam dar Iran* [The History of Photography and Pioneer Photographers in Iran]. Tehran: Shirkat-i Intisharat-i Ilmi va Farhani, 1997.

Lenders to the Exhibition

England

Koushna Navabi, LONDON

Germany

Staatsbibliothek zu Berlin, Preußischer Kulturbesitz, BERLIN

Iran

Ali Akbar Sadeghi and Shirin Gallery, TEHRAN
Parviz Tanavoli, TEHRAN
Tirafkan Cultural Foundation, TEHRAN

Switzerland

Mohammed Afkhami Foundation, SWITZERLAND

United Arab Emirates

Lamees Hamdan, DUBAI
The Farjam Foundation, DUBAI
The Farook Collection, DUBAI

United States of America

Pouya Afshar, CAMBRIDGE, MASSACHUSETTS
Babak Beheshti, LOS ANGELES
Brooklyn Museum, NEW YORK
Freer Gallery of Art and Arthur M. Sackler Gallery, Smithsonian Institution, WASHINGTON, D.C.
Shirin Neshat and Gladstone Gallery, NEW YORK AND BRUSSELS
Emily and Teddy Greenspan, LOS ANGELES
Grey Art Gallery, New York University
The Kimia Foundation, LOS ANGELES
Shoja Azari and Leila Heller Gallery, NEW YORK
Library of Congress, WASHINGTON, D.C.
Los Angeles County Museum of Art
Metropolitan Museum of Art, NEW YORK
Bahman and Yasmin Mossavar-Rahmani, RIVERSIDE, CONNECTICUT
The Museum of Contemporary Art, LOS ANGELES
Massoud Nader, NEW YORK
Shulamit Nazarian, LOS ANGELES
Nicky Nodjoumi, NEW YORK
Houman M. Sarshar, LOS ANGELES
Dr. Sep Sarshar, LOS ANGELES
Azita Bina-Seibel and Elmar W. Seibel, BOSTON
Leila Taghinia-Milani Heller, NEW YORK
University of Chicago Library
Joan ValaNejad, LAGUNA NIGUEL, CALIFORNIA
Yale University Library, NEW HAVEN, CONNECTICUT
Anonymous lender, NORTH BEND, OREGON

Photography Credits

Unless otherwise noted below, all images are photo © Museum Associates/LACMA.

Front cover, pp. 65 (detail), 92–102: © Siamak Filizadeh; back cover, 133 (detail): © Estate of Reza Mafi; pp. 4, 5: © Koushna Navabi; pp. 8, 28, 206 (top and bottom): © Pouya Afshar; p. 11: photo by Kaveh Kazemi/Getty Images; p. 15: photo courtesy Golestan Palace Library and Archive, Tehran, Iran; p. 16: photo courtesy The Khalili Collection; pp. 29, 39, 40, 44, 106 (right), 109, 207: photos courtesy Staatsbibliothek zu Berlin; pp. 34 (details), 36–38 (details), 108, 190: digital images © The Metropolitan Museum of Art. Image Source: Art Resource, NY; p. 43: © Mirzabaygi; p. 46, 128, 129, 172 (top): © Estate of Kaveh Golestan; p. 53: © Charles Hossen Zenderoudi, digital image © The Museum of Modern Art/SCALA/Art Resource, NY; p. 54: © Parviz Tanavoli, photo courtesy Walker Art Center; p. 57: © Mohammad Memarzadeh, photo courtesy Tehran Museum Contemporary; p. 58: © Iman Safaei; p. 61 (top and bottom): © Mehran Mafi Bordbar, photos courtesy the artist; pp. 72, 112 (left and right), 113, 148, 162: photos courtesy Freer Gallery of Art and Arthur M. Sackler Gallery, Smithsonian Institute, Washington, D.C.; pp. 87 (detail), 174: © Estate of Ardeshir Mohassess; pp. 90 (detail), 126, 202–203: © Shoja Azari; pp. 103, 104: © Fereydoun Ave; pp. 106 (left), 136, 163: photos courtesy The Metropolitan Museum of Art; p. 110: © Fataneh Dadkhah; pp. 114, 124, 125: © Parviz Tanavoli; pp. 116 (left and right), 117: photos courtesy Institute for the Study of the Ancient World, New York University; pp. 118–19: © Estate of Hosein Ghollar Aghasi; pp. 120 (left and right), 123 (right): © Shirin Neshat, photos courtesy the artist and Gladstone Gallery, New York and Brussels; p. 122: © Estate of Ardeshir Mohassess, photo courtesy of Asia Society; pp. 123 (left), 165 (top and bottom), 168 (top), 170 (top and bottom): © Abbas; p. 130: © Taravat Talapasand, photo courtesy of the artist; pp. 131, 179, 180: © Ali Akbar Sadeghi; p. 132: © Siah Armajani, photo courtesy Parasol unit foundation for contemporary art; pp. 134–35: © Yasmin Sinai; pp. 138–39: all © Shadi Ghadirian; p. 140: © Sadegh Tirafkan, photo courtesy Brooklyn Museum; p. 141: © Afsoon, photo courtesy Leila Heller Gallery; pp. 142, 208 (detail): © Ramin Haerizadeh, courtesy Gallery Isabelle van den Eynde; p. 143: © Asad Faulwell; pp. 144–45: © Koushna Navabi; pp. 146–47, 149, 150: © Khosrow Hassanzadeh, photos courtesy Leila Heller Gallery; p. 152 (top and bottom): © Estate of Bahman Jalali; p. 153: © Nicky Nodjoumi; p. 154, 166 (left and right): © Nicky Nodjoumi, photos courtesy of the artist and Taymour Grahne Gallery; pp. 156, 157: © Malekeh Nayiny; p. 158: © Kourosh Golnari; p. 159: © Shahpour Pouyan; pp. 160, 161: photos courtesy the Kimia Collection; p. 164: © Estate of Kimon Evan Marengo, (bottom right) courtesy Yale University Library; p. 167: Farshid Mesghali; pp. 168 (bottom), 169, 171 (right), 172, 173: © Maryam Zandi; p. 171 (left): © Ahmad Aali; pp. 174–177: © Estate of Ardeshir Mohassess, photos courtesy Library of Congress; p. 178: © Estate of Noureddin Zarrinkelk; p. 181: © Pouya Afshar and Souroush Rezaee; pp. 182 (detail), 191: © Khosrow Hassanzadeh; p. 184: © Faramarz Pilaram, photo courtesy of the artist; p. 185: © Charles Hossen Zenderoudi, photo courtesy Grey Art Gallery, New York University Art Collection; pp. 186, 187: © Mohsen Yazidipour; pp. 188, 189: © Rana Javadi, photos courtesy the artist; p. 192: © Newsha Tavakolian, photo courtesy Thomas Erben Gallery; p. 194: © Sadegh Tirafkan, photo courtesy Brooklyn Museum; p. 195: © Tamineh Monzavi, photo courtesy the artist; pp. 196–99: all © Shoja Azari, courtesy of Leila Heller Gallery; p. 200: © Kazeem Chalipa, photo courtesy University of Chicago Library, Special Collections Research Center; p. 201: © Habibollah Sadeghi.

FRONT COVER Siamak Filizadeh, *Anis al-Daula* from the series Underground, 2014 (PLATE 1B)

PAGES 4–5 Koushna Navabi, *Mussy Duck*, detail, 2016 (PLATE 40)

PAGE 8 Pouya Afshar, *Mourn Baby Mourn*, 2017 (PLATES 93A–B)

PAGE 65 Siamak Filizadeh, *Shah and the British Ambassador* from the series Underground, 2014 (SEE PLATE 1C)

PAGE 88 Maryam Zandi, *Untitled*, 1979 (PLATE 71)

PAGE 90 Shoja Azari, *Idyllic Life*, detail, 2012 (PLATE 27)

PAGE 182 Khosrow Hassanzadeh, *Untitled*, detail, 2001 (PLATE 84)

PAGE 208 Ramin Haerizadeh, *He Came, He Left, He Left, He Came*, detail, 2010 (PLATE 38)

BACK COVER Reza Mafi, *Siyah mashq*, detail, 1971 (PLATE 32)

OPPOSITE Ardeshir Mohassess, *Religious Prohibition of the Caviar Fish*, detail, 1972 (PLATE 72)

Published in conjunction with the exhibition
In the Fields of Empty Days: The Intersection of Past and Present in Iranian Art
at the Los Angeles County Museum of Art,
May 6–September 9, 2018.

This exhibition was organized
by the Los Angeles County Museum of Art.

Major support for the catalogue comes from Houman M. Sarshar and Sylvester Angel Cetina, with additional support provided by Romanov Investments Inc. The project is also supported in part by an award from the National Endowment for the Arts.

Copublished in 2018 by

Los Angeles County Museum of Art
5905 Wilshire Boulevard, Los Angeles, CA 90036
www.lacma.org

and
DelMonico Books • Prestel
DelMonico Books is an imprint of Prestel,
a member of Verlagsgruppe Random House GmbH

Prestel Verlag
Neumarkter Strasse 28, 81673 Munich

Prestel Publishing Ltd.
14–17 Wells Street, London W1T 3PD

Prestel Publishing
900 Broadway, Suite 603, New York, NY 10003
www.prestel.com

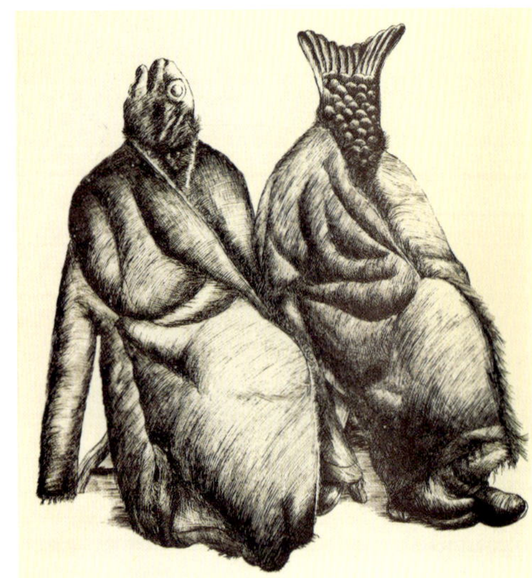

In the Fields of Empty Days

PUBLISHER
Lisa Gabrielle Mark

EDITORS
Erica Wrightson, with Claire Crighton

DESIGNER
Lorraine Wild and Xiaoqing Wang
for Green Dragon Office

TYPESETTING (PERSIAN)
Faye Vahdani

RIGHTS & REPRODUCTIONS
Christina Zeek

PHOTOGRAPHY
Peter Brenner, Steve Oliver, and Jonathan Urban

RESEARCH/FACT-CHECKING SUPPORT
Laura Horan and Terri Morris

PRODUCTION DIRECTOR
Karen Farquhar for DelMonico Books • Prestel

COLOR SEPARATIONS
Echelon Color, Santa Monica, California

Printed and bound in China

TYPEFACES
Greta Text Pro, Greta Arabic, and Cronos Pro

ISBN: 978-3-7913-5738-6

Library of Congress Cataloging-in-Publication Data

Names: Komaroff, Linda, 1953- | Los Angeles County Museum of Art, organizer, host institution.
Title: In the fields of empty days : the intersection of past and present in Iranian art / Linda Komaroff ; with addition contributions by Sheila R. Canby, Sheida Dayani, Hamid Keshmirshekan, Hani Khafipour, Vali Mahlouji, Shabnam Rahimi-Golkhandan, Shadi Shafiei, and Sandra Williams.
Description: Los Angeles : Los Angeles County Museum of Art ; Munich ; New York : DelMonico Books/Prestel, 2018. | Includes bibliographical references.
Identifiers: LCCN 2017048257 | ISBN 9783791357386 (hardback)
Subjects: LCSH: Art and history--Iran--History--20th century--Exhibitions. | Art and history--Iran--History--21st century--Exhibitions. | Art, Iranian--20th century--Exhibitions. | Art, Iranian--21st century--Exhibitions. | BISAC: ART / Middle Eastern. | ART / Collections, Catalogs, Exhibitions / Group Shows. | ART / History / Contemporary (1945-).
Classification: LCC N72.H58 I5 2018 | DDC 700.959/0904--dc23 LC record available at https://lccn.loc.gov/2017048257

A CIP catalogue record for this book is available from the British Library.

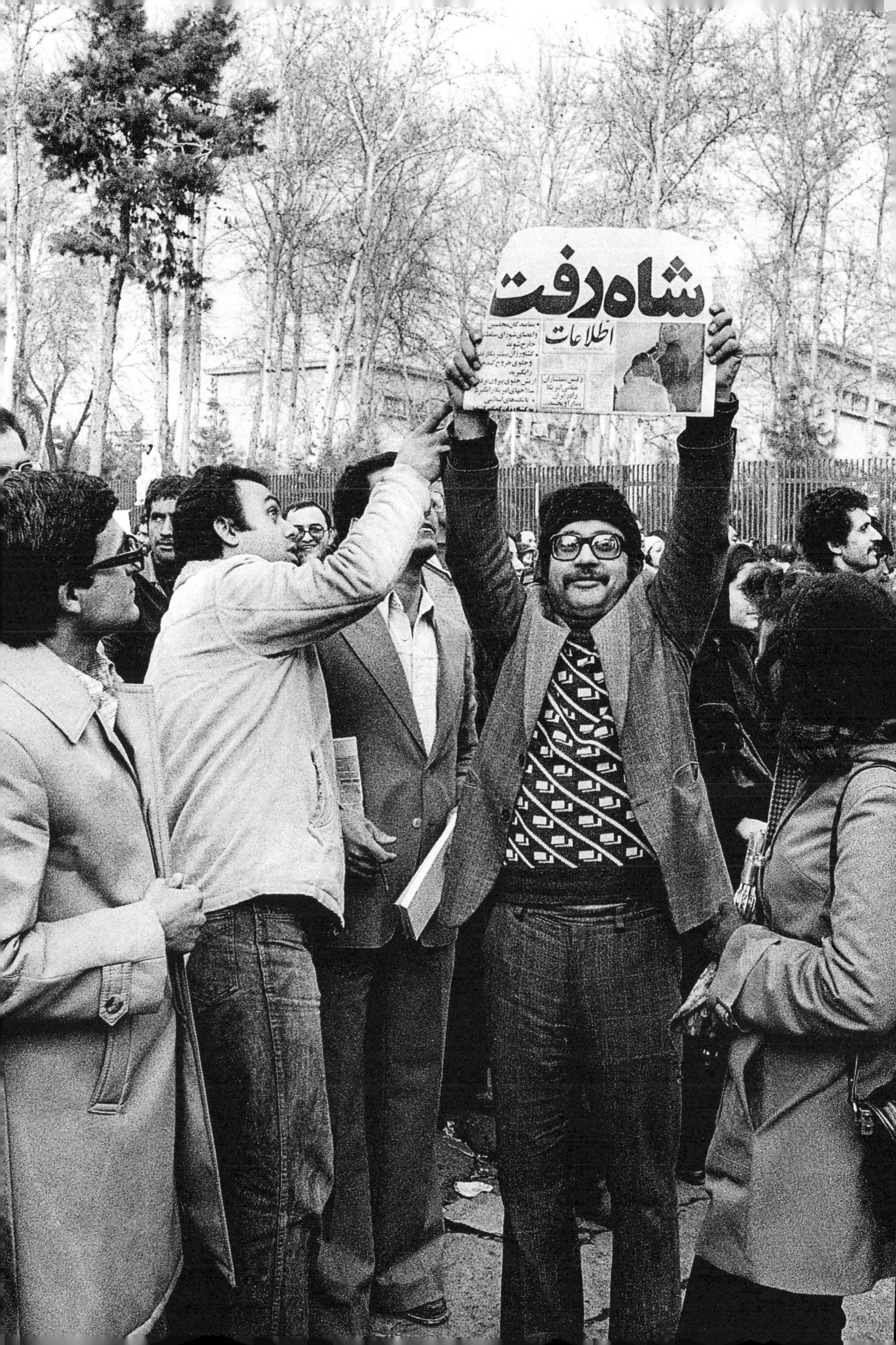
شاه رفت
اطلاعات

آخر شاهنامه

مهدی اخوان ثالث

تهران . مهر ۱۳۶۶

این شکسته چنگِ بی قانون،
رامِ چنگِ چنگی شوریده رنگِ پیر،
گاهَ گویی خواب می بیند
خویش را در بارگاهِ پر فروغ مهر
طرفه چشم‌انداز شاد و شاهدِ زرتشت،
یا پریزادی چمان سرمست
در چمنزاران پاک و روشنِ مهتاب می بیند.
روشنی‌های دروغینی
کاروانِ شعله‌های مرده در مرداب
بر جبینِ قدسیِ محراب می بیند.
یاد ایّام شکوه و فخر و عصمت را،
می‌سراید شاد،
قصه غمگین غربت را

"هان، کجاست؟
پایتخت این کج آئین قرنِ دیوانه؟
با شبانِ روشنش چون روز،
روزهای تنگ و تارش، چون شب اندر قعرِ افسانه.
با قلاعِ سهمگینِ سخت و ستوارش،
با لئیمانه تبسم کردنِ دروازه‌هایش، سرد و بیگانه.

هان، کجاست؟
پایتختِ این دژ آئین قرنِ پرآشوب.
قرنِ شکلک چهر.
بر گذشته از مدارِ ماه،
لیک بس دور از قرارِ مهر.
قرنِ خون‌آشام،
قرنِ وحشتناکترِ پیغام،
کاندران با فضله‌ی موهومِ مرغِ دور پروازی
چار رکنِ هفت اقلیم خدا را در زمانی برمی‌آشوبند.
هر چه هستی، هر چه پستی، هر چه بالایی
سخت می‌کوبند.
پاک می‌روبند.

هان، کجاست؟
پایتخت این بی‌آزرم و بی‌آیین قرن.
کاندران بی‌گونه‌ای مهلت
هر شکوفه‌ی تازه رو بازیچه باد است.
همچنانکه حرمتِ پیرانِ میوه‌یْ خویش بخشیده
عرصه‌ی انکار و وهن و غدر و بیداد است.

پایتختِ اینچنین قرنی
کو؟
بر کدامین بی‌نشان قلّه‌ست،
در کدامین سو؟
دیدبانان را بگو تا خواب نفریبد.
بر چکادِ پاسگاهِ خویش، دل بیدار و سر هشیار،
هیچشان جادوییِ اختر،
هیچشان افسونِ شهرِ نقره مهتاب نفریبد.
بر به کشتی‌هایِ خشم بادبان از خون،
ما، برایِ فتح سویِ پایتختِ قرن می‌آییم.
تا که هیچستانِ نُه تویِ فراخِ این غبارآلودِ بی‌غم را
با چکاچاک مهیبِ تیغ‌هامان، تیز
غرّش زهره درانِ کوسهامان، سهم
پرّش خارا شکافِ تیرهامان، تند؛
نیک بگشاییم
شیشه‌های عمر دیوان را
از طلسم قلعه پنهان، ز چنگِ پاسدارانِ فسونگرشان،
جَلد بربائیم
بر زمین کوبیم.
ور زمین گهواره فرسوده آفاق
دستِ نرم سبزه‌هایش را به پیش آرد،
تا که سنگ از ما نهان دارد،
چهره‌اش را ژرف بشخاییم.
ما
فاتحانِ قلعه‌هایِ فخرِ تاریخیم،
شاهدانِ شهرهایِ شوکتِ هر قرن.
ما
یادگارِ عصمتِ غمگینِ اعصاریم.
ما
راویانِ قصه‌هایِ شاد و شیرینیم.
قصه‌هایِ آسمانِ پاک.
نورِ جاری، آب.
سردِ تاری، خاک.
قصه‌هایِ خوش‌ترین پیغام.
از زلالِ جویبارِ روشن ایّام
قصه‌هایِ بیشه انبوه، پشتش کوه، پایش نهر.
قصه‌هایِ دستِ گرمِ دوست در شب‌هایِ سردِ شهر.
ما
کاروانِ ساغر و چنگیم
لولیانِ چنگمان افسانه‌گویِ زندگیمان، زندگیمان شعر و افسانه.
ساقیانِ مستِ مستانه
هان، کجاست؟
پایتختِ قرن؟
ما برای فتح می‌آییم،
تا که هیچستانْش بگشاییم..."

این شکسته چنگِ دلتنگِ محال اندیش،
نغمه پردازِ حریم خلوتِ پندار،
جاودان پوشیدهَ از اسرار،
چه حکایت‌ها که دارد روز و شب با خویش
ای پریشانگویِ مسکین! پرده دیگر کن
پوردستان جانَ ز چاهِ نابرادر در نخواهد برد.
مُرد، مُرد، او مُرد،
داستانِ پورِ فرّخزاد را سر کن.
آنکه گویی ناله‌اش از قعرِ چاهی ژرف می‌آید
نالد و موید،
موید و گوید
"آه، دیگر ما
فاتحانِ گوژپشت و پیر را مانیم،
بر به کشتی‌هایِ موج بادبان از کف.
دل به یادِ برّه‌هایِ فرّهی، در دشت ایّامِ تهی، بسته،
تیغ‌هامان زنگ خورد و کهنه و خسته،
کوسهامان جاودان خاموش،
تیرهامان بال بشکسته.
ما
فاتحانِ شهرهایِ رفته بر بادیم.
با صدایی ناتوان‌تر زانکه بیرون آید از سینه،
راویانِ قصه‌هایِ رفته از یادیم.
کس به چیزی، یا پشیزی، برنگیرد سکّه‌هامان را
گویی از شاهی‌ست بیگانه.
یا ز میری دودمانش منقرض گشته.
گاه گه بیدار می‌خواهیم شد زین خواب جادویی،
همچو خواب همگنانِ غار،
چشم می‌مالیم و می‌گوئیم: آنک، طرفه قصرِ زرنگارِ صبحِ شیرینکار.
لیک بی‌مرگ است دقیانوس!
وای، وای، افسوس."

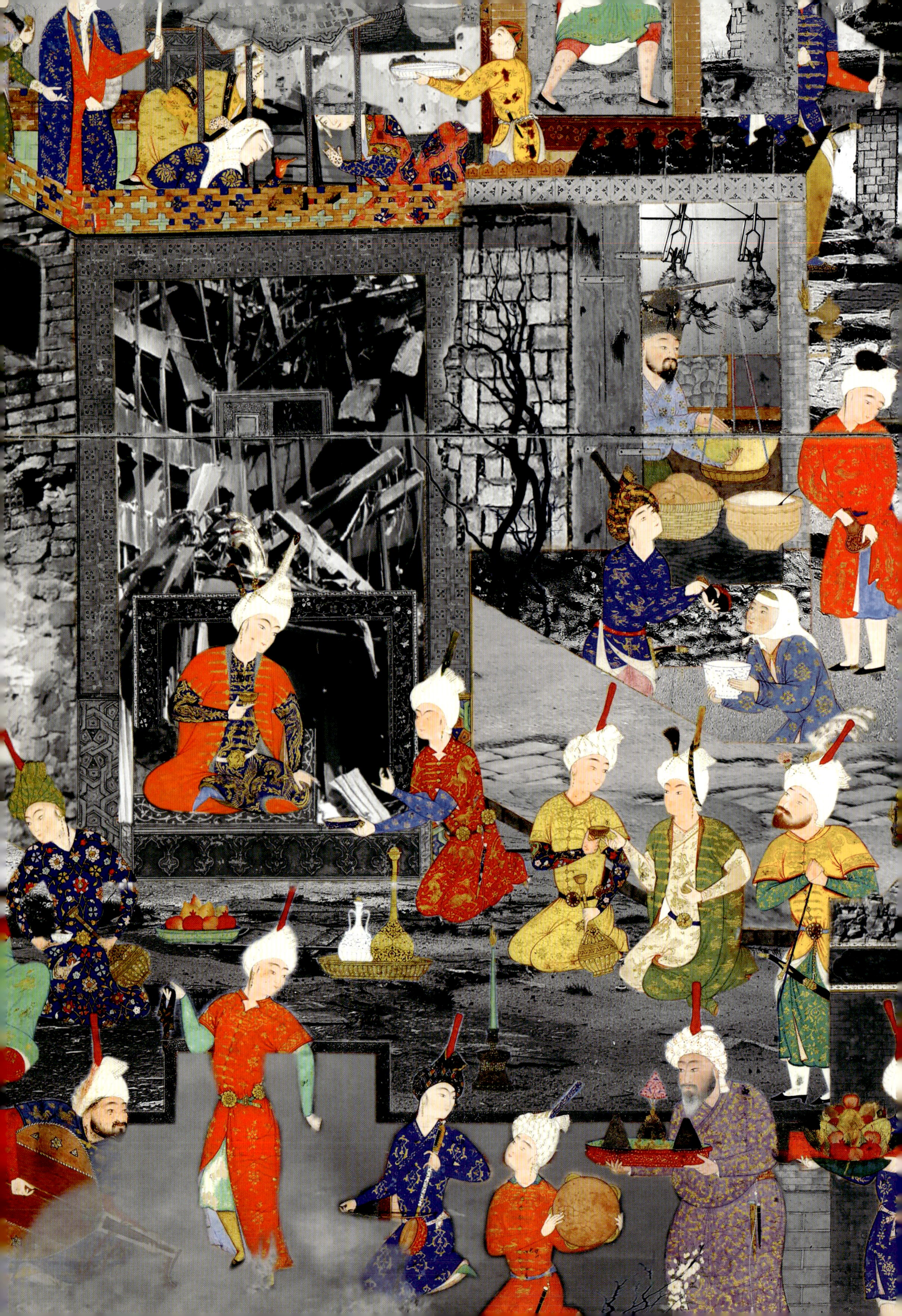

Kings *and* Heroes

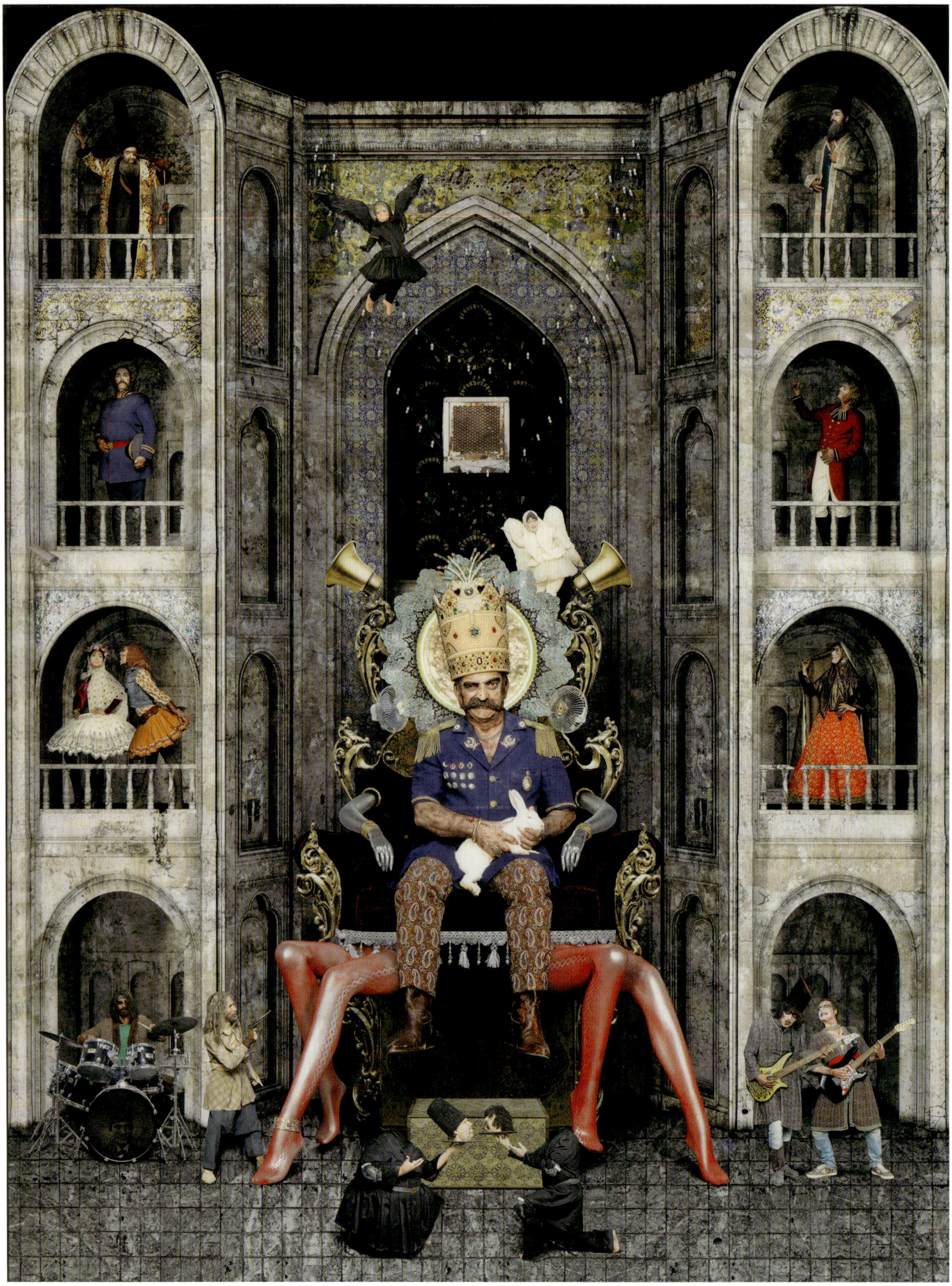

PLATE 1A

Siamak Filizadeh
***Coronation*, 2014**
FROM THE SERIES **Underground**

The series Underground takes as its theme the long reign of Nasir al-Din Shah (r. 1848–96), who was assassinated just short of his fiftieth jubilee. In Siamak Filizadeh's telling of the tale, Nasir al-Din rules an underground city for fifty-year intervals, dies, is resurrected, and governs again exactly as before. While the narrative is ostensibly set in the past, its siting and meaning reference present-day Iran. Although Nasir al-Din came to the throne as a teenager, he is depicted in this coronation scene, and throughout the series, in middle age.

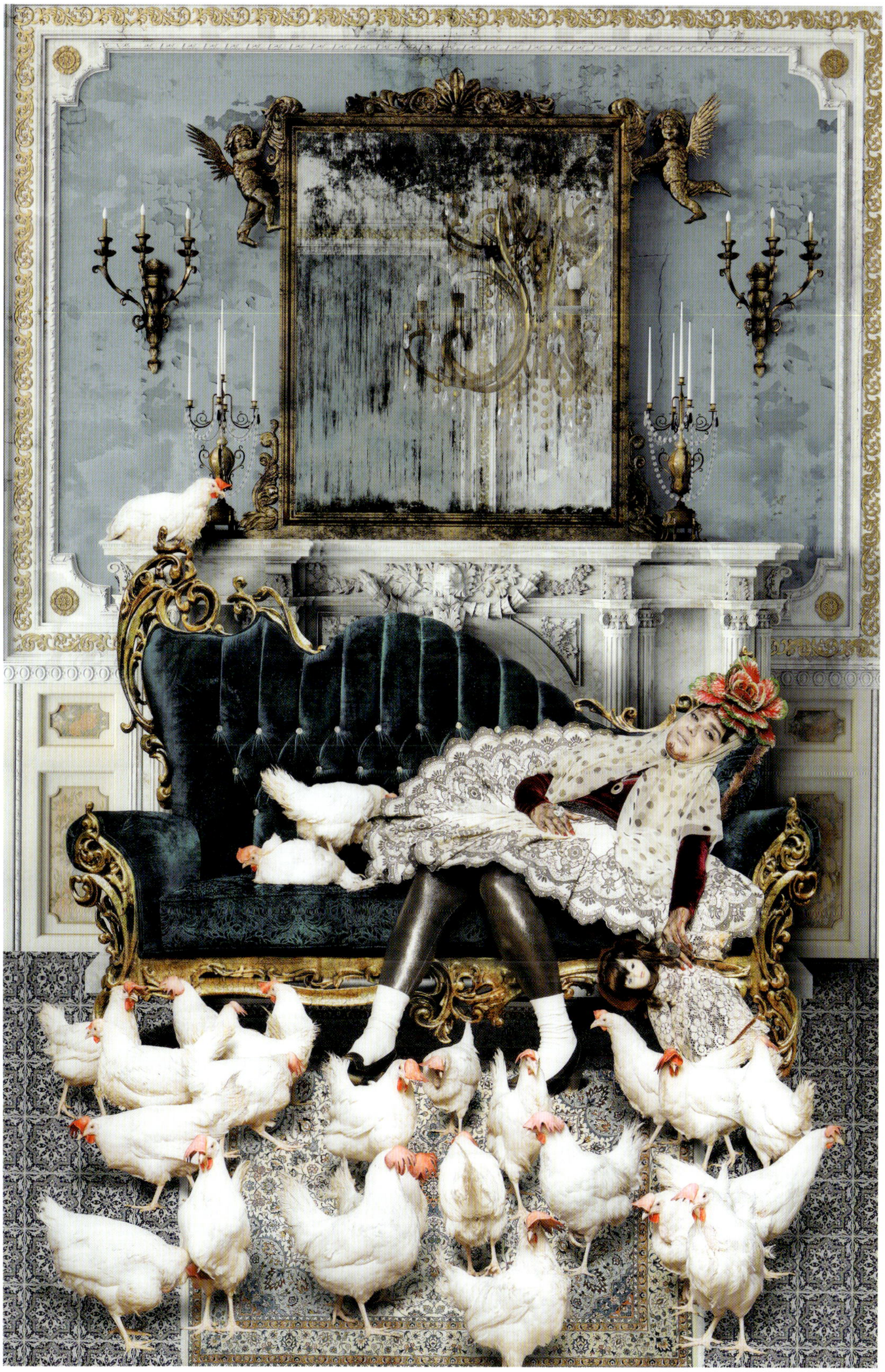

PLATE 1B

Siamak Filizadeh
Anis al-Daula, 2014
FROM THE SERIES Underground

This intriguing composition was inspired by two photographs Nasir al-Din Shah made of his wife, Anis al-Daula: in one, she reclines on a settee, and in the other, she holds a European doll. In Siamak Filizadeh's version, the royal spouse is surrounded by chickens (perhaps a reference to her humble origins) in a room evocative of the French-inspired interiors preserved in Nasir al-Din-era photographs and in paintings of the Golestan Palace, in Tehran.

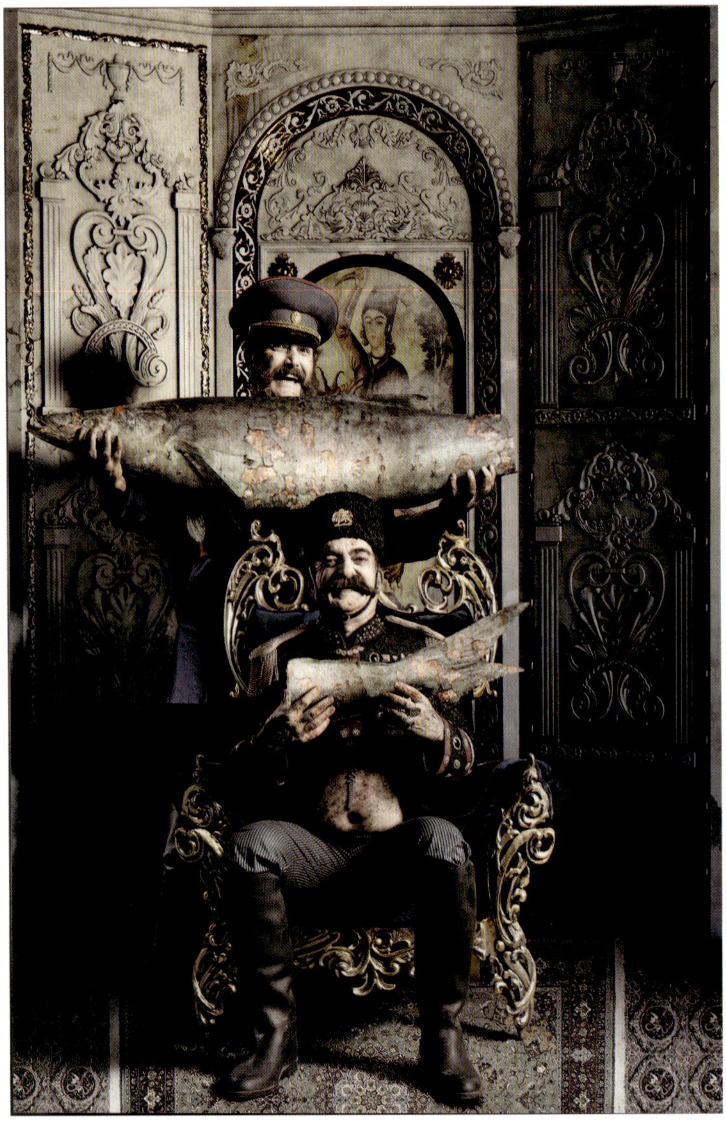

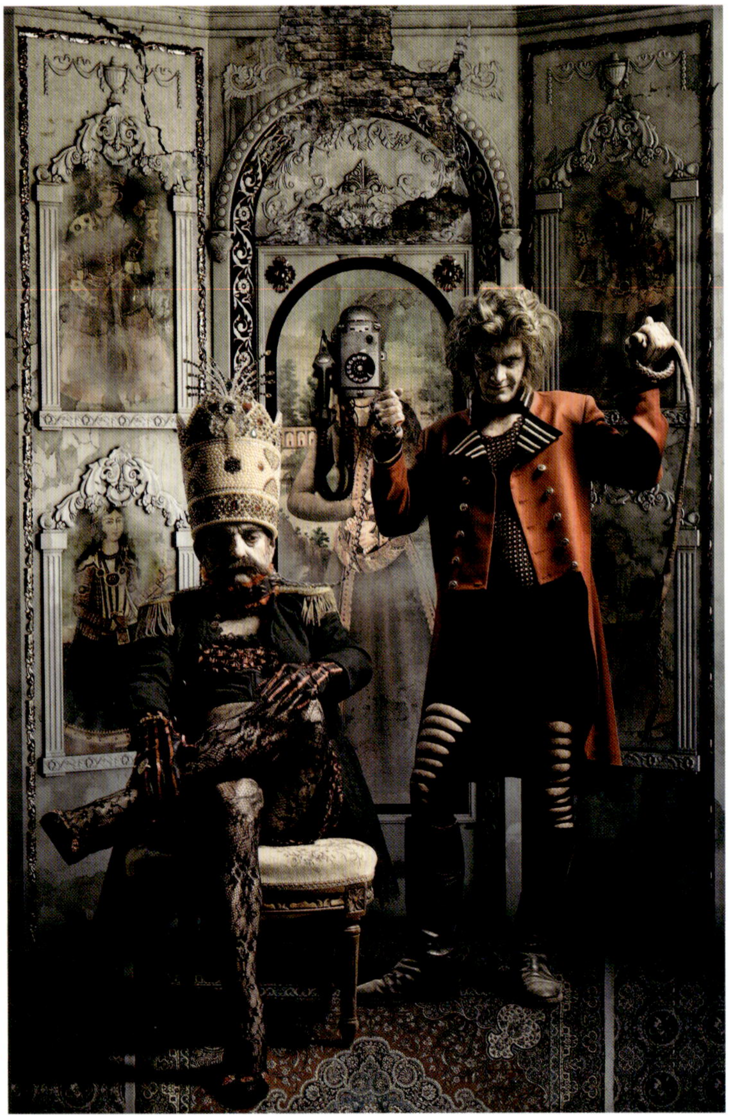

PLATES 1C–D (RIGHT TO LEFT)

Siamak Filizadeh
***Shah and the British Ambassador*, 2014**
***Shah and the Russian Ambassador*, 2014**
FROM THE SERIES Underground

One of the many challenges of Nasir al-Din's reign was the escalating interference of England and Russia as each sought control over traditional Persian territories. This pair of prints ironically emphasizes the shah's impotence against such foreign domination, personified by the ambassadors. The British ambassador uses a leash and whip to control the shah, feminized and sexualized by black lace stockings; the Russian ambassador smugly holds aloft the better part of a large sturgeon from the Caspian Sea, while Nasir al-Din happily makes do with the tail end.

By using ironic imagination as a form of resistance toward grand narration of the past, I desperately try to move beyond both past and present. This approach takes into account the gap(s) hidden in history—the ones that in my opinion narrate the main essence of history—in order to challenge the weight of history on my shoulders. I look to reread, reevaluate, re-research, and revise this history.

Siamak Filizadeh

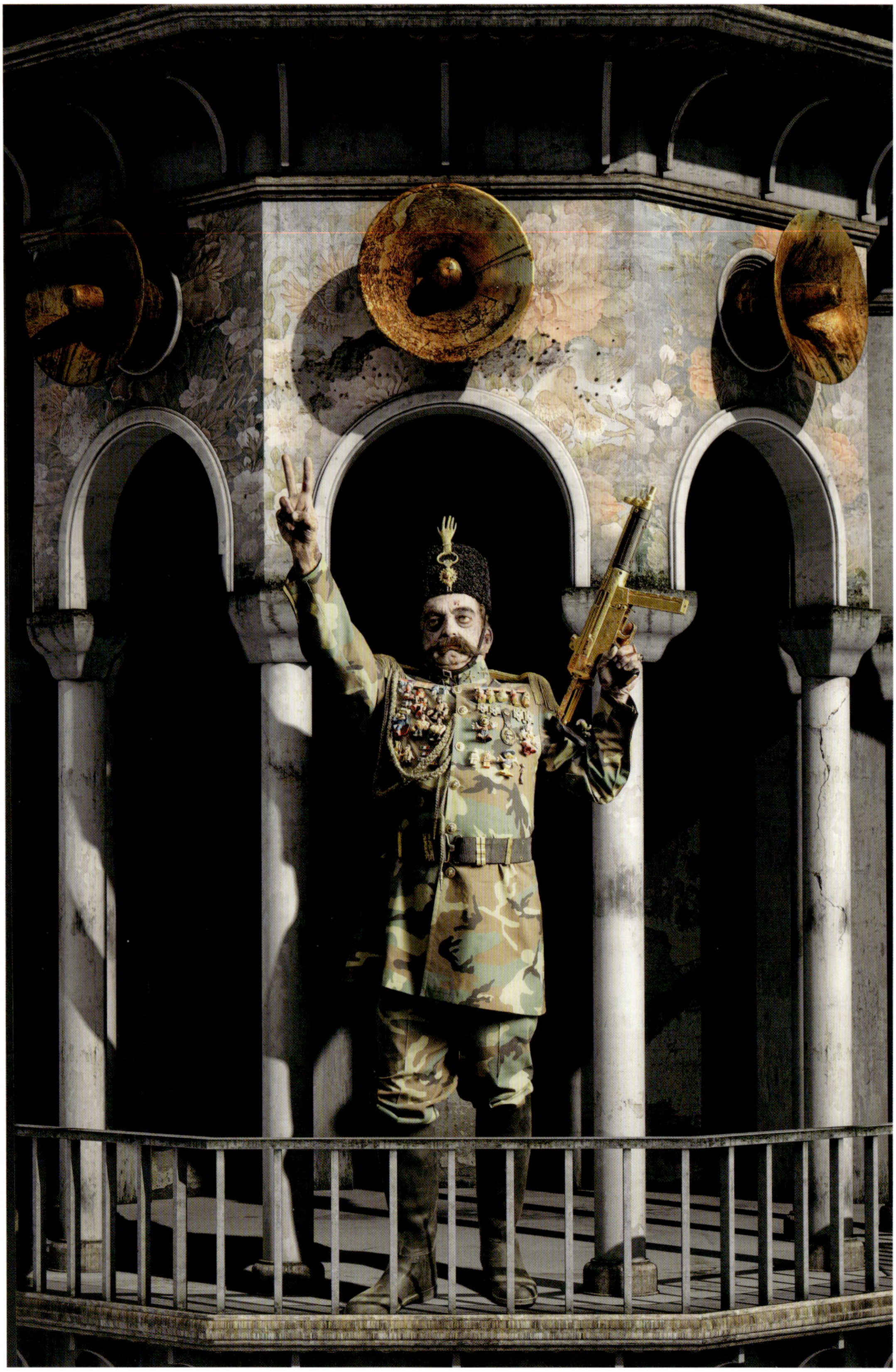

PLATE 1E

Siamak Filizadeh
***Vigor*, 2014**
FROM THE SERIES Underground

Clothed in camouflage gear decorated with children's pins rather than medals and military insignia, and armed with an Uzi, the shah gives the victory symbol from a balcony. The scene perhaps suggests Nasir al-Din's bravura, self-delusion, and public deception, for his adventures generally ended in defeat. Modern-day elements, including the submachine gun, serve as reminders that this type of prevarication for political ends is not restricted to the past.

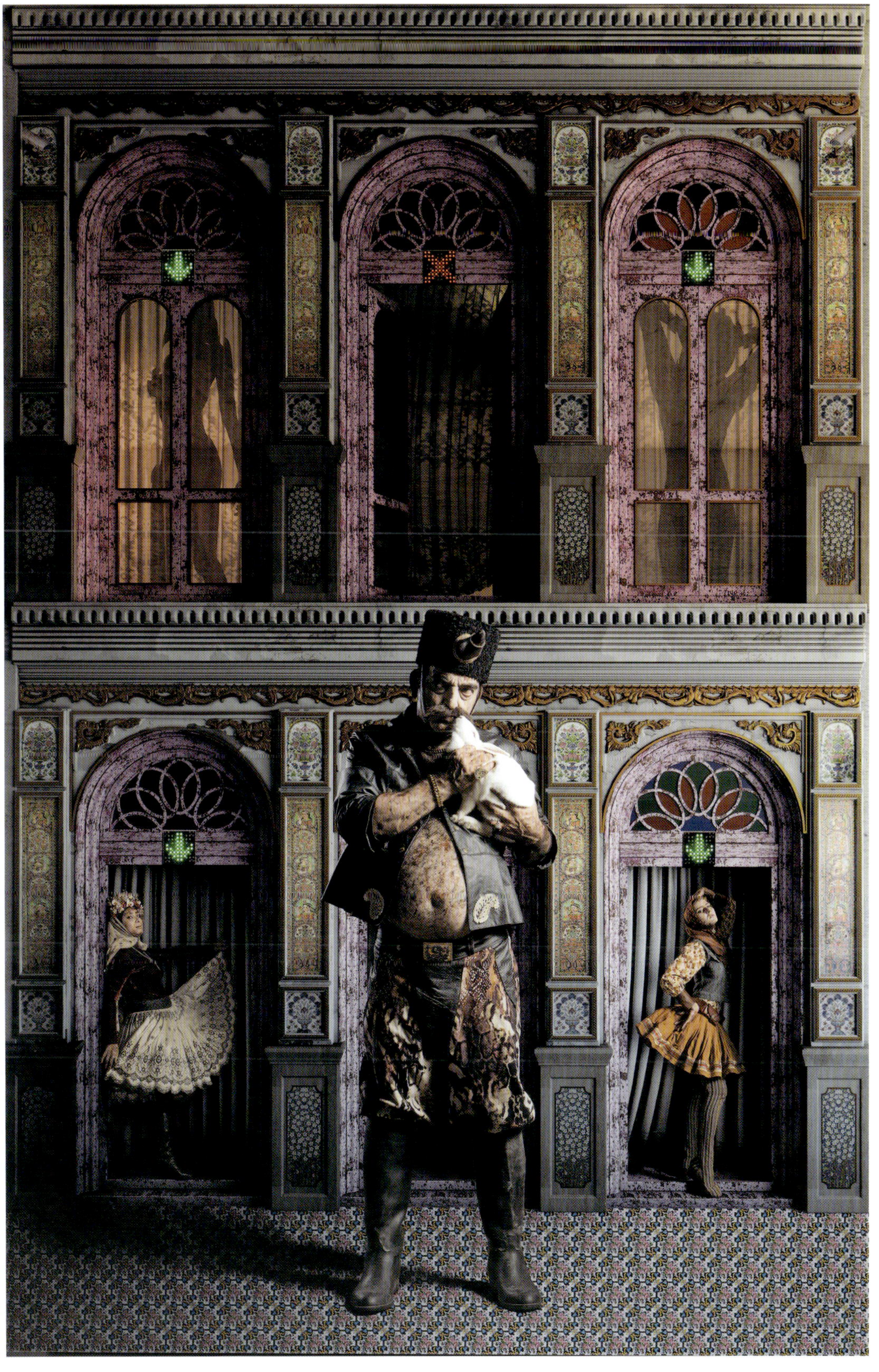

PLATE 1F

Siamak Filizadeh
Harem, 2014
FROM THE SERIES **Underground**

Details of Nasir al-Din's family life and loves are preserved in a variety of sources, his own photographs of the royal harem among them. Women, and not only his domineering mother, Mahd Ulya, but also several of his wives, left their mark on his reign. Here the artist imagines the harem as a bordello, although the shah is more interested in his rabbit than in the temptations of his wives.

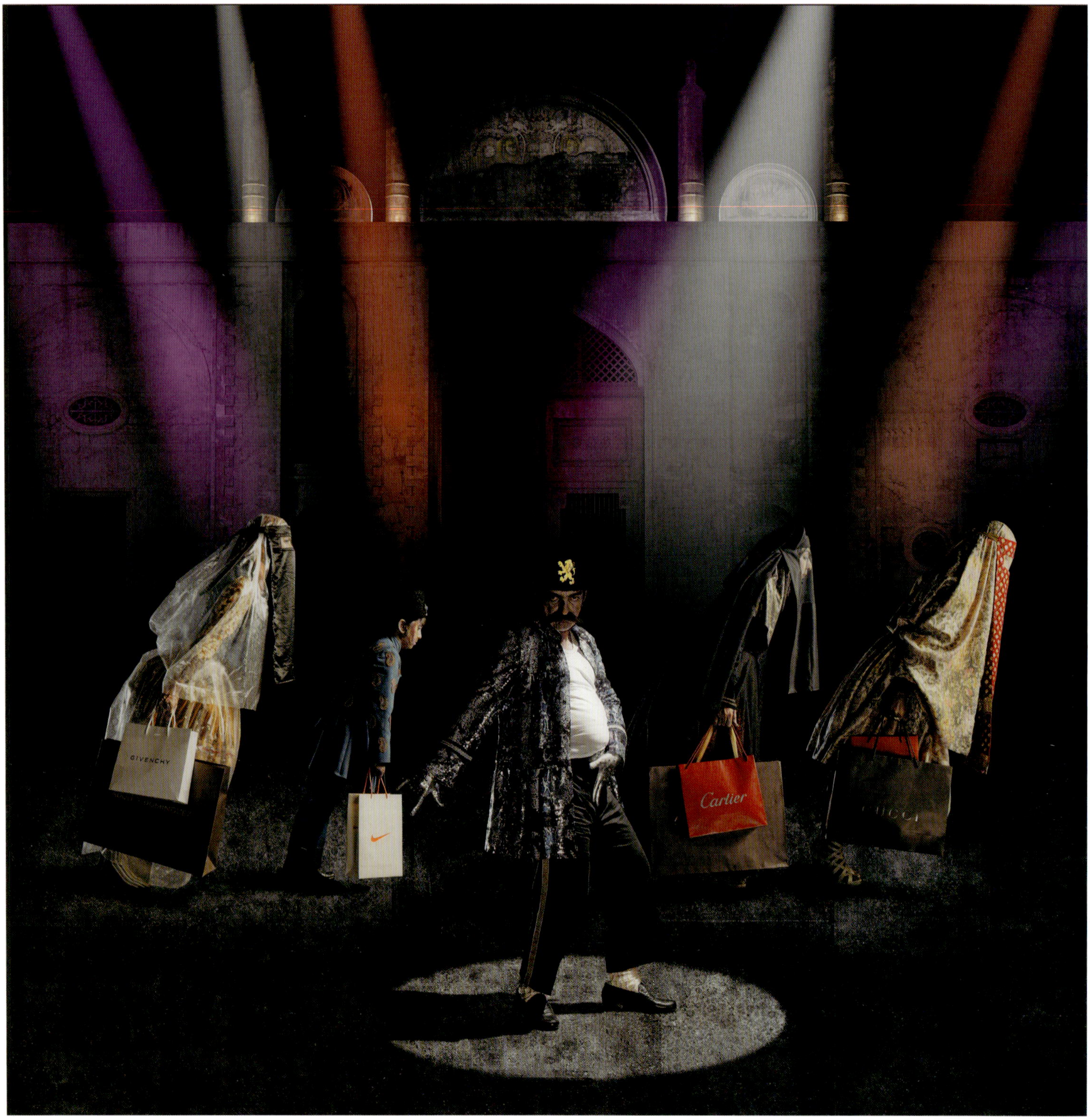

PLATE 1G

Siamak Filizadeh
***Return from Europe*, 2014**
FROM THE SERIES Underground

Nasir al-Din was the first Iranian ruler to visit Europe; he made three trips in all. In Siamak Filizadeh's rendering of the return from one such journey, the shah's family members are shown in a darkened courtyard bending forward under the burden of their luxury goods. At center, lit by a spotlight, the king is clothed and posed as Michael Jackson. The irony of this seemingly gently derisive scene is that the actual European tours were bracketed historically by social and religious unrest and armed government retaliation.

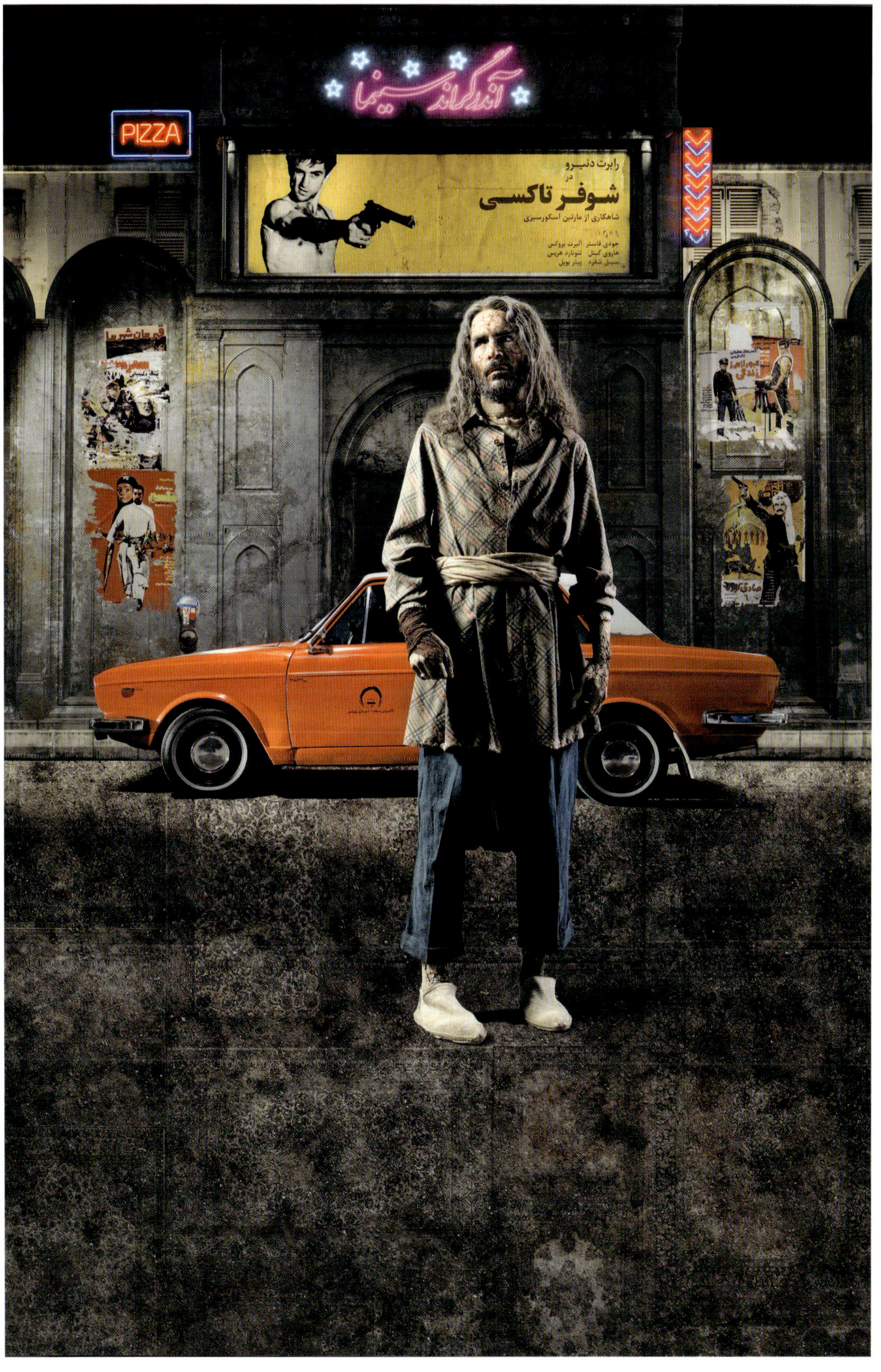

PLATE 1H

Siamak Filizadeh
***Mirza Riza Kirmani*, 2014**
FROM THE SERIES **Underground**

Mirza Riza Kirmani, the shah's assassin, is the subject of several prints—the first of which shows him in the guise of Travis Bickle, the lonely and depressed antihero of the film *Taxi Driver*. The rumpled and slightly deranged Mirza Riza stands in nighttime Tehran outside a movie theater where *Taxi Driver* is playing, while parked behind him is an antique Paykan taxi. Several surviving photographs of Mirza Riza (c. 1850–1896) picture him as a ragged, chained prisoner.

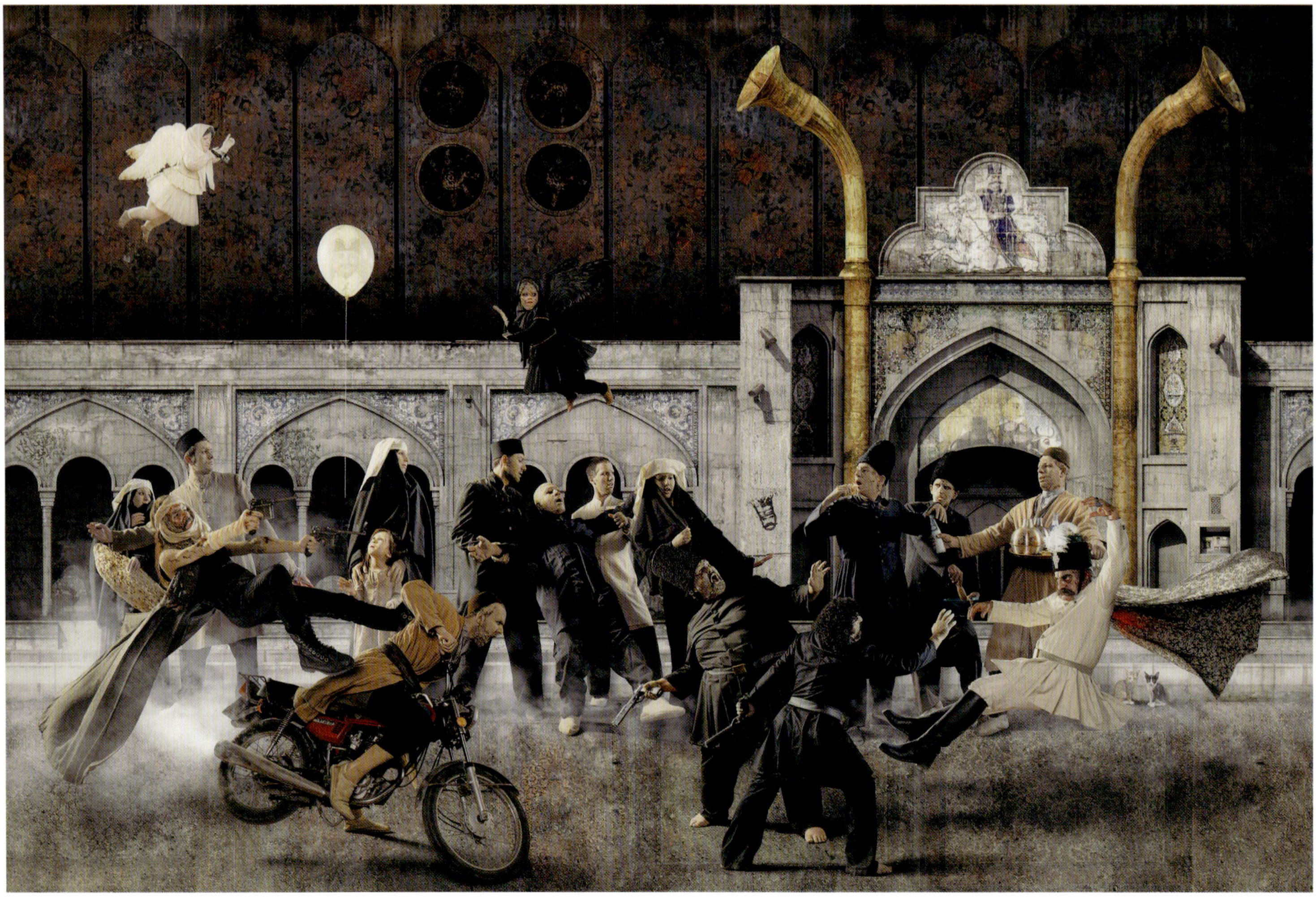

PLATE 11

Siamak Filizadeh
***Assassination*, 2014**
FROM THE SERIES Underground

The shah's assassination is envisioned in this photograph like a scene from an action film and with elements inspired by *The Matrix*. Here, however, the two main sections, in which the assassin and the shah each are propelled backward, were photographed separately and then digitally united. The dramatic narrative is enlivened by playful elements such as the Nasir al-Din balloon and the pair of onlooking kittens.

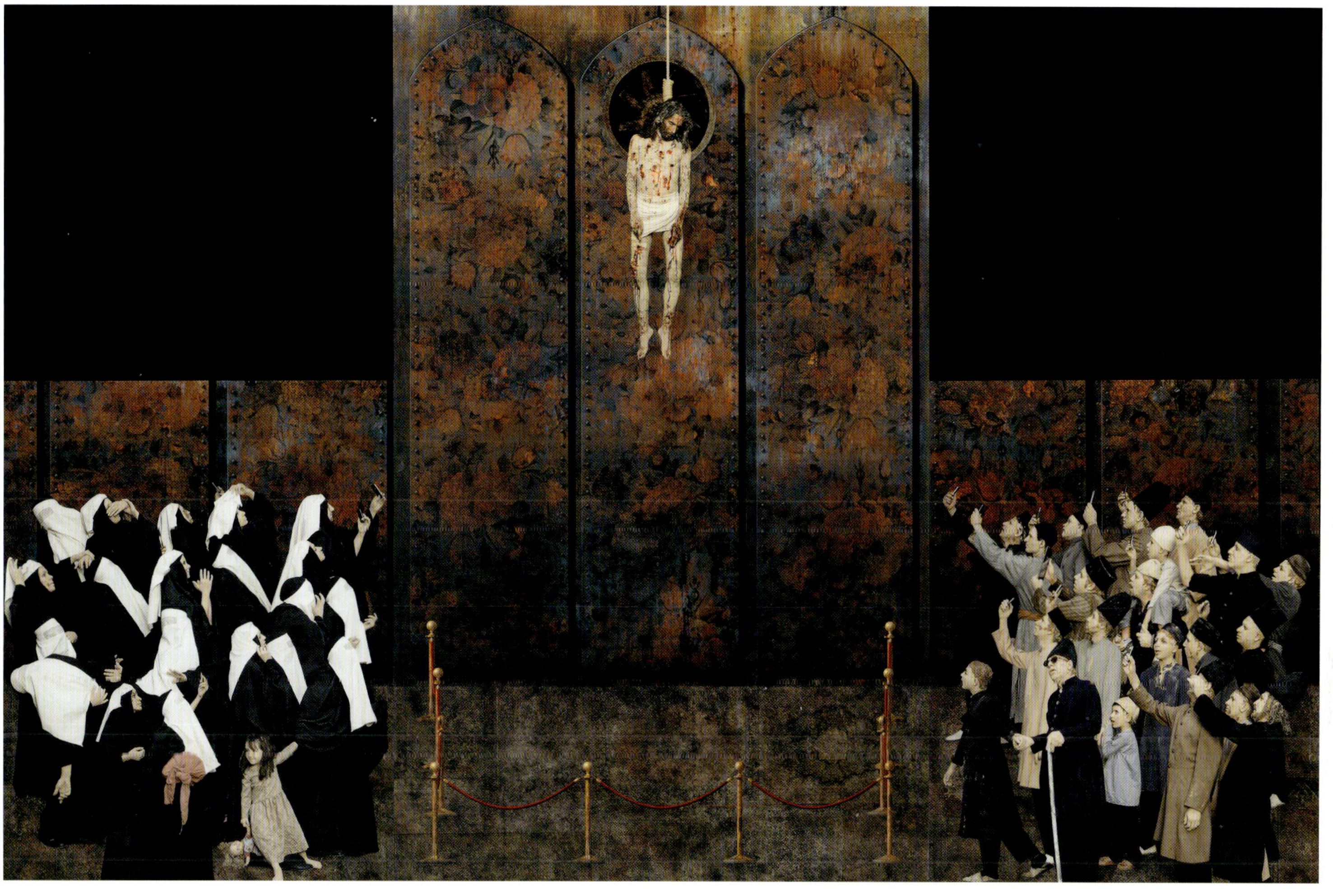

PLATE 1J

Siamak Filizadeh
***Execution*, 2014**
FROM THE SERIES Underground

The series concludes with the assassin's public hanging conceived as a grand triptych. The bloody, Christlike figure of Mirza Riza hangs limply at the center; a velvet-roped stanchion below helps hold back the assembly of onlookers who crowd the two side panels. Segregated by gender, the mob experiences the execution in an entirely contemporary manner—through cell phone cameras—except for a single blind man, who seems unaware of the fateful event.

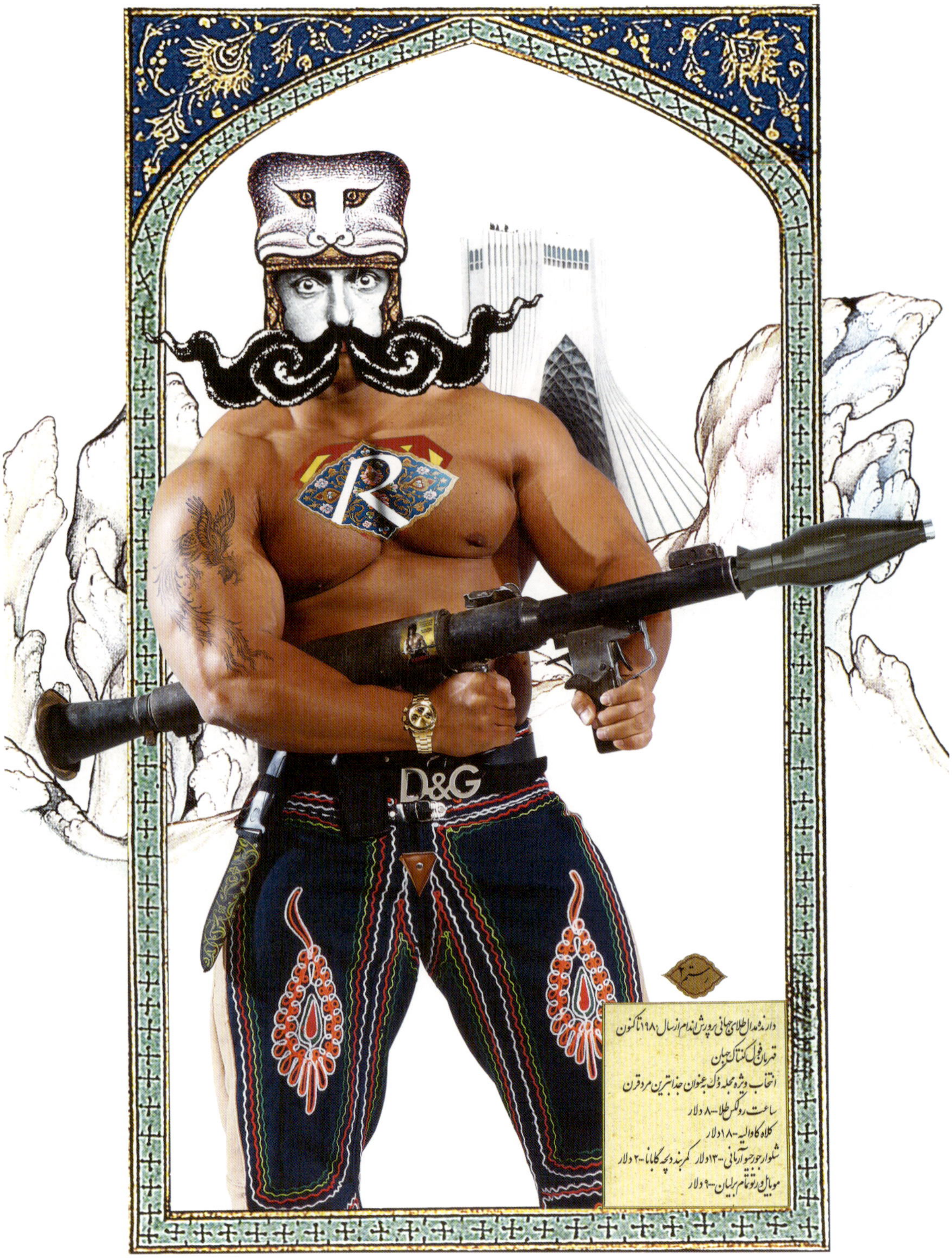

PLATE 2

Siamak Filizadeh
***Rostam II returns at age of 30 having been brought up abroad*, 2009**

Rustam, the great Iranian hero of the *Shahnama* (Book of Kings), is represented as a bazooka-toting, bare-chested bodybuilder, his bulging thighs clothed in the type of short pants worn by members of the *zurkhana*, the traditional "house of strength." In the composition's lower right, a text box emulates the text blocks in manuscripts of the *Shahnama*, but instead of rhymed Persian couplets, this version itemizes Rustam's deluxe consumer goods and lists his bodybuilding awards.

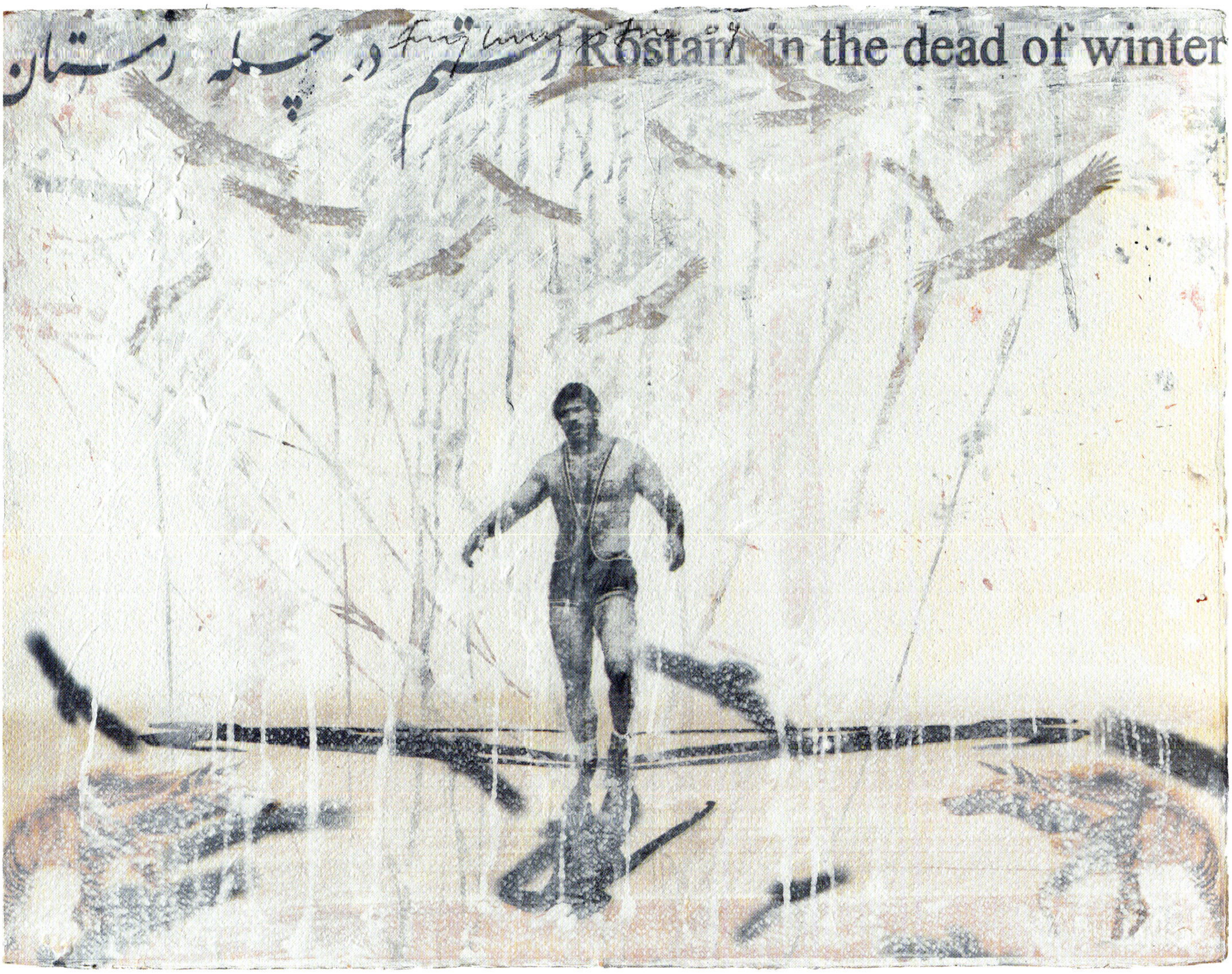

PLATE 3

Fereydoun Ave
***Rostam in the Dead of Winter*, 2009**

Fereydoun Ave has created several series featuring the epic hero Rustam represented by photographs of Abbas Jadidi, an Iranian wrestler who won the 1996 Olympic silver medal. While Rustam is portrayed as triumphant in other works, here, in a hostile environment populated by hyenas and vultures, he is bereft. The ominous splashes of red paint, the wild animals, and Rustam's isolation and visible exhaustion suggest an unfavorable end for the diminished hero.

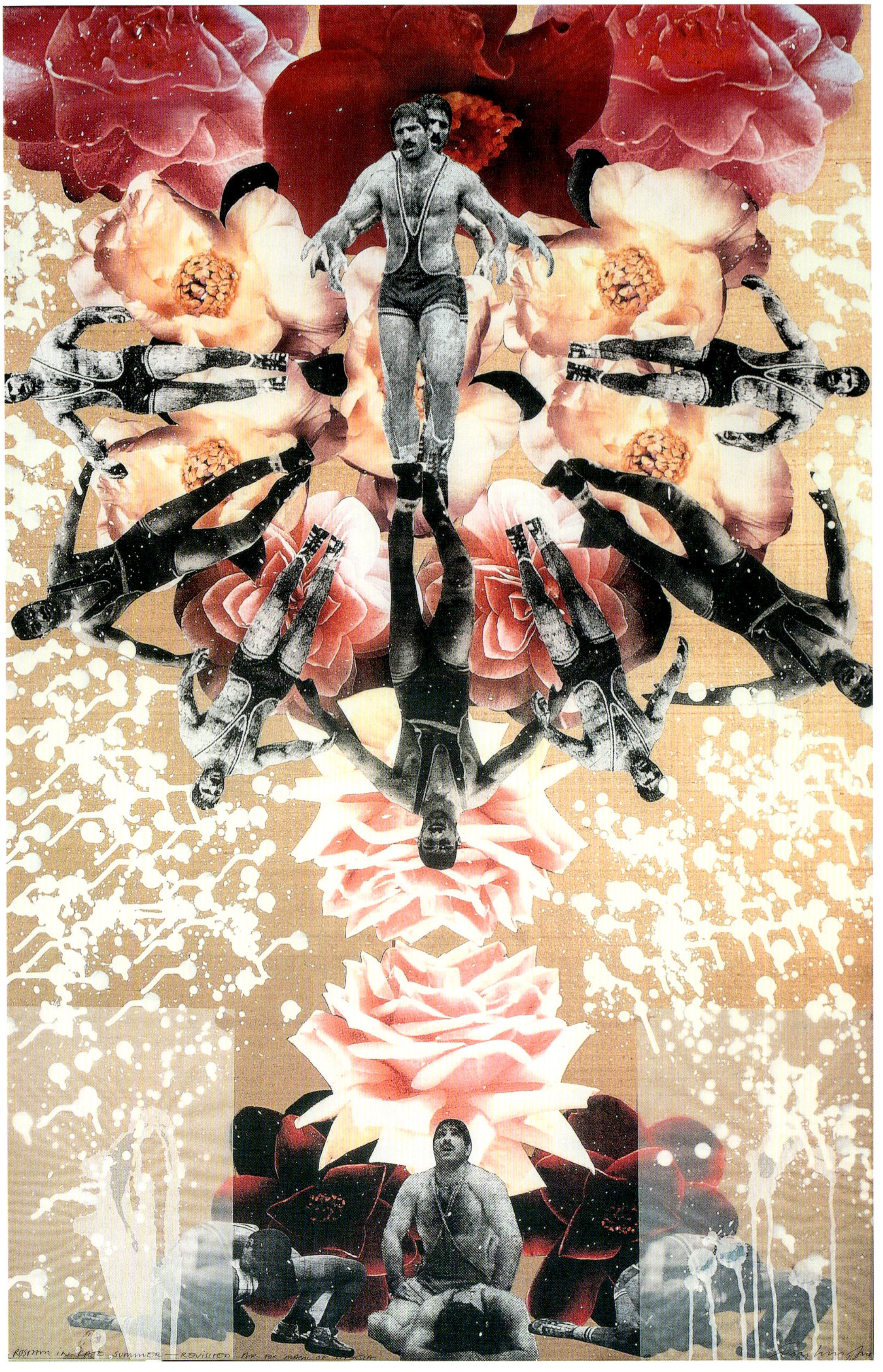

PLATE 4

Fereydoun Ave
***Untitled*, 2009**
FROM THE SERIES Rostam in Late Summer—Revisited

Fereydoun Ave, a key contributor to Iran's art scene since the 1960s, in recent years has built a body of work around Rustam, the great warrior of the Persian epic, the *Shahnama*. In this print based on an original collage, Ave uses images of a contemporary wrestler to symbolize Rustam and shows him in multiples that form an intimidating army. The flowers in full bloom convey a sense of hopefulness, while Rustam's defeat of an opponent emphasizes the hero's superiority.

*My Iranianness comes from
my complex relationship with
Iran's mythology and
archetypes, and so, naturally,
does my work.*

Fereydoun Ave

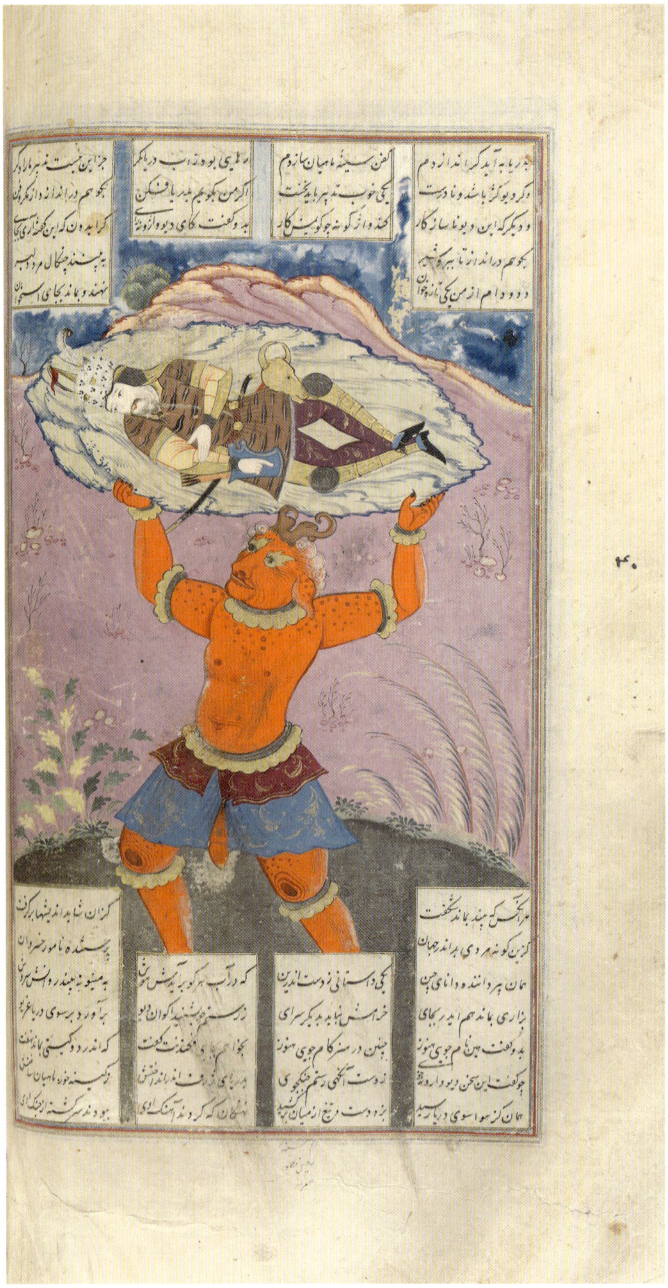

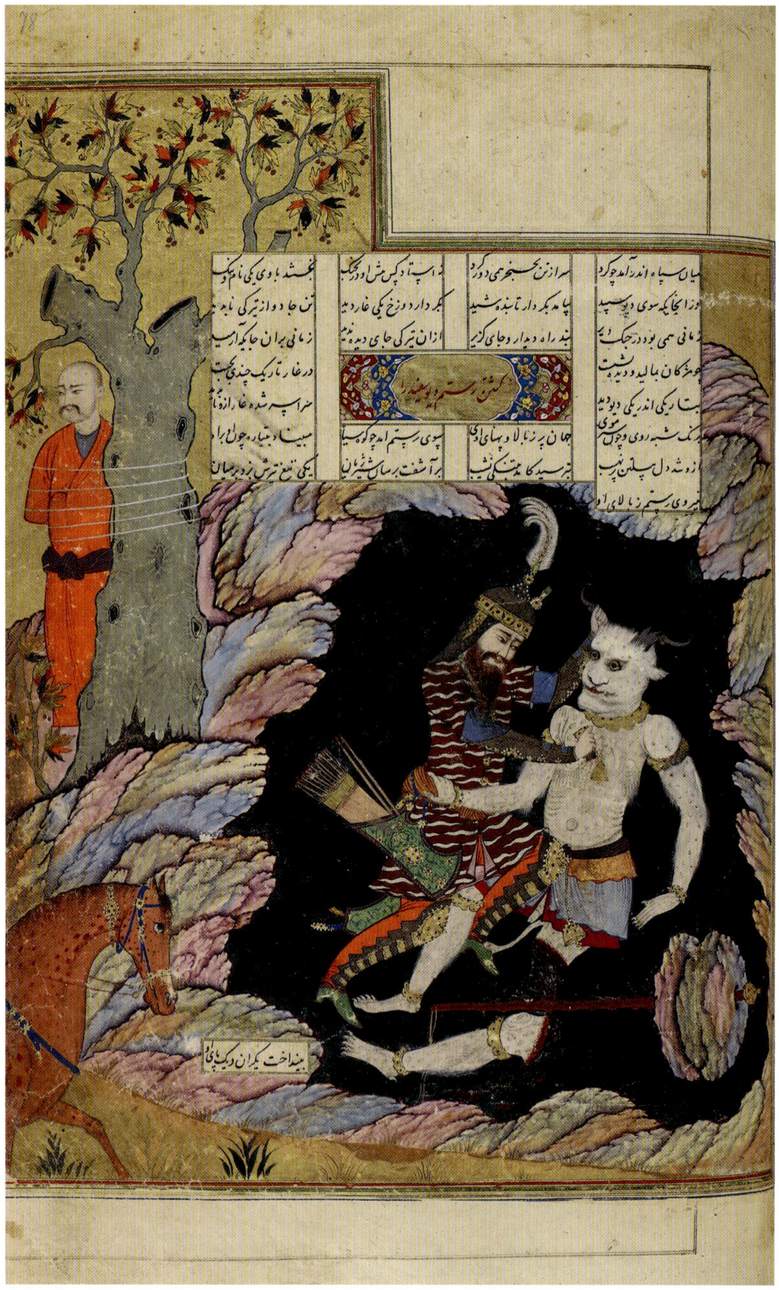

PLATES 5–6 (RIGHT TO LEFT)

***Rustam's Seventh Labor: He Kills the White Div*, c. 1670**
FROM the *Shahnama* of Firdausi

PAINTING BY **Mu'in Musavvir**
***The Div Akvan Carries Rustam to the Sea*, 1660s**
FROM the *Shahnama* of Firdausi

These paintings from two different manuscripts of Iran's national epic, the *Shahnama*, focus on the great hero Rustam, who succeeds by strength and cunning. In order to save the ruler Kai Kavus, Rustam was forced to undergo seven labors, the last of which is depicted in one painting, where he slays the White Div (demon). In the other, the Div Akvan lifts the sleeping Rustam, along with the boulder he rests on, and threatens to discard him into, his choice, either the sea or the mountains.

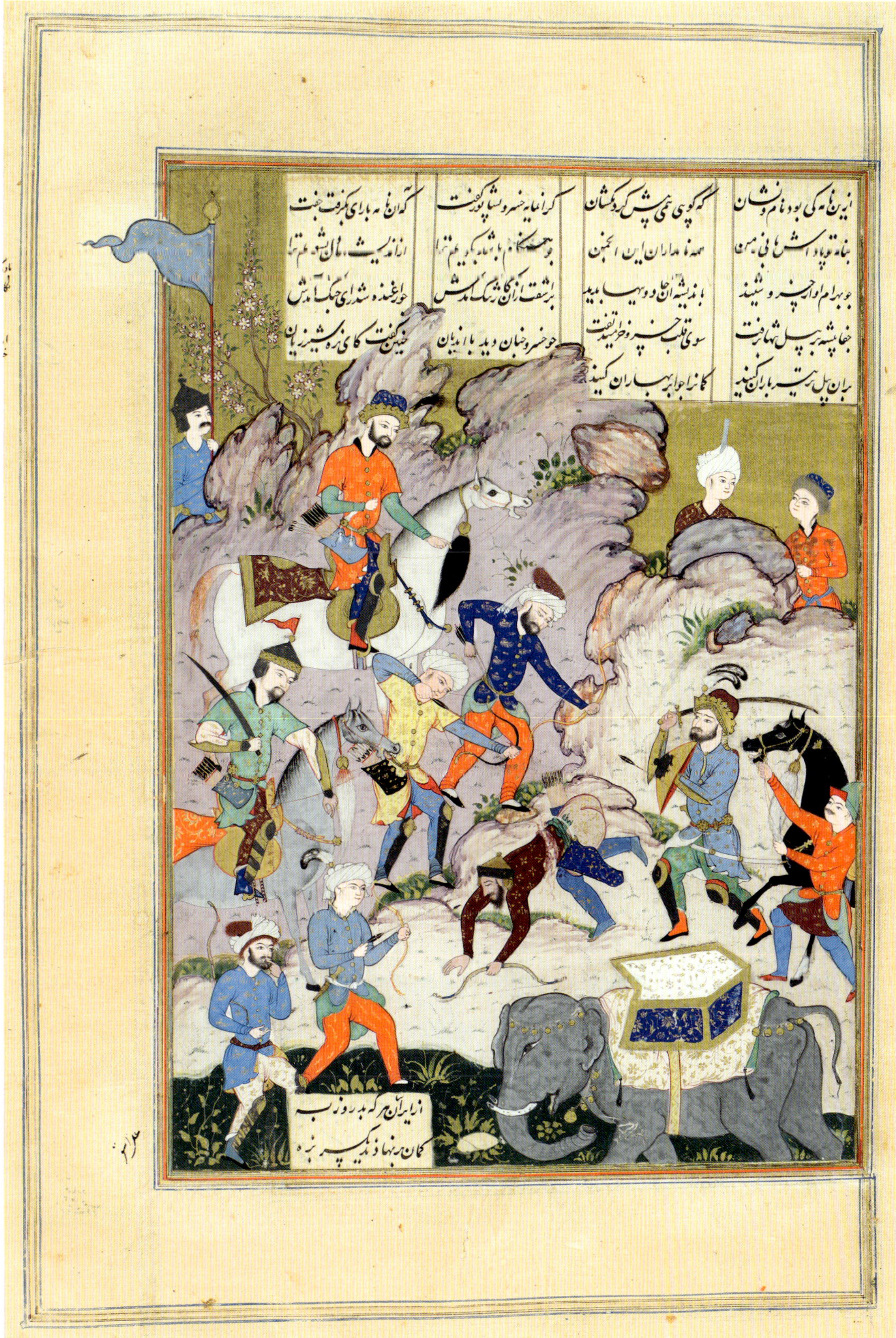

PLATE 7

ATTRIBUTED TO **Ali Asghar**
***The Combat of Khusrau Parviz and Bahram Chubina*, c. 1577**
FROM the *Shahnama* of Firdausi for Shah Isma'il II (r. 1576–77)

This depiction of an epic battle cheekily includes, at the center of the page, a figure who has fallen, leaving his buttocks exposed. The humiliated man perhaps can be understood as representing an out-of-favor courtier, thereby drawing the centuries old battle between the Sasanian ruler Khusrau Parviz (r. 590–628) and his would-be usurper, Bahram Chubina, into the contemporary world of the manuscript's creation.

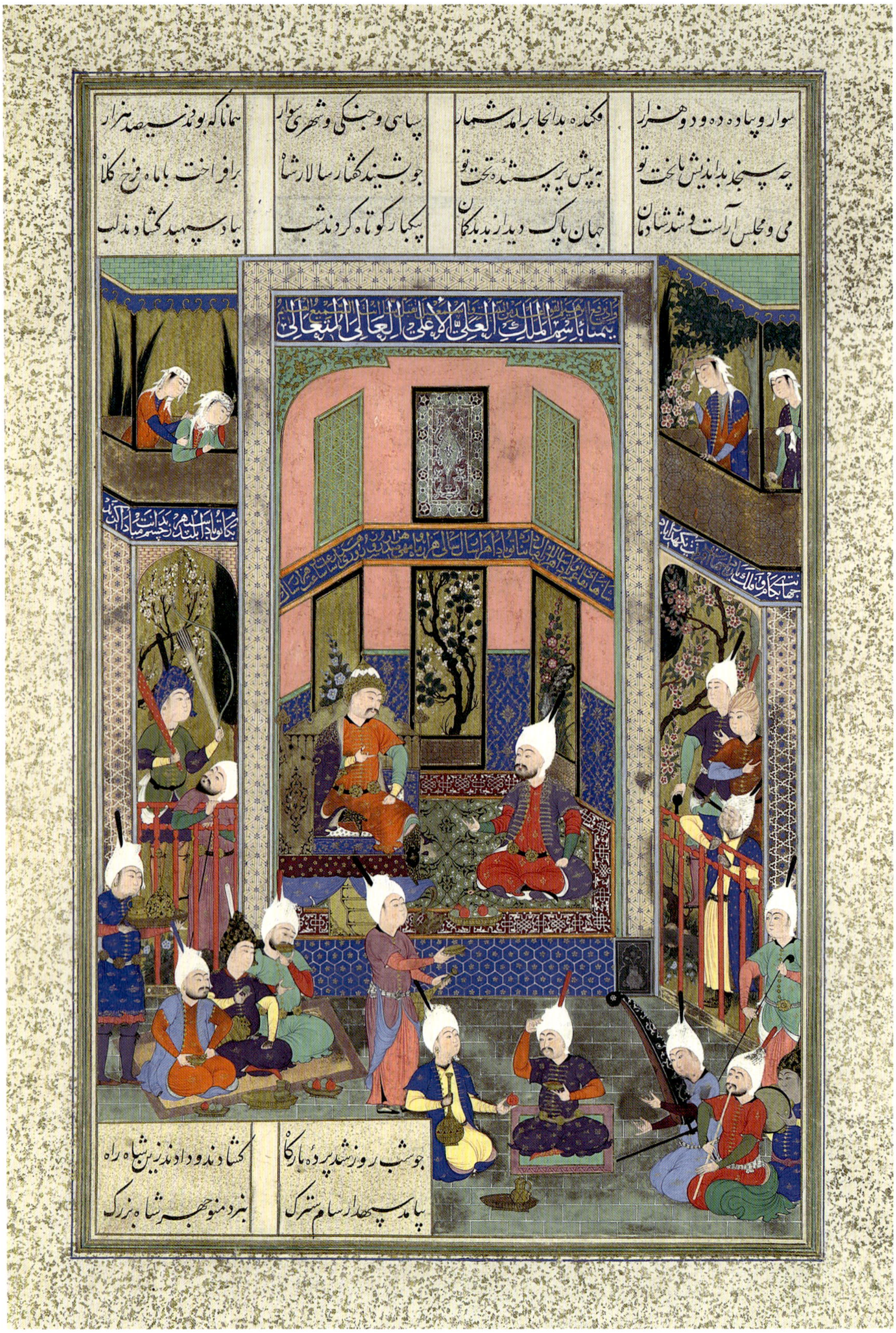

PLATE 8

PAINTING ATTRIBUTED TO **Abdul-Aziz**
Manuchihr Welcomes Sam
***but Orders War upon Mihrab*, c. 1525**
FROM the *Shahnama* of Firdausi

This page was once part of a manuscript commissioned by Shah Tahmasp (r. 1524–76) that is considered one of the most opulent and luxurious *Shahnama*s ever made. It depicts the festive arrival of the warrior Sam at Shah Manuchihr's palace, for which the king has ordered a celebration. However, the merry atmosphere will soon sour when Sam requests that his son be allowed to marry the daughter of the king's enemy. Ultimately, the union does take place and produces one of the most prominent *Shahnama* heroes, Rustam.

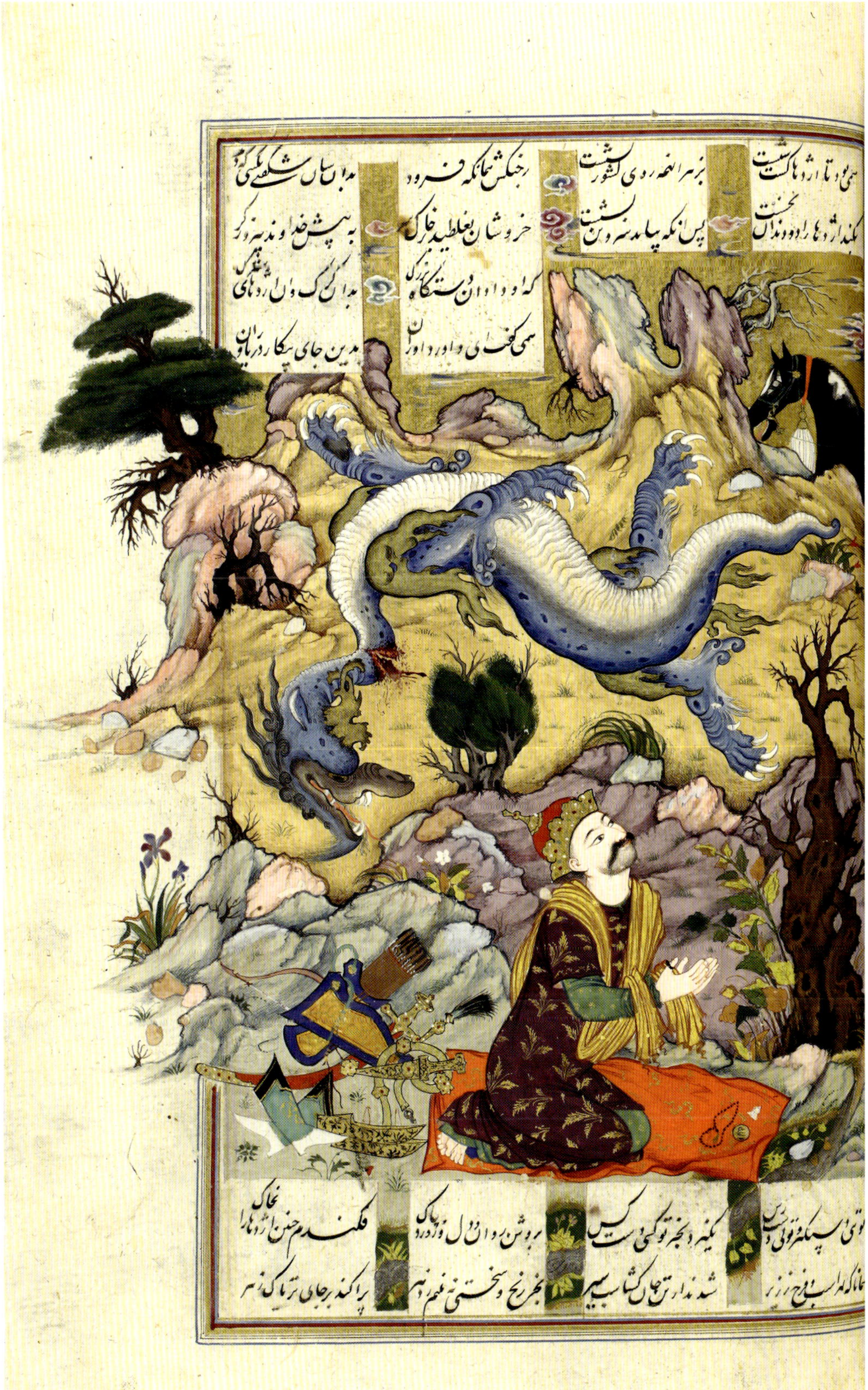

PLATE 9

***Gushtasp and the Dragon of Mount Sakila,* AH 1014/1605**

FROM the *Shahnama* of Firdausi

This illustration of the ancient Prince Gushtasp praying after slaying a dragon so he can marry the daughter of a high-ranking official is reframed in the Islamic culture of the book's making. Gushtasp's garb is that of a seventeenth-century Safavid courtier; he is shown praying in the manner of a Shi'ite Muslim, with prayer beads and the *muhr* (a disc made of clay from Karbala to which the worshipper touches his head).

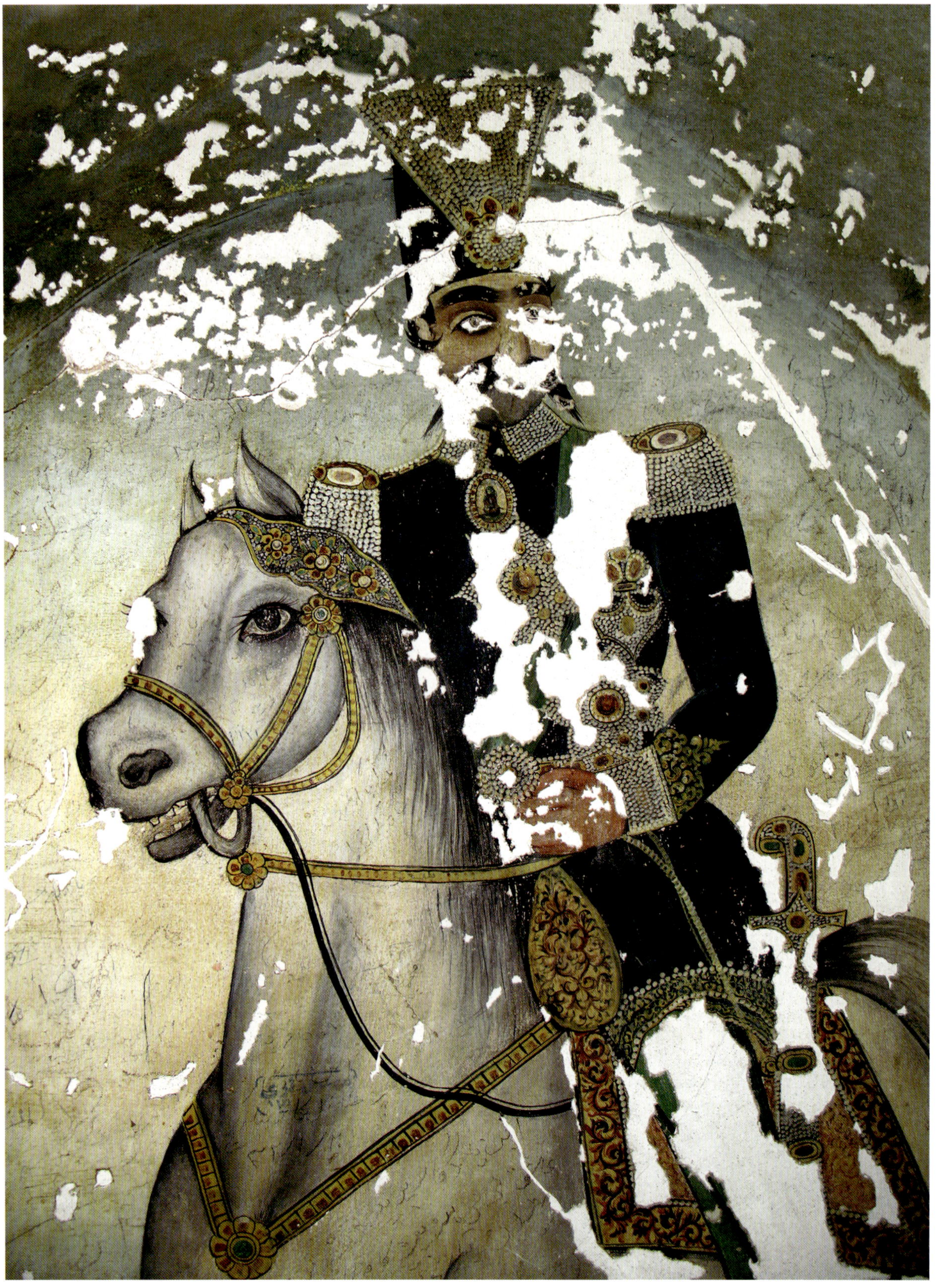

PLATE 10

Fataneh Dadkhah
***Untitled*, 2006**
FROM THE SERIES Destruction

In her series Destruction, Fataneh Dadkhah recorded decaying architectural elements in Iran, from worn wooden doors to walls covered in mangled advertisements to chipped tile revetment. This print captures a nineteenth-century mural most likely portraying a young Nasir al-Din Shah (r. 1848–96). As depicted in the photograph, the mural has suffered equally from the ravages of time and from intentional defacement, including graffiti. In its ruined state, the image of the mural has become a visual metaphor for the transformation of historical memory.

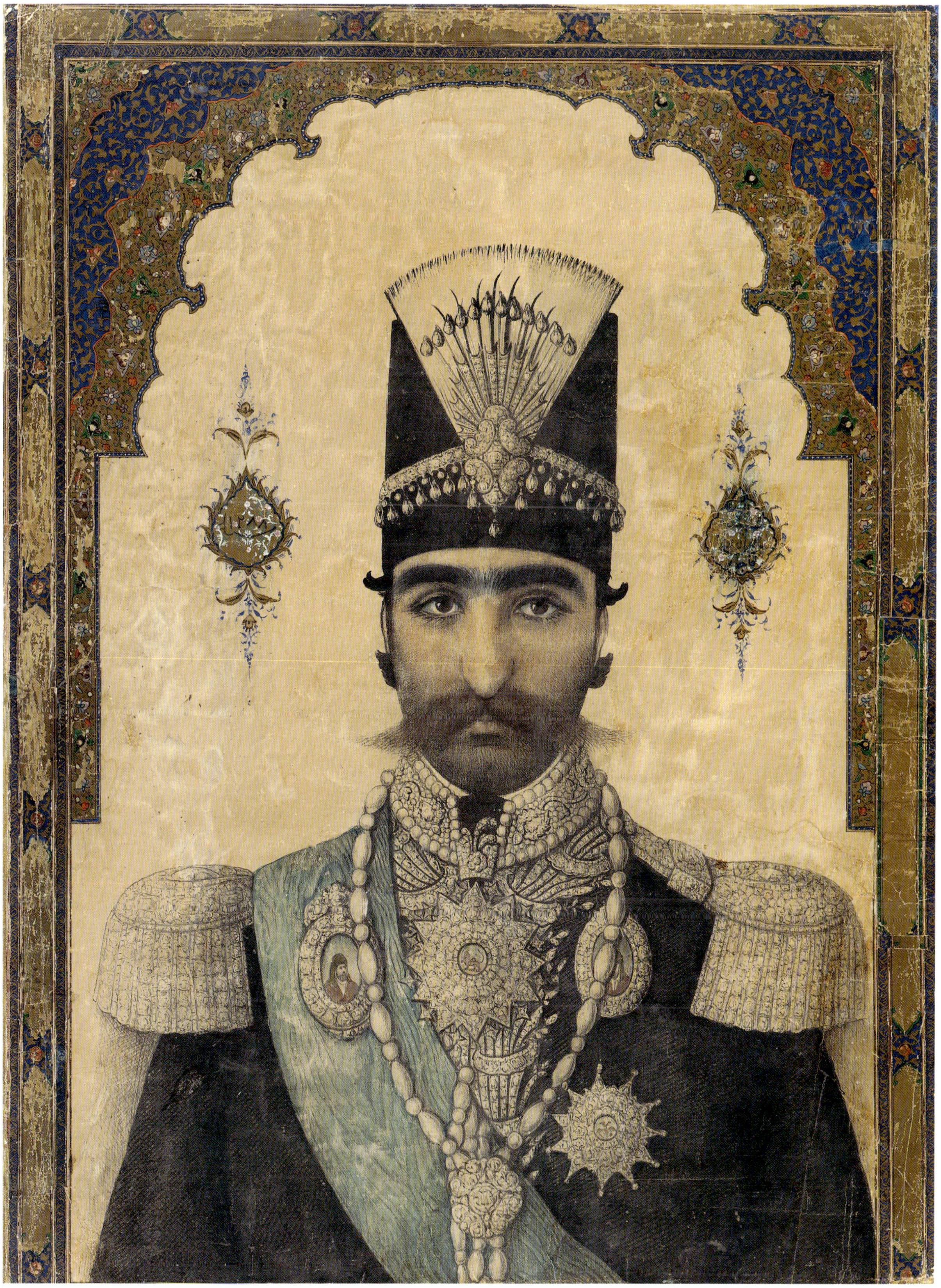

PLATE 11

***Early Portrait of Nasir al-Din Shah** (r. 1848–96)*, **c. 1850**

Likenesses were made of Nasir al-Din, as no other Iranian ruler before him, documenting his teenage years up to the time of his death. The shah is shown here at perhaps just nineteen or twenty years of age, wearing jeweled portraits of the Shi'ite Imams, probably Ali and Hasan, along with royal insignia. The archlike illuminated frame references the past, while the realistic depiction reflects more recent Western influences, including the advent of portrait photography.

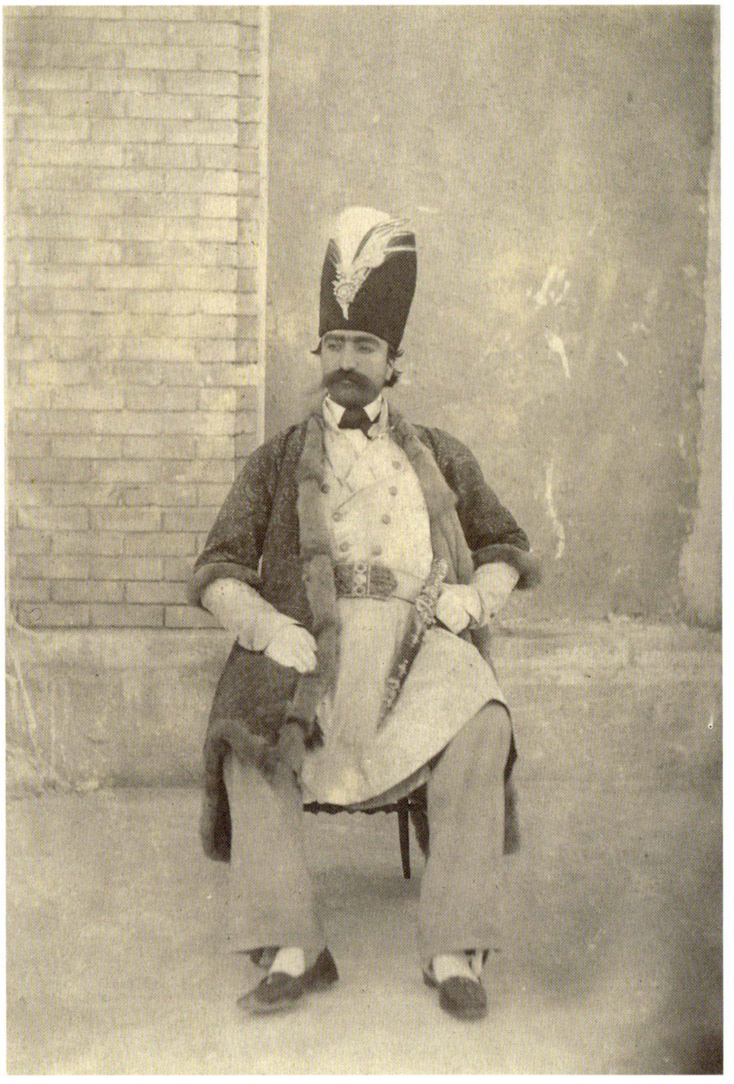

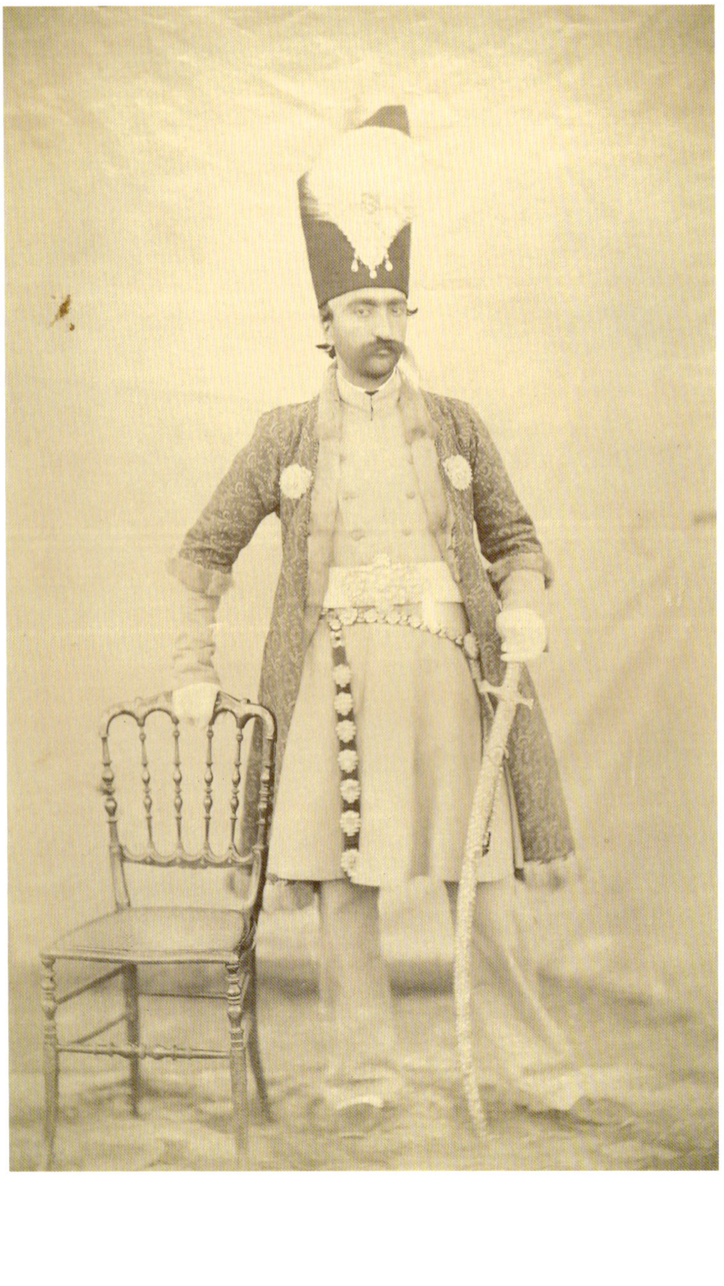

PLATES 12–13 (RIGHT TO LEFT)

POSSIBLY **Luigi Pesce**
Nasir al-Din Shah, **c. 1855–58**

Nasir al-Din Shah, **c. 1852–55**

Shortly after its invention, photography came to Iran through a pair of cameras gifted by European diplomats to the Qajar court sometime between 1839 and 1842. The crown prince and later shah, Nasir al-Din, developed a passion for the new medium. In addition to practicing photography himself and encouraging the training of local photographers, the young shah invited foreigners to take his portrait, which resulted in these two early images, one of them possibly taken by the Italian Colonel Luigi Pesce.

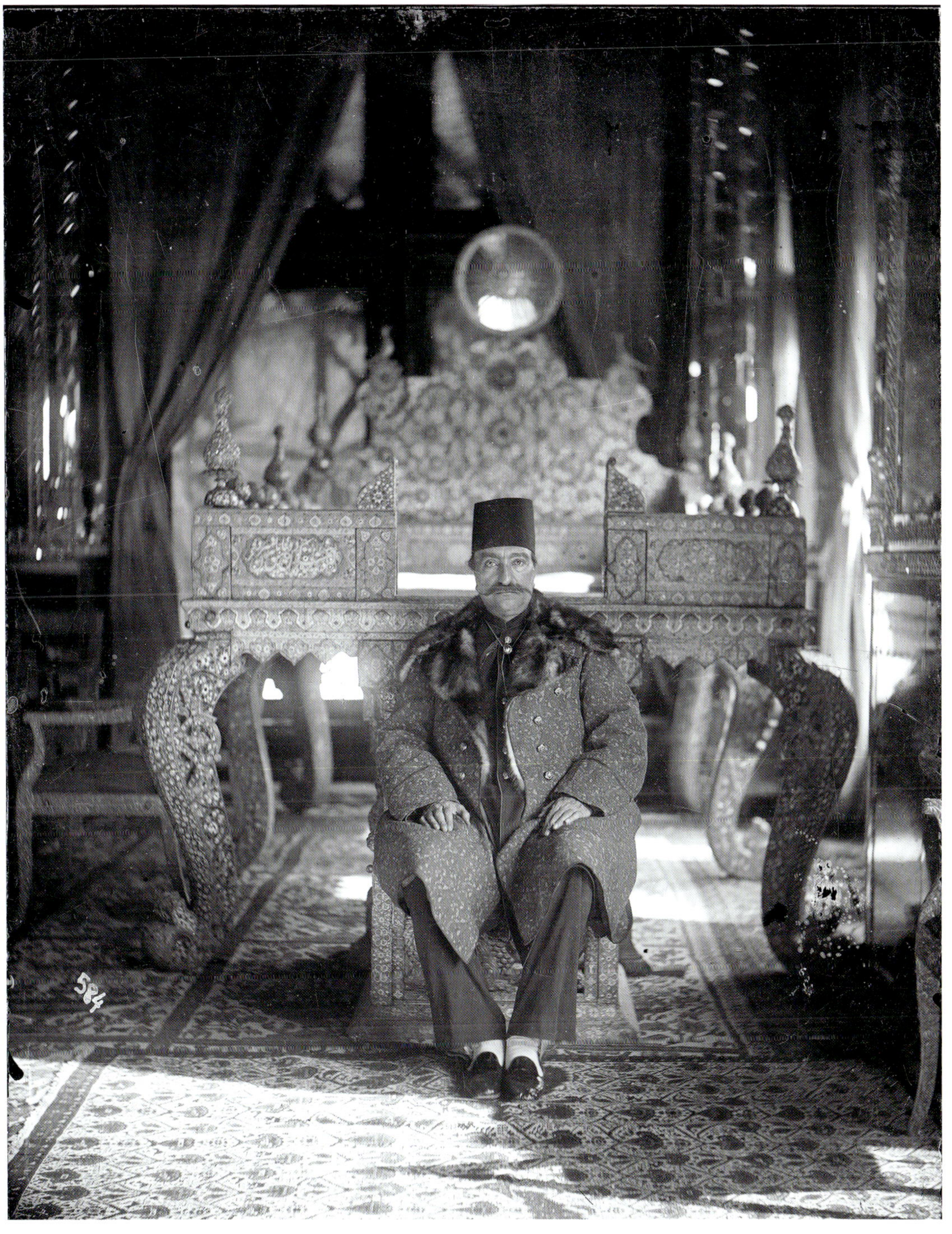

PLATE 14

Antoin Sevruguin
***Nasir al-Din Shah Sitting on the Lower Step of Takht-i Tavus or the Peacock Throne,* late 19th century**

In the nineteenth century, increased contact with Europe and shifting global markets led to an influx of Western technologies, styles, and ideas into Iran. This portrait of Nasir al-Din by Antoin Sevruguin captures the period's blend of old and new. Recorded in the then-novel medium of photography rather than in a traditional portrait painting, the shah sits in a Western-style coat on the lower step of Takht-i Tavus, or the Peacock Throne, Iran's historic seat of power under the Qajars.

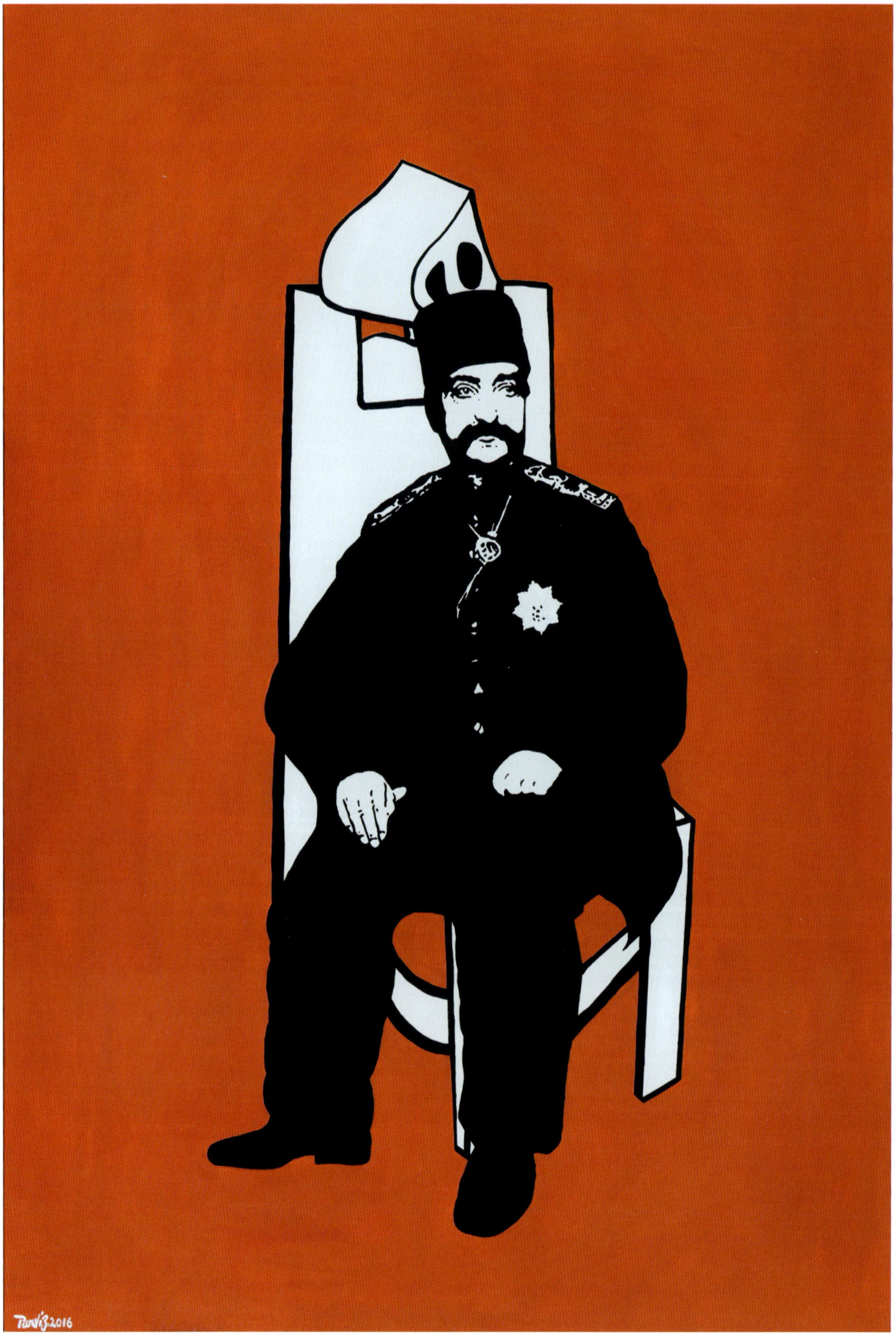

PLATE 15

Parviz Tanavoli
***Nassereddin Shah*, 2016**
FROM THE SERIES **Universal Icons**

Pioneer of Iranian modern art Parviz Tanavoli explores celebrity in his recent body of work Universal Icons. For *Nassereddin Shah*, Tanavoli repurposed a photograph of Nasir al-Din from 1889 and translated it into the flat graphic style characteristic of the Pop art aesthetic. In a further update to the past, Tanavoli seats the shah on a chair that features the artist's own seminal sculpture, *Heech*—Persian for "nothing," which perhaps serves here as a commentary on the value of celebrity icons.

Iran is amassed with layers and layers of thoughts and imageries. How could one be involved with one layer and ignore the rest?

Parviz Tanavoli

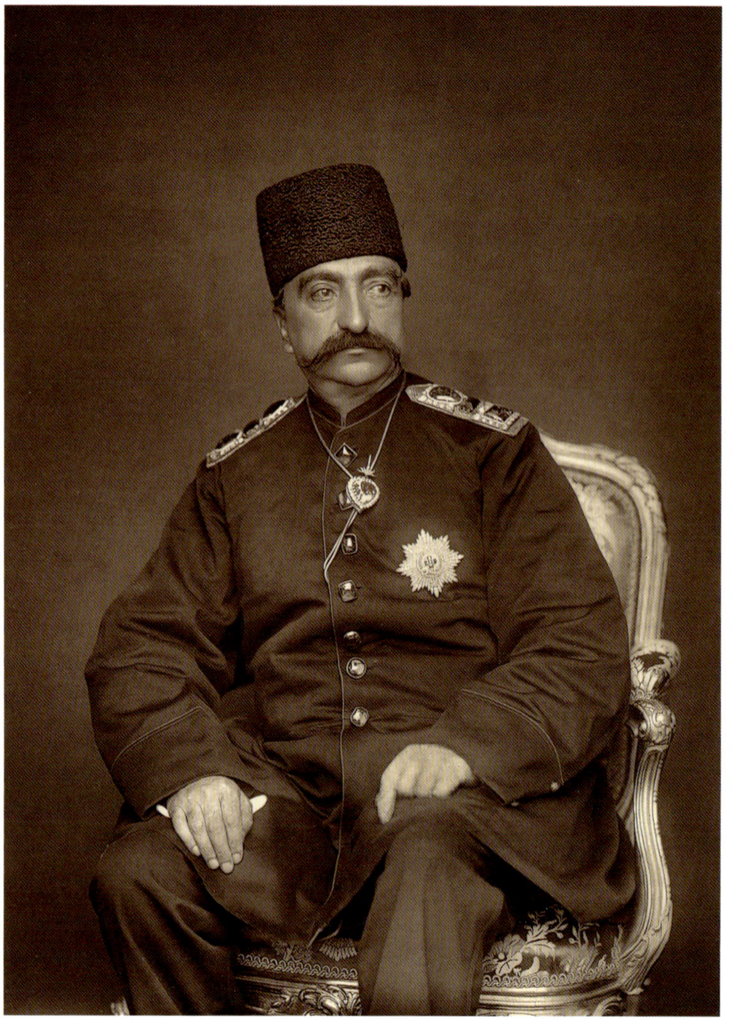

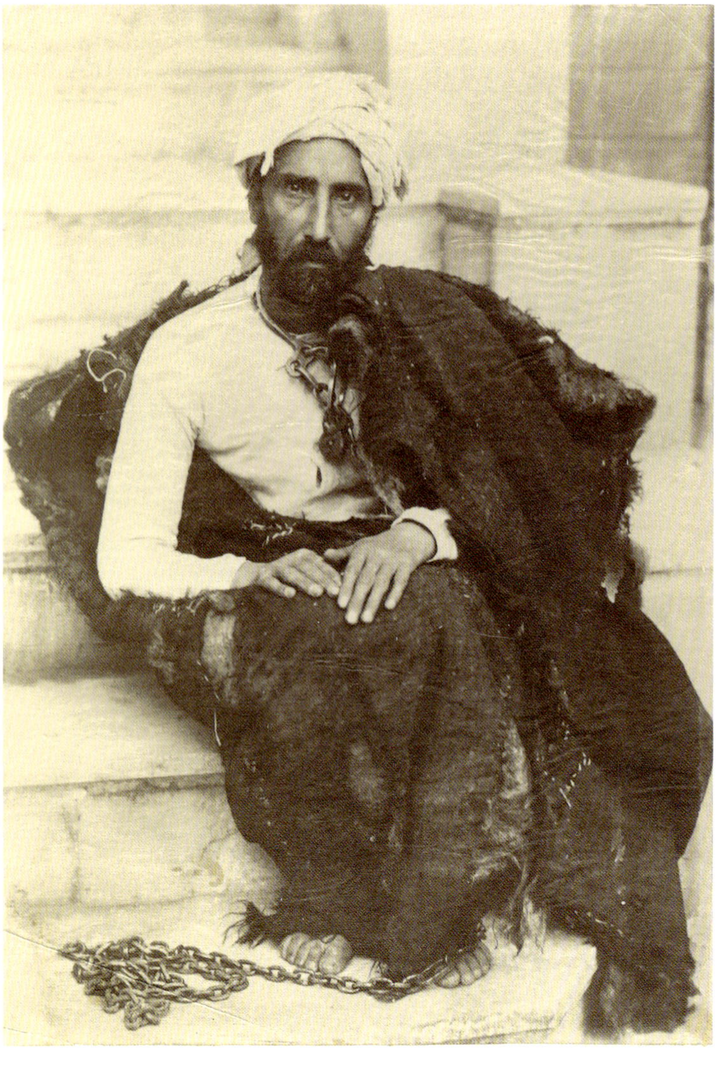

PLATES 16–17 (RIGHT TO LEFT)

Herbert Rose Barraud
***Portrait of Nasir al-Din Shah Wearing Formal Attire*, 1889**

Antoin Sevruguin
***Mirza Riza Kirmani, Nasir al-Din Shah's Assassin*, 1896**

On his third and final trip to Europe, Nasir al-Din Shah sat for this portrait by British photographer Herbert Rose Barraud. Not long after Nasir al-Din's return to Iran, economic and political turbulence encouraged secular and religious factions to unite against him and ultimately spawned a plot to end his life. While visiting a shrine in the spring of 1896, the shah was shot and killed by a discontented merchant, Mirza Riza Kirmani, shown here shackled.

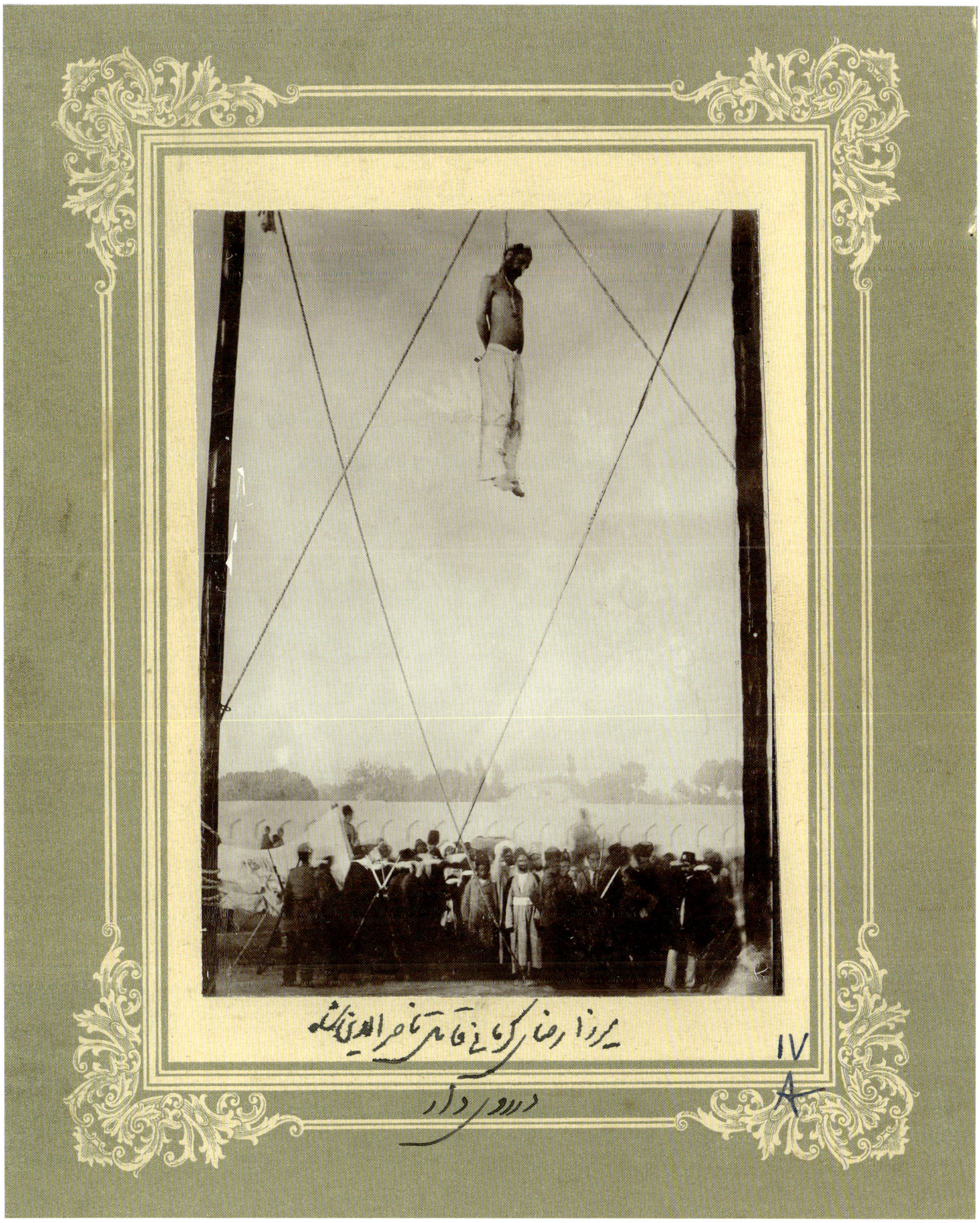

PLATE 18

Execution of Mirza Riza Kirmani, Nasir al-Din Shah's Assassin, 1896

Shortly after his assassination of Nasir al-Din Shah, the bankrupt merchant Mirza Riza Kirmani was hanged. However, the societal dissatisfaction that precipitated the shah's murder did not diminish with either death, and instead was fueled by the ineptitude and corruption of the shah's successors. Within a decade, this discontent bubbled forth into a constitutional revolution, and by 1925 the greatly weakened Qajar dynasty came to an end.

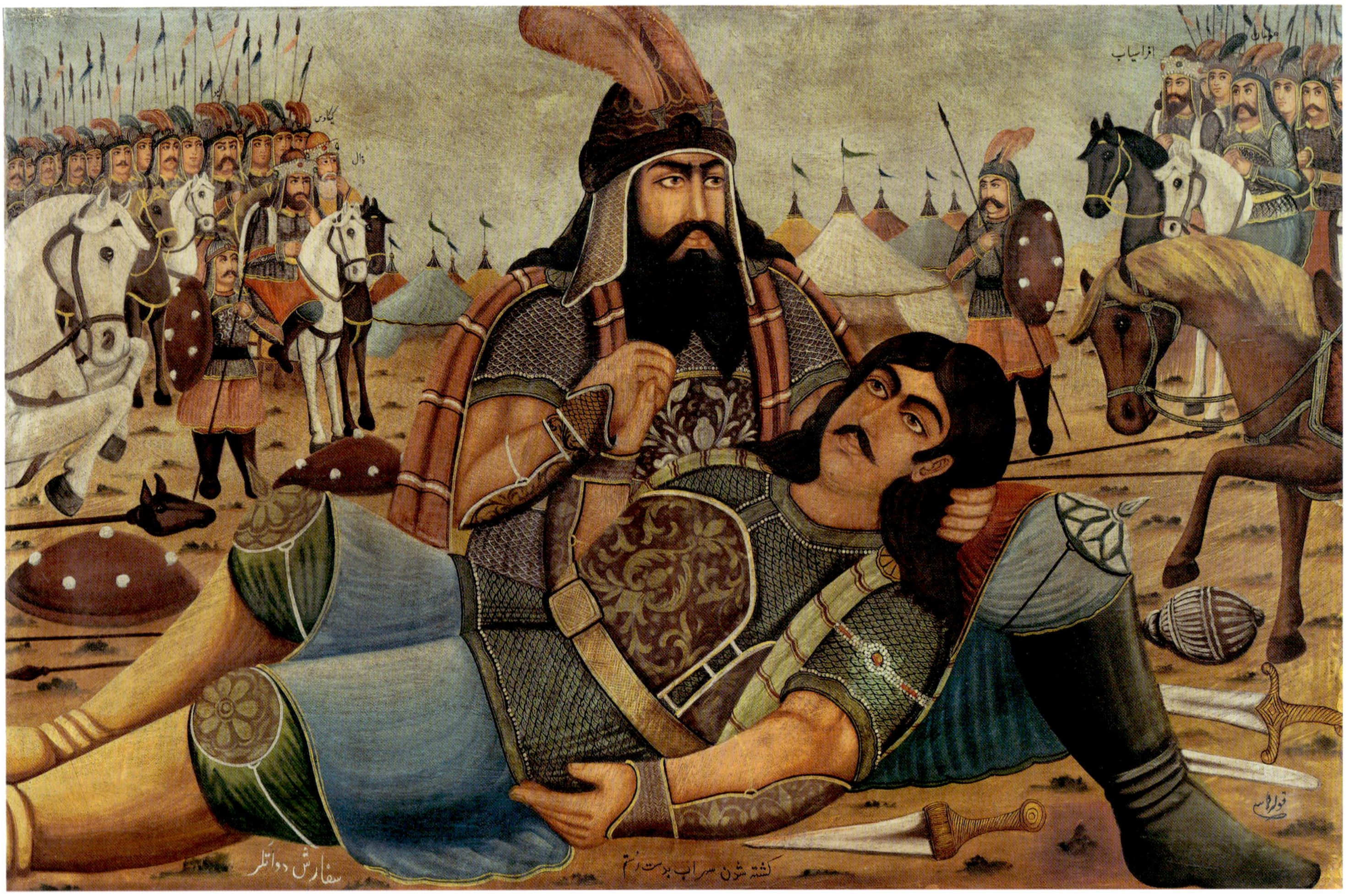

PLATE 19

PROBABLY **Hussein Qular Aqasi**
***Rustam with Suhrab*, mid-20th century**

One of the most tragic episodes of the *Shahnama* is that of Rustam mistakenly slaying his son Suhrab, as shown in this painting. Rustam notices too late the amulet that he had gifted the boy's mother affixed to Suhrab's arm, and thus realizes he has killed his son. Visualized through large-scale paintings, the story's imagery is comparable to representations of Imam Husain cradling his dying son, Ali Akbar, martyred at Karbala, thereby bridging the divide between religious ritual and secular art.

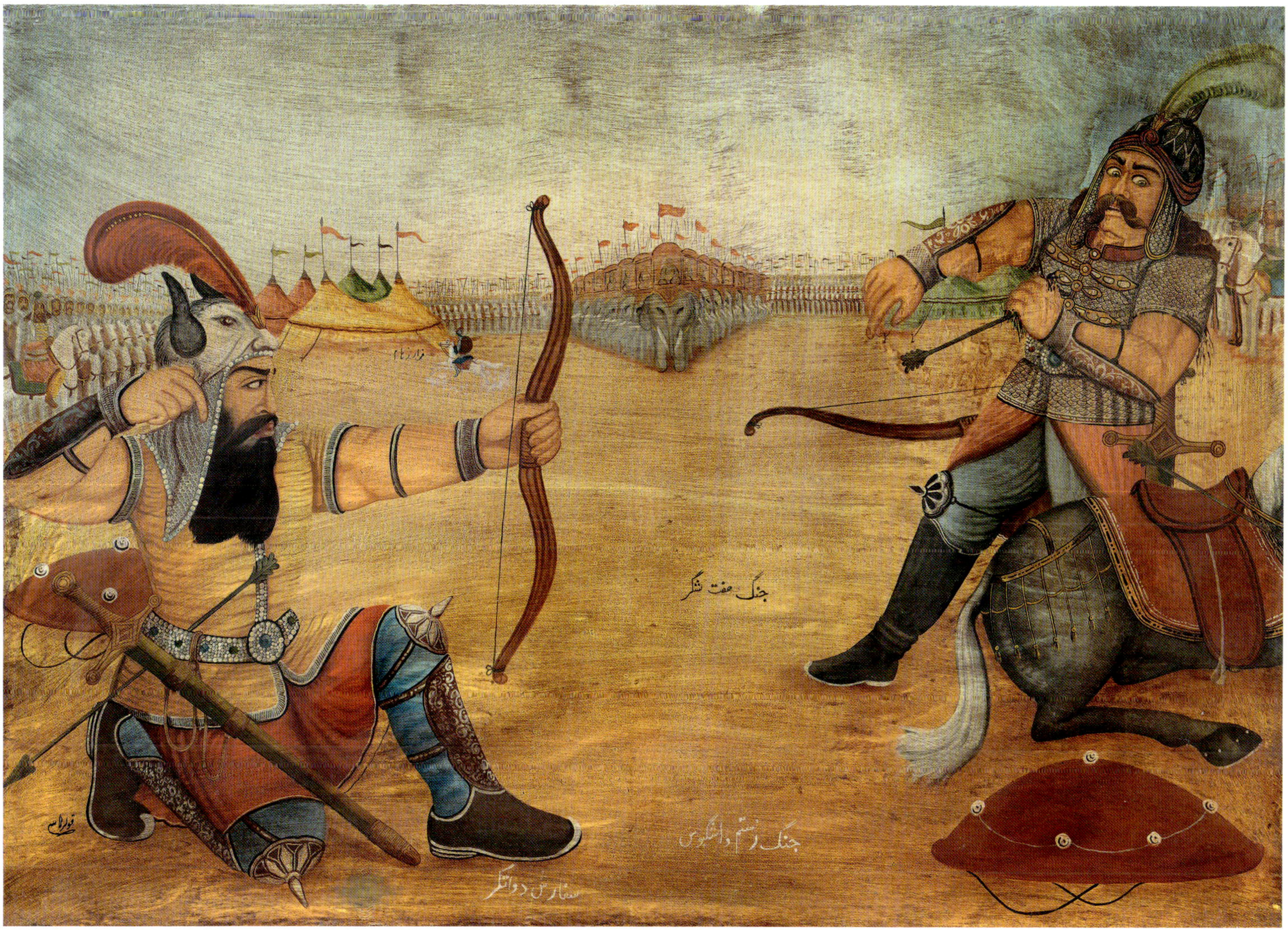

PLATE 20

PROBABLY **Hussein Qular Aqasi**
***Rustam Battling Ashkbus*, mid-20th century**

So-called coffeehouse or *parda* paintings served as one of the first forms of public art in Iran and brought pictorial narrative outside the royal courts and into the general public eye. The paintings were transported by itinerant storytellers or hung in public spaces, such as coffeehouses. Inspiration for this new type of art sprang from traditional sources, such as religious stories and the national epic, the *Shahnama*. Depicting a scene from the epic poem, this work illustrates the battle between the Iranian hero Rustam and his Turanian counterpart, Ashkbus.

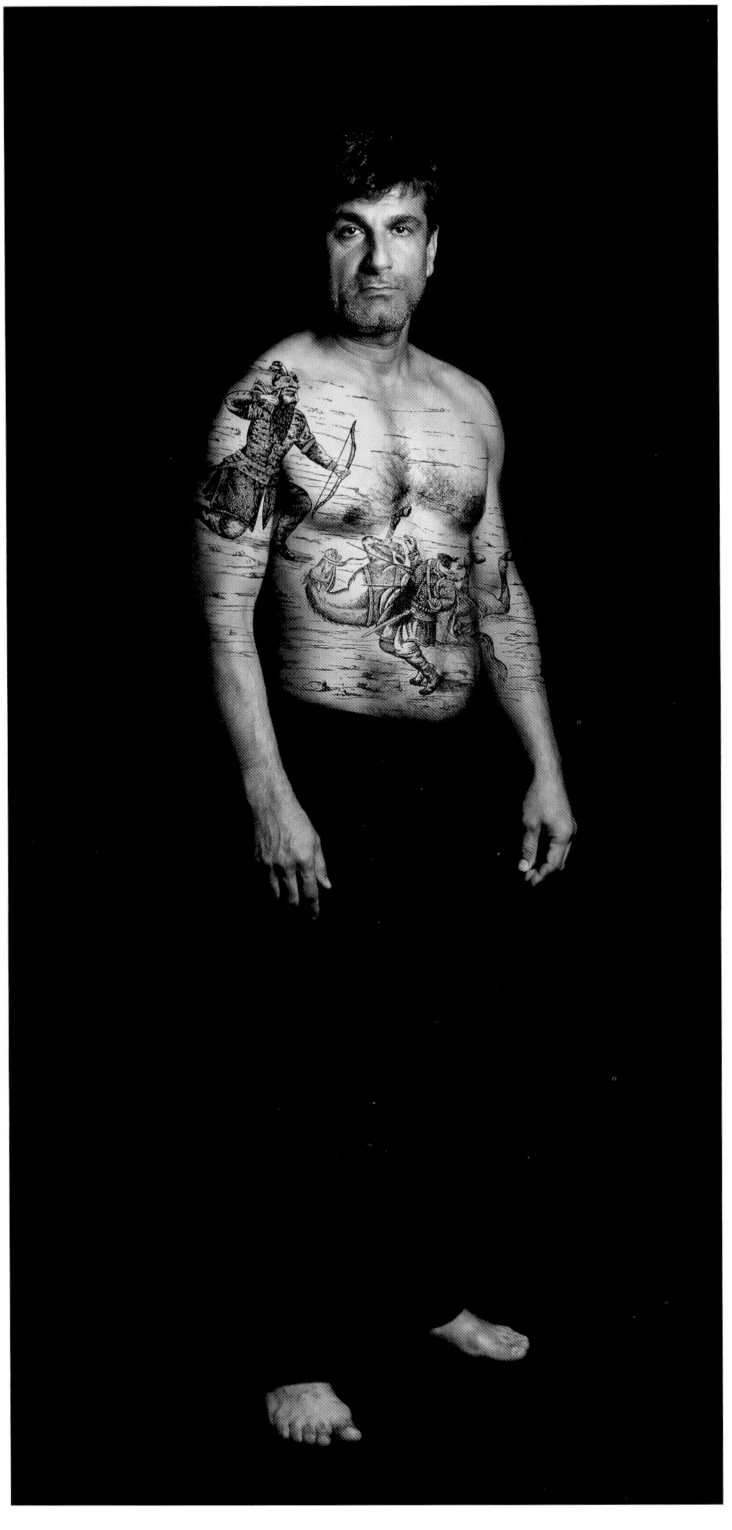

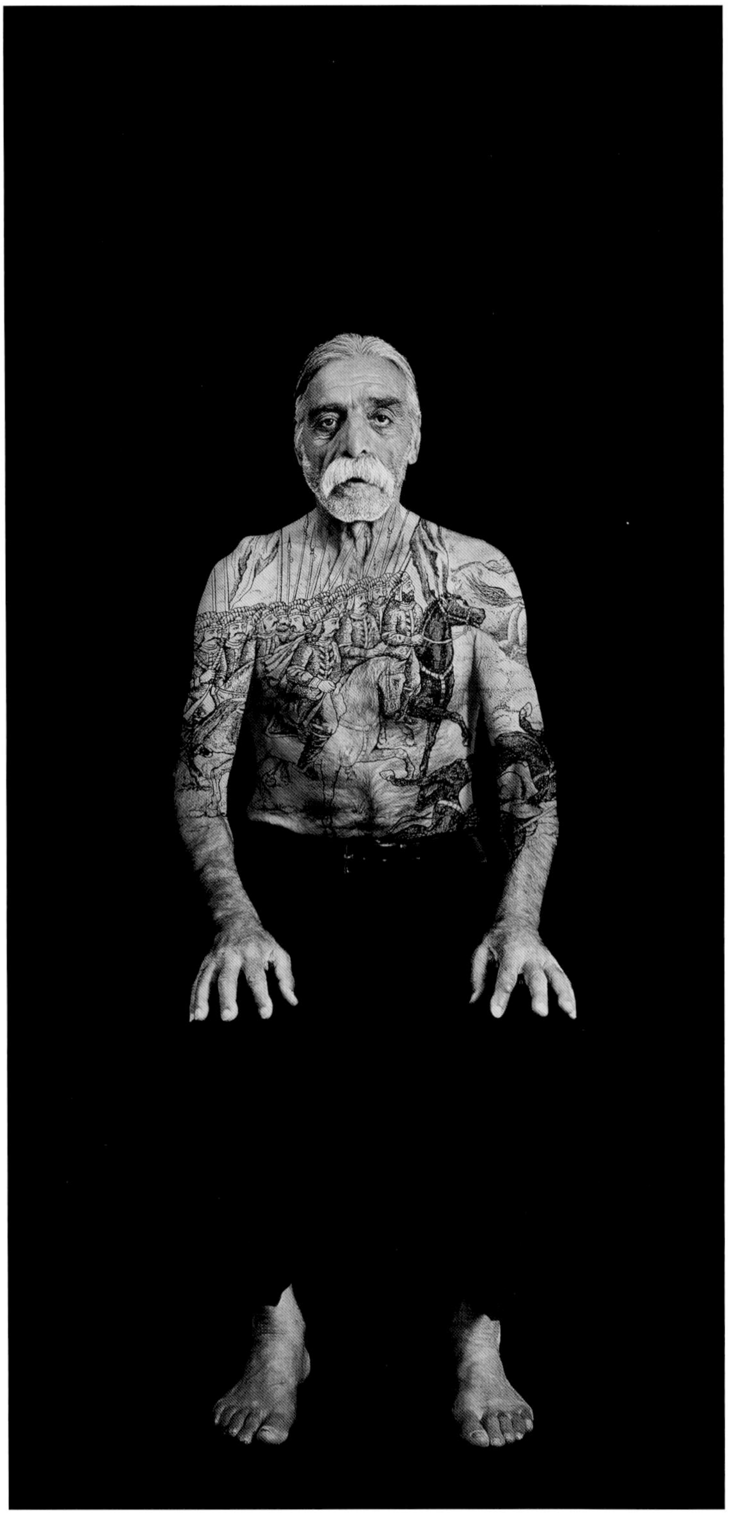

PLATES 21A–B (RIGHT TO LEFT)

Shirin Neshat
***Bahram* (Villains), 2012**
***Amir* (Villains), 2012**
FROM THE SERIES **The Book of Kings**

Shirin Neshat is the best-known artist of the Iranian diaspora. In her series The Book of Kings, she brings forward to the present the inherent nationalism of the *Shahnama*, the Iranian national epic, using portraits of friends and acquaintances with hands crossed diagonally over their hearts to depict patriots. She also created a smaller group of villains, as seen here, represented by full-length male portraits with tattoo-like battle scenes from the *Shahnama* covering their bare upper torsos, for which Neshat relied on her copy of an early-twentieth-century lithograph edition of the *Shahnama*.

My art has always been about bridging my own personal existential issues together with the larger sociopolitical and historical realities of the world I inhabit.

Shirin Neshat

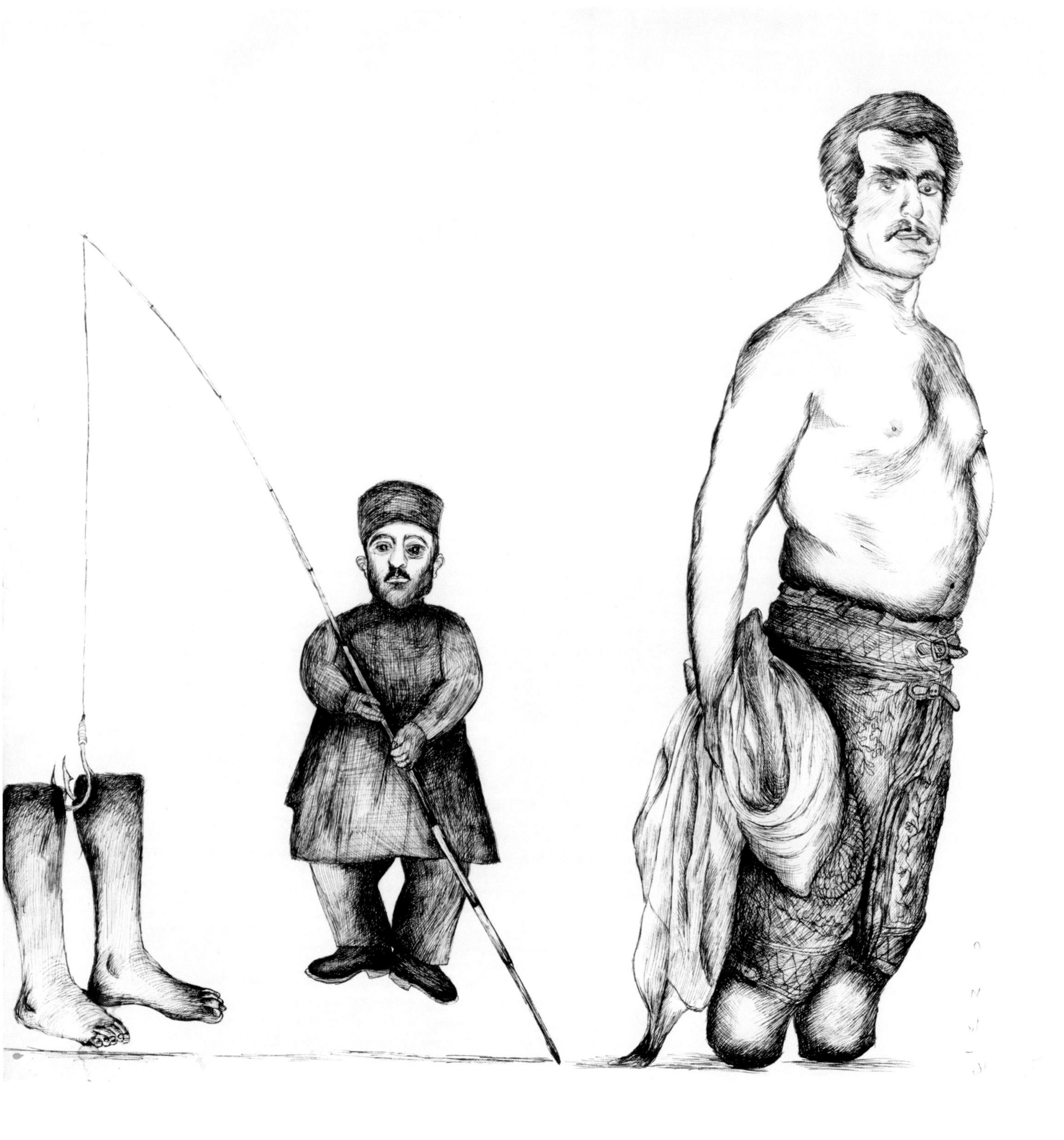

PLATE 22

Ardeshir Mohassess
***Untitled*, 1972**

Ardeshir Mohassess's black-ink drawings are divisible into two types: the first characterized by simple outlines drawn with a brisk detachment, and the second by intricately detailed and heavily shaded rendering, as in this work. Its jolting subject matter is characteristic of the artist's interest in the macabre: a dwarf clothed in Qajar costume catches a pair of legs with his fishing pole; the legs belong to a bare-chested figure clothed in the type of short pants worn by members of the *zurkhana* (the traditional "house of strength," somewhat akin to a gymnasium).

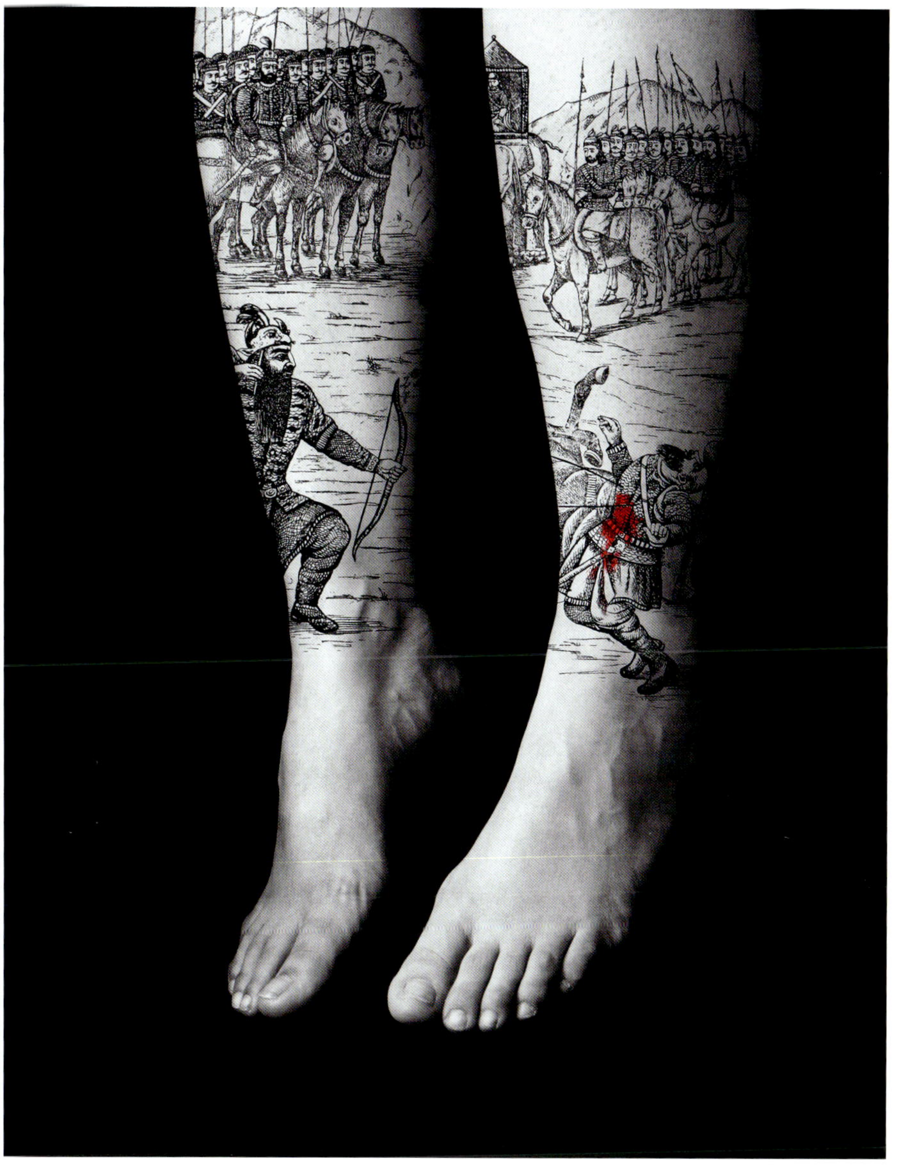

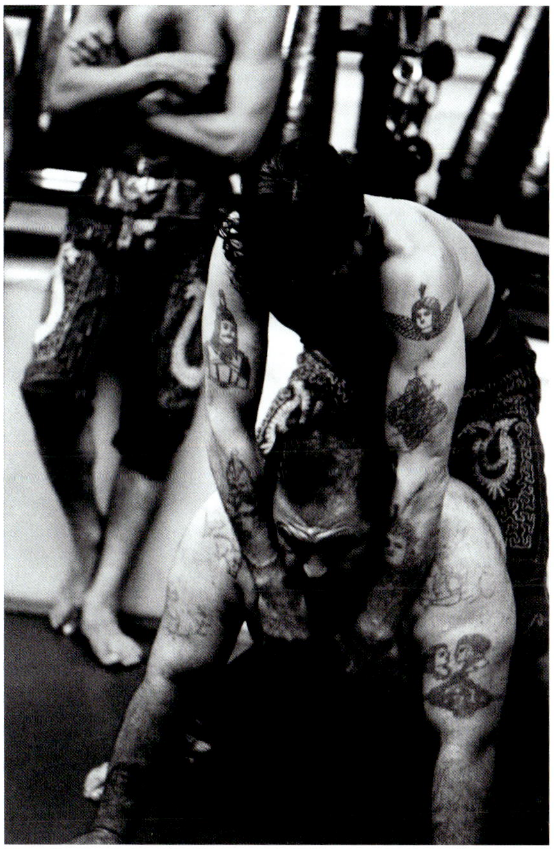

PLATES 23–24 (RIGHT TO LEFT)

Shirin Neshat
***Divine Rebellion*, 2012**
FROM THE SERIES The Book of Kings

Abbas
***Wrestlers at training*,**
***wearing old traditional trousers*, 1971**

Although the story line for the series The Book of Kings is derived from the *Shahnama*, which was written more than a millennium earlier, Shirin Neshat also was inspired by such contemporary events as the protests and demonstrations that defined the Green Movement (which followed the 2009 Iranian presidential election) and the Arab Spring (demonstrations that began in 2010). Here, dangling legs are covered with tattoo-like images of an ancient battle scene featuring the hero Rustam (ABOVE RIGHT). In the documentary photograph, the heavily tattooed wrestlers of the *zurkhana* suggest another possible source of inspiration for Neshat.

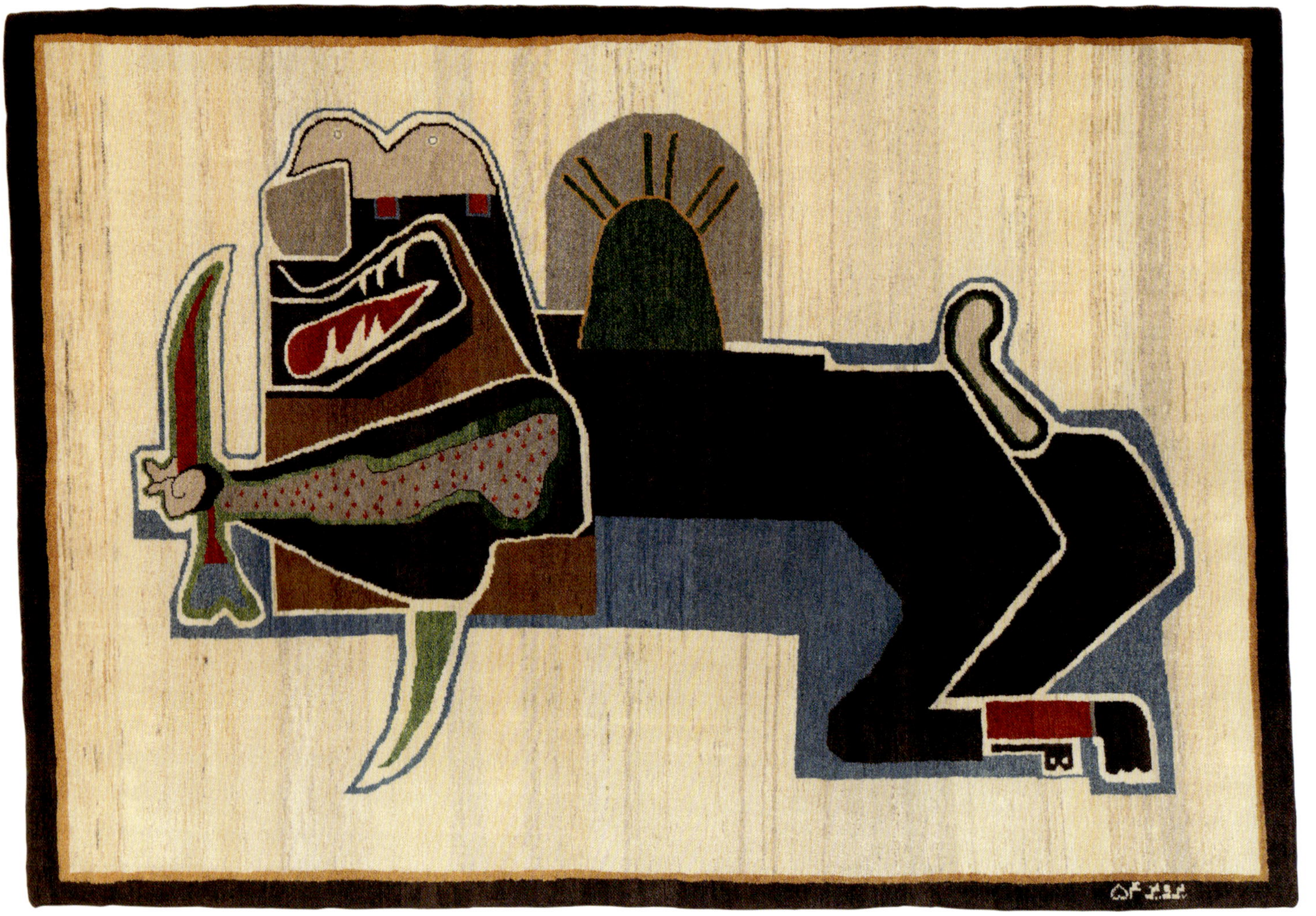

PLATE 25

Parviz Tanavoli
***Lion and Sword III*, 1976**

One of the founders of the Saqqakhana school, Parviz Tanavoli, in his "lion and sword" carpets, made use of a typically Persian medium while focusing on a traditional emblem of kingship and the Iranian state—a lion with the sun rising from its back. Given that the lion and sun with sword was the symbol of Pahlavi Iran, its use in the carpets, including with what appears to be an antique lock on the animal's hind leg, suggests a subtle form of political commentary; it also reinforces the inherent Shi'ism of the image.

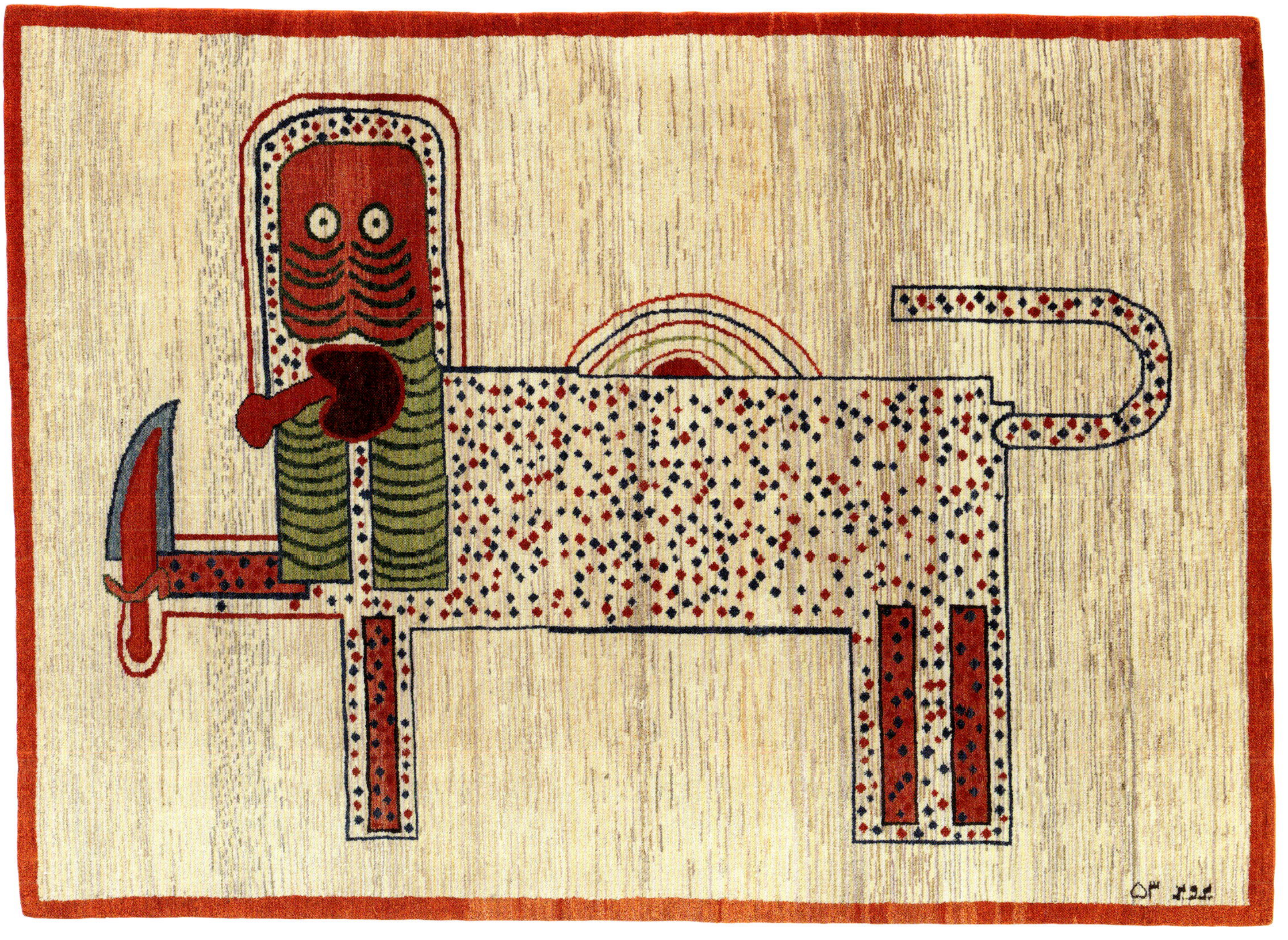

PLATE 26

Parviz Tanavoli
***Lion and Sword II*, 1975**

Parviz Tanavoli has a long-standing fascination with lions, which he has rendered in a variety of media and forms. He began collecting tribal rugs decorated with lions in the early 1970s, and these inspired some of his own work. Here, the combination of lion and sword, which became a state symbol of first the Qajar dynasty and subsequently Pahlavi Iran, also has strong Shi'ite connotations, as both lion and sword are associated with Imam Ali.

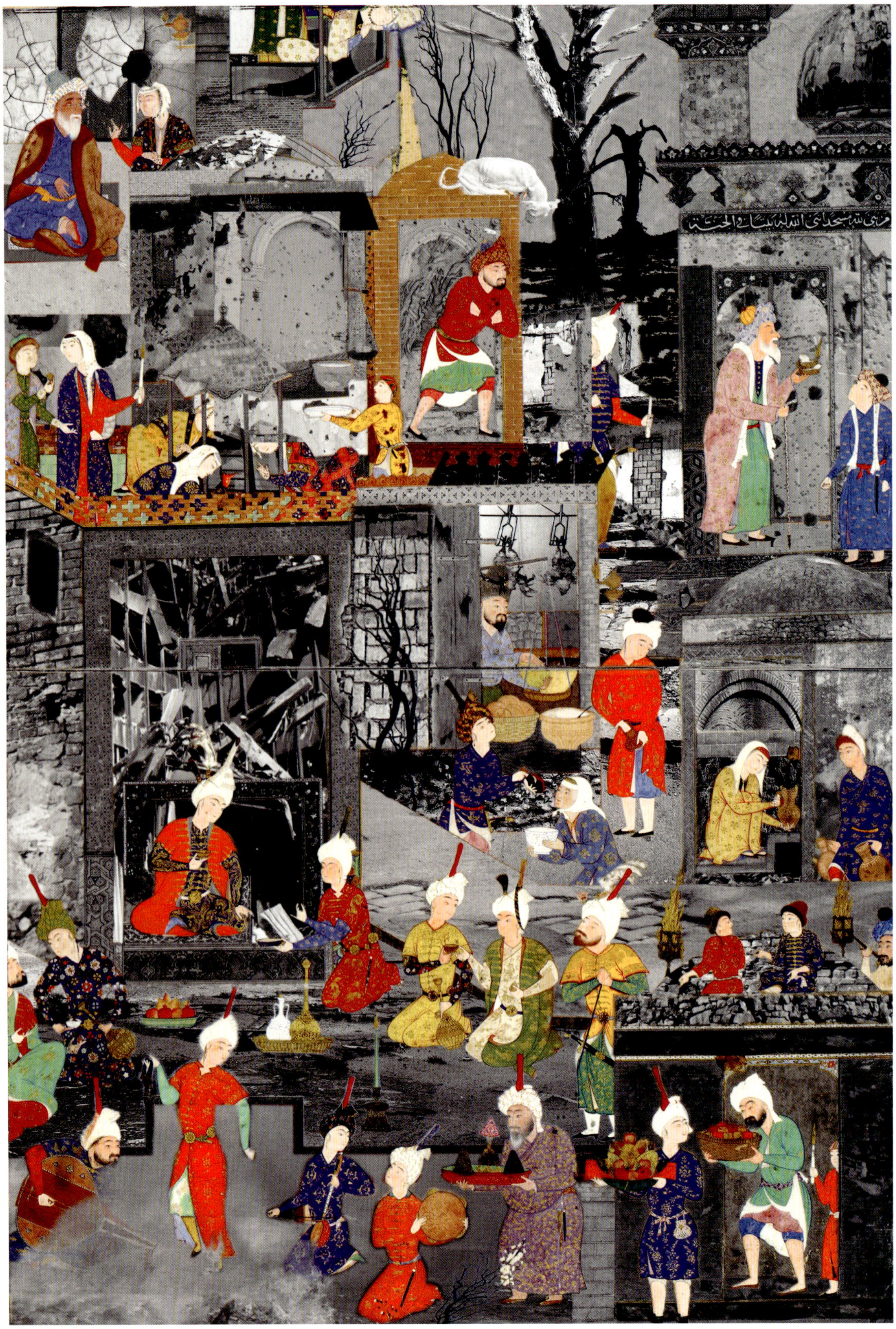

PLATE 27

Shoja Azari
***Idyllic Life*, 2012**

The starting point of Shoja Azari's powerful video is a Persian miniature painting of an unknown scene. Detached from a sixteenth-century manuscript, it depicts a palace in a bustling town. However, the pleasant setting is interrupted by the sound of a trapped bird as the video devolves into a series of sometimes violent vignettes of grainy images presenting scenes of fervor and conflict. Like the manuscript illustration, the exact story behind each video clip is ambiguous, and the viewer is left to intuit the narrative of Azari's dark and disquieting vision.

We humans construct our myths, heroes, and demons to infuse our lives with meaning in the face of the great absurdity of life and the terror of death. Such constructs provide us with a sense of worth, permanence, and immortality. Each generation takes the tread of the past, reimagines or builds upon it, and then passes it on to the next. Without such continuum, a people or culture will cease to exist.

Shoja Azari

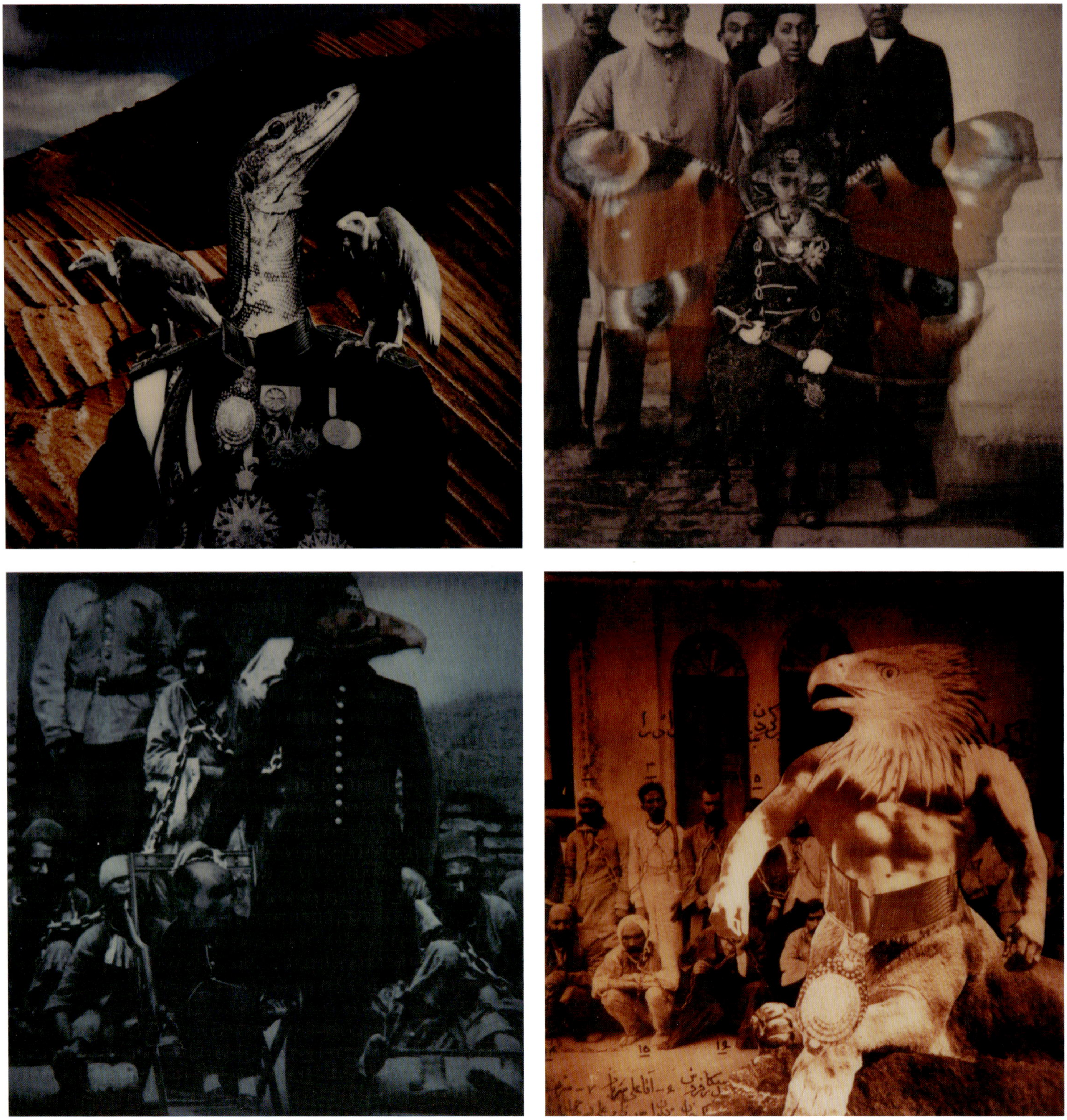

PLATES 28 A–D
(RIGHT TO LEFT, TOP TO BOTTOM)

Kaveh Golestan
***Untitled*, 1976**
FOUR POLAROIDS FROM THE SERIES Az Div o Dad

Kaveh Golestan's series Az Div o Dad (Of Demon and Beast) appropriates nineteenth- and early-twentieth-century photographs to produce fantastical pictures that reference both the late Qajar era of the early 1900s and the Pahlavi 1970s. These works, which represent the satirical manipulation of historical figures—most notably members of the Qajar royal family, including a young prince given butterfly wings (probably the son of Nasir al-Din Shah)—have prompted a new generation of artists to employ images of deposed kings as a means of questioning and critiquing their own present-day leaders.

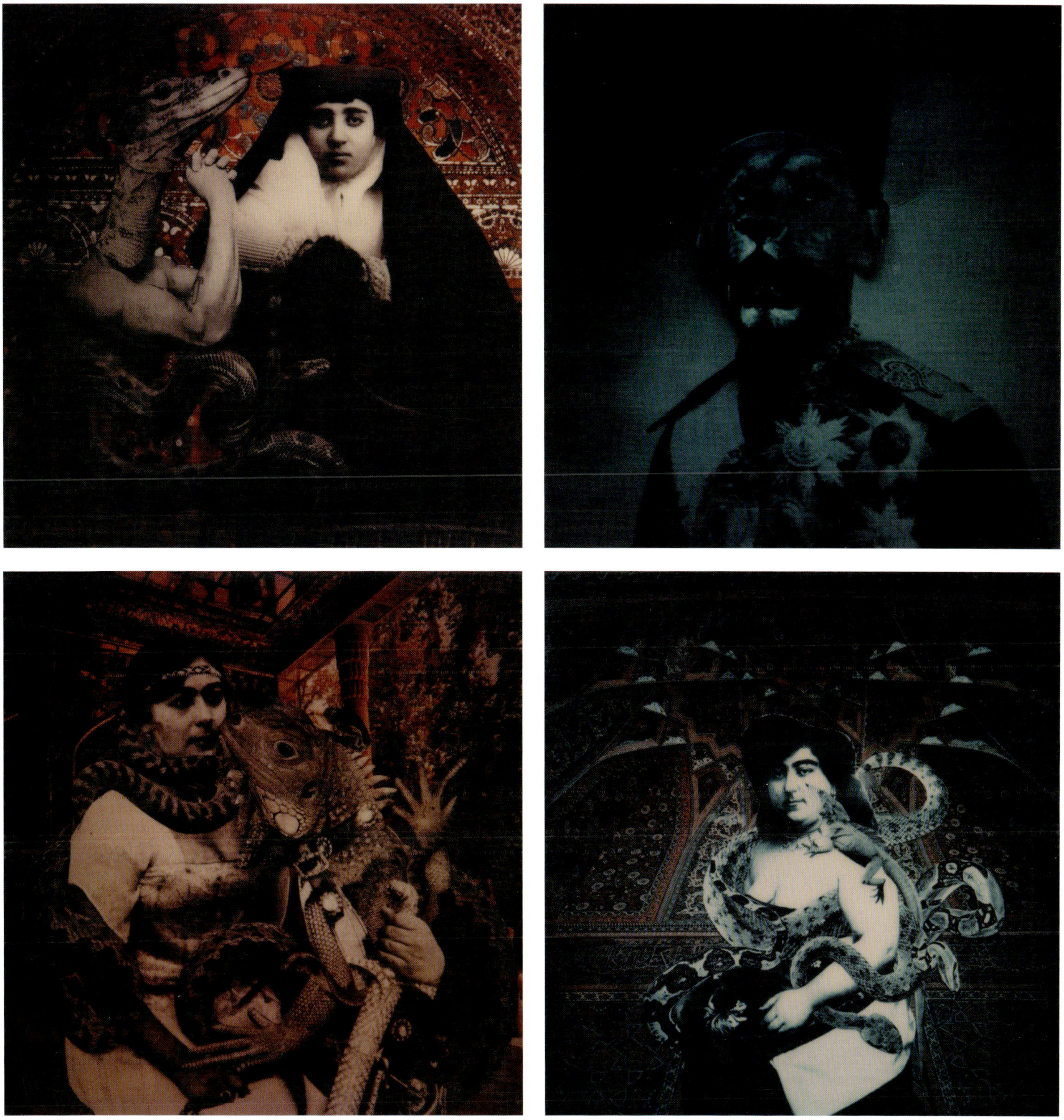

PLATES 28 E–H
(RIGHT TO LEFT, TOP TO BOTTOM)

Kaveh Golestan
***Untitled*, 1976**
FOUR POLAROIDS FROM THE SERIES Az Div o Dad

In 1976 photojournalist Kaveh Golestan departed from documentary-style photography to create a series of surrealistic collages composed of appropriated nineteenth- and early twentieth-century photographs shot on Polaroid film. Titled Az Div o Dad (Of Demon and Beast), it presents lizard and leonine heads replacing the faces of kings and princes, while women, including Nasir al-Din Shah's daughter Taj al-Sultana, are wrapped in or seduced by serpents and lizards. The bizarre and menacing world that Golestan creates can be interpreted as a reaction to political life in prerevolutionary Iran.

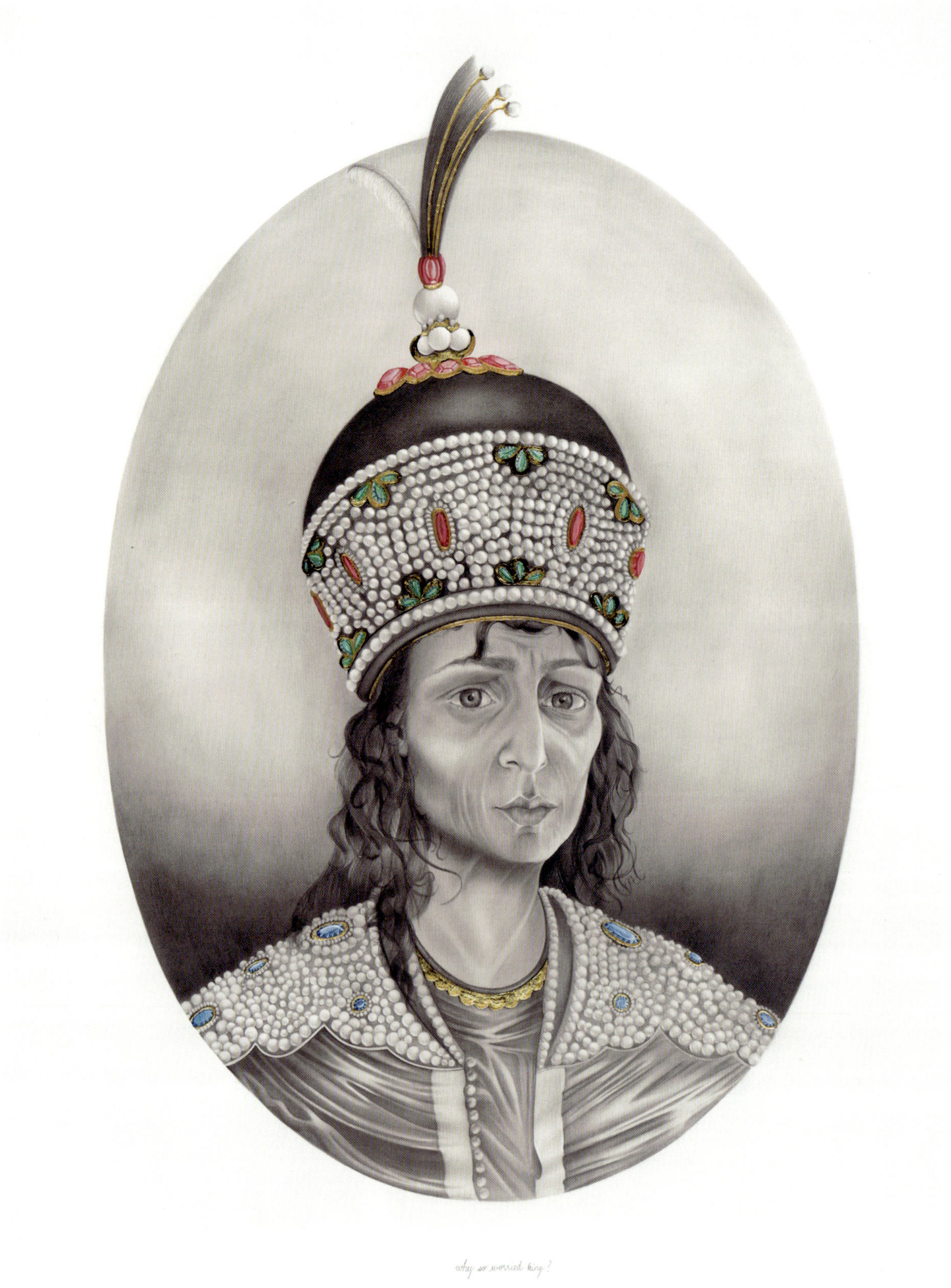

PLATE 29

Taravat Talepasand
***Why So Worried King?*, 2009**

This work belongs to a larger group in which Taravat Talepasand reimagines portraits of Qajar men and women as self-portraits; here, she transforms an image of the first Qajar king, Agha Muhammad Khan (r. 1789–97). A fierce military leader and brutal ruler, he was also noted for being beardless (caused by his castration as a teenager at the hands of an enemy leader), an affect Talepasand magnifies by adding long hair to the bald ruler. Agha Muhammad Khan's visible worry may be a prescient concern for the fate of Iran.

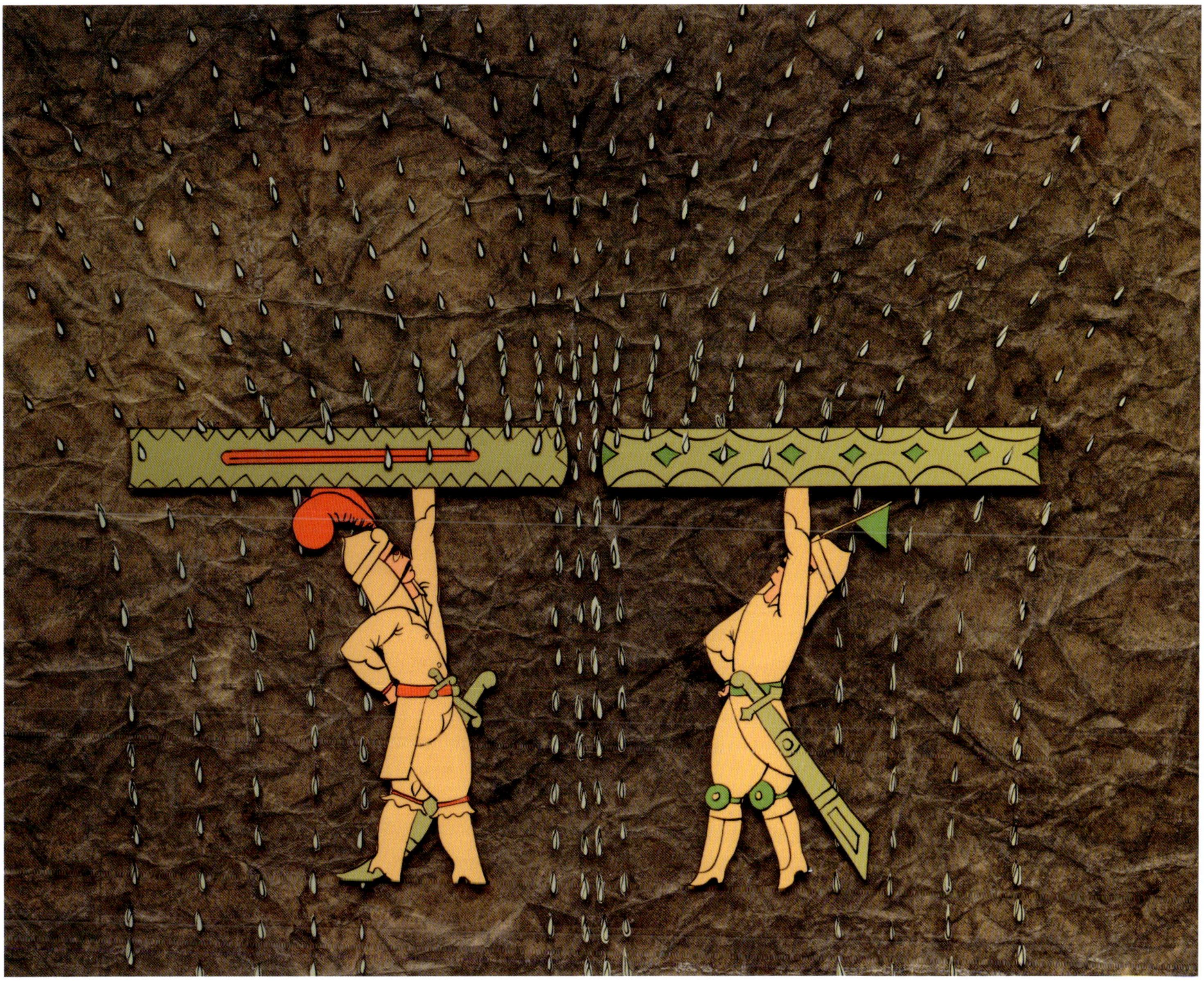

PLATE 30

Ali Akbar Sadeghi
Boasting XVIII, 1973

Painter and illustrator Ali Akbar Sadeghi, an artist of long-standing stature in Iran, is perhaps best known for his animations from the 1970s. The film *Boasting*, for which this animation cell was produced, reflects the chaotic state of Iran in the early 1970s. Here, the competing political factions of the day, in the guise of medieval warriors, come together in the end for a common cause. Sadeghi appears to have prophesied the times leading up to the 1979 Iranian Revolution, when various political parties united briefly to help depose the shah.

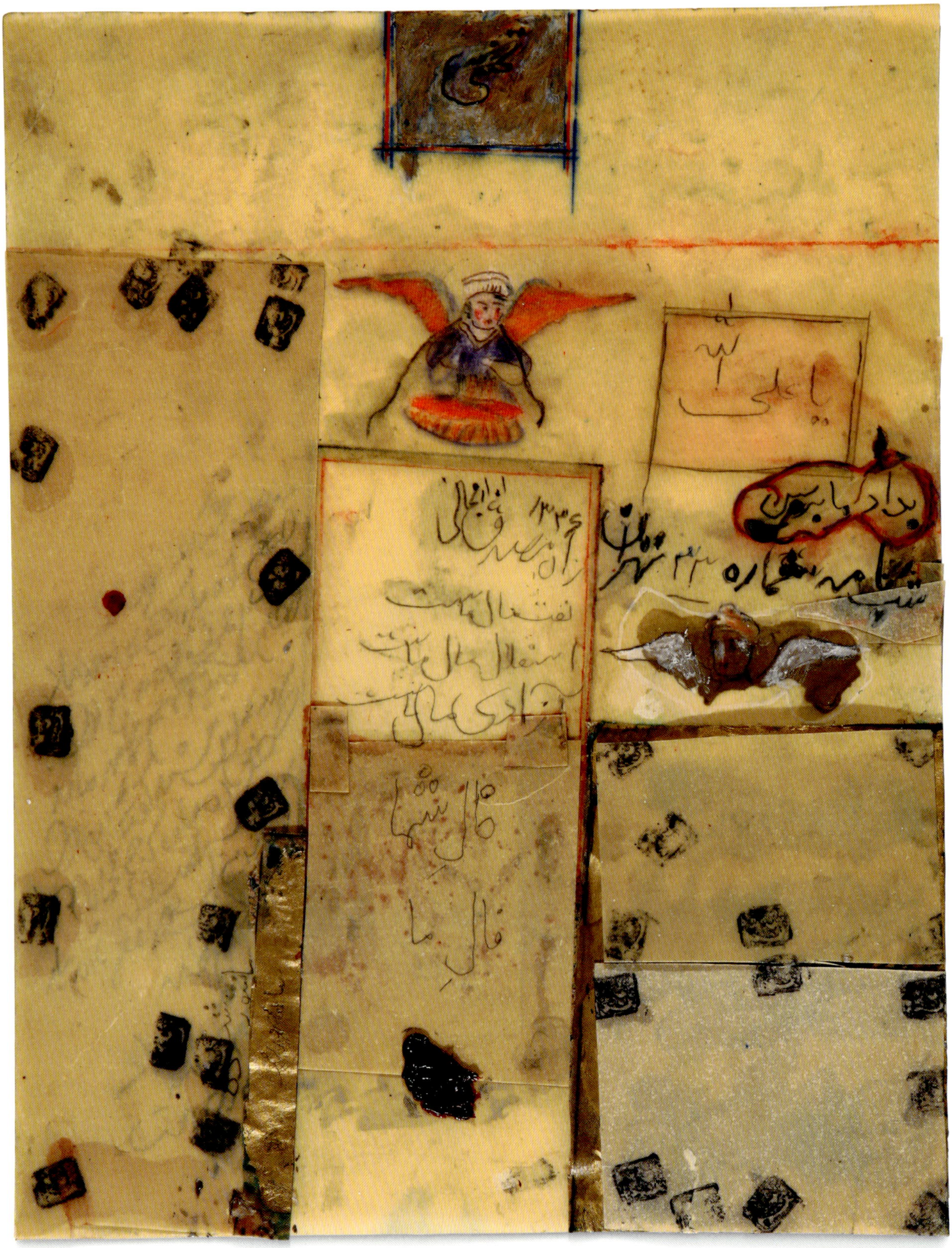

PLATE 31

Siah Armajani
***Night Letter #1*, 1957**

Before he left Iran in 1960, Siah Armajani, renowned in America for his monumental sculpture, produced a small body of works on paper and canvas, including *Night Letter #1*, which references a type of political leaflet distributed only under cover of night. The text includes slogans from the Mossadeq period (1951–53), an invocation to Imam Ali, and the name of famed Olympic wrestling gold medalist Takhti. The angelic imagery derives from popular culture. Combining politics, faith, and heroism, this work reflects the patriotism, idealism, and discontent of the young artist.

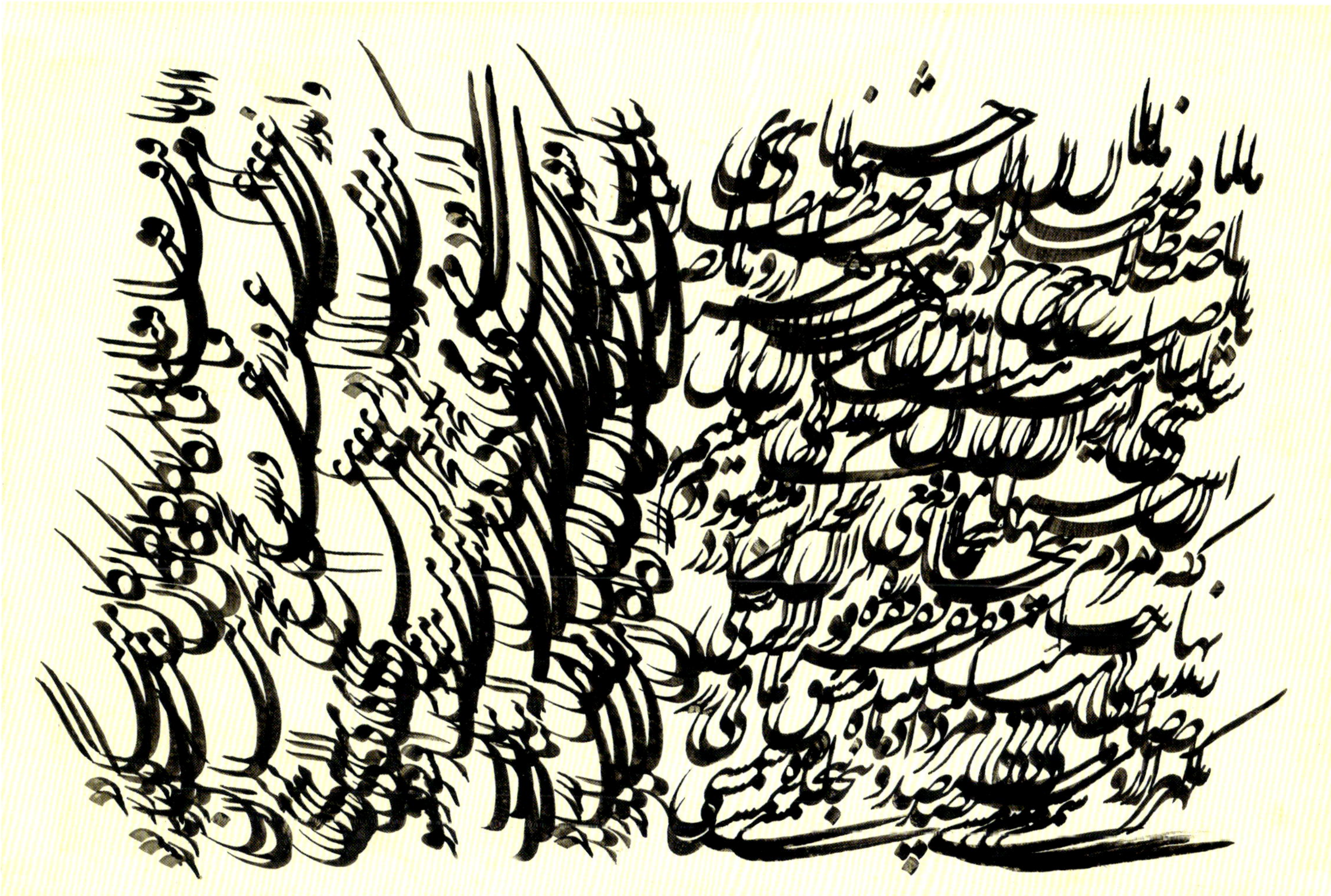

PLATE 32

Reza Mafi
Siyah mashq, 1971

Siyah mashq (literally "black writing") describes the practice sheet with which traditional Iranian calligraphers prepared before beginning a more highly finished piece. Here, the classically trained calligrapher Reza Mafi subverts the *siyah mashq* for political purposes. A Persian poem that customarily would be copied as an exercise but is rendered here with virtuoso skill occupies the left side of the page; on the right appear the artist's own words, in which he condemns the extravagance of the shah's 2,500th-anniversary celebrations of the monarchy while many Iranians were living in poverty.

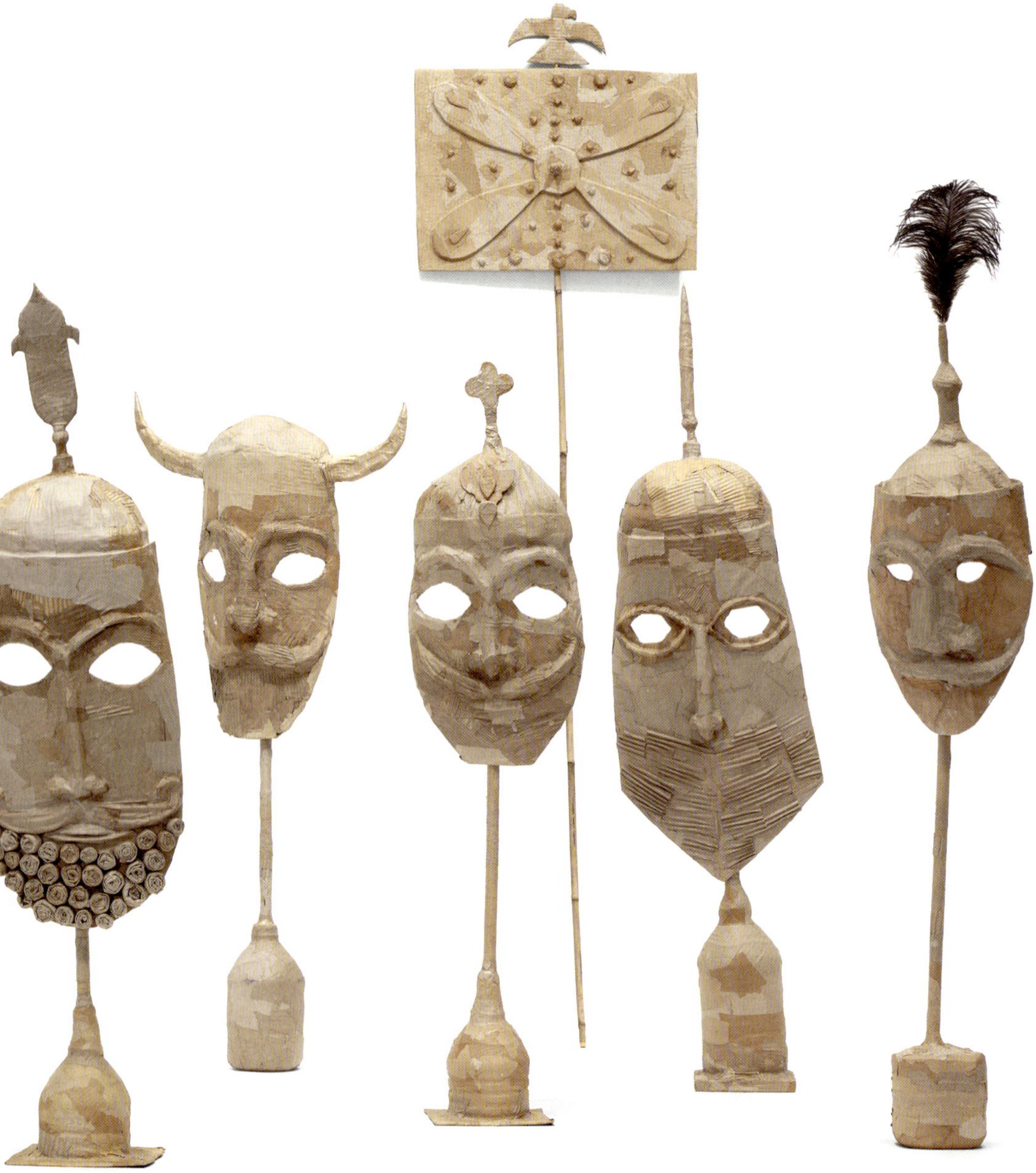

PLATE 33

Yasmin Sinai
***The Act of Gurdafarid, the Female Warrior*, 2015**

Yasmin Sinai here reinterprets the story of a great woman warrior in the *Shahnama*: Gurdafarid is the daughter of a petty ruler whose fortress guards the border between Iran and Turan. When her father's chief champion is captured by the invading Turanian army, Gurdafarid dons armor and rides out to challenge the enemy's leader. Sinai dramatically visualizes this story for a contemporary audience as a reminder of the significant roles women have played—past and present—in Iran. The two faces of Gurdafarid, the puppet head and the mounted warrior, are self-portraits of the artist.

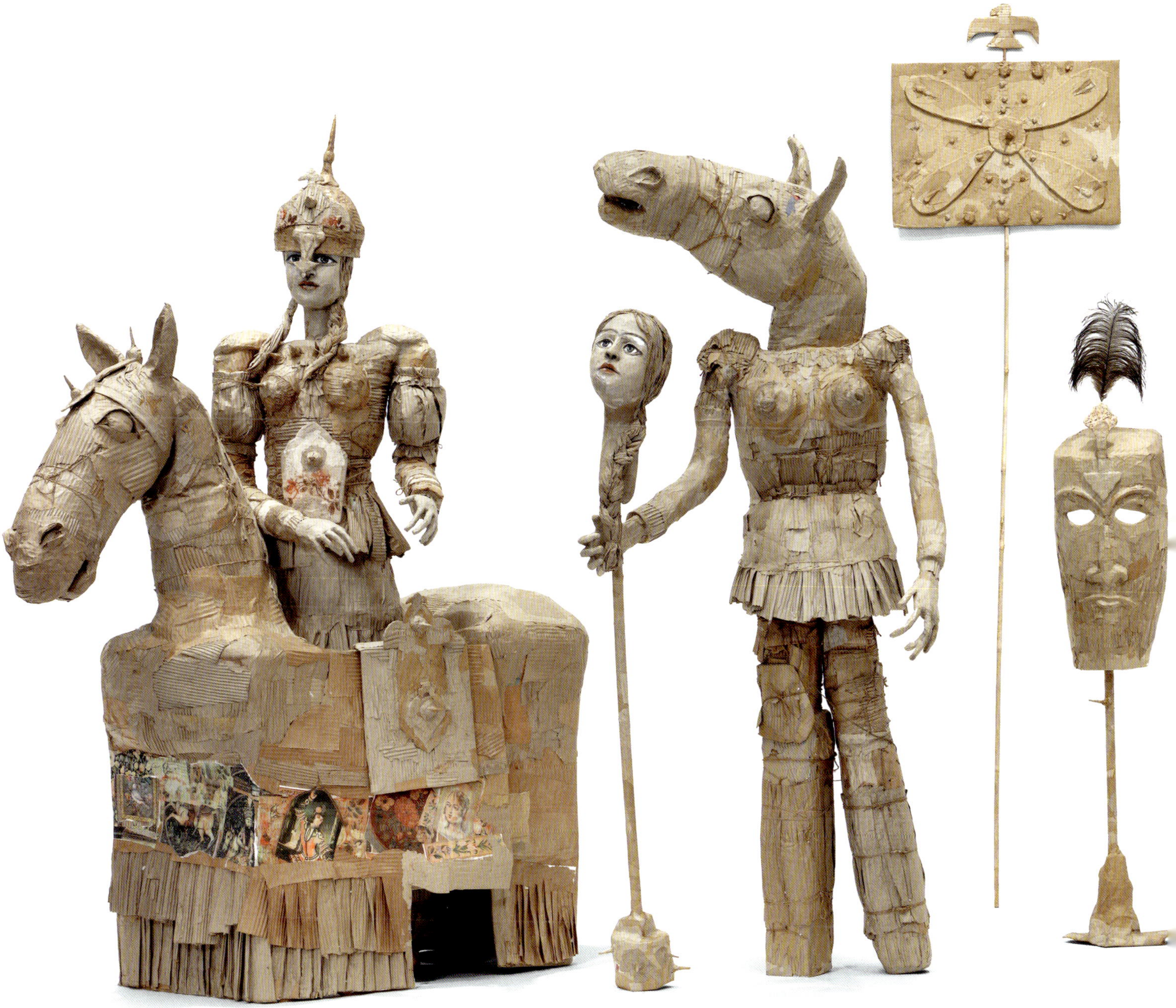

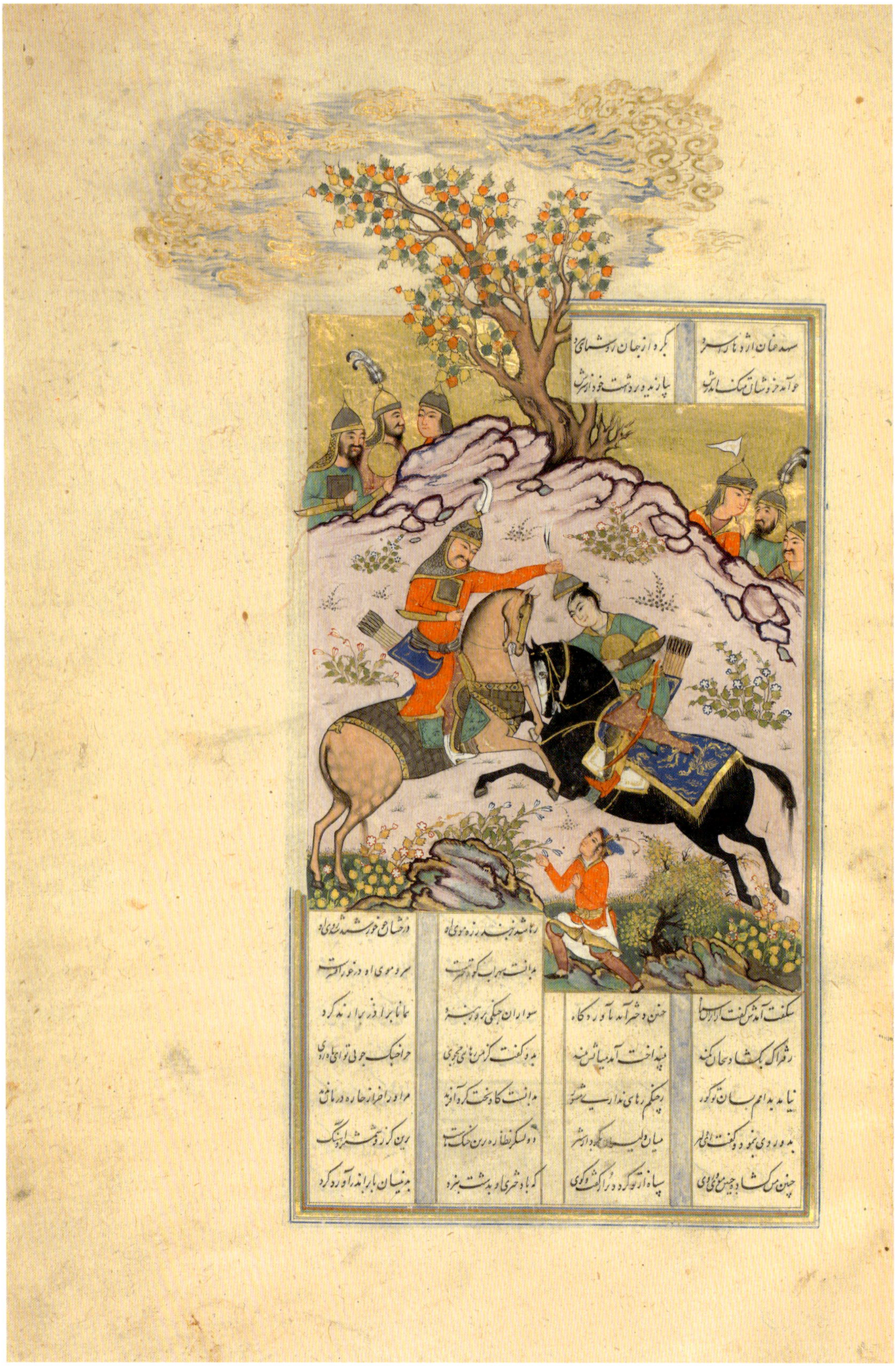

PLATE 34

***Suhrab Fights Gurdafarid*, AH 1014/1605–7**

FROM the *Shahnama* of Firdausi

This manuscript illustration depicts the moment when the identity of the heroine, Gurdafarid, who dressed as a man to protect her family's castle, is revealed. Her foe, Suhrab, removes her helmet and upon seeing her beauty, falls in love; Gurdafarid, in turn, utilizes this to defend her troops. The only female portrayed as a valiant protector of the Iranians in the *Shahnama*, she continues to represent the ideals of strength and wisdom.

I am Gurdafarid, the female
warrior among the kings!

My battlefield is called life!

My armor is my past made of
my scars, pain, and tears!

My sword is my love and
passion is my shield!

My horse is my freedom!

I ride today, free and wild
toward the future!

Yasmin Sinai

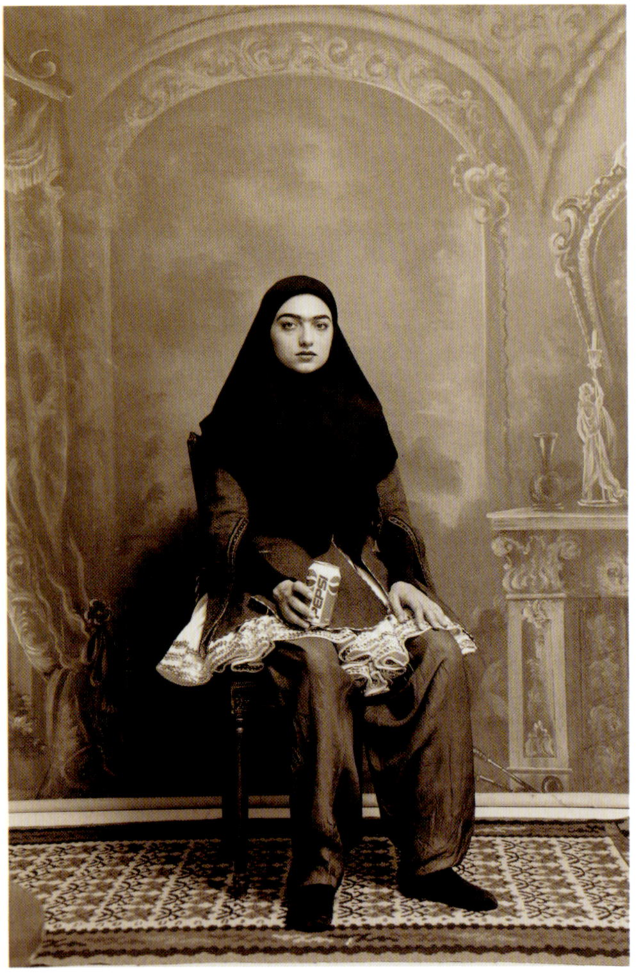

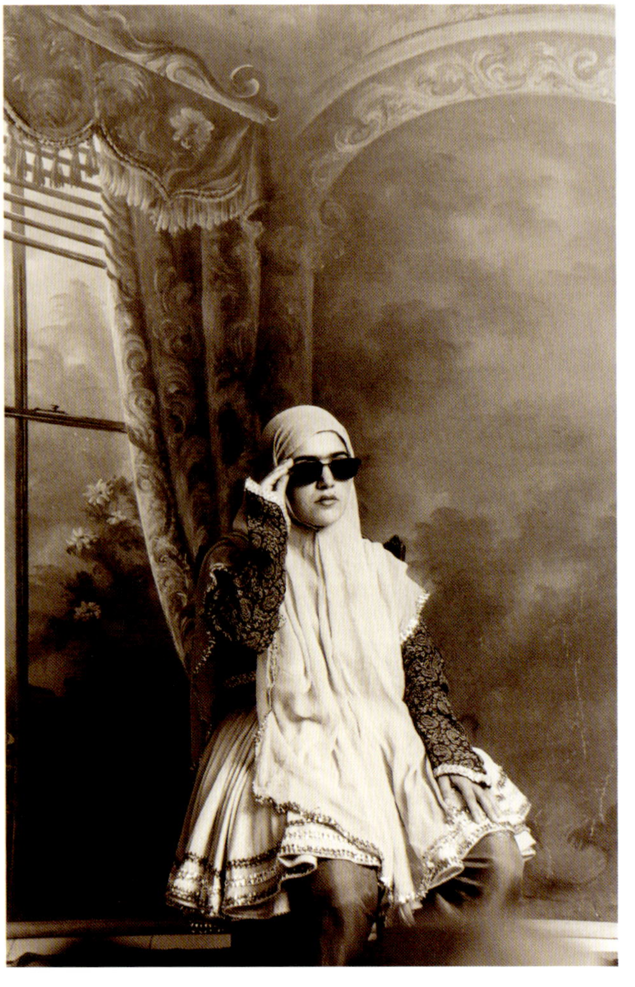

PLATES 35 A–D (RIGHT TO LEFT)

Shadi Ghadirian
***Untitled*, 1998**
FOUR PHOTOGRAPHS FROM THE SERIES Qajar

Inspired by the studio portraiture of the late nineteenth century, Shadi Ghadirian re-created the earlier settings in a set of thirty-three photographs known as the Qajar series. She employed painted backdrops and dressed her models in vintage clothes to emulate the fashion of the day—headscarves and short skirts worn over baggy trousers, and thick, black eyebrows. She added modern-day elements, such as a pair of sunglasses, a Pepsi can, and a single-lens reflex camera to create ironic imagery that reflects the tension between tradition and modernity in Iranian society.

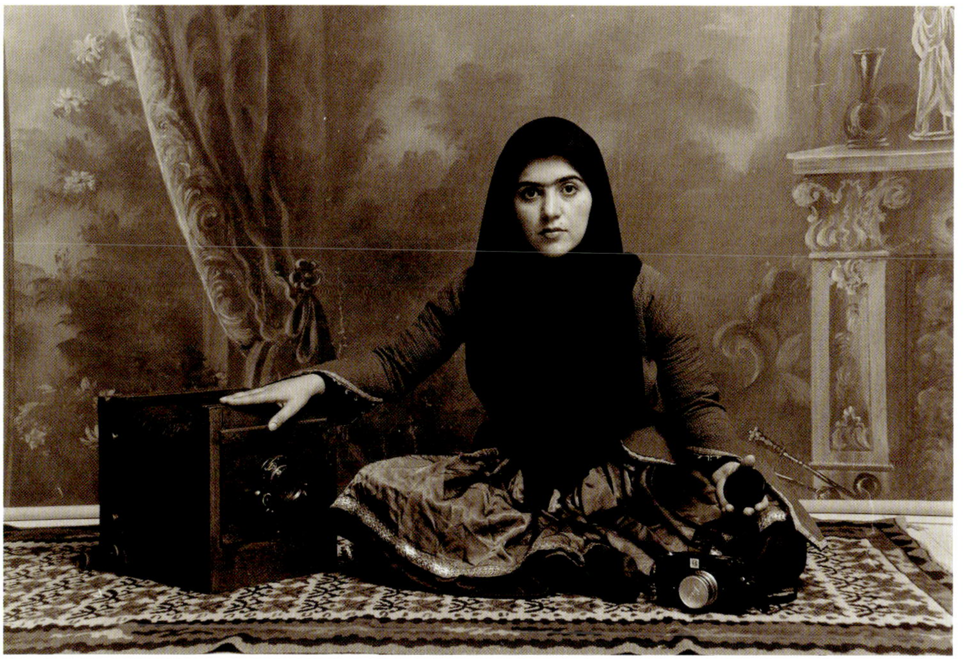

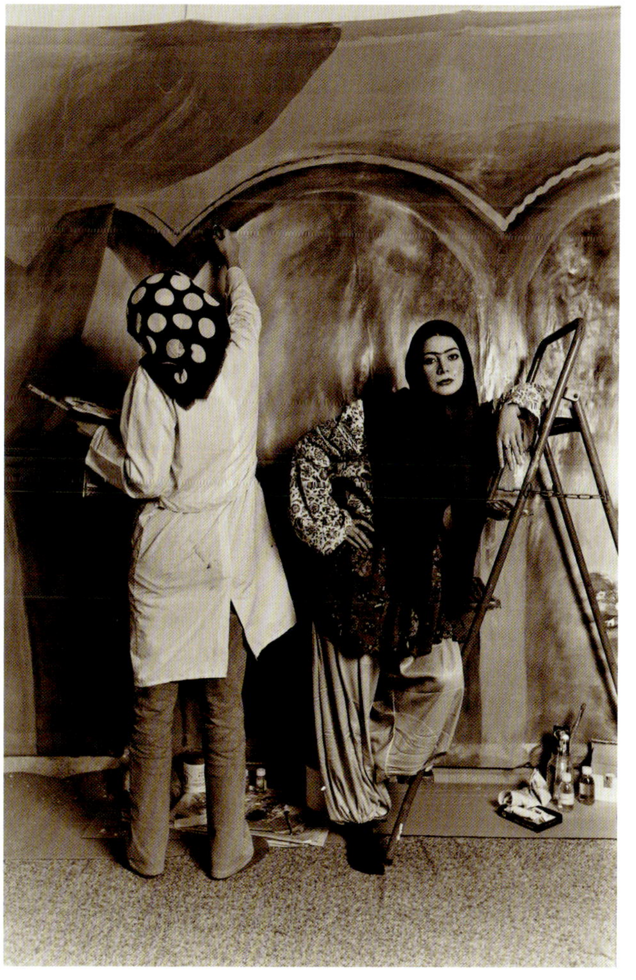

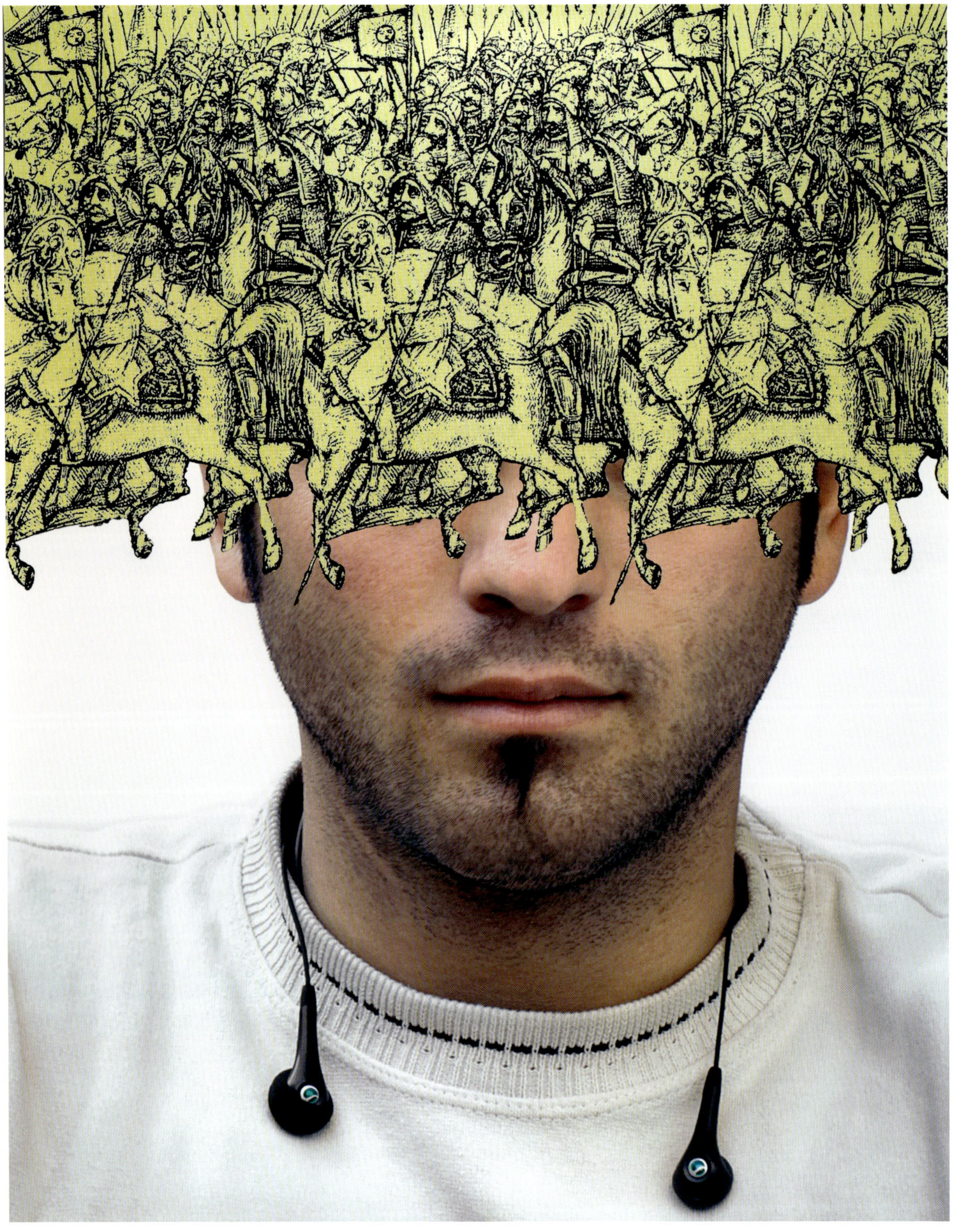

PLATE 36

Sadegh Tirafkan
***The Loss of Our Identity #1 (Boy)*, 2007**
FROM THE SERIES The Loss of Our Identity

In the series The Loss of Our Identity, Sadegh Tirafkan addresses the notion of self-identity for Iran's youth, as defined by the parameters of global culture. In this print, a young man with earbuds is pictured as though he is tuning out of a fading past and tuning in to an attractive "modern" life.

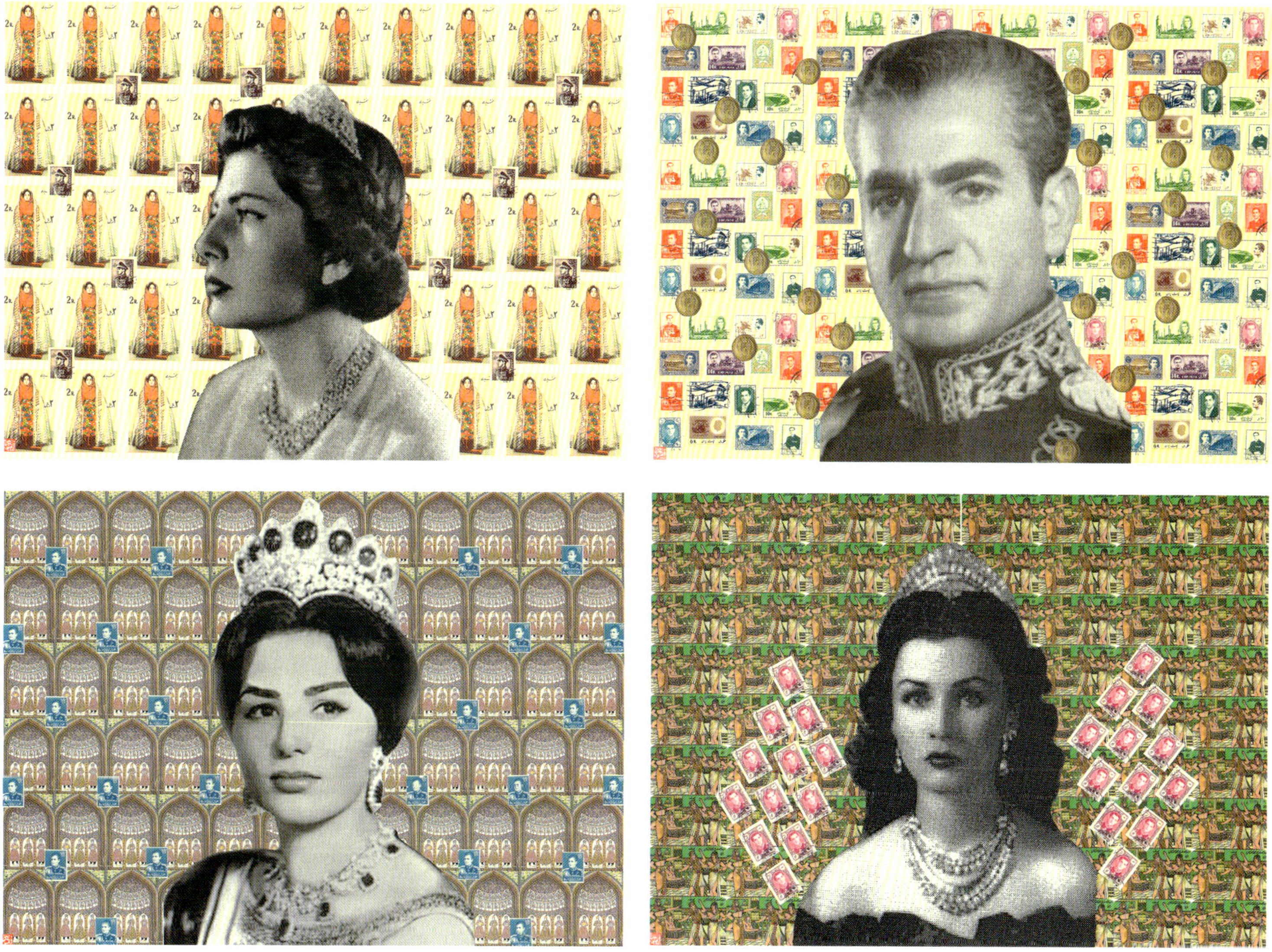

PLATE 37

Afsoon

***Shah and His Three Queens*, 2009**

FROM THE SERIES **Fairytale Icons**

Afsoon's *Shah and His Three Queens* belongs to a series in which the artist reconsiders her childhood heroes and their fates, probing the idea of "happily ever after" and its attainability. Here, Mohammad Reza Shah is shown alongside his wives: Princess Fawzia of Egypt and Soraya Esfandiary Bakhtiari, both of whom he divorced, and Farah Diba, who remained with him throughout the Iranian Revolution, their subsequent exile in 1979, and his death from cancer a year later.

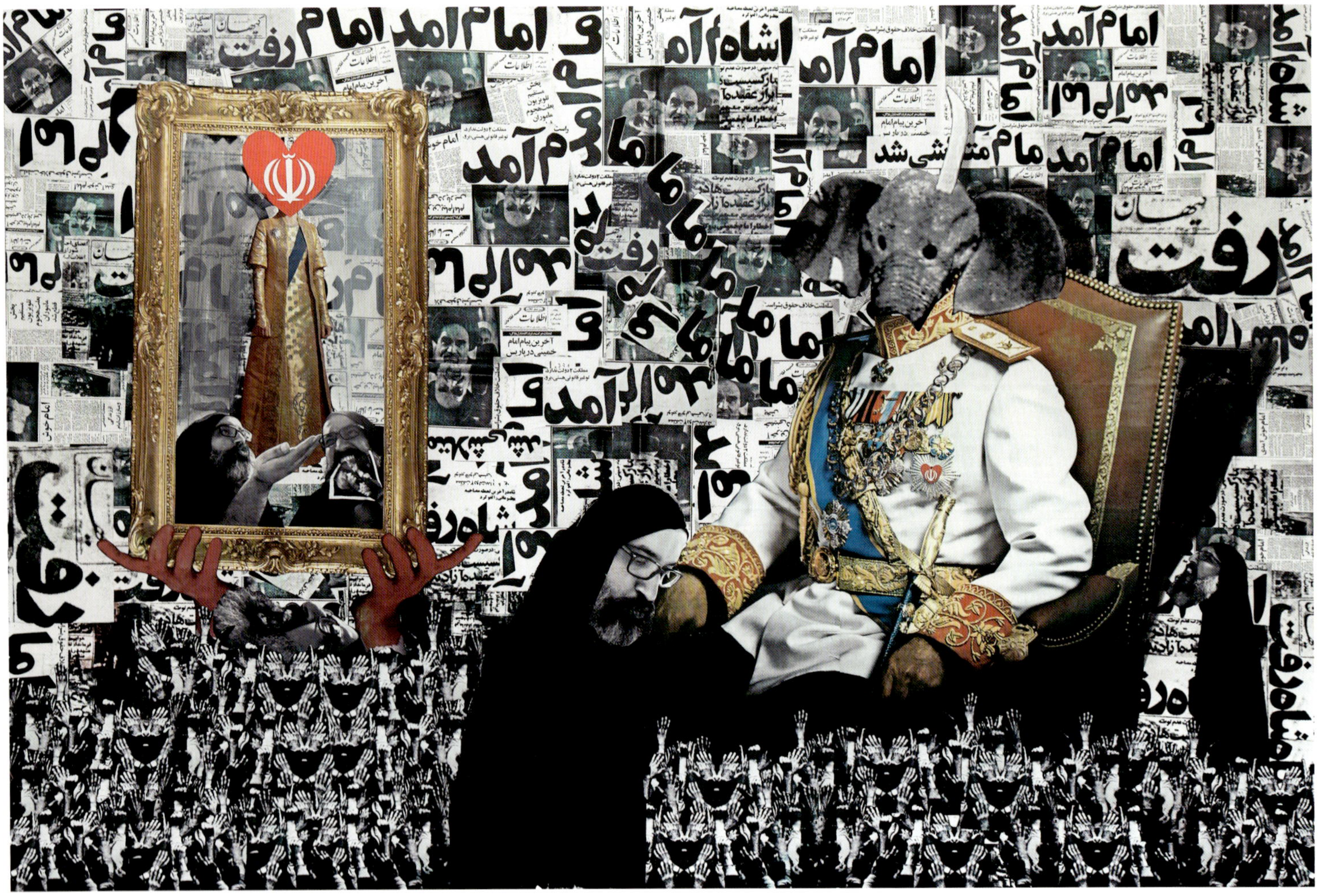

PLATE 38

Ramin Haerizadeh
***He Came, He Left, He Left, He Came*, 2010**

Using photography, drawing, painting, film, and animation but especially collage, Ramin Haerizadeh creates multilayered works that reclaim and transform found images into cleverly unsettling scenes. Here the artist mixes the now-iconic Iranian newspaper headline from January 16, 1979, that announced the shah's departure with the headline declaring Ayatollah Khomeini's arrival two weeks later. Covered with a black chador, the artist ironically inserts himself into the scene, kneeling before the king and worshipping the queen.

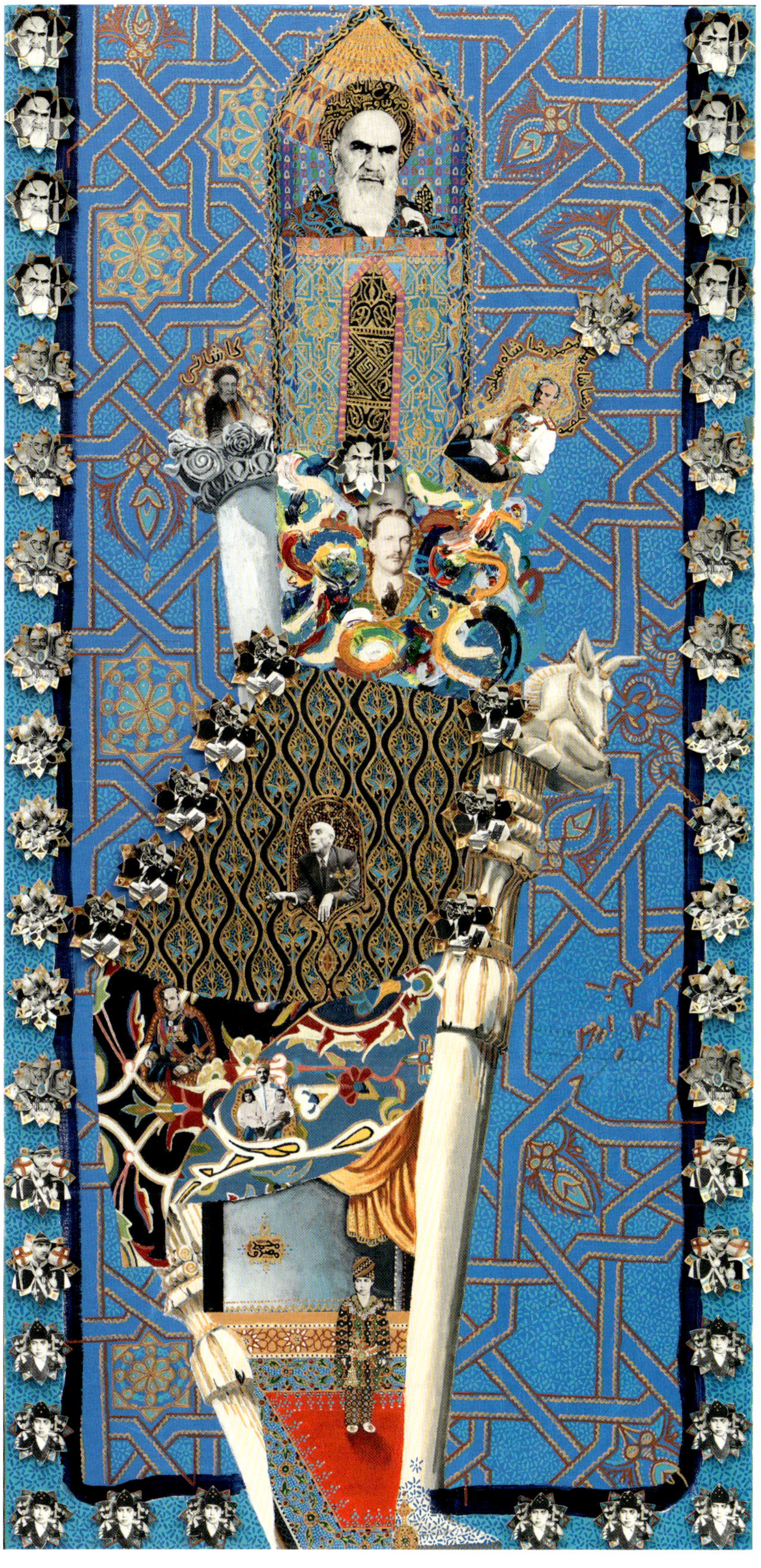

PLATE 39

Asad Faulwell
***Pillars—Iran (1882–1989)*, 2009**

Pillars—Iran (1882–1989) is composed of painted pre-Islamic architectural elements and Islamic patterns paired with collaged portraits of seminal figures in Iran's recent history, including Mohammad Reza Shah, Mohammad Mossadeq, and Ayatollah Ruhollah Khomeini. The result is a distorted two-dimensional pillar, an eclectic and unstable monument to Iran's turbulent history, which continues to define present-day Iran.

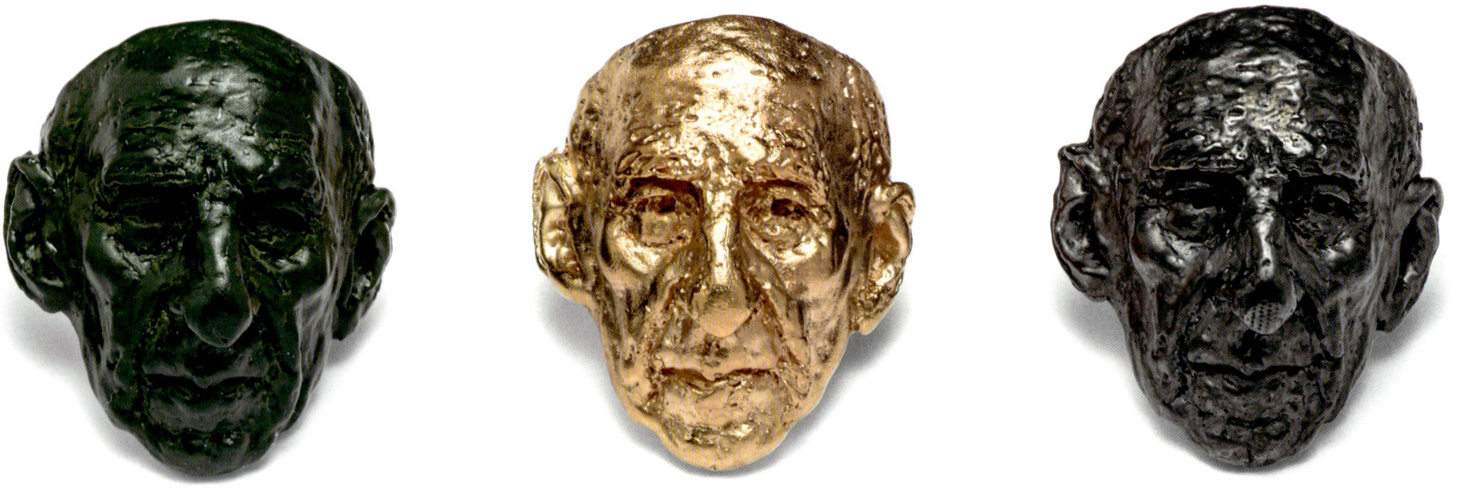

PLATE 40

Koushna Navabi
***Mussy Duck*, 2016**

These rings by Koushna Navabi are small yet detailed busts of Mohammad Mossadeq, Iran's prime minister from 1951 to 1953. In 1952 Mossadeq, a staunch nationalist, ended the British oil concession in Iran, which triggered a confrontation that would lead to his overthrow the following year by a British-and-American-led coup. In contrast with large-scale public monuments, Navabi's rings function as a personal and portable form of adoration.

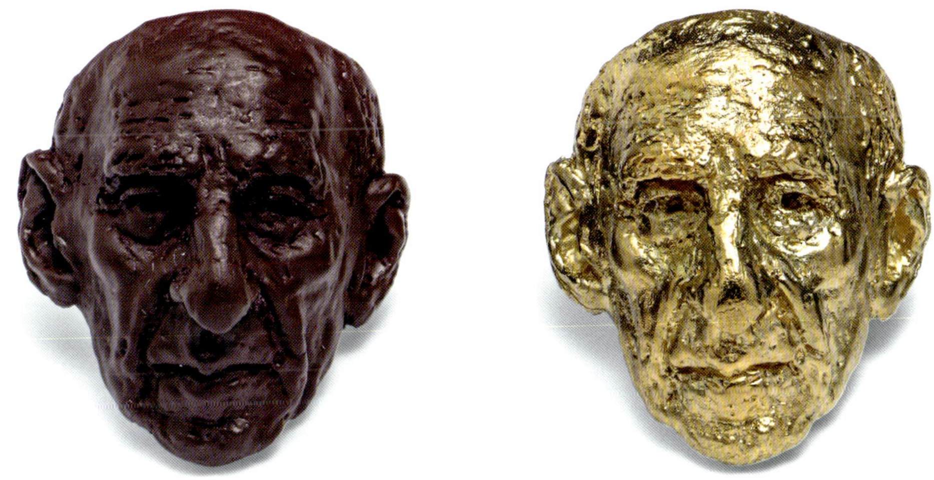

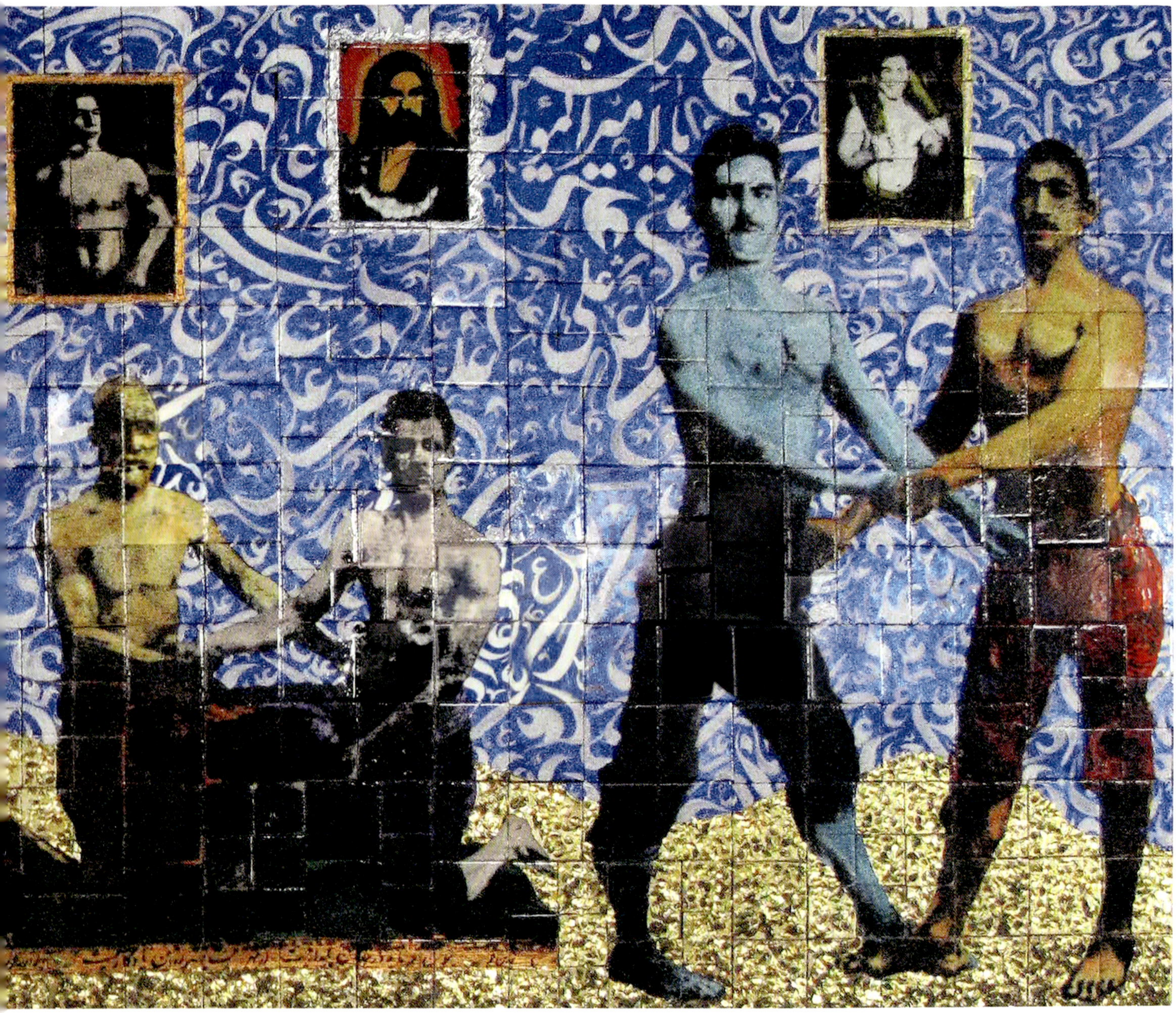

PLATE 41

Khosrow Hassanzadeh
***Remember*, 2010**

One of Iran's foremost contemporary artists, Khosrow Hassanzadeh frequently focuses on the image of the *pahlavan*, a champion of high moral character. Here, he uses tilework—the traditional Iranian form of architectural decoration—to express his favorite theme. Based on vintage photographs, these pahlavans are clothed as members of the *zurkhana*, a traditional system of athletics originally used to train warriors in Iran that combines martial arts, calisthenics, and strength training with music and religious chanting.

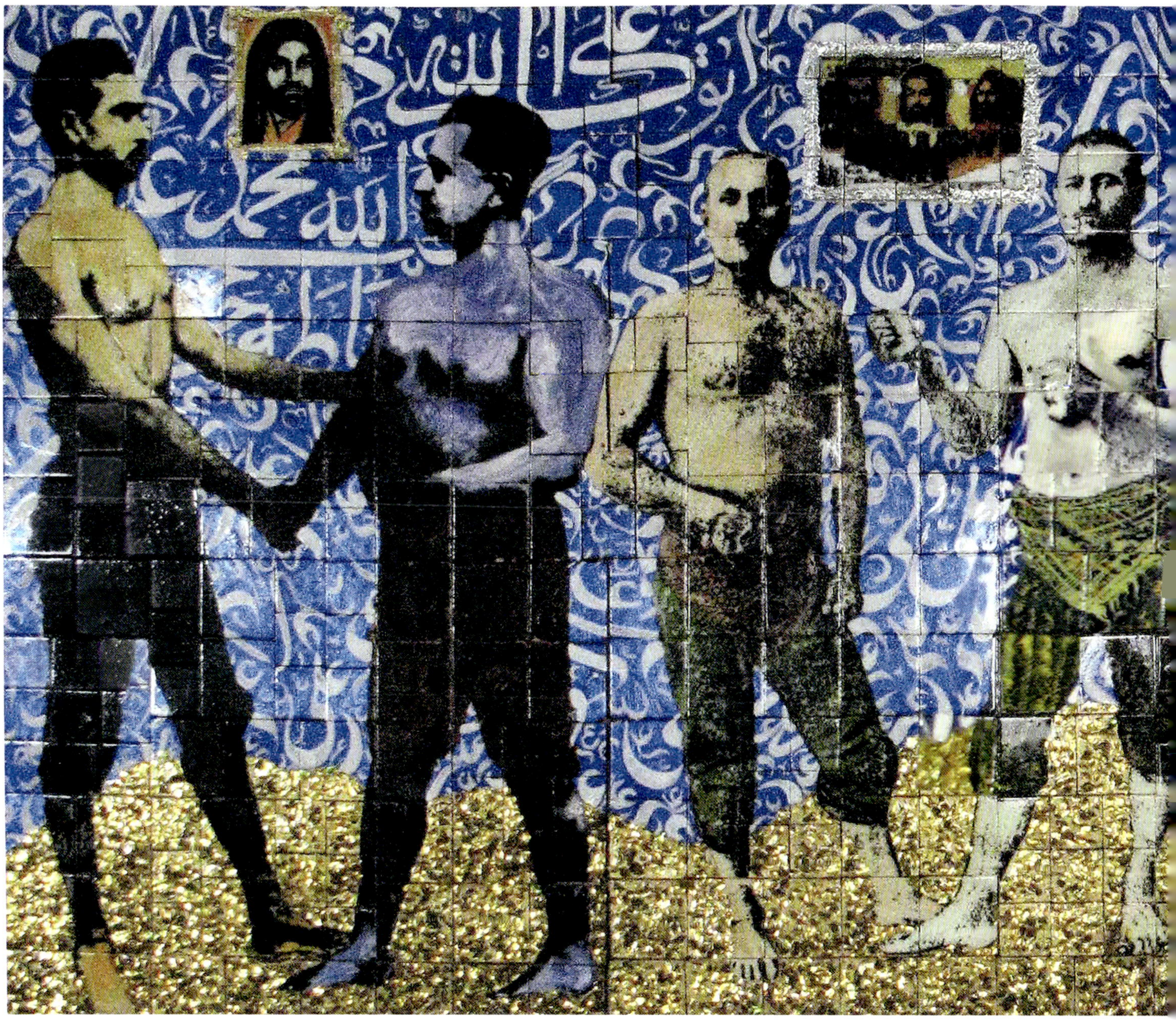

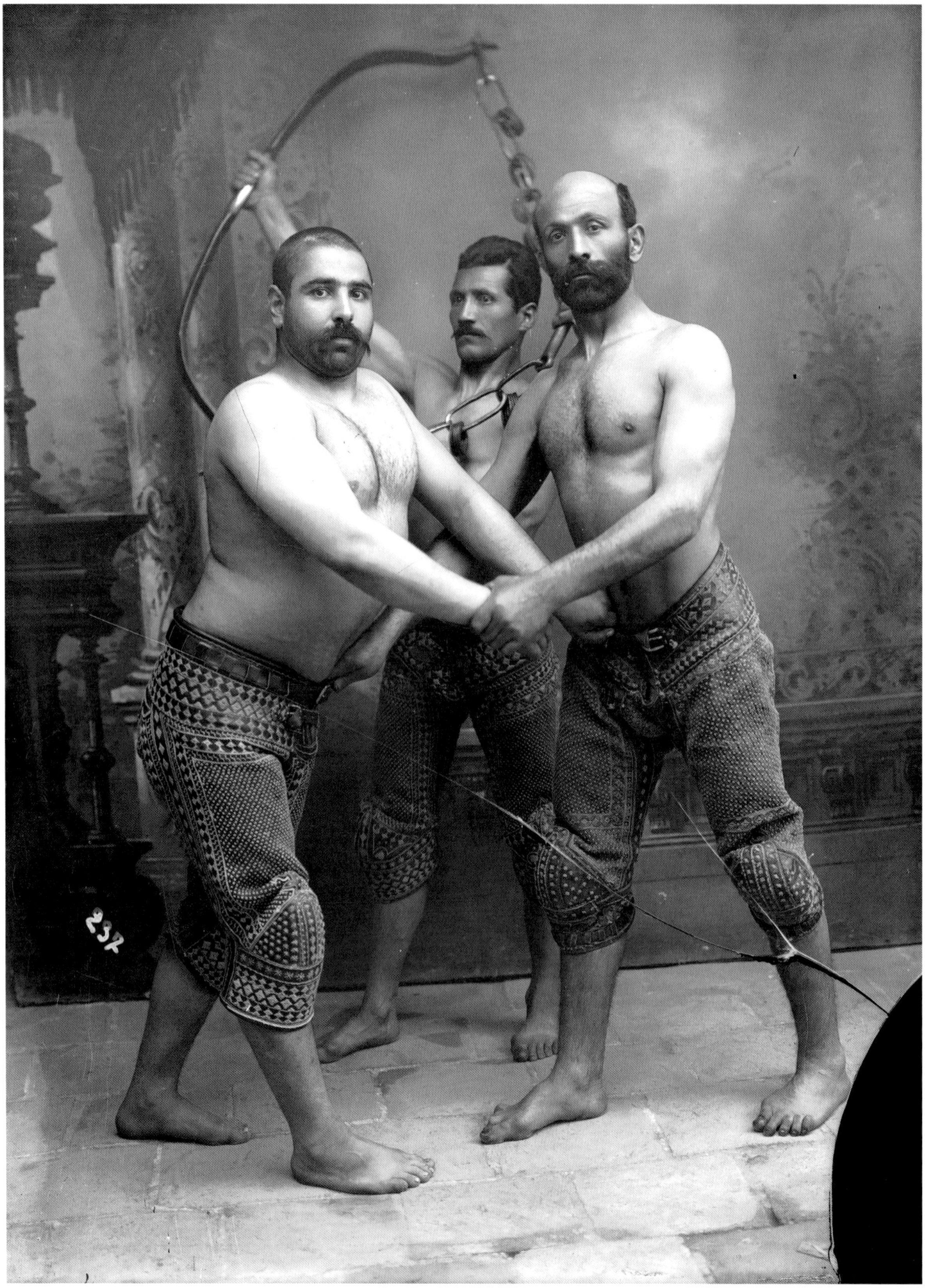

PLATE 42

Antoin Sevruguin
Studio Portrait: Three Wrestlers Taking the Pose, late 19th century

The men shown here, athletes of a type of traditional wrestling still practiced in Iran, are easily identified by the short patterned pants they are wearing and the *kabbada*, a heavy iron bow used during training, like the one lifted by the man in the back. Contemporary Iranian artists like Khosrow Hassanzadeh have used images such as this one to create works that memorialize a bygone era.

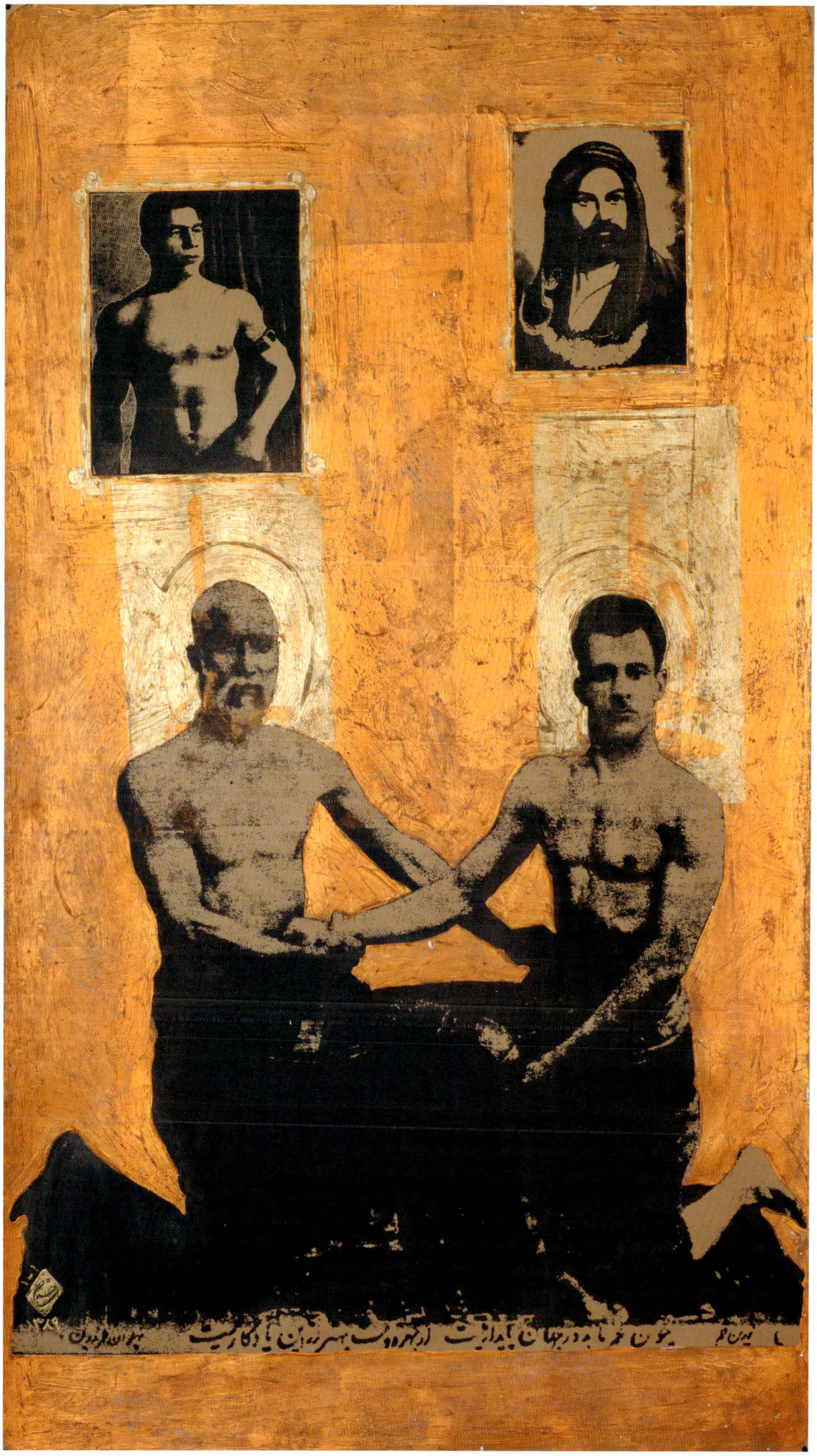

PLATE 43

Khosrow Hassanzadeh
***Untitled III*, 2010**
FROM THE SERIES Remember

The *pahlavan*, the traditional Iranian strongman known for his virtue and bravery, is a favorite theme for Khosrow Hassanzadeh. Here, based on a vintage photograph, two pahlavans are clothed and posed as members of the *zurkhana* beneath more recent framed images of Imam Ali and Takhti, the famed Olympic gold medalist in wrestling.

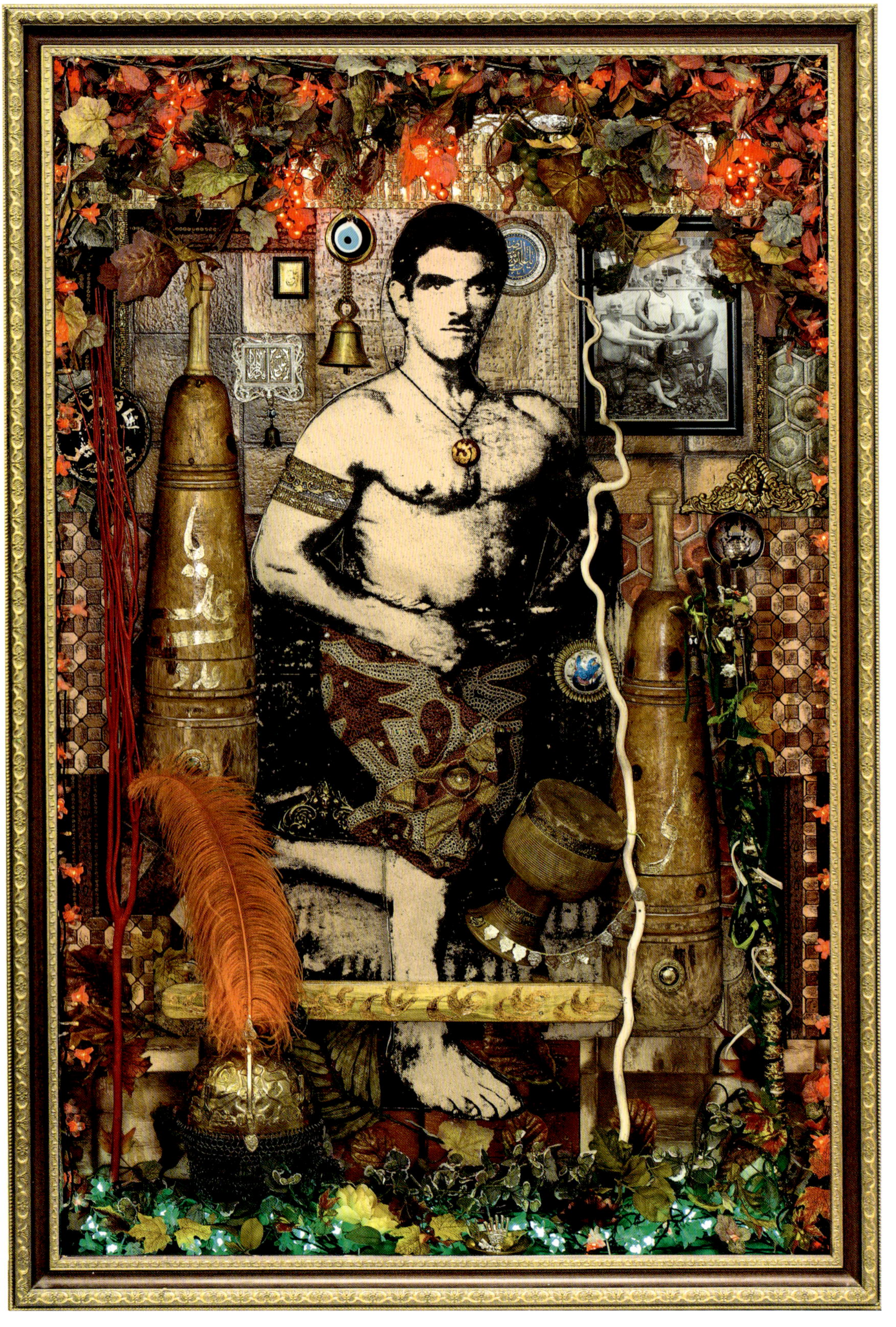

PLATE 44

Khosrow Hassanzadeh
***Pahlavan II, Ready to Order*, 2008**

This mixed-media box provides a contemporary take on Iranian history, culture, and religion. Its focal point is an image of a *pahlavan* (or champion) based on a vintage photograph. The pahlavan is clothed as a member of the *zurkhana* and enclosed, along with actual objects associated with the zurkhana, in a shrine-like structure decorated with internal lights, perhaps to emulate the Iranian tradition of erecting temporary memorials to commemorate the dead.

My art celebrates the icons of ordinary people. I believe the most sacred symbols of Persian culture have endured through them.

Khosrow Hassanzadeh

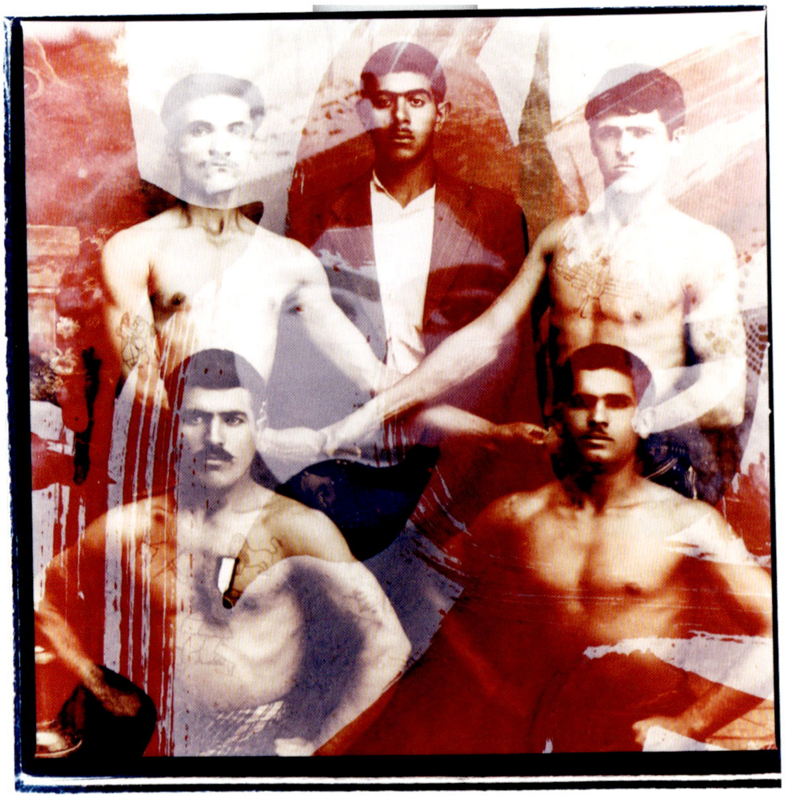

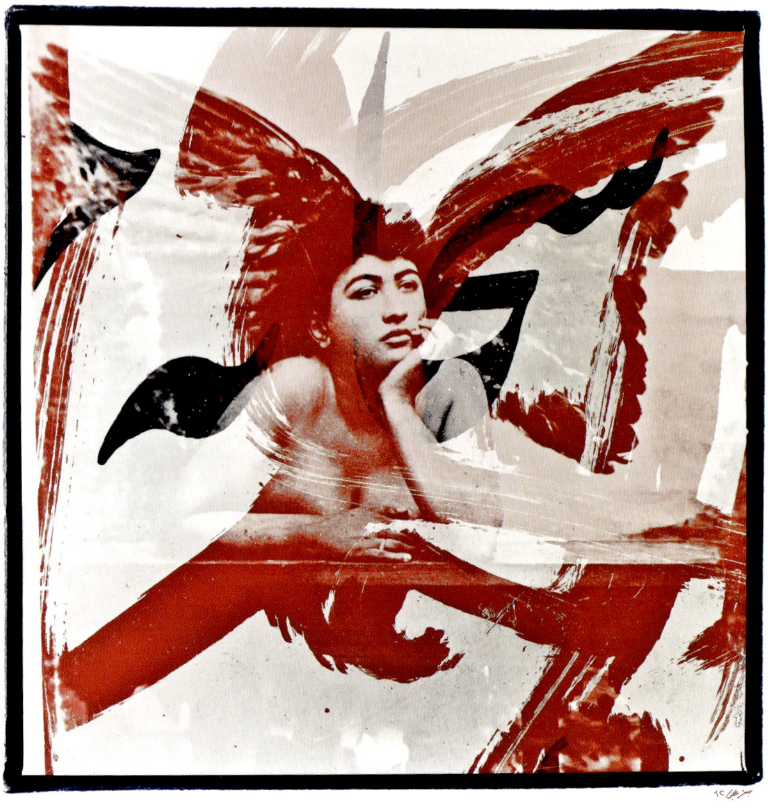

PLATES 45 A–B

Bahman Jalali
***Untitled*, 2003**
***Untitled*, 2003–5**
FROM THE SERIES Image of Imagination

In the series Image of Imagination, Bahman Jalali employs photomontage to fuse two distinct Iranian legacies, the Qajar dynasty and the 1979 Iranian Revolution, into one coexisting image. By layering earlier photographic portraits recovered from Nasir al-Din Shah's Golestan Palace and documentary footage of a photography studio sign defaced during the revolutionary period, Jalali investigates the complex relationship between Iran's past and present. The vintage photographs and the photo studio sign belong to the past, while the colorful defacement represents the present day.

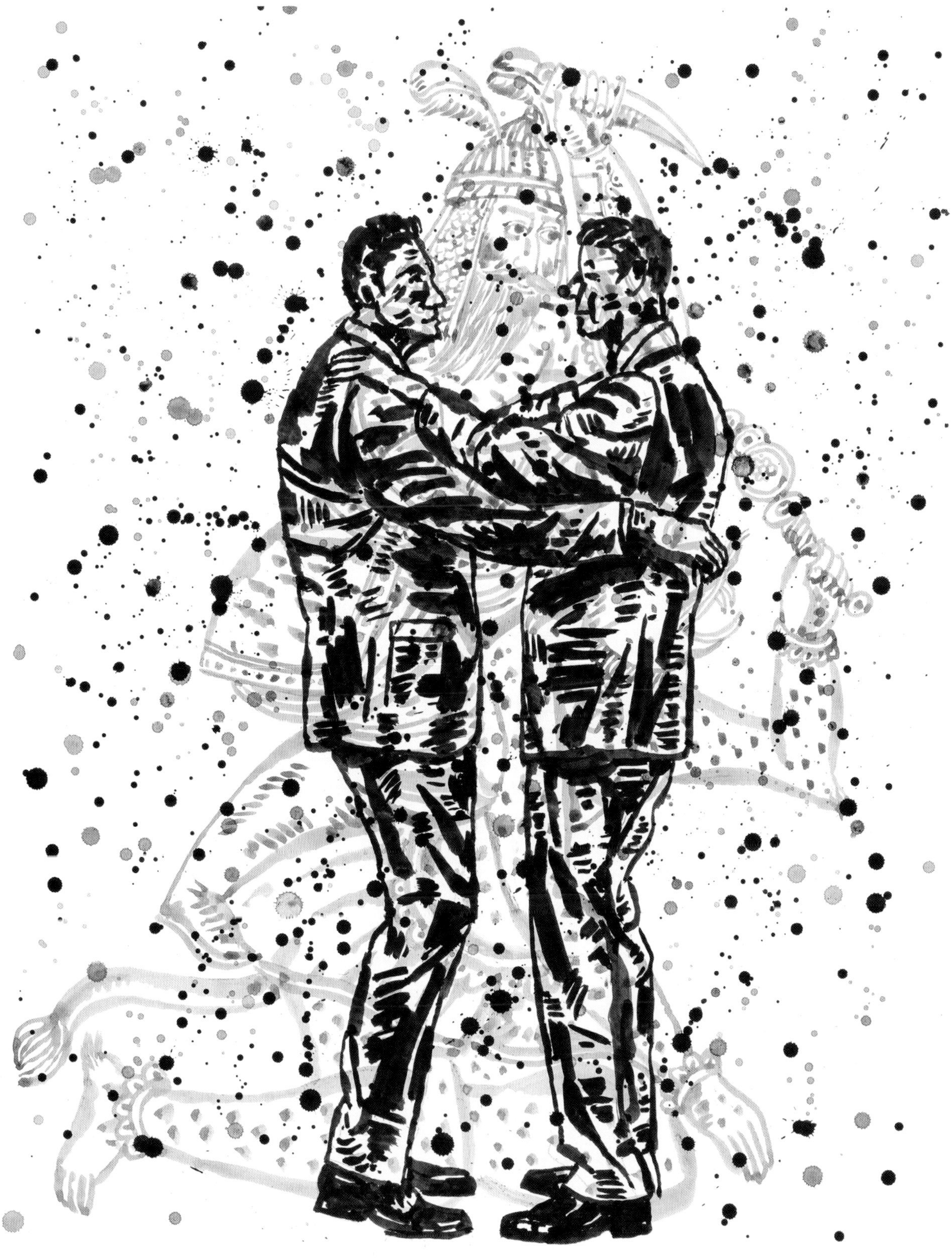

PLATE 46

Nicky Nodjoumi
***Untitled*, 2015**

Nicky Nodjoumi's compositions are often oddly unsettling, as though some unknown calamity threatens. Adding to this sense of disquiet, his works are frequently conceived as two moments in time existing simultaneously, as here. In the foreground, a pair of men in suits, archetypal politicians, embrace in agreement as they perhaps decide the fate of some far-off country, maybe Iran, thus relating to the artist's own history of dislocation. In the background, a well-known scene from the Iranian national epic in which the mythical hero Rustam slays the White Div plays out.

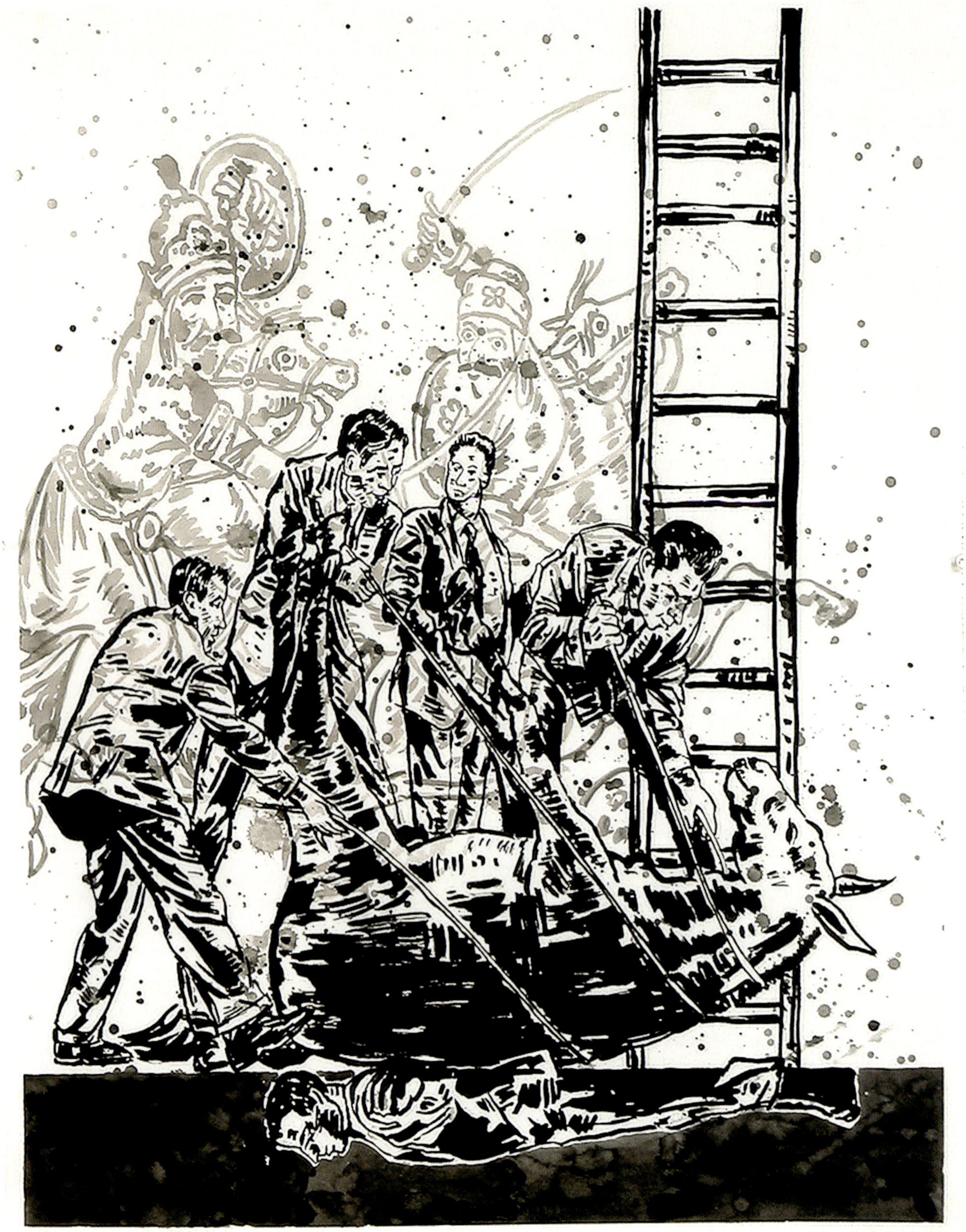

PLATE 47

Nicky Nodjoumi
Study for Inspector's Scrutiny, 2012

Nicky Nodjoumi is renowned in the world of contemporary Iranian art for his searing and satirical critiques of modern life. The political nature of Nodjoumi's work began in earnest in the 1970s, when, as a young teacher at Tehran University of Fine Arts, he joined in the opposition to Mohammad Reza Pahlavi and created posters lambasting the shah. Nodjoumi's recent work depicts suited men in surreal landscapes, at times fighting with one another, sealing deals with a handshake, or tying up animals, as portrayed here.

For many years, I have worked with imagery that deals with two opposing views in the same painting or drawing. Embedded culturally, this duality may be real or unreal, foreground or background, historical or contemporary. Utilizing this dual construct, I have been trying to manifest and portray the hybrid nature of my cultural and existential history.

Nicky Nodjoumi

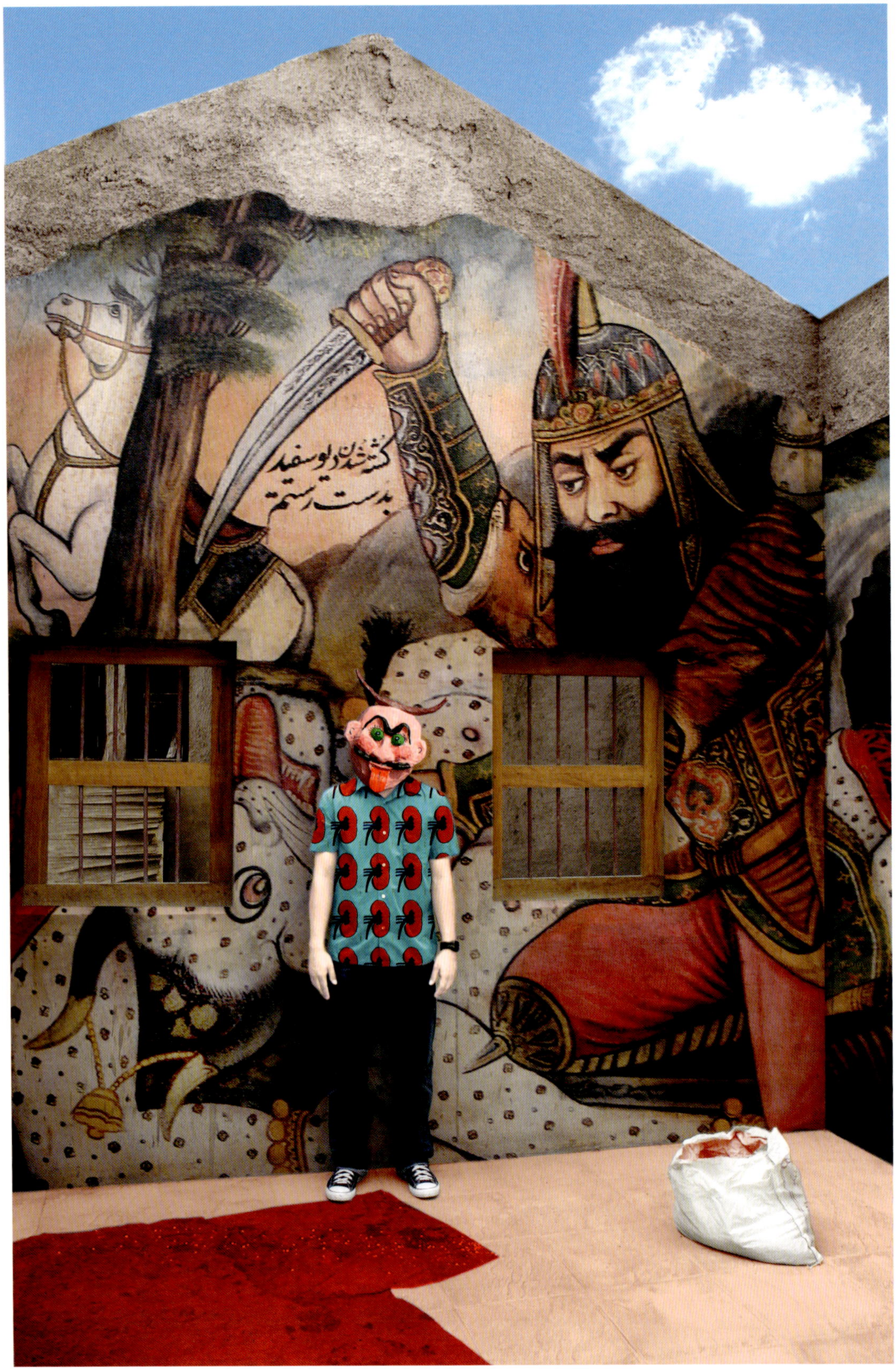

PLATE 48

Malekeh Nayiny
***A Ruin from the Past*, 2007**

The Paris-based artist Malekeh Nayiny draws upon the great Iranian hero Rustam in a pair of works that pertains both to the universal notion of confronting one's demons and to the specifically regional theme of the Iranian national epic, the *Shahnama*. In terms of the latter, the demons are those defeated by Rustam, as depicted here in the scene in which he kills the White Div, a monstrous demon, re-created as a wall mural and announced in the Persian caption beneath the hero's raised dagger.

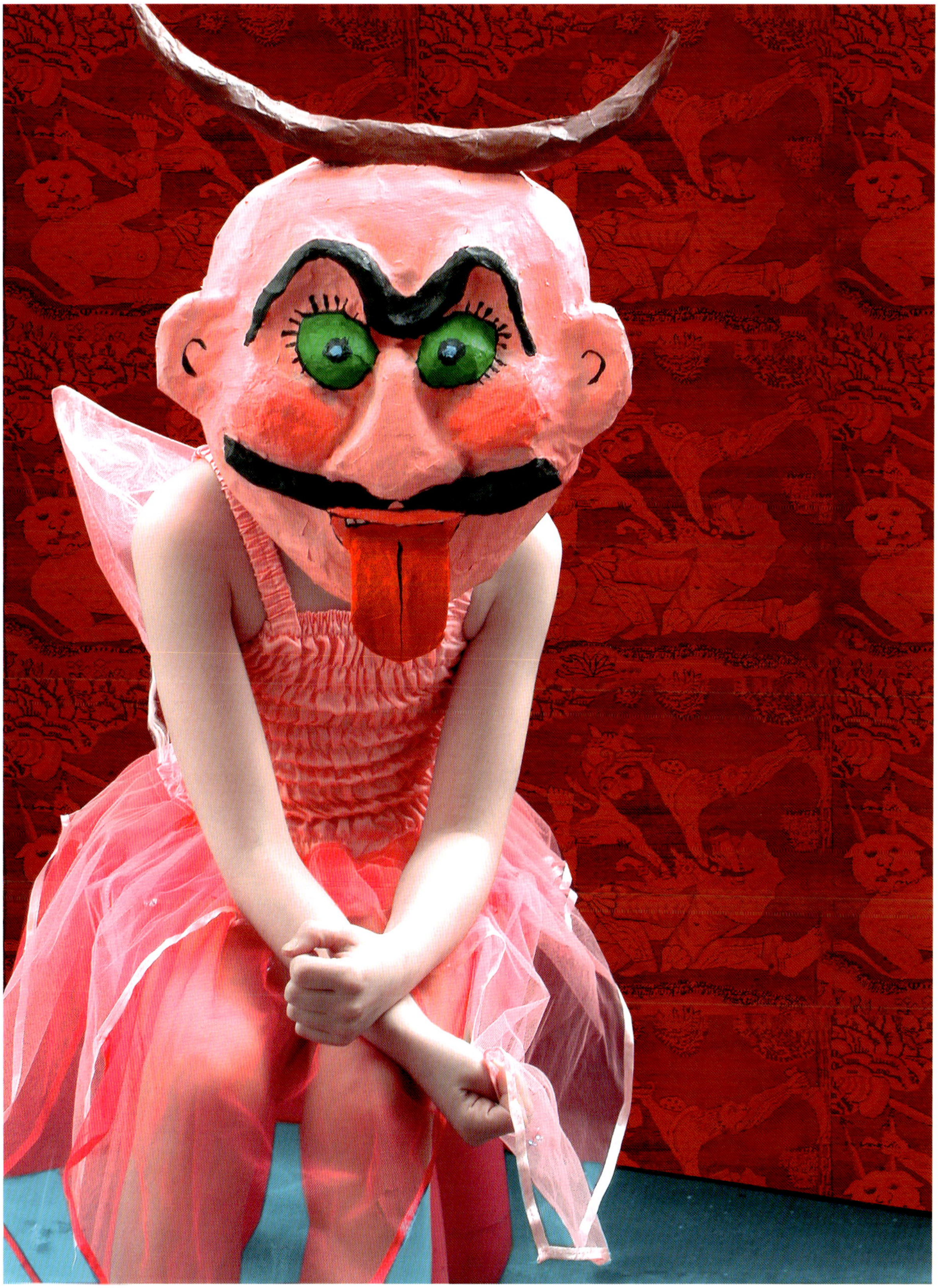

PLATE 49

Malekeh Nayiny
***All in Pink*, 2007**

Here, Rustam combatting the White Div, the same vignette as in Malekeh Nayiny's *A Ruin from the Past*, is re-created and repeated like wallpaper behind the horned demon. The humorous playfulness of both these Nayiny prints only partially conceals an implied darkness—the conquering of one's own demons—and raises the question, whose face is hidden behind the grotesque pink mask? Perhaps it's our own.

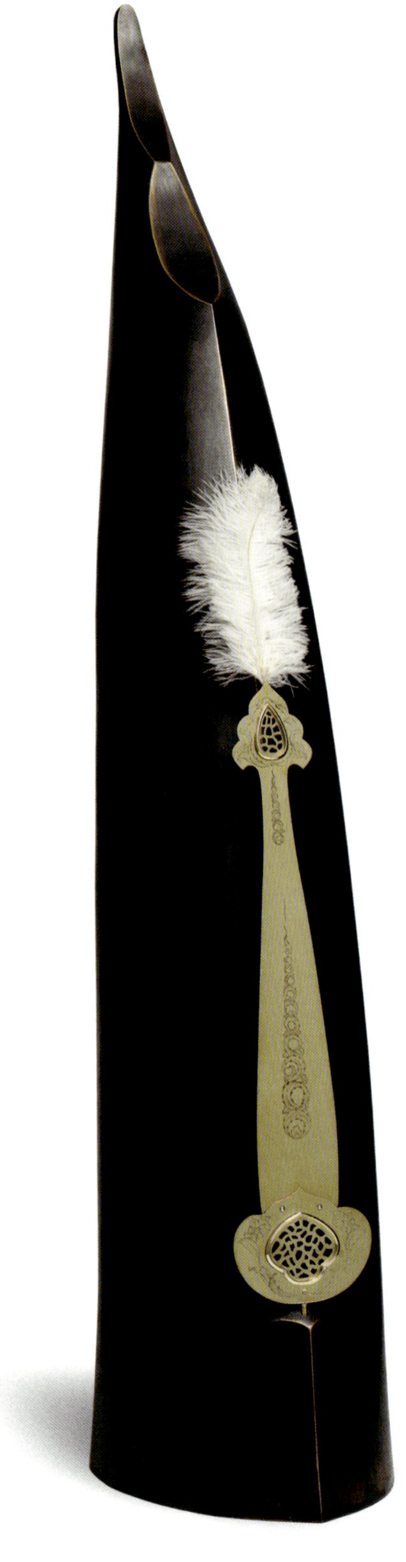

PLATE 50

Kourosh Golnari
***The Renowned Sovereign*, 2017**

In this sculpture, Tehran-based artist Kourosh Golnari references Iran's Qajar dynasty by refashioning into metal, and on a grand scale, a style of tall cap made from lamb fleece and worn by leading members of the court, most notably the shah. The intriguing work provides a three-dimensional representation of nineteenth-century royal images and imagery presented in two-dimensional works elsewhere in this catalogue. More than a sculpture of a hat, it personifies and monumentalizes the shah and as such is perhaps intended to provoke debate about Iran's past rulers.

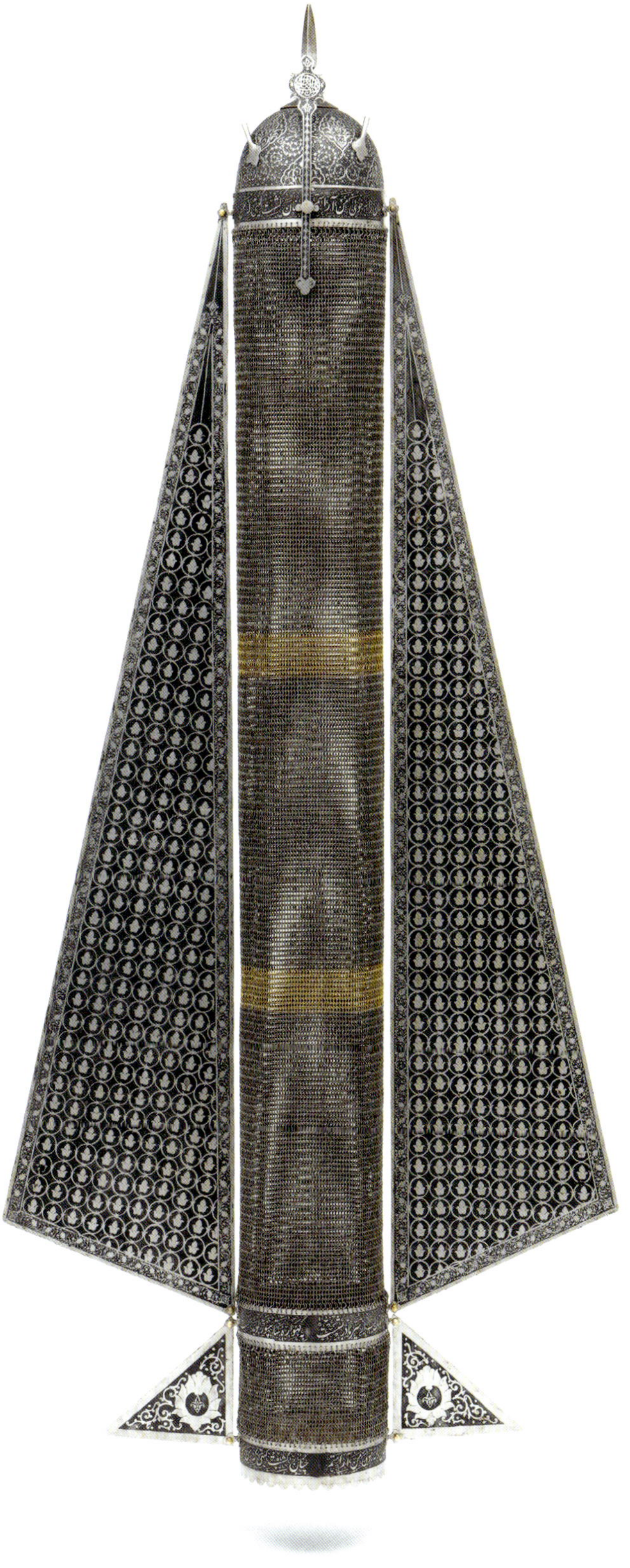

PLATE 51

Shahpour Pouyan
***Projectile 8*, 2012**

Like a warrior standing at the ready, this sculpture by New York-based Shahpour Pouyan features a traditional battle helmet with chain mail transformed into a missile. The work's anthropomorphism is enhanced by its life-size scale and suspension from the ceiling, which allows for subtle movement. To create his projectiles, Pouyan worked with traditional metalsmiths who create armor costumes for actors in *ta'ziya* (passion plays memorializing the death of Imam Husain).

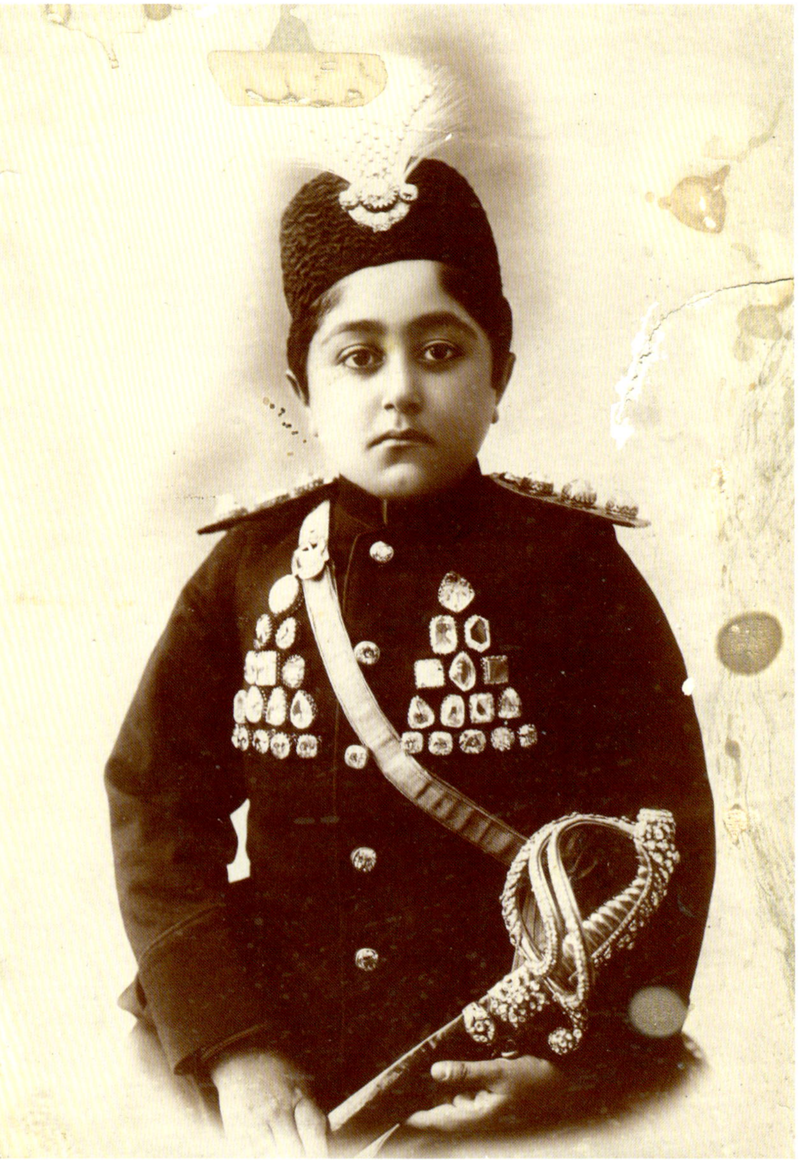

PLATE 52

Antoin Sevruguin
***Portrait of Ahmad Shah*, c. 1909**

The twilight years of the Qajar dynasty were marked by several decades of unrest and political turmoil, during which separatist forces and Western intervention repeatedly threatened Iran's sovereignty. On the same day as his father was deposed in 1909, the twelve-year-old Ahmad Shah was crowned king and inherited a greatly weakened Iran. Following the chaos of World War I, a military coup led by Reza Khan stripped the young shah of his power, and in 1925 the Qajar dynasty was formally dissolved by parliamentary decree.

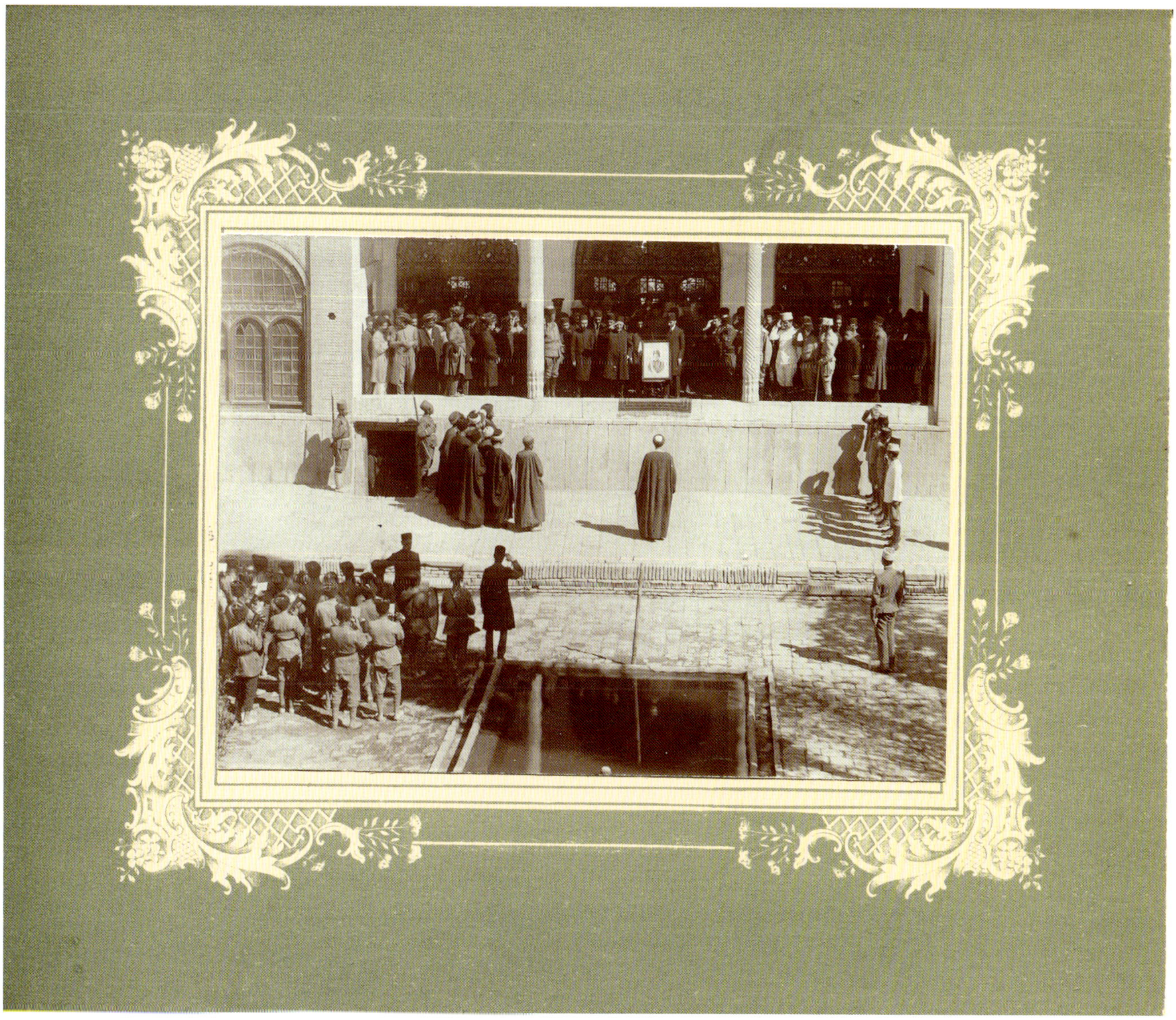

PLATE 53

***Salam Ceremony in Front of Ahmad Shah's Portrait*, early 20th century**

In the Qajar period, salam ceremonies were important displays of power and pomp in which courtiers, military officials, and foreign dignitaries expressed their deference to the shah. The decline of the dynasty in the twentieth century, however, saw the simultaneous decline in such ceremonies. This photograph records one such ceremony; the young Ahmad Shah (r. 1909-25) not present, is represented by a portrait.

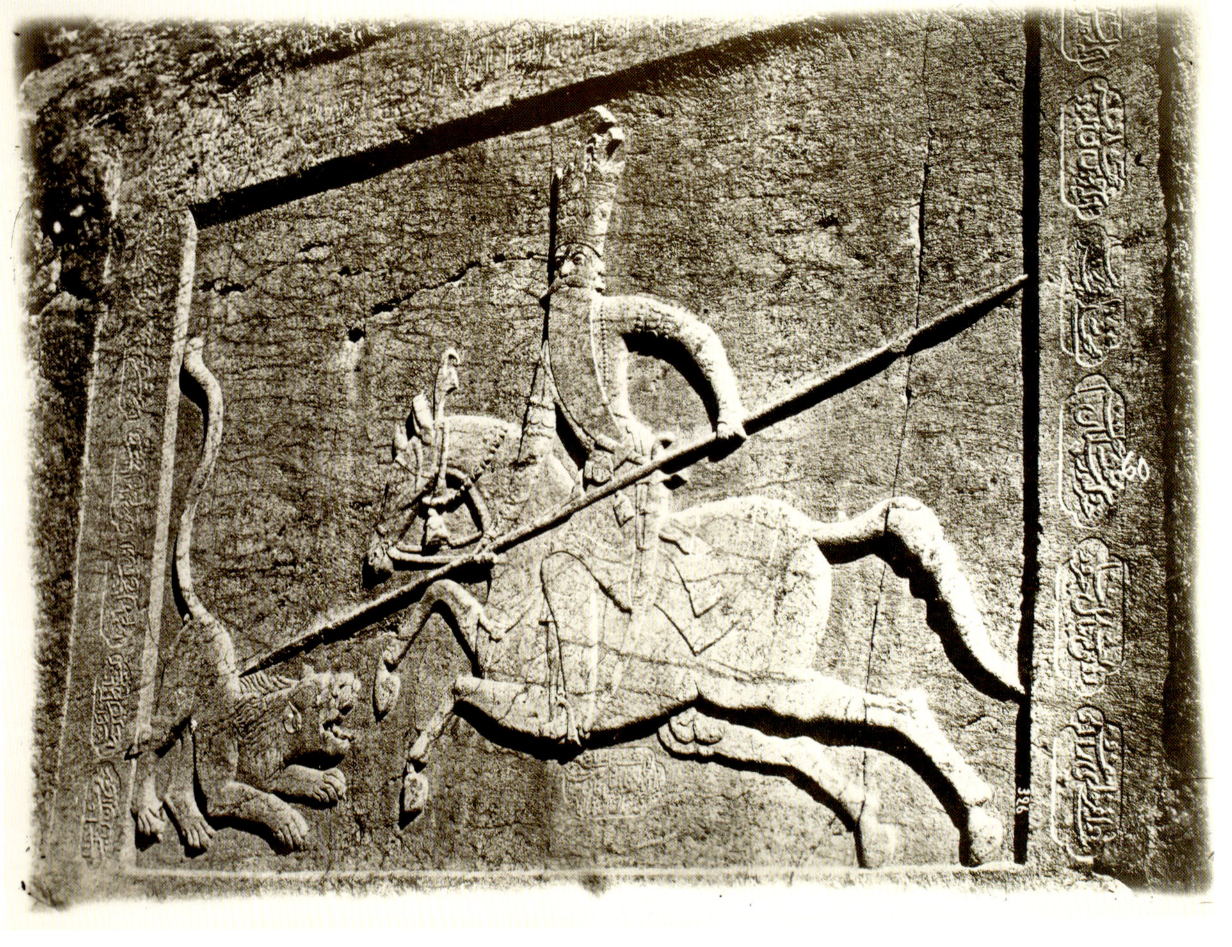

PLATE 54

Antoin Sevruguin
***Qajar Rock Relief Depicting Fath Ali Shah near Rayy*, late 19th century**

The rock-cut relief, though it depicts a nineteenth-century shah, harks back to pre-Islamic royal reliefs celebrating the prowess of the king. Photographs were commissioned, sometimes by members of the ruling Qajar dynasty, to commemorate both the pre-Islamic and the more recent monumental relief sculptures of Iran.

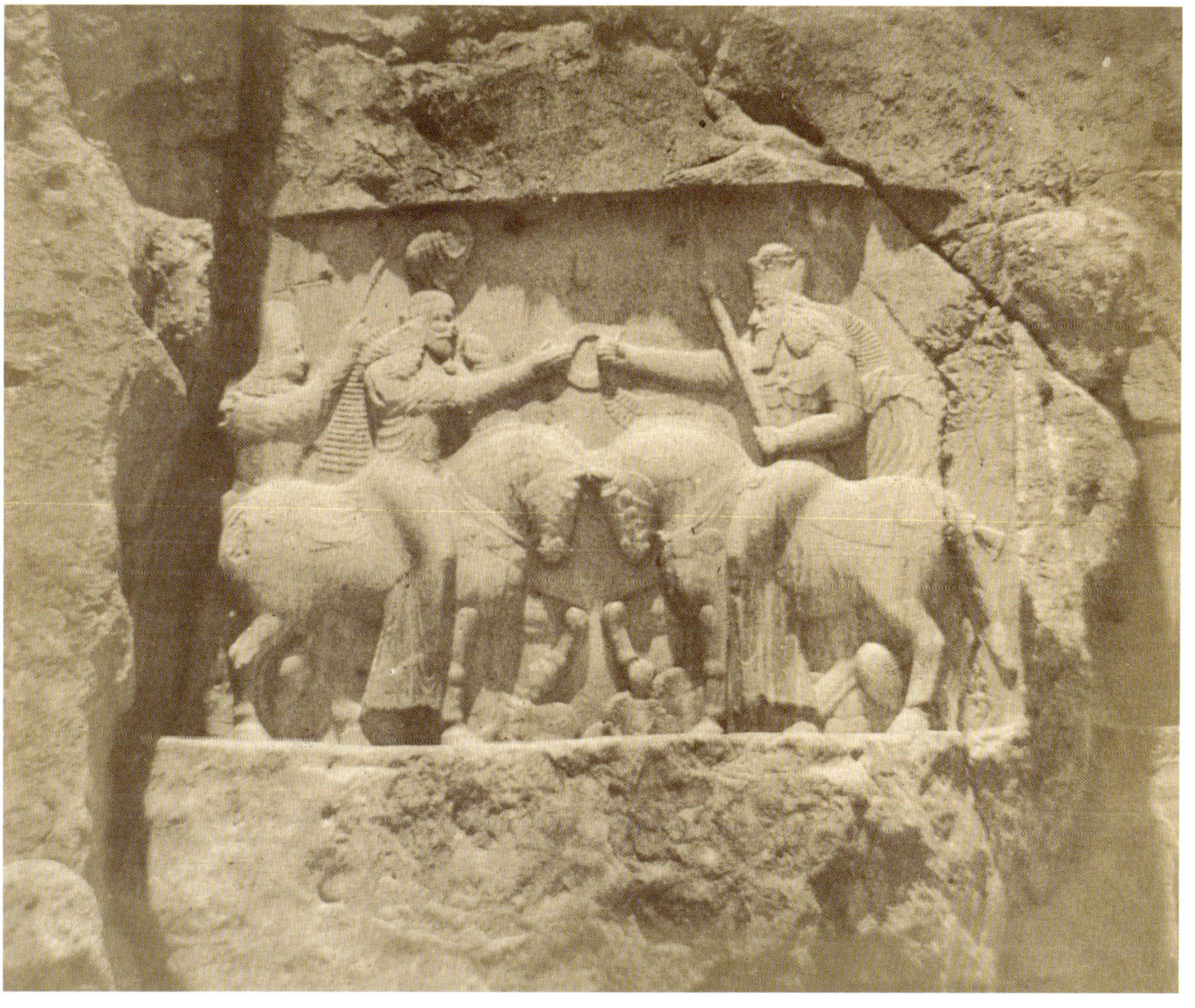

PLATE 55

Luigi Pesce
***Bas Relief at Nakshi Rustam*, 1858**

In the second half of the nineteenth century, a growing interest in Iran's ancient past, combined with the new medium of photography, inspired foreign and local photographers to document the country's historical sites. The Italian colonel Luigi Pesce carried out just such a trip to Naqsh-i Rustam, an Achaemenid (550–330 BC) necropolis that also features Sasanian Empire (224–651) rock-cut reliefs. This photograph, the first ever made at the site, depicts the investiture of the Sasanian king, Ardashir I, by the Zoroastrian god Ahura Mazda.

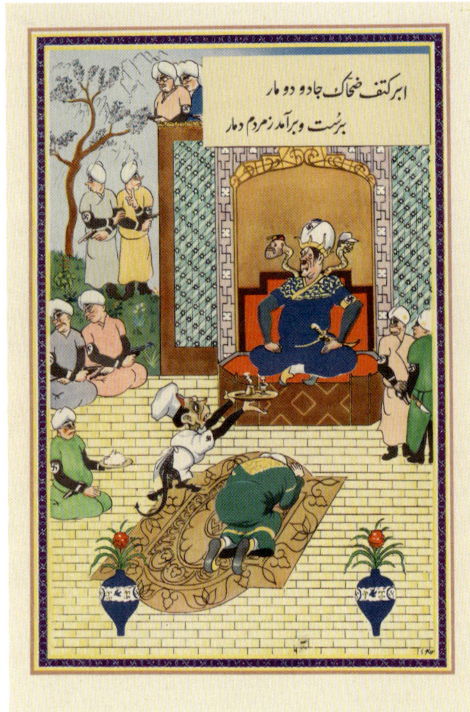

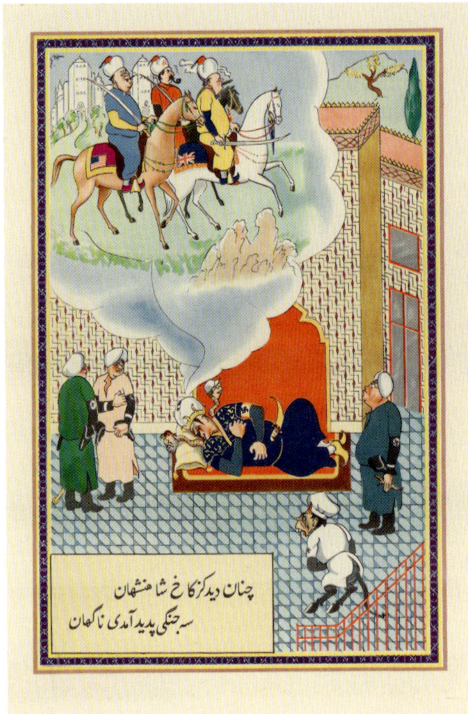

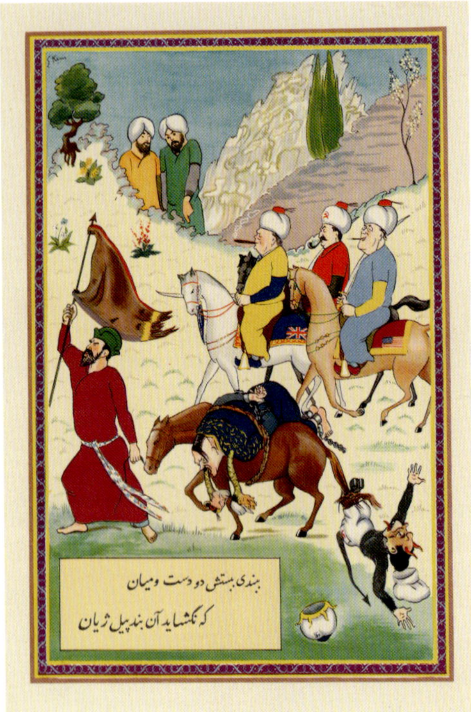

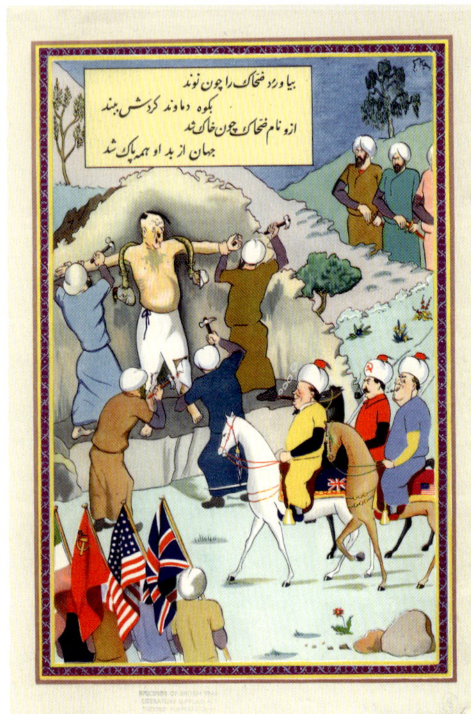

PLATES 56 A–D
(RIGHT TO LEFT, TOP TO BOTTOM)

Kimon Evan Marengo
***Ahriman-Goebbels, disguised as Zahhak-Hitler's cook, causes serpents with the faces of Mussolini and Tojo to grow out of his shoulders*, 1942**

***Zahhak-Hitler's dream about the three warriors who will cause his demise—here depicted as Churchill, Stalin, and Roosevelt*, 1942**

***The arrival of the promised warriors, Churchill, Stalin, and Roosevelt, led by the symbol of Iranian national liberation, Kava*, 1942**

***Zahhak-Hitler is nailed to Mt. Damavand by the liberated Iranian people*, 1942**

During World War II, as part of an effort to promote popular support for the Allies in Iran, the British government commissioned propaganda posters that utilized a key episode from the Iranian national epic, the *Shahnama*: the story of the wicked King Zahhak. Here and throughout the series, Hitler is portrayed as the evil Zahhak, who has a pair of snakes growing from his shoulders with the heads of Mussolini and Tojo; the chief minister of Nazi propaganda, Goebbels, is represented as Satan, in the guise of Zahhak-Hitler's cook.

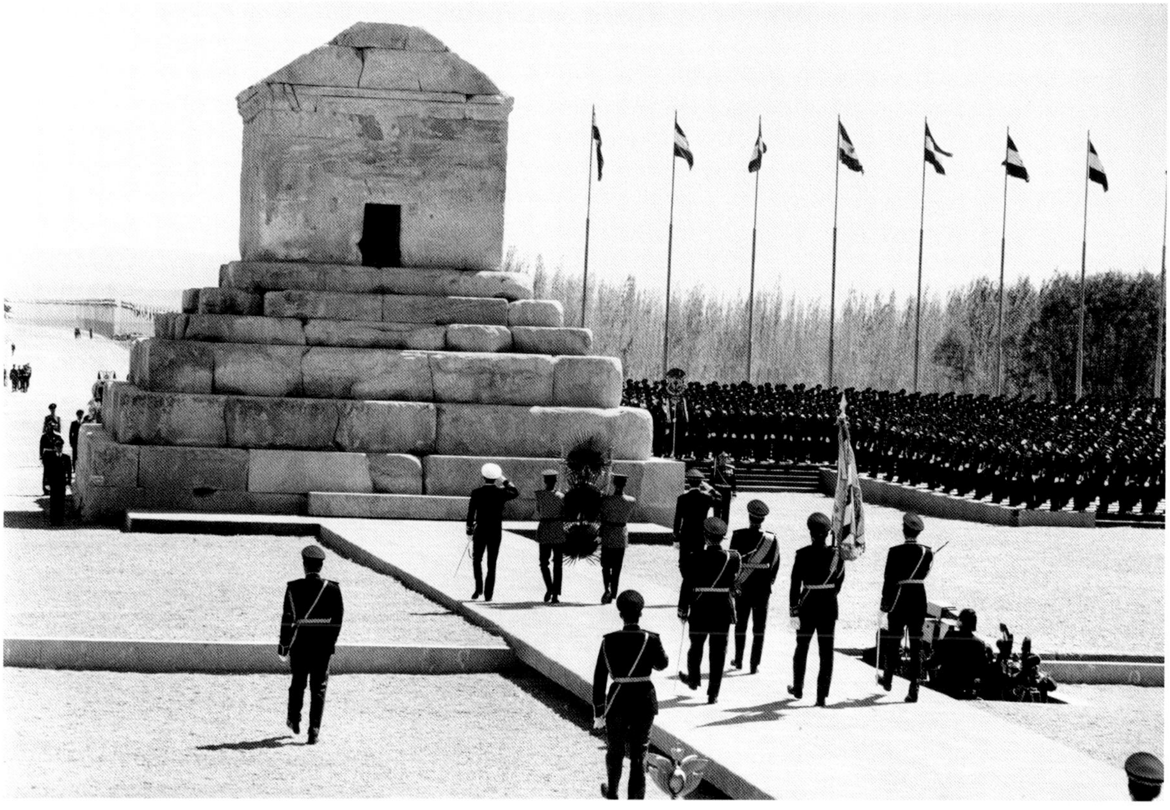

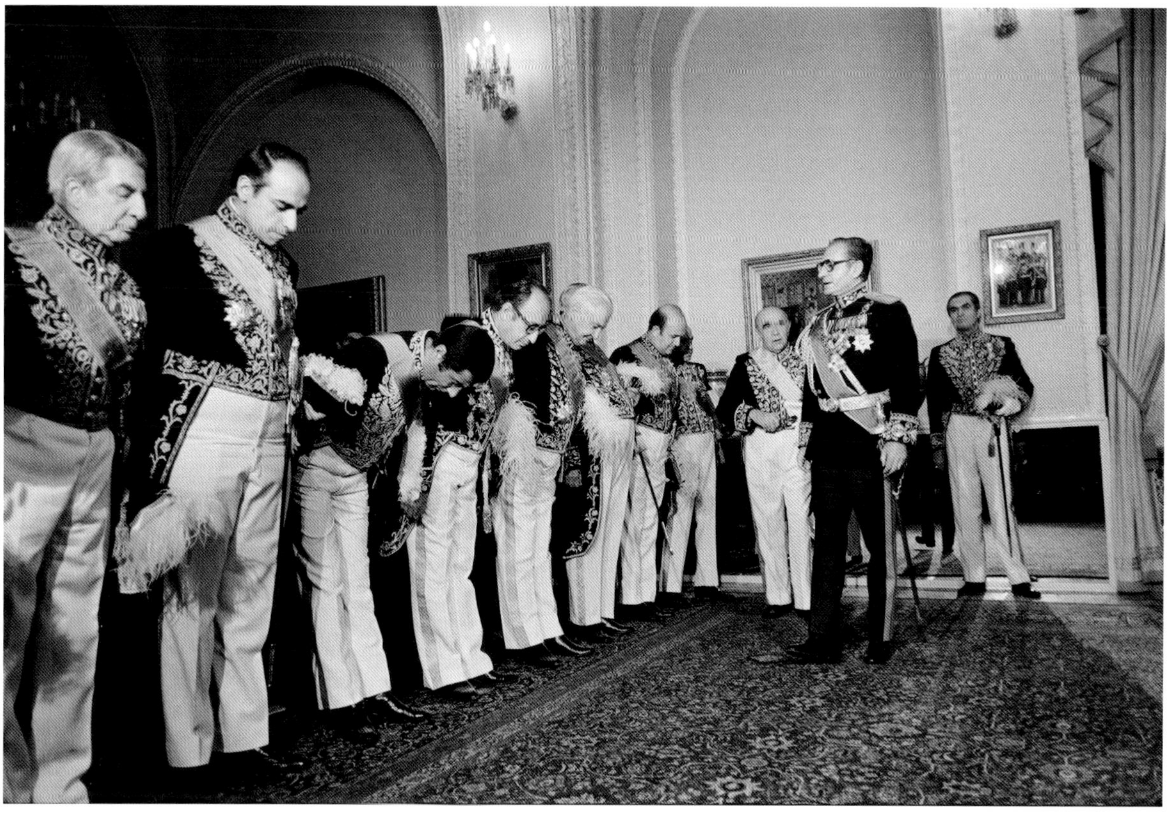

PLATES 57–58

Abbas

***At the tomb of Cyrus the Great, celebrations of the 2500th anniversary of the monarchy,* 1971**

***The shah with Hoveyda's cabinet,* 1977**

These two images capture moments in the official life of Mohammad Reza Pahlavi (r. 1941–79). In one, the shah pays homage to Cyrus the Great at the opening ceremony of the lavish festivities associated with the 2,500th anniversary of the founding of the Imperial State of Iran and First Persian Empire on October 12, 1971. In the second, chief courtiers and military officials assemble to offer their respects on the occasion of the shah's fifty-eighth birthday. Amir-Abbas Hoveyda, Iran's longest-serving prime minister (1965–77), stands to the shah's right.

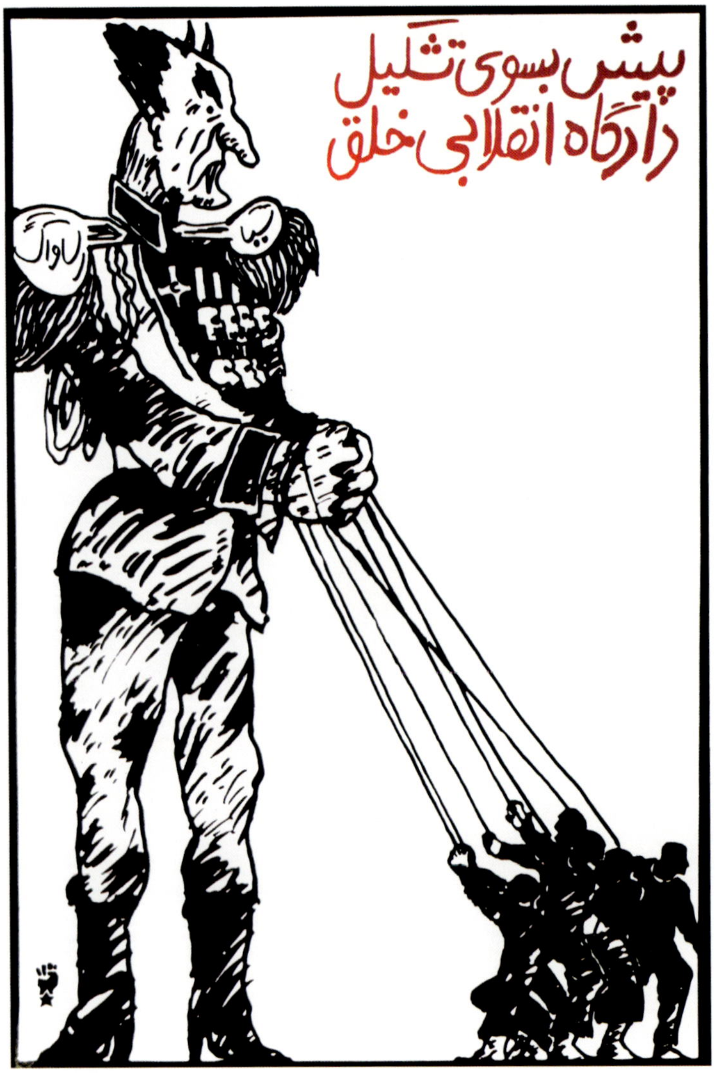

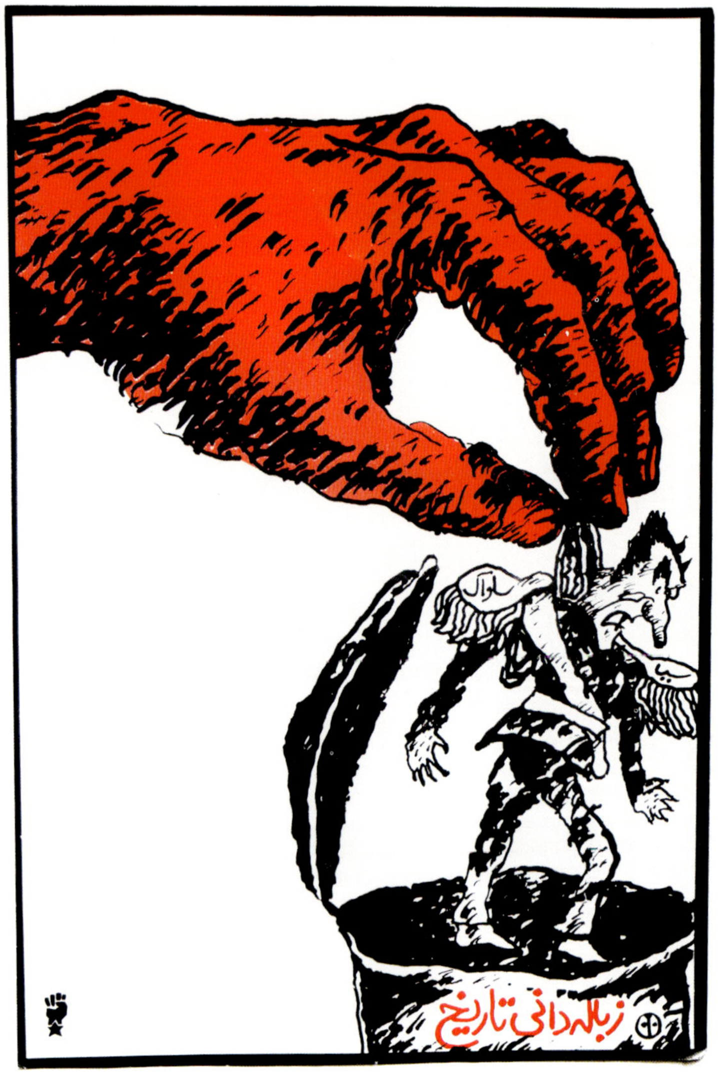

PLATES 59–60 (RIGHT TO LEFT)

Nicky Nodjoumi
***The Trash Can of History*, c. 1979**

***Forward to Establish a People's Revolutionary Court*, c. 1979**

Nicky Nodjoumi, now based in Brooklyn, was one of the foremost members of Group 57, which designed political posters that were shown at a scandalous exhibition at Tehran University in December 1979. As the graphic quality of the medium required, the posters are rendered simply and with straightforward messages. In one, the shah is depicted being discarded into the trash bin of history; in the other, revolutionaries lead the handcuffed shah to the "People's Court" for justice.

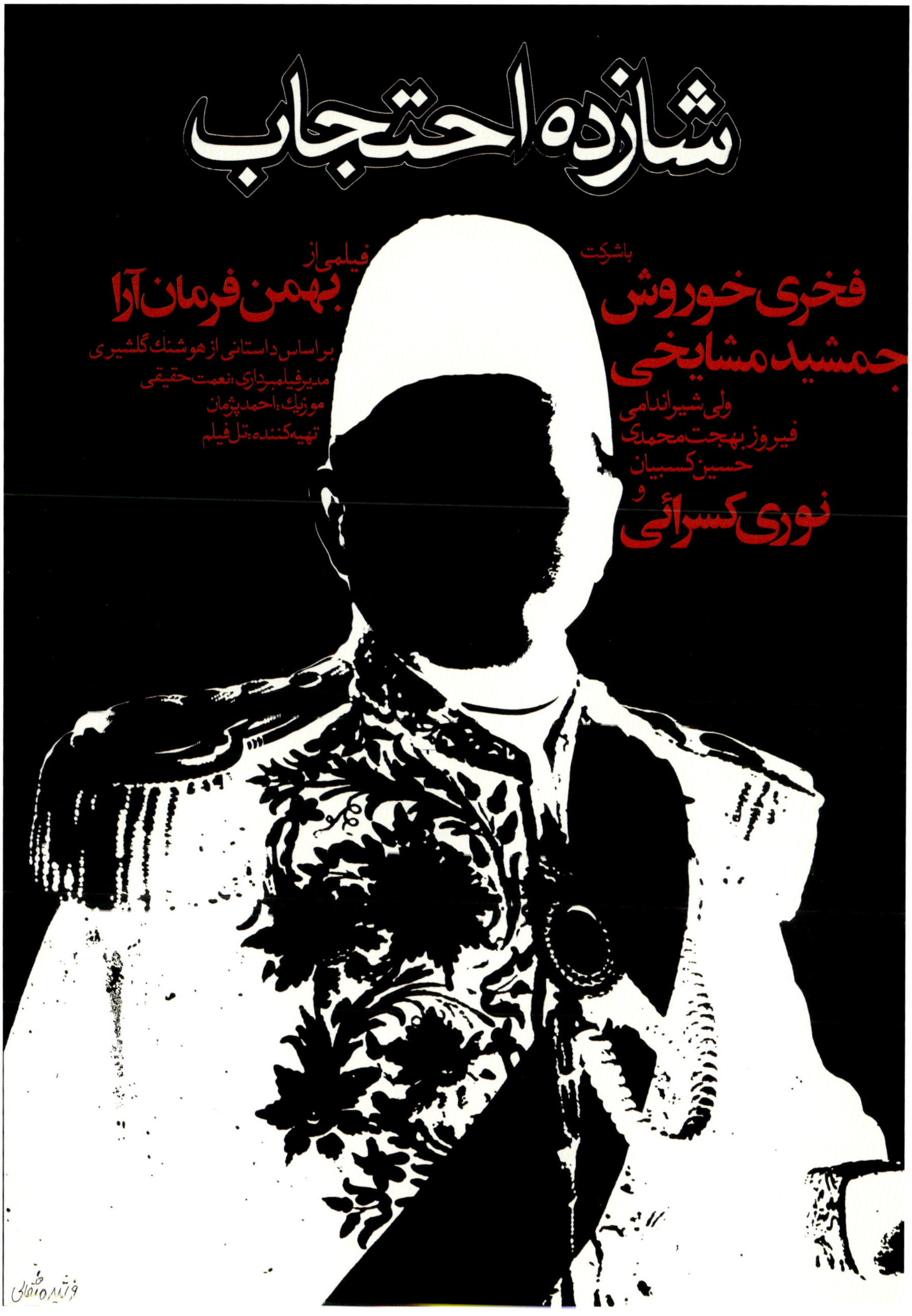

PLATE 61

Farshid Mesghali
***Shazdeh Ehtejab*, 1974**

The acclaimed 1969 novel *Shazdeh Ehtejab* by Houshang Golshiri was made into a film in 1974 by Bahman Farmanara. The movie poster was created by Iran's foremost illustrator and graphic designer, Farshid Mesghali. The book, film, and poster collectively mark significant milestones in literature, cinema, and graphic design. In this poster, Mesghali masterfully captures the core idea of the story by presenting its protagonist as a faceless Qajar prince whose anonymous character encourages viewers to identify him with symbols of royalty and power, both past and present.

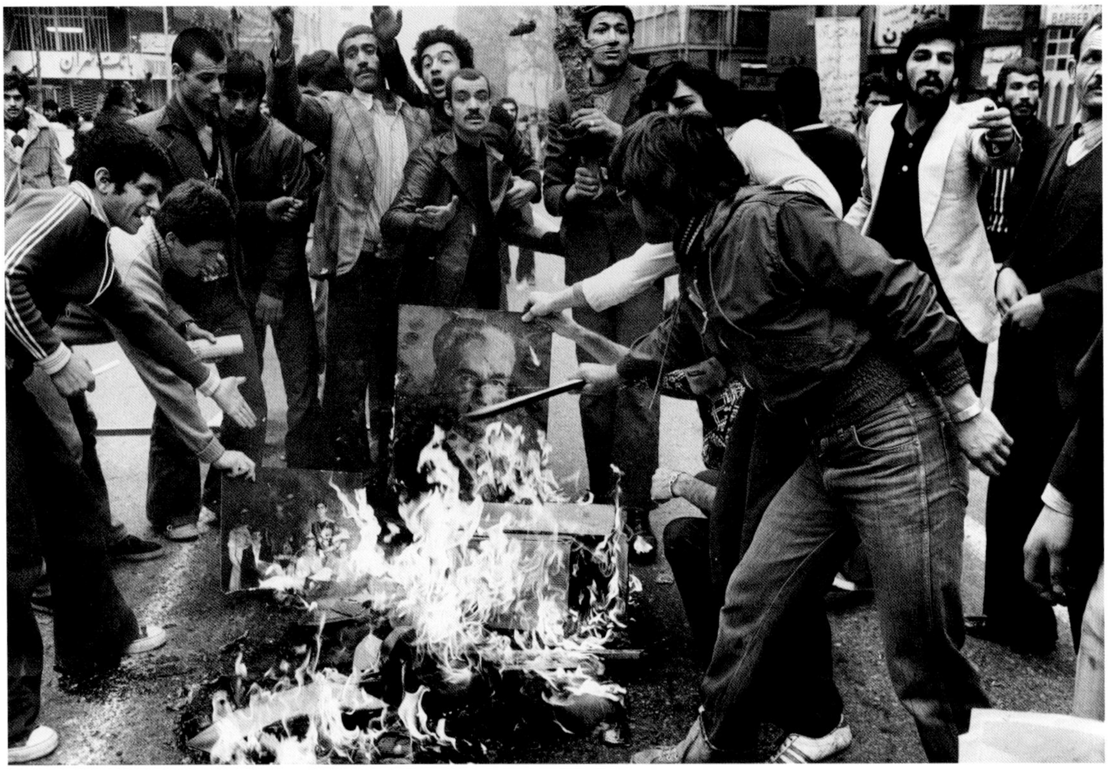

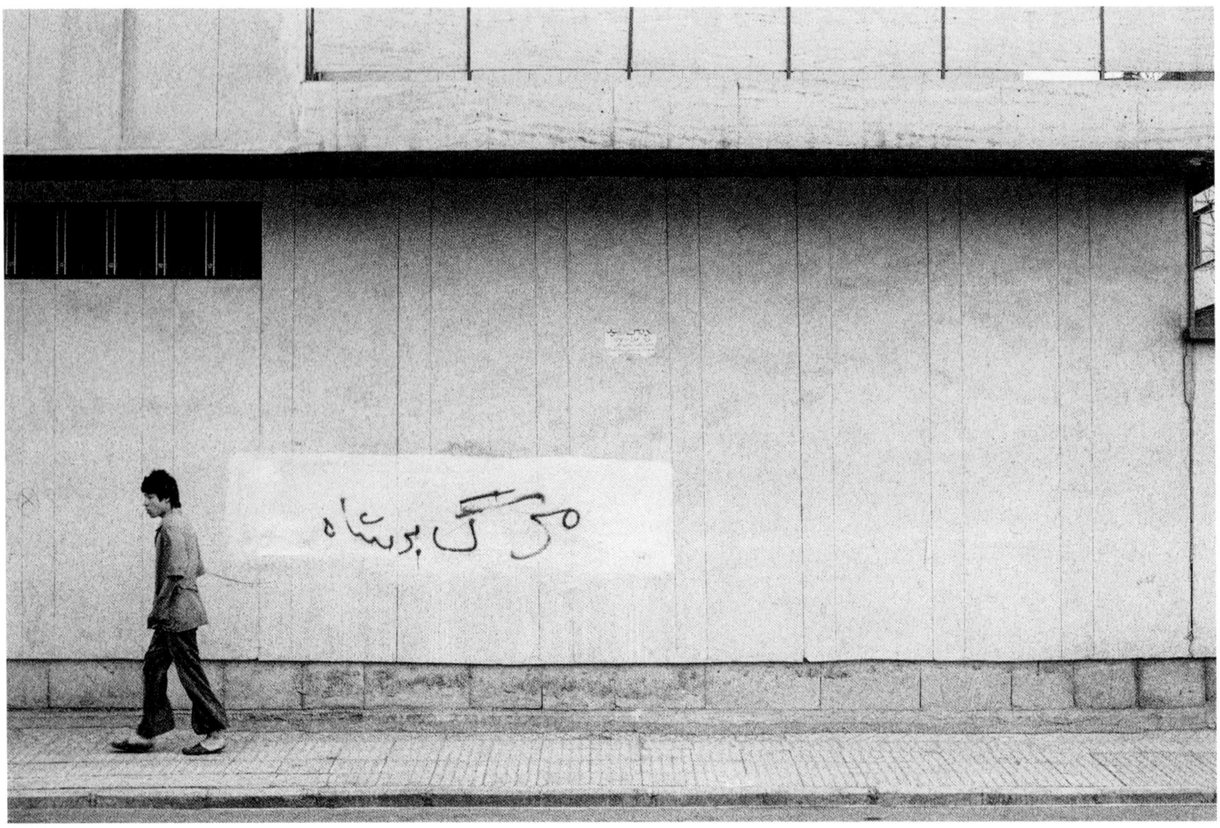

PLATES 62–63

Abbas
***Men burning a portrait of the shah*, 1978**

Maryam Zandi
***Mural News / Streets of Tehran*, 1979**

The greatest public demonstrations in the history of Iran, directed against the shah, took place in December 1978. The photograph by Abbas, the best-known photographer of the Iranian Revolution, of men burning the shah's portrait, captures the turbulence of the time. Maryam Zandi was one of the few women photojournalists to document the revolution. Her photograph of a man walking past graffiti reading, "Down with the Shah," which was painted over an earlier whitewashed message, is typical of the deliberate manner in which she selects and frames her compositions.

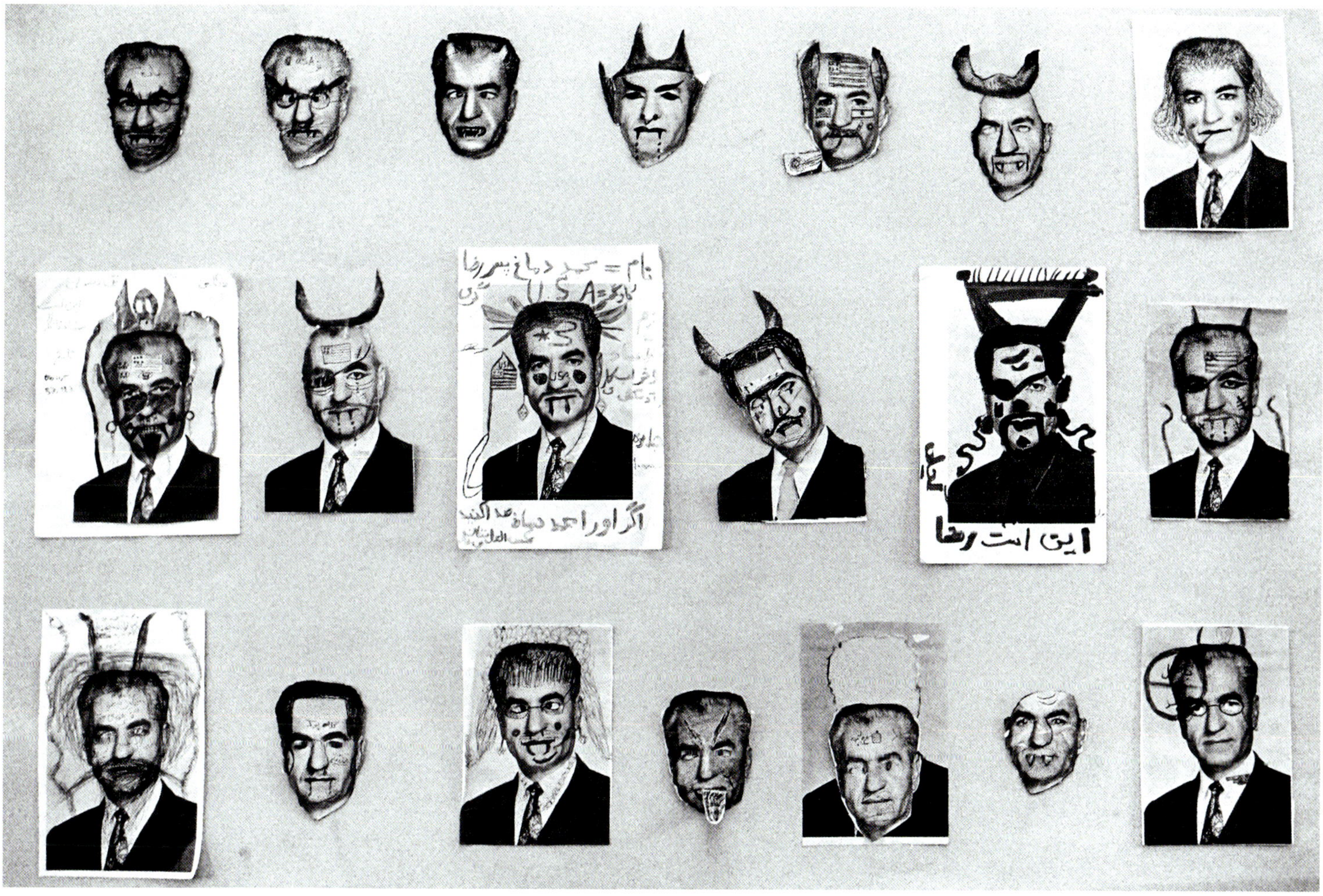

PLATE 64

Maryam Zandi
Untitled, 1979

This photograph recording a collage of cutout and defaced images of the shah, mocking him as a demonic agent of the United States, was probably the work of students at Tehran University. Shot in early 1979, the playfulness and audacity of the anti-shah messaging, which gave way to scenes of violence, factionalism, and fear in the photographs Maryam Zandi made slightly later that year.

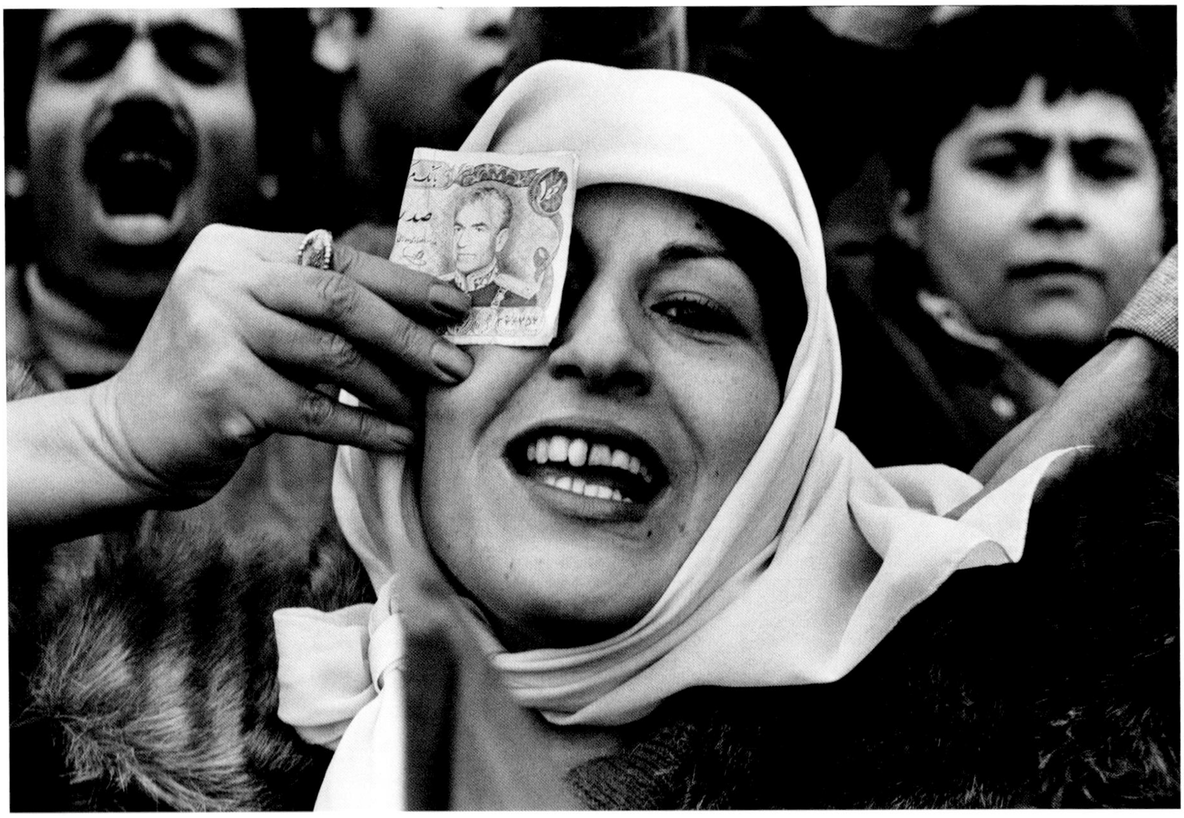

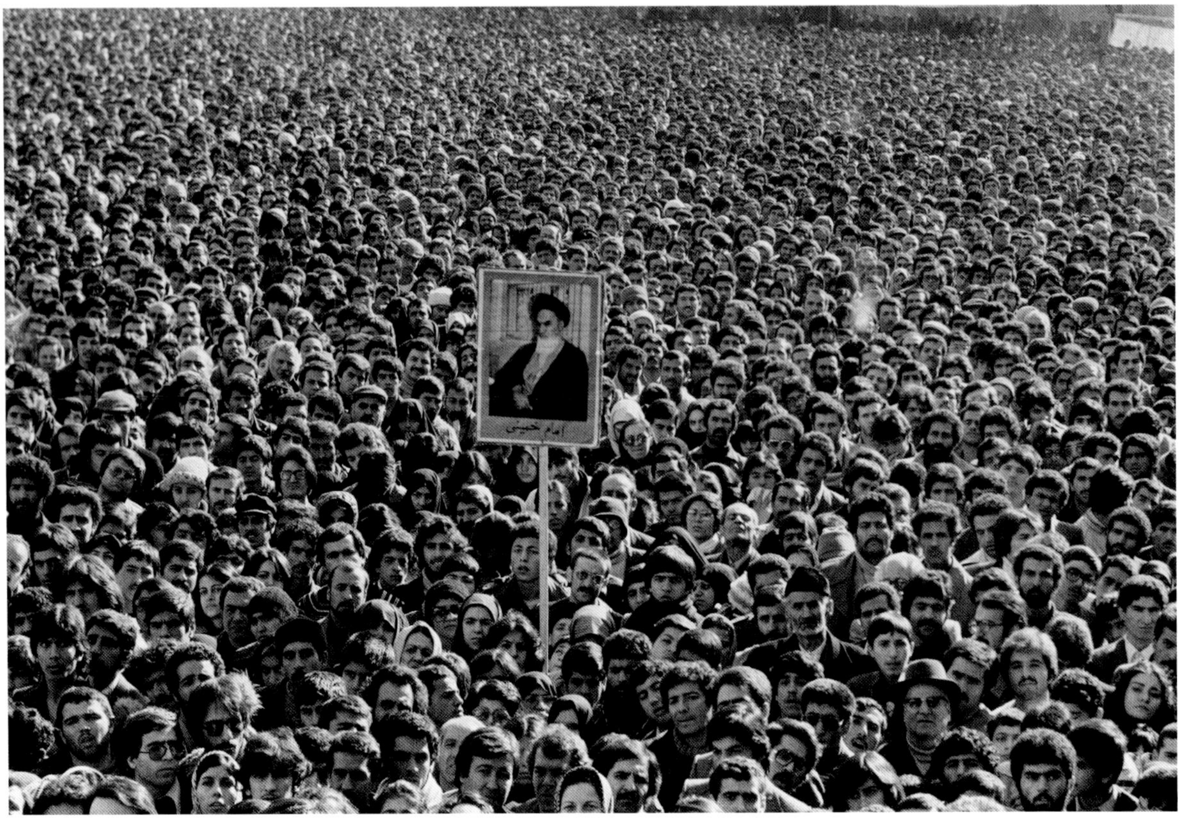

PLATES 65–66

Abbas

***Woman at a pro-shah demonstration*, 1979**

***Ayatollah Ruhollah Khomeini's portrait is exhibited by the crowd attending the opening of the Tehran University*, 1979**

In the tumultuous penultimate days of the shah, protests and strikes paralyzed the nation. Schools and universities were closed, newspapers suspended, and public assembly prohibited. This photograph, in which Ayatollah Khomeini's portrait is exhibited by a crowd, was taken on January 14, 1979, at the reopening of Tehran University, two days before the shah left Iran. Throughout the turbulent political transition, anti- and pro-shah demonstrations continued, as recorded in the photograph of a woman holding to her eye currency depicting the shah, indicating her support for the absent ruler.

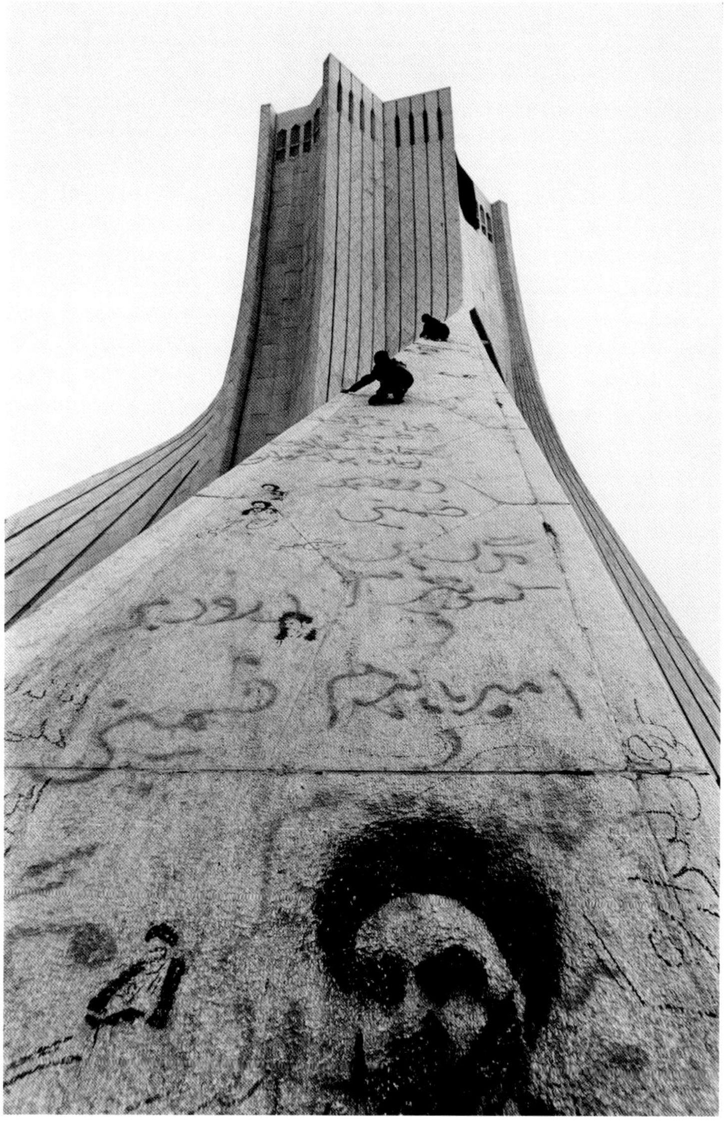

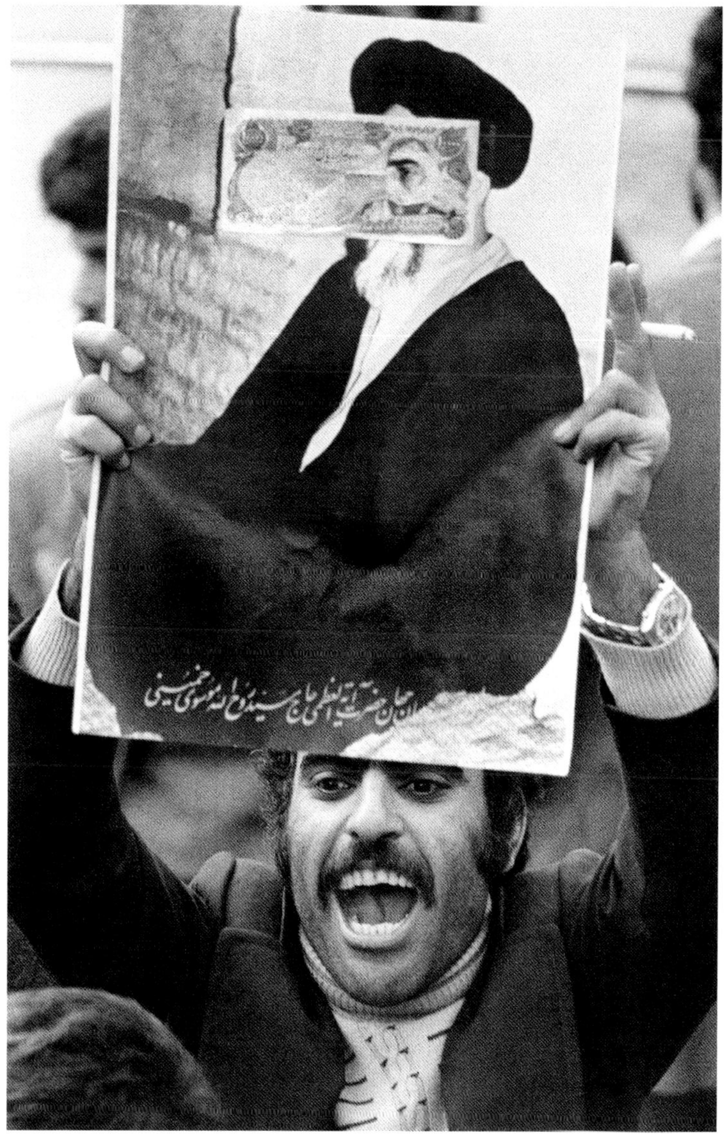

PLATES 67–68 (RIGHT TO LEFT)

Maryam Zandi
***Untitled*, 1979**

Ahmad Aali
***Tehran, 1979*, 1979**

Maryam Zandi sought to compose a photographic memoir documenting the progression of the revolution and its aftermath. Her image of a man holding a Khomeini poster belongs to the period that marked the departure of the shah and predates the return of the Ayatollah. Ahmad Aali, who has been an active force in the Iranian art world since the early 1960s, succinctly captured Iran's new postrevolutionary world in his photograph, which encapsulates the shattering transfer of power. Here the famed Shahyad Tower has been rebranded with the stenciled image of Khomeini.

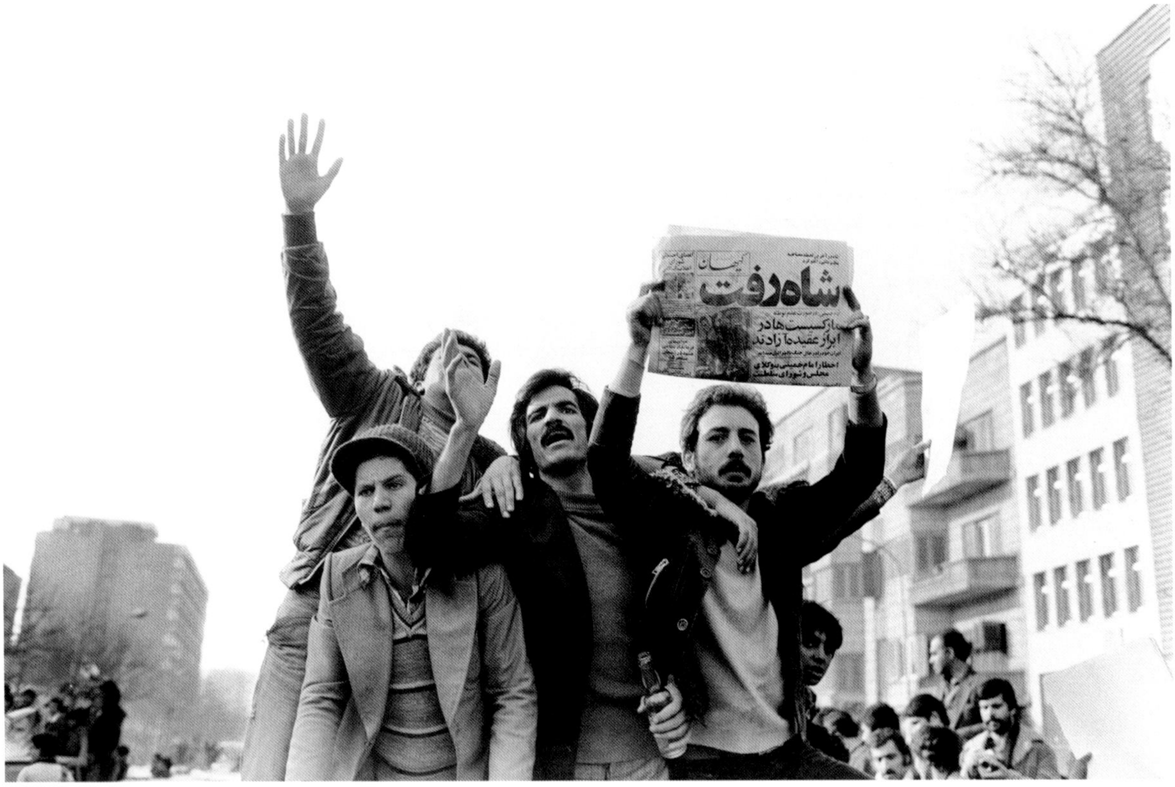

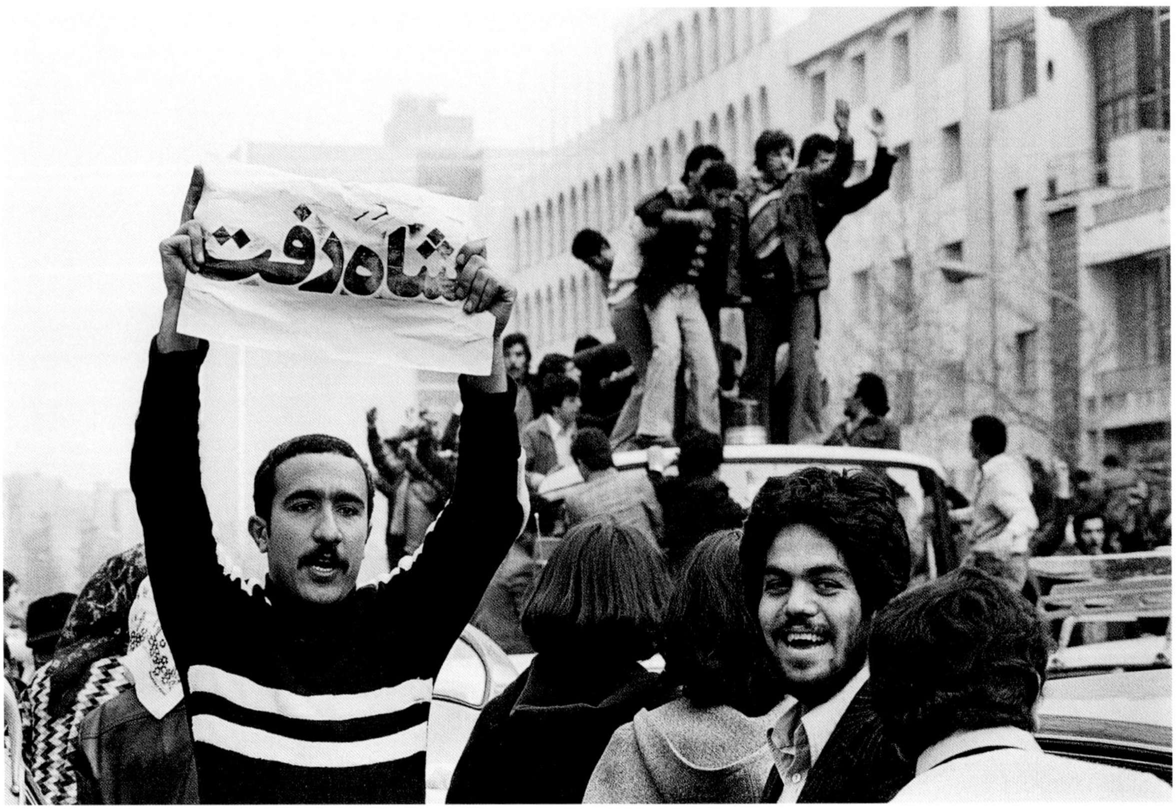

PLATES 69–70

Kaveh Golestan
***The Shah Left*, 1979**

Maryam Zandi
***Happiness of People on the Day the Shah Left Iran, Enghelab and Other Streets*, January 16, 1979**

Best known as a documentary photographer, Kaveh Golestan in 1979 was awarded the Robert Capa Gold Medal for his brilliant visual account of the Iranian Revolution. This photograph is from that body of work and records the jubilant throngs (a member of which holds aloft a newspaper featuring the historic headline, "The Shah Left") that filled Tehran's streets following the departure of the shah. Maryam Zandi's contemporaneous photograph likewise documents the elated crowds on January 16, 1979.

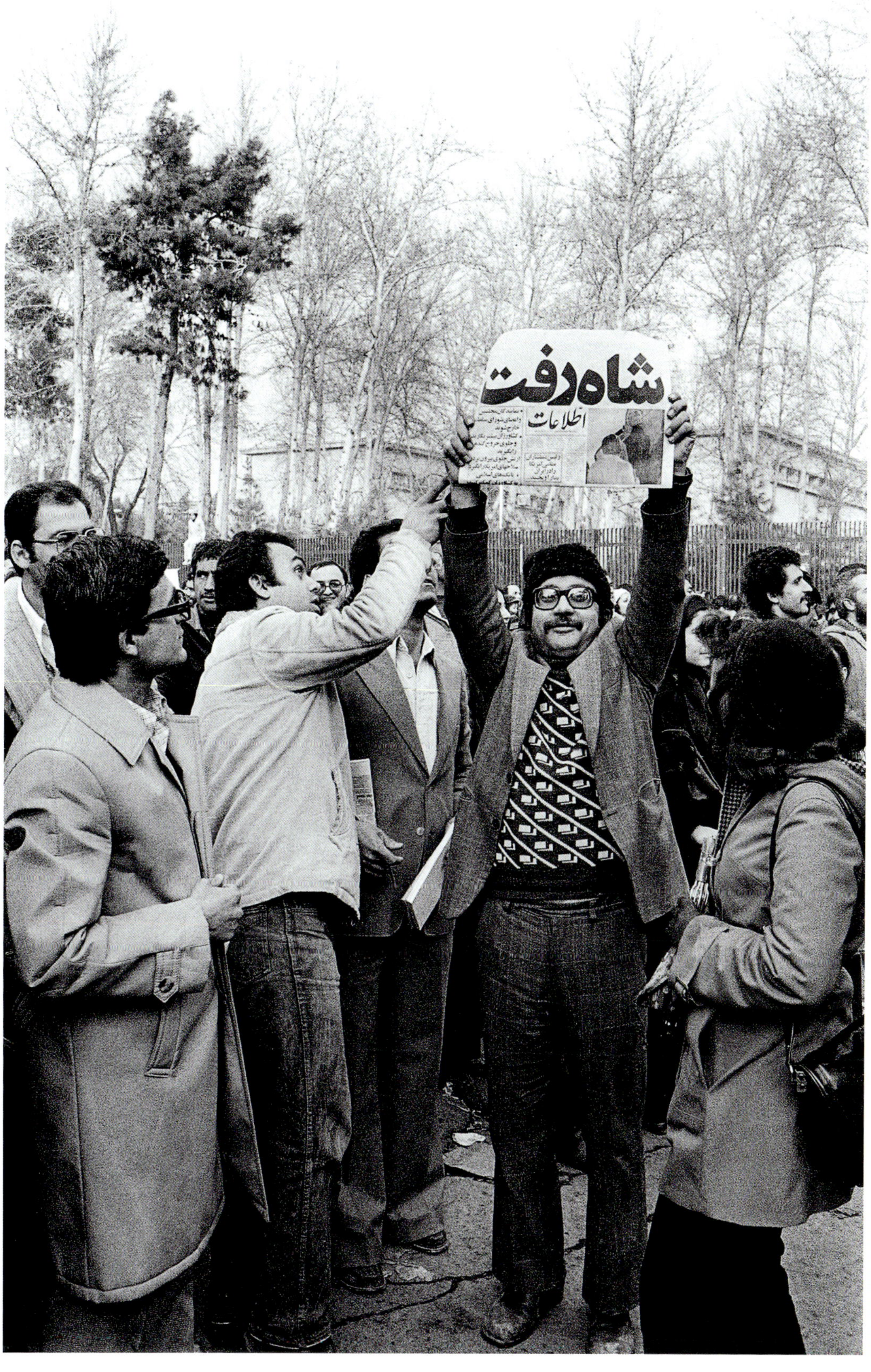

PLATE 71

Maryam Zandi
***Untitled*, 1979**

Maryam Zandi's cool eye for choosing her subjects is particularly evident in this image of a man ecstatically holding a newspaper with the headline, "The Shah Left." There is something both charming and sad in this scene of unrestrained happiness, for, within a few months, many of the newspapers proclaiming the glad tidings of the shah's departure would be shuttered by the new leadership.

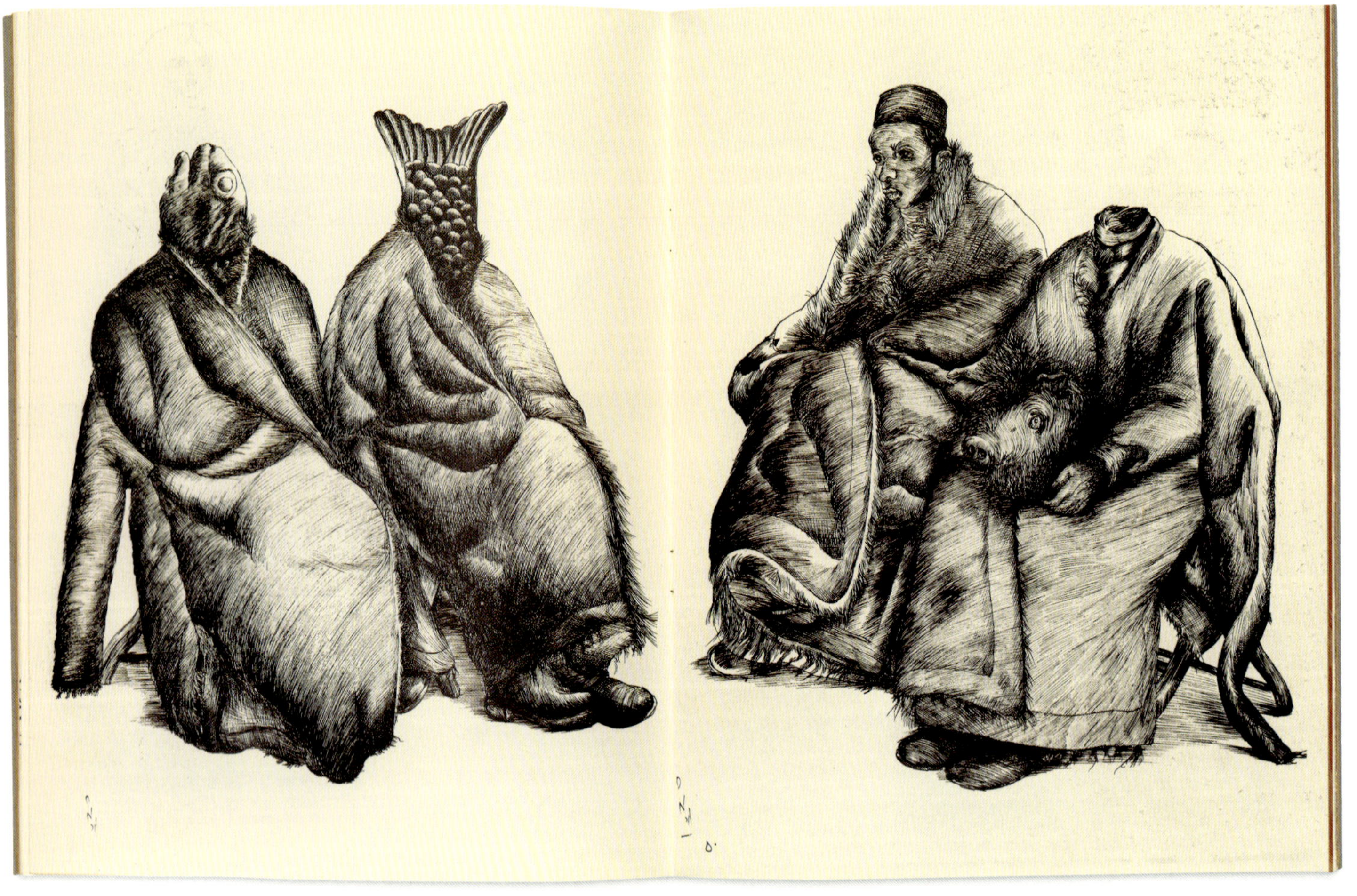

PLATE 72

Ardeshir Mohassess
Religious Prohibition of the Caviar Fish **(LEFT) and an untitled drawing (RIGHT)**

Within Iran's burgeoning modern art scene in the 1960s and 1970s, Ardeshir Mohassess emerged as a vocal social critic. A self-taught artist with an academic background in law and political science, Mohassess often used grotesqueries and dark humor to express his distaste for oppression and corruption, even among the hallowed religious class. Reproduced in a 1972 exhibition catalogue, this pair of drawings (now missing) depicts mutated clerics: the men are shown with their heads missing or replaced by fish parts; one holds a pig's head in his lap.

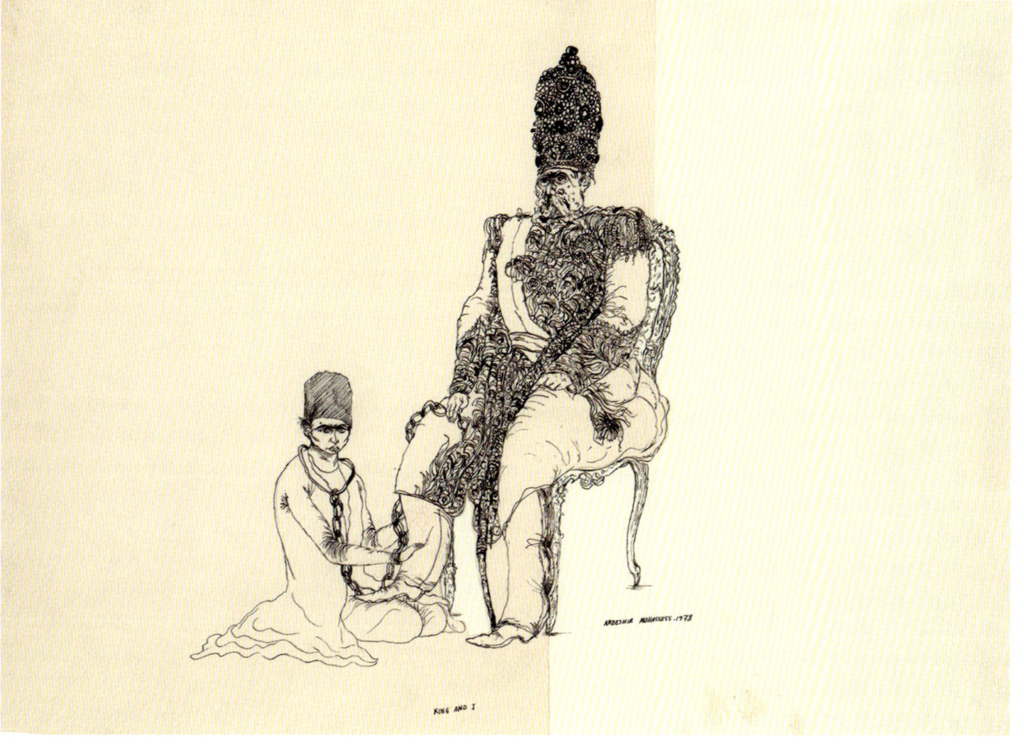

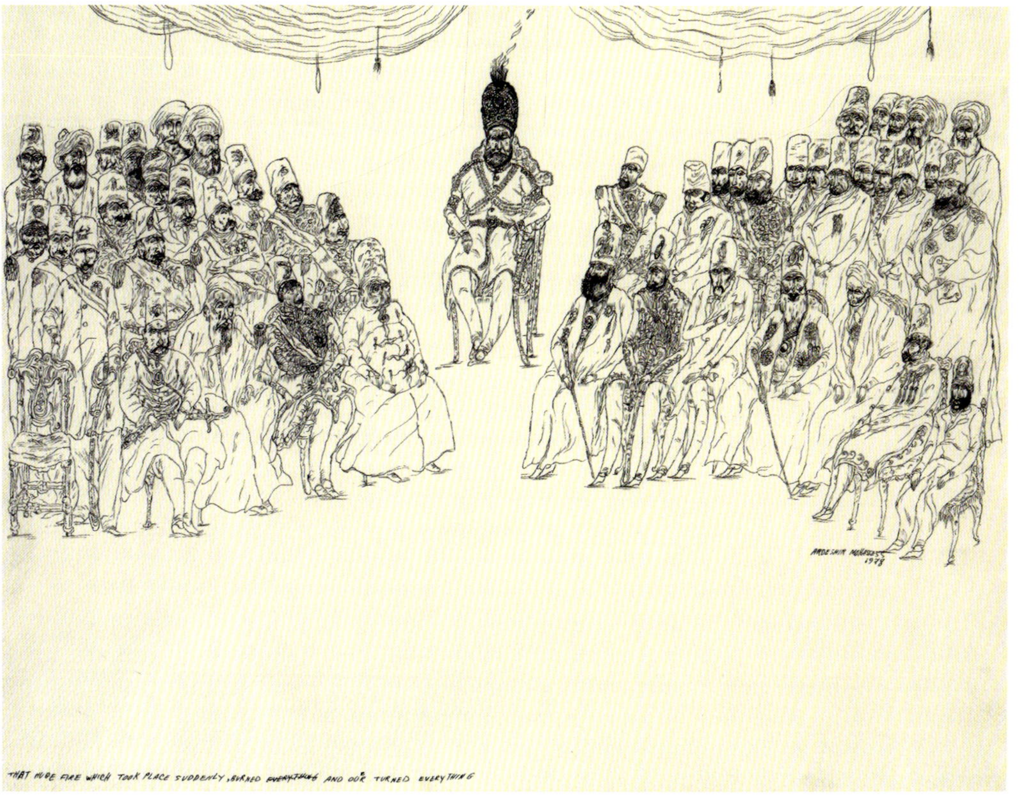

PLATES 73 A–B

Ardeshir Mohassess
***King and I*, 1978**
FROM THE SERIES Life in Iran

***That huge fire which took place suddenly, burned and over turned everything*, 1978**
FROM THE SERIES Life in Iran

Ardeshir Mohassess was known for his illustrations that blended humor and social commentary. Though he left Iran in 1976, he closely followed the events leading up to the Iranian Revolution and its aftermath, which are reflected in his series Life in Iran (1977–79). Mohassess sets his compositions in the later nineteenth century, but he clearly is referencing recent events. In one drawing, he illustrates a tragic event from 1978 at Cinema Rex, a movie theater in Abadan that was set ablaze, causing four hundred deaths.

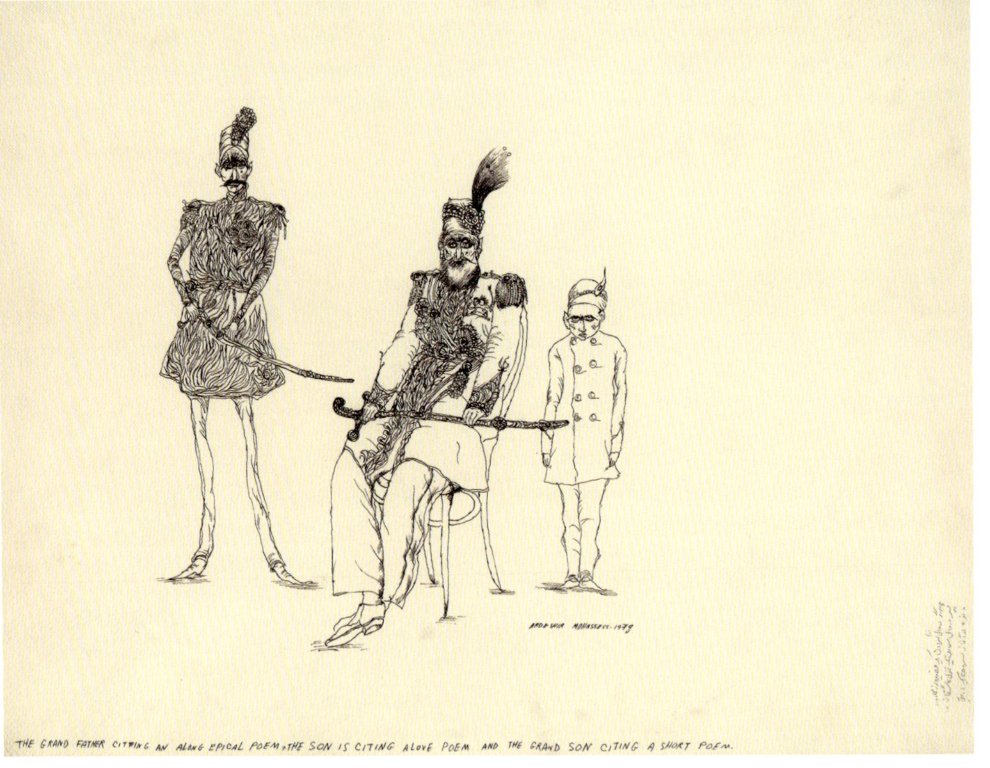

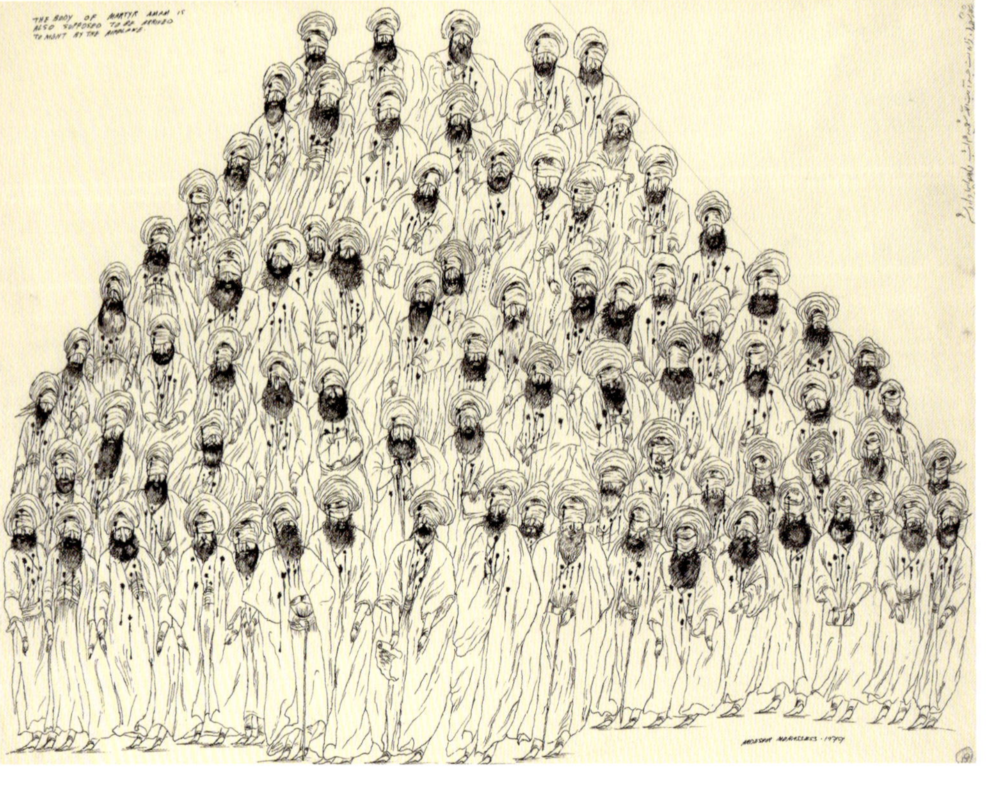

PLATES 73 C–D

Ardeshir Mohassess
***The grand father citing an along* [sic] *epical poem, the son is citing a love poem and the grand son citing a short poem*, 1978**
FROM THE SERIES Life in Iran

***The body of martyr Imam is also supposed to be arrived* [sic] *tonight by the airplane*, 1977**
FROM THE SERIES Life in Iran

In the first drawing, Ardeshir Mohassess represents three generations of Pahlavi rulers in the guise of three Qajar kings who lose their cultural ties with each passing generation. In the second image, he utilized a nineteenth-century photograph of a group of clerics posing in front of a religious school as a foundation for his work. In criticism of the Pahlavi regime, Mohassess depicts traces of bullet holes in the figures' chests, symbolizing their honorable deaths as martyrs, awaiting their (martyred) leader.

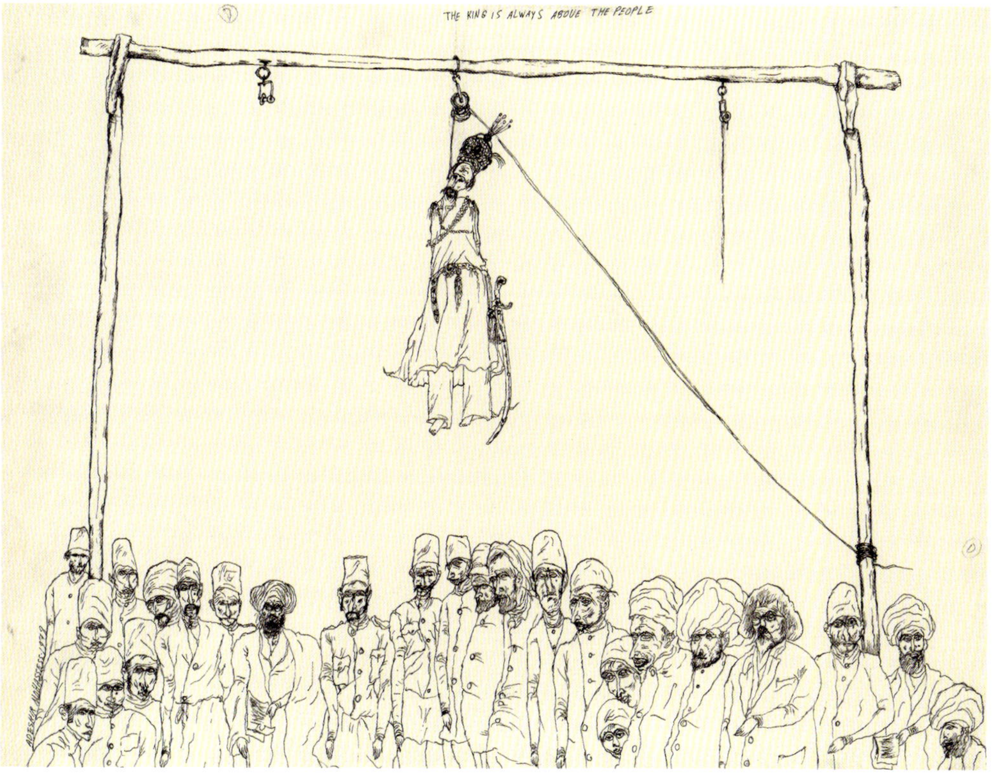

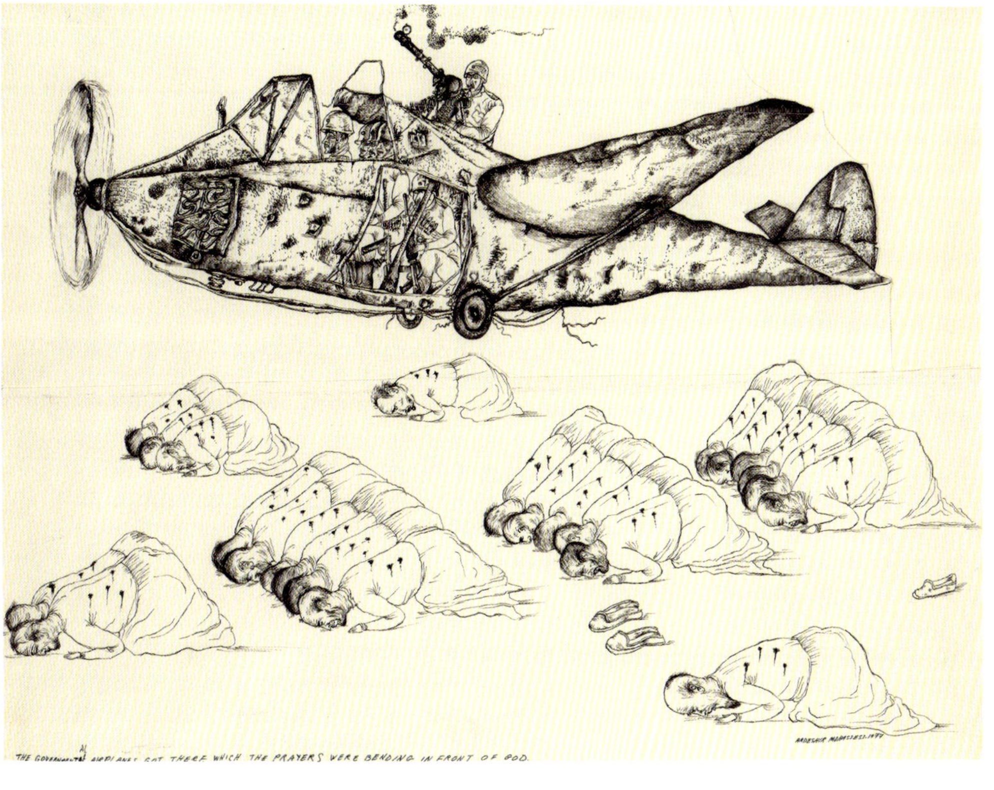

PLATES 73 E–F

Ardeshir Mohassess
***The king is always above the people*, 1978**
FROM THE SERIES Life in Iran

***The governmental airplanes got there which* [sic] *the prayers were bending in front of God*, 1977**
FROM THE SERIES Life in Iran

In depicting a Qajar king hanging above all others, Ardeshir Mohassess humorously interprets the notion of the tyrant's supremacy, literally and morbidly. This illustration, which bears resemblance to a late-Qajar photograph of a bandit's execution, reveals the artist's astute choice of Qajar imagery to symbolize the current shah's demise. The drawing illustrating men at prayer with bullet holes in their backs references the frequent raids on mosques prior to the 1979 Iranian Revolution. The dilapidated aircraft suggests the exhaustion of the shah's army in its battle against the people.

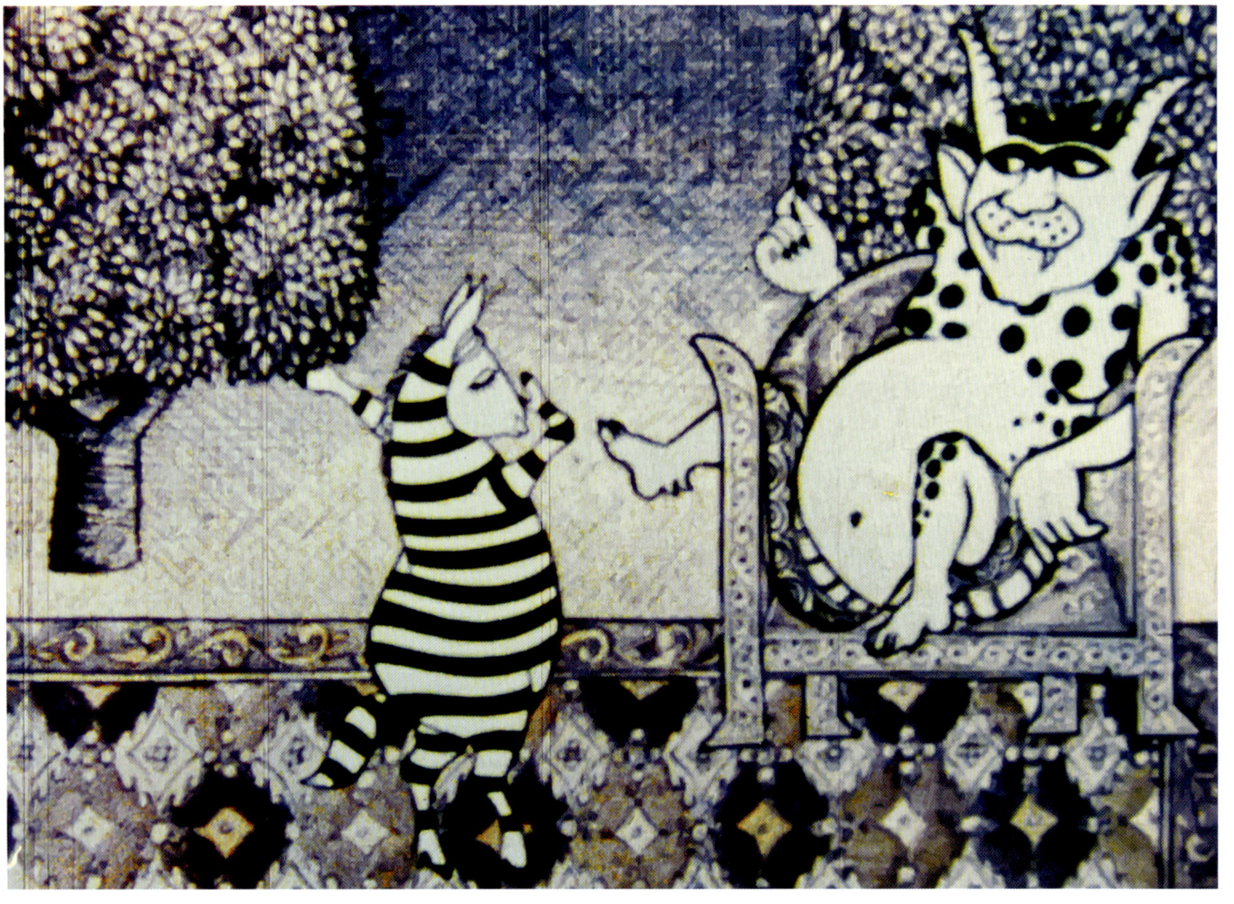

PLATE 74

Noureddin Zarrinkelk
***Amir Hamza the Lover and the Dancing Zebra,* 1977**

This animation presents a traditional tale of magic, villainy, and thwarted love, and visually blends nineteenth-century furnishings and costumes with contemporary (1977) elements. It includes a segment of a dancing zebra, actually an enchanted princess, whose stripes move uncannily with her body. The figure of the horned demon who bewitched the princess was based on Amir-Abbas Hoveyda, Iran's prime minister from 1965 to 1977.

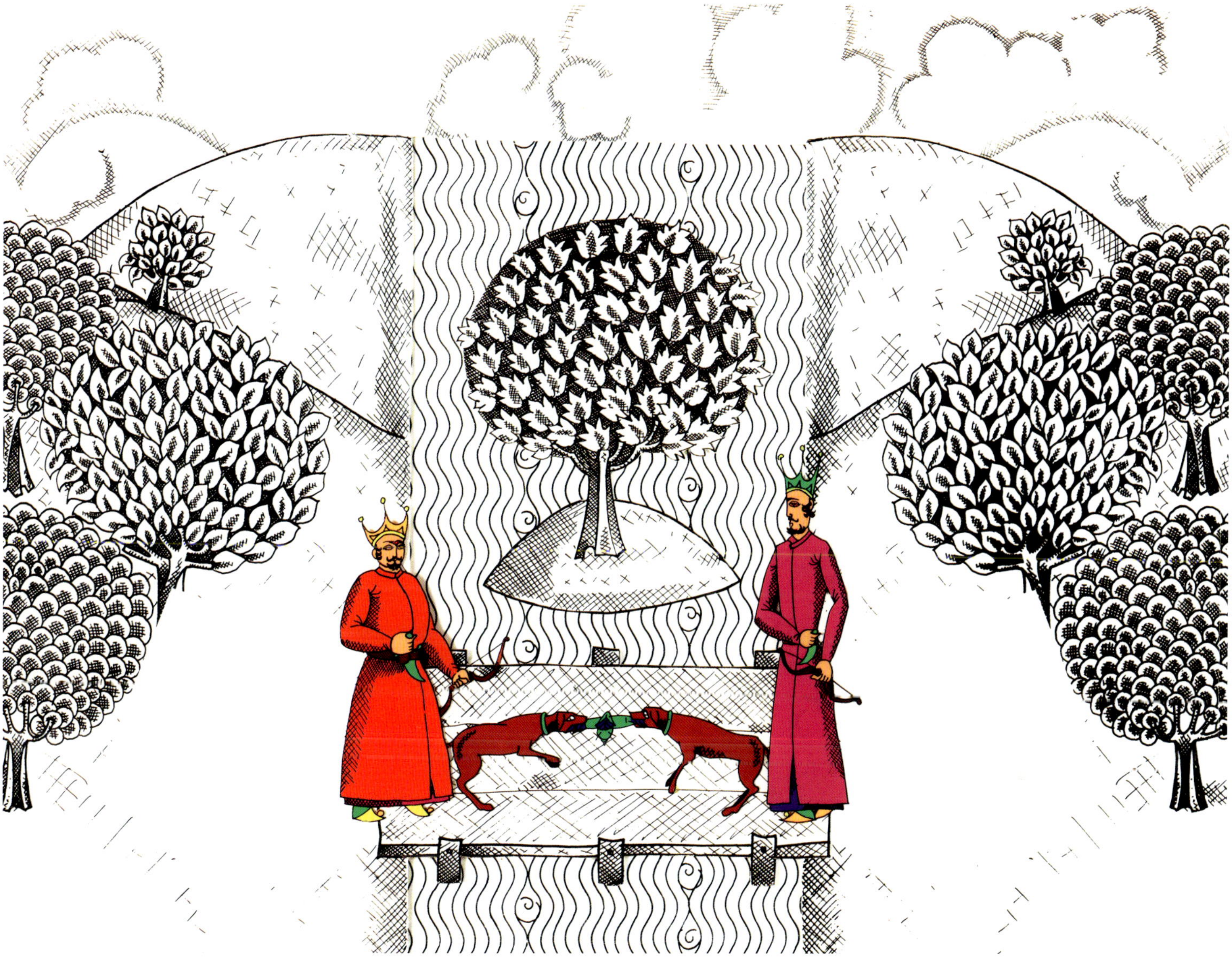

PLATE 75

Ali Akbar Sadeghi
***Flower Storm*, 1972**

Flower Storm is the second film by one of the Iran's pioneers of animation, Ali Akbar Sadeghi. The images, rendered in a style loosely based on traditional Persian manuscript painting, recount the story of the personal conflict between two kings that eventually leads to war. Through the secret collaboration of the children from both lands, the warheads are replaced with flowers and birds and are showered upon the kingdoms; this also references the Persian expression *sarzamin-i gul u bulbul* (the land of bird and flower), meaning a peaceful land.

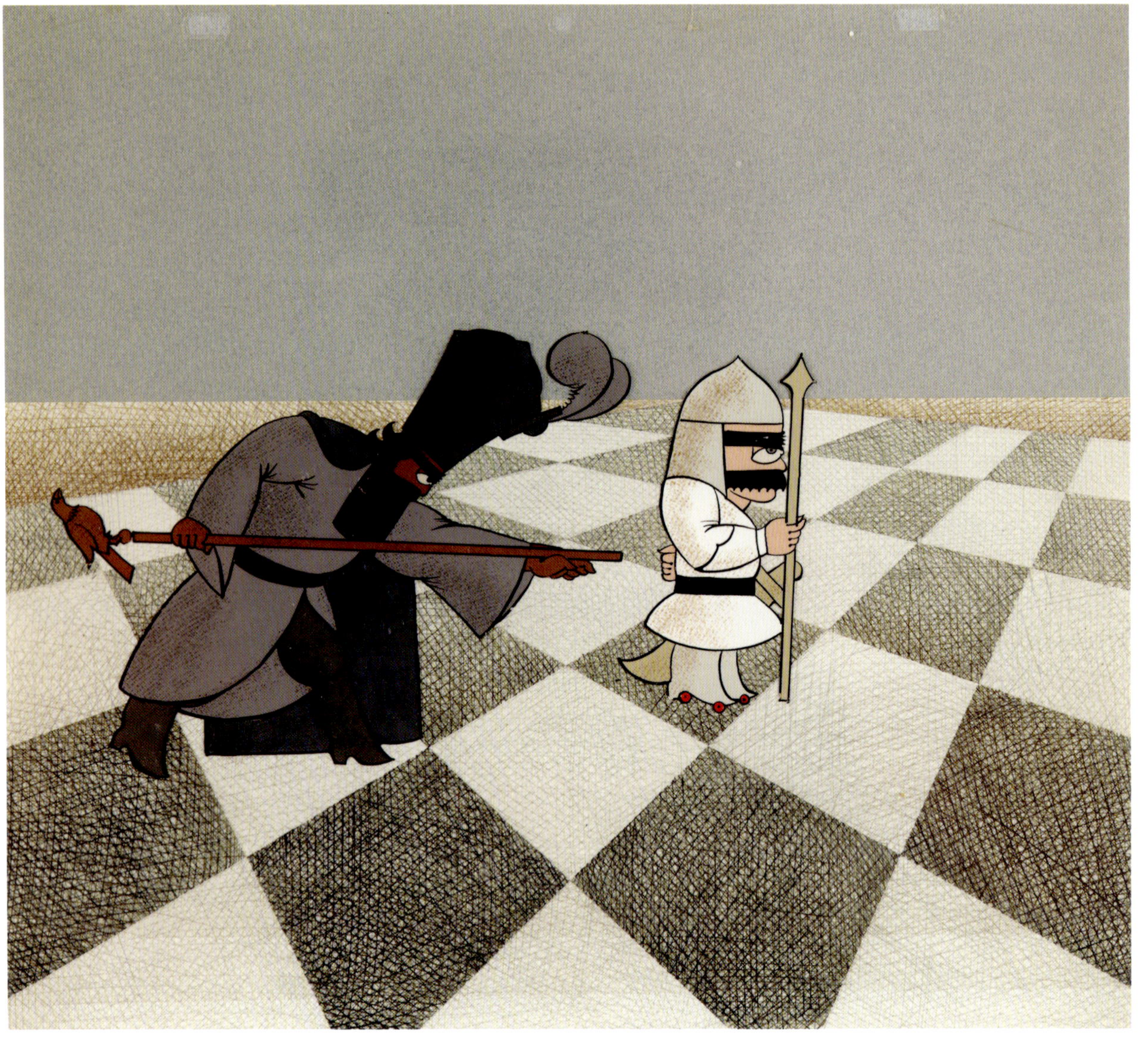

PLATE 76

Ali Akbar Sadeghi
***The Rook*, 1974**

The Rook, by Ali Akbar Sadeghi, playfully embodies the modern subject of war through the classic game of chess. Persian-looking figures stand in as chess pieces. Sadeghi portrays ignorant leaders playing at war, and common people representing the pawns, castles, and knights, who are the first to be slayed. The deceptive statesmen or viziers (traditional queens) use their positions to serve the shahs (kings), while the *rukhs* (rooks—*rukh* is Persian for war chariot) roll through the battlefield/chessboard.

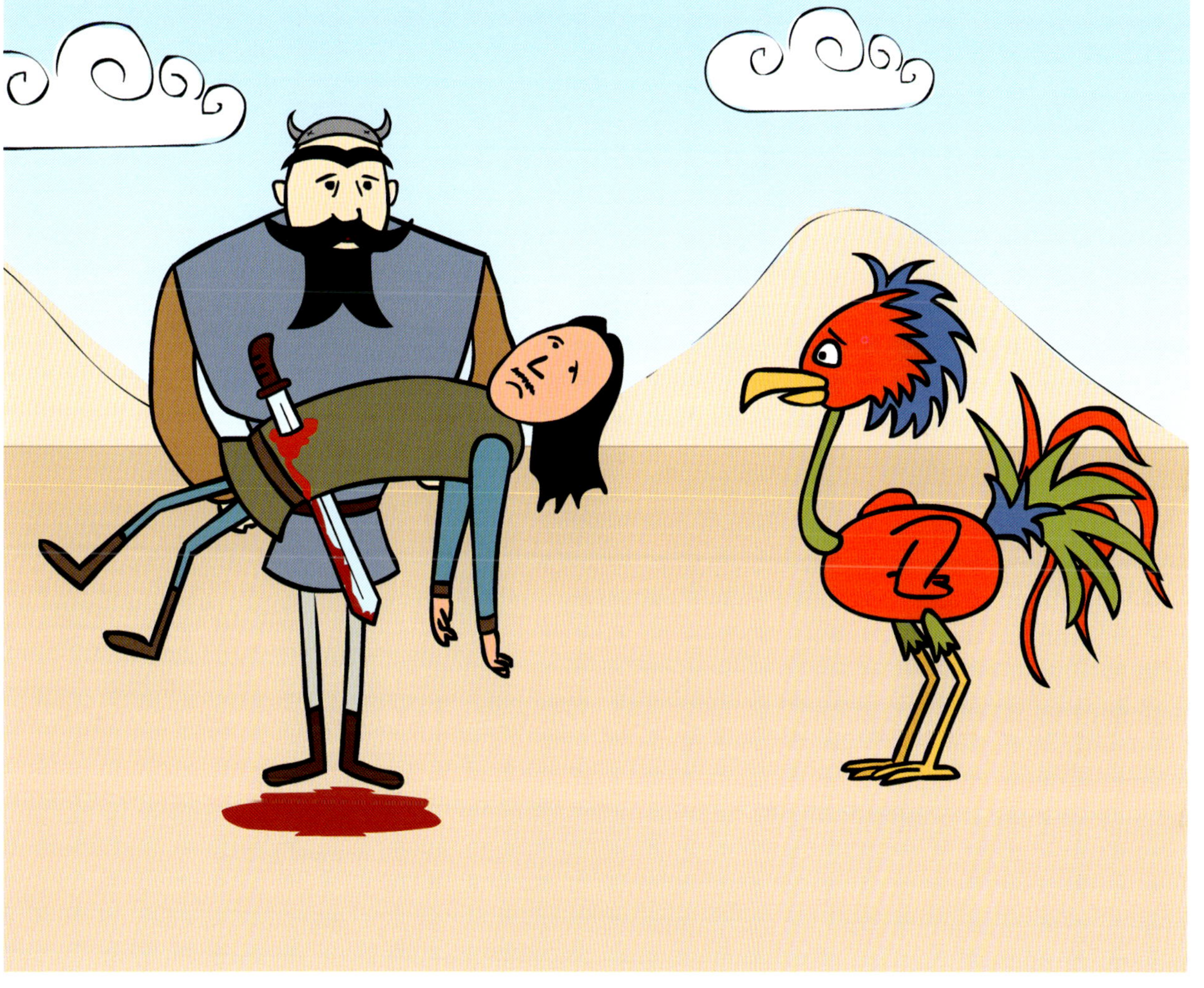

PLATE 77

Pouya Afshar and Soroush Rezaee
***Rostam in Wonderland*, 2012–14**

Rostam in Wonderland—a five-episode collaboration between Pouya Afshar, a multimedia artist, and Soroush Rezaee, an animator—transports the legendary warrior of the *Shahnama* to twenty-first-century Iran. The once-deft hero fumbles through trials of contemporary life that are both comically absurd and all too realistic, including the pitfalls of inflation, a drug epidemic, and the effects of economic sanctions. The artists dryly critique contemporary Iranian society by making light of these issues through Rustam's naïveté and shock at the changed ways of his beloved Iran.

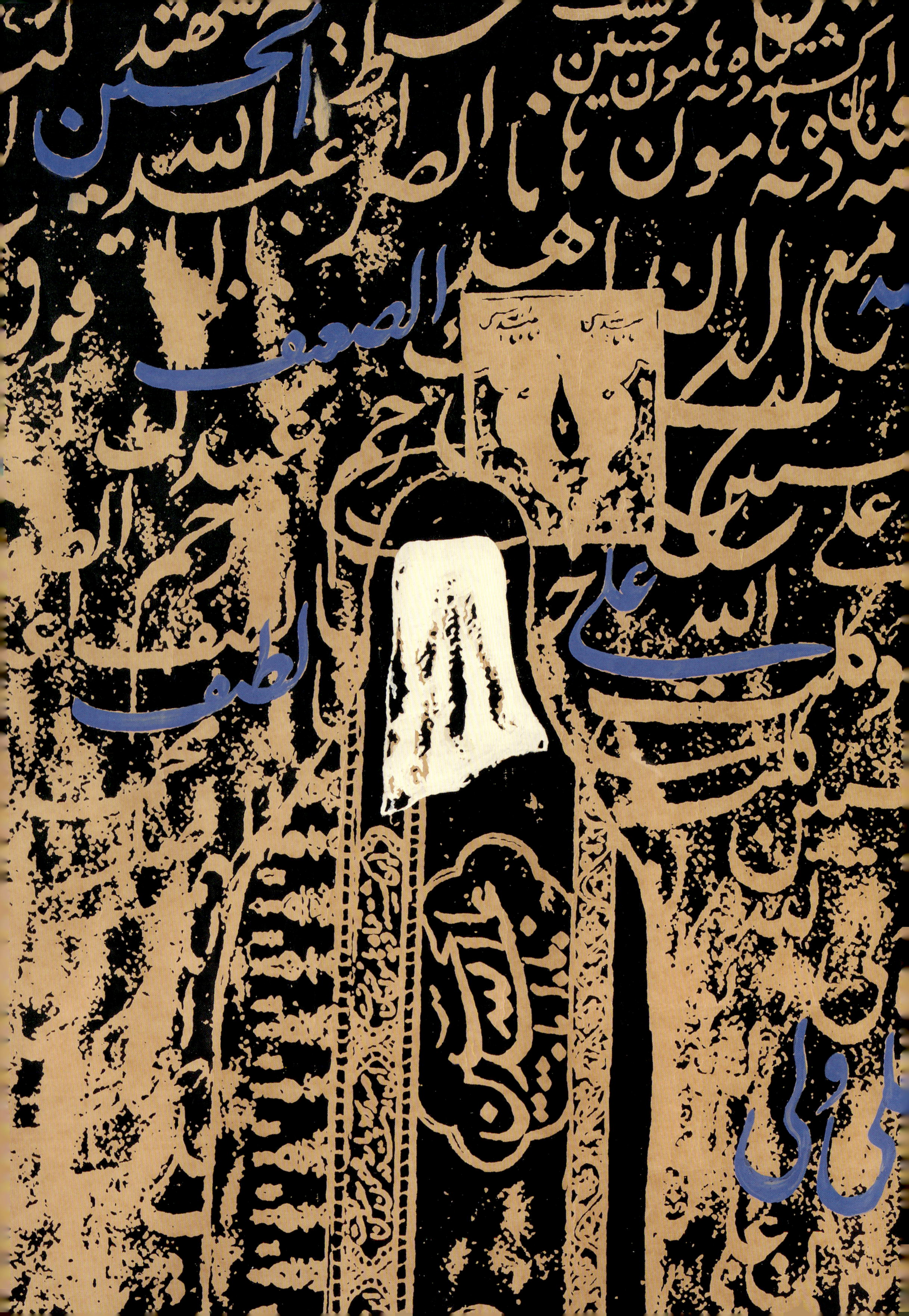

Saints *and* Martyrs

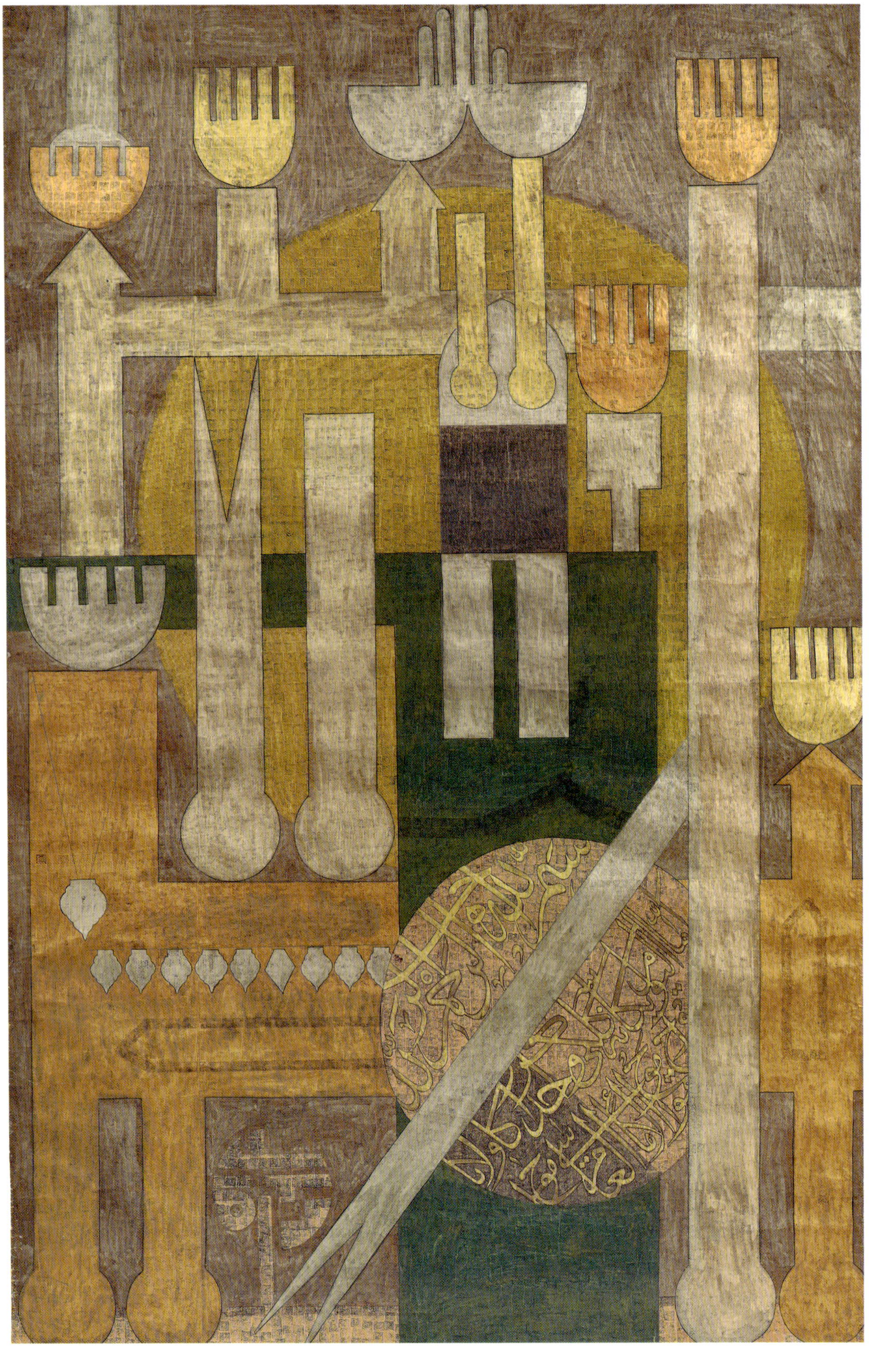

PLATE 78

Faramarz Pilaram
***Imam*, c. 1962**

This painting encapsulates many of the characteristics of the Saqqakhana movement, which blended Shi'ite themes and motifs with modern art aesthetics into a uniquely Iranian style. Here, Faramarz Pilaram, a pioneer of the movement, abstractly references Imam Ali through the bifurcated-sword-like shapes. The geometrized hands reference the severed hands of Abbas, who was killed along with Imam Husain at Karbala in 680; the hand was also a feature of small public water fountains known as *saqqakhana*, for which the movement was named.

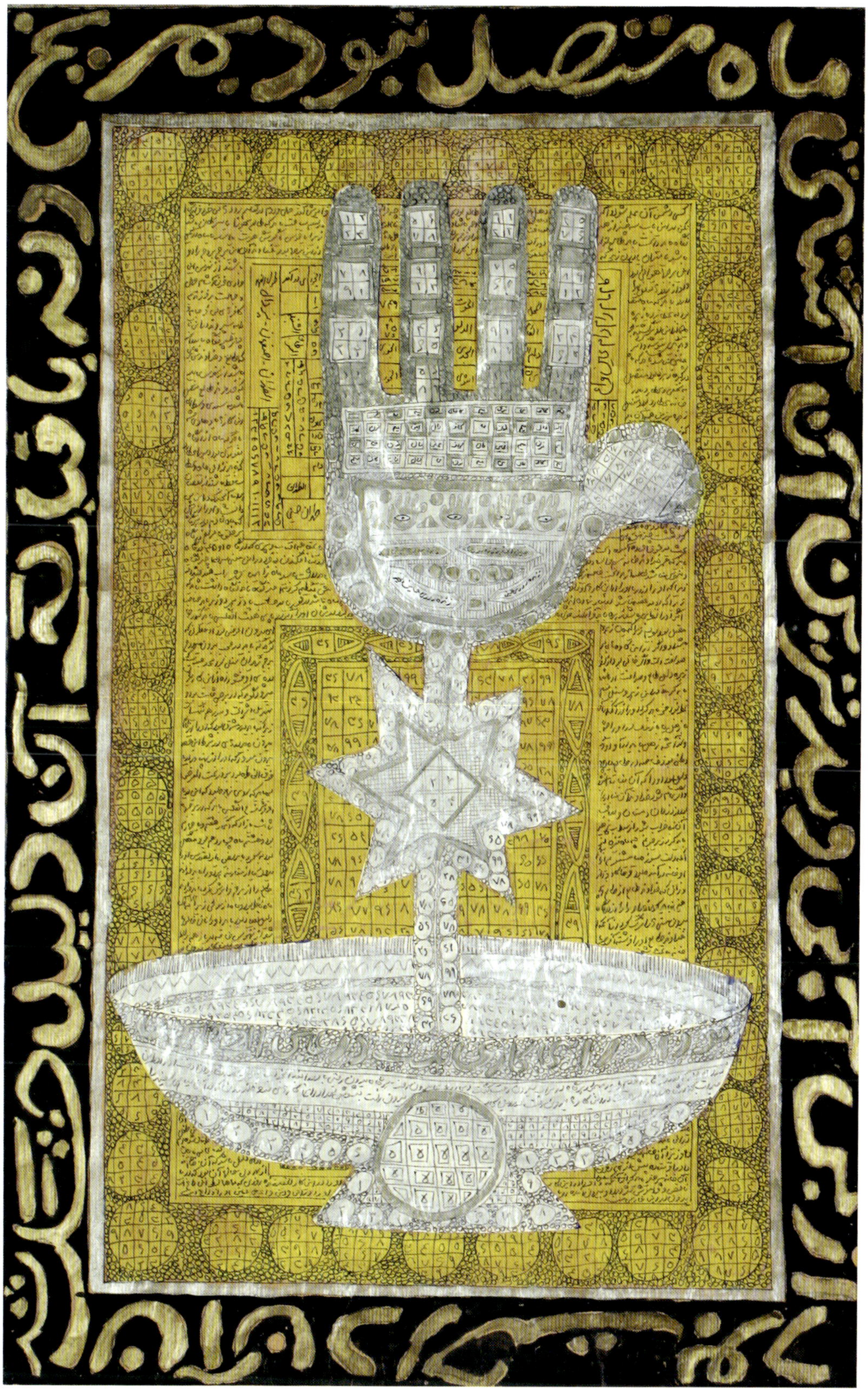

PLATE 79

Charles Hossein Zenderoudi
The Hand, **1960–61**

One of the pioneers of Iranian modernism, Zenderoudi is especially associated with the Saqqakhana movement, so called for Shi'ite-themed public drinking fountains. Expressed in the visual language of modern art, the collage's subject matter and symbolism are closely tied to the *saqqakhana* itself. An upraised hand of flat brass typically surmounts the fountain, as a reminder of the mutilation of Abbas, half-brother and standard-bearer of Imam Husain, and drinking bowls attached by chains to the water tank prompt users to recall the thirst of Husain and his followers at Karbala.

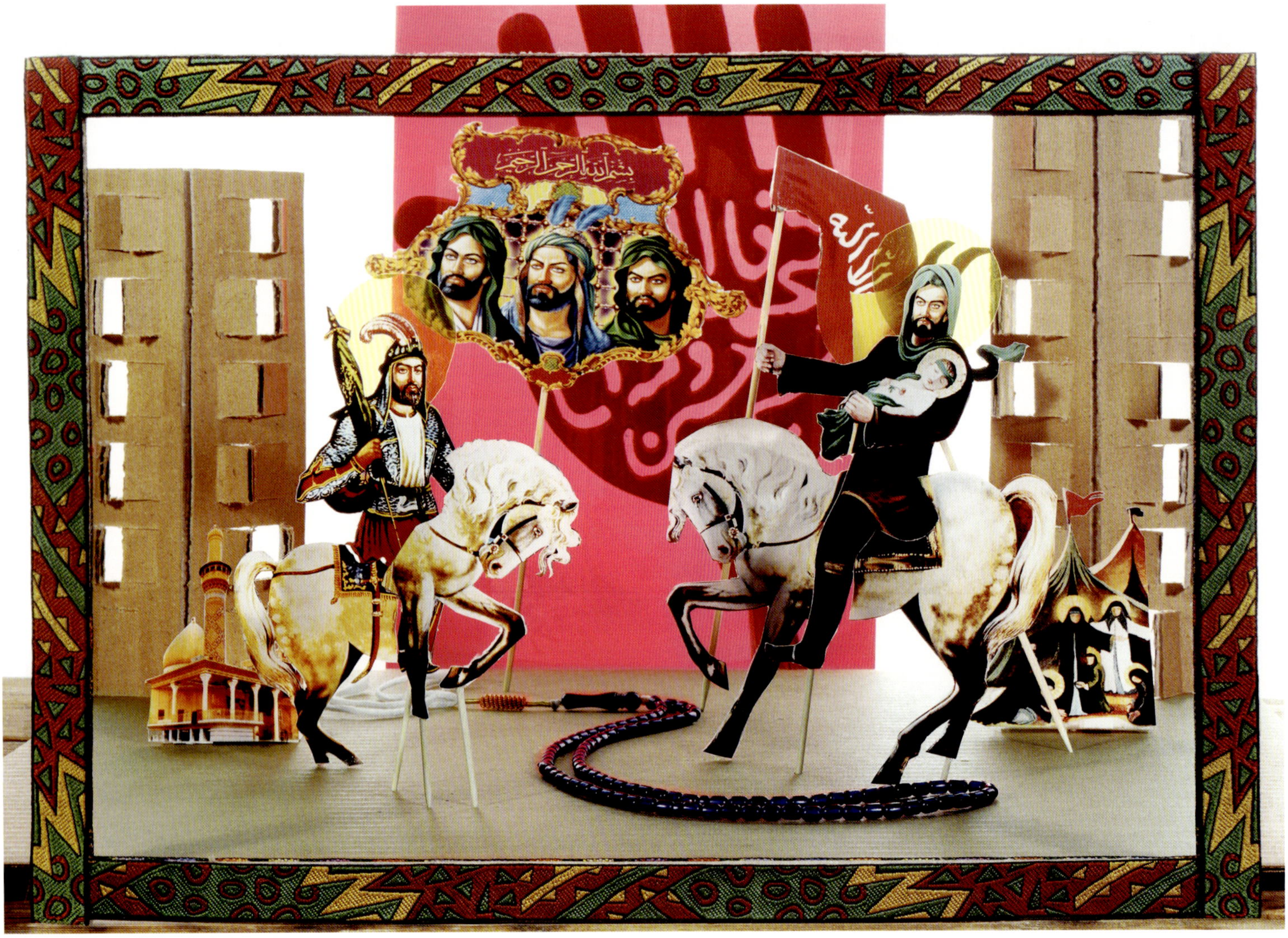

PLATE 80 A

Mohsen Yazdipour
***Untitled*, 2008**
FROM THE SERIES A Play with Feelings

Ashura imagery, as facetiously recontextualized here, is meant to remove any barriers between past and present so that the viewer can experience the events of Karbala in real time. Here, the horseman at right is Imam Husain with his infant son Ali Asghar, shot with an arrow in the throat while his father held him aloft pleading for water. At left is the imam's standard-bearer and half-brother, Abbas, who was mutilated and killed while attempting to fetch water from the Euphrates.

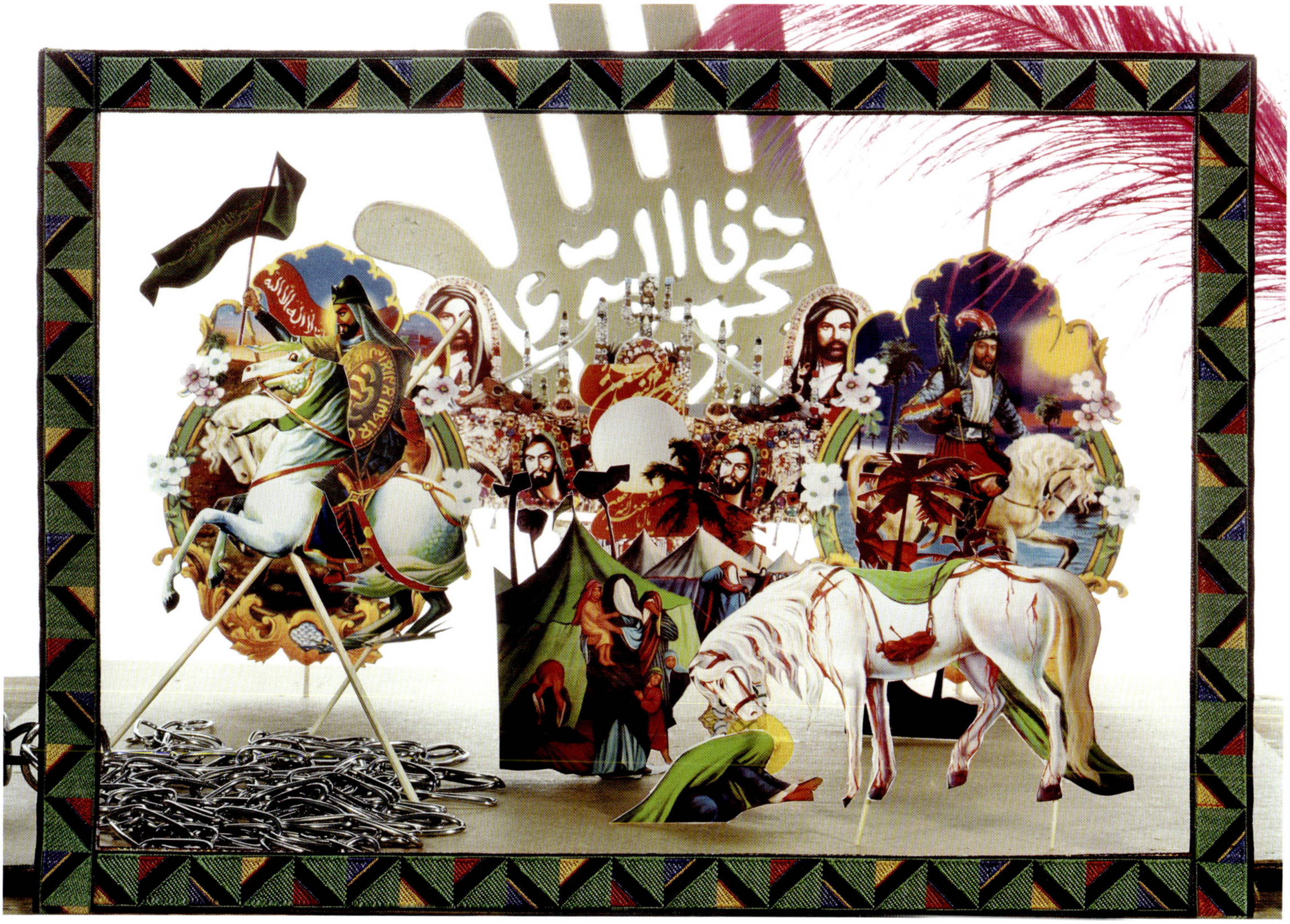

PLATE 80 B

Mohsen Yazdipour
***Untitled*, 2008**
FROM THE SERIES **A Play with Feelings**

This print is from a series in which the artist collages and photographs popular images (now proscribed in Iran) commemorating the massacre of Imam Husain and his family at Karbala in 680. Such Shi'ite imagery remains readily recognizable in Iran in much the same way that depictions of martyred Christian saints were commonplace in premodern Europe and are still well known in many places.

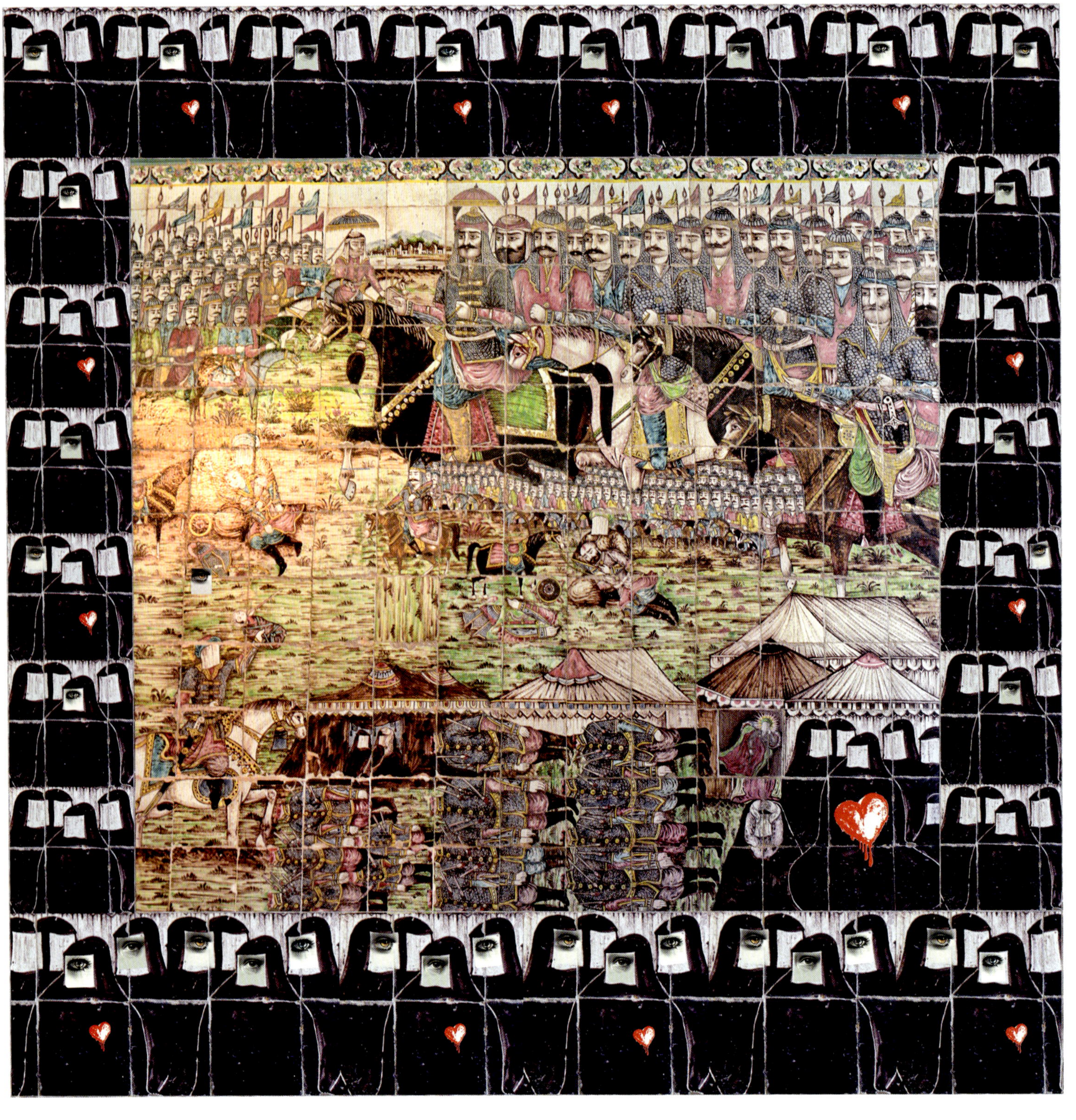

PLATE 81

Rana Javadi
Never Ending Chaos 7, 2013

Rana Javadi, along with other female photojournalists, was banned from covering the front line of the Iran-Iraq War (1980–88). In this later work, Javadi offers an account of the war through digital collage, using images from early-twentieth-century Karbala-themed tiles in the Mu'avin al-Mulk *takiyya*. These prints emphasize the recycling of shared experience across time and space. Javadi uses images of women as a frame, a reminder of her own marginalization and that of her female colleagues, whose only accepted role in war is to have saddened, blood-dripping hearts and tearful eyes.

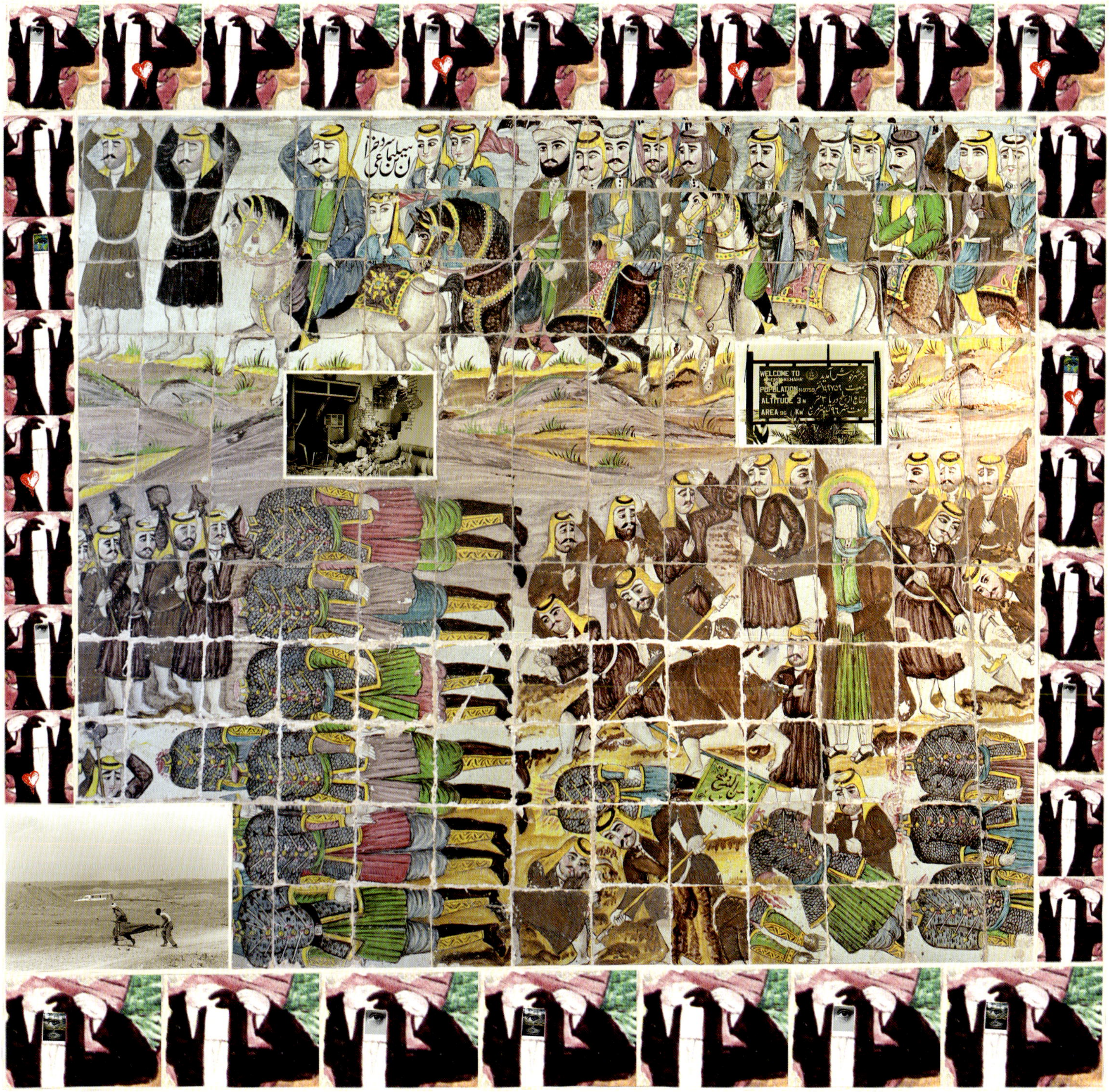

PLATE 82

Rana Javadi
***Never Ending Chaos 2*, 2013**

In this photo collage print, photojournalist Rana Javadi draws a strong comparison between the violent battle of Khorramshahr, a major engagement in the Iran-Iraq War in 1980, and the battle of Karbala, at which Imam Husain and his family were martyred in 680. This message is conveyed through the juxtaposition of images of demolished houses and deceased soldiers in Khorramshahr shot by Javadi's late husband, Bahman Jalali, and the artist's own photographs of the Karbala-themed tiles of the Mu'avin al-Mulk *takiyya* in Kermanshah.

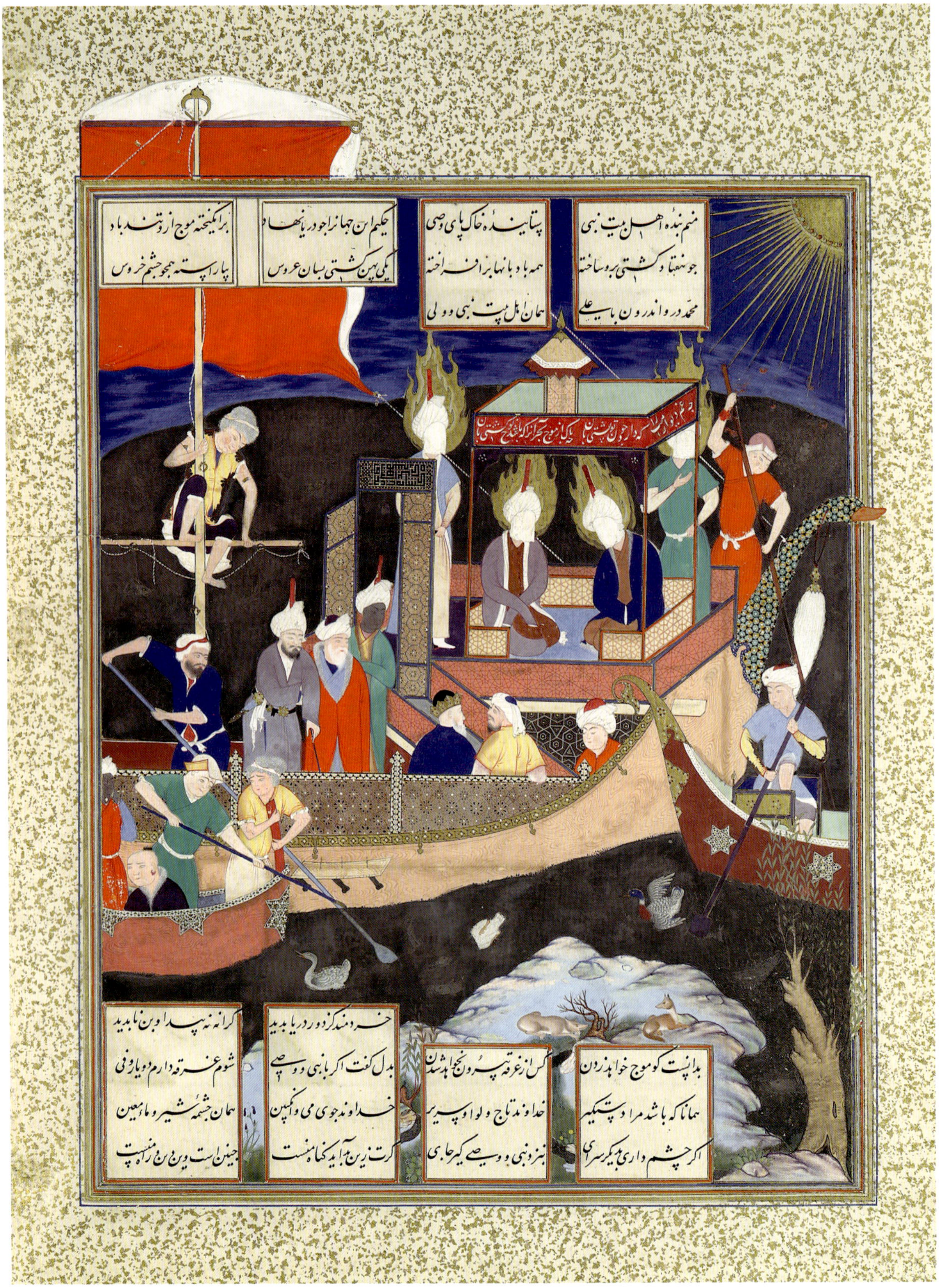

PLATE 83

PAINTING ATTRIBUTED TO **Mirza Ali**
***Parable of the Ship of Shi'ism*, c. 1530–35**
FROM the *Shahnama* of Firdausi

This manuscript illustration and associated imagery bring the seventh-century Shi'ite Imams into the early Safavid period. It was under the Safavid dynasty (1501–1722) that Shi'ite Islam became the state religion of Iran, and this painting, from a royally sponsored manuscript, emphasizes the new orthodoxy. The four veiled figures with flaming haloes depicted in the bow of the central ship are members of the *ahl-i bait-i nabi*, the family of the house of the Prophet: Muhammad and Ali (kneeling), and Ali's sons Hasan and Husain.

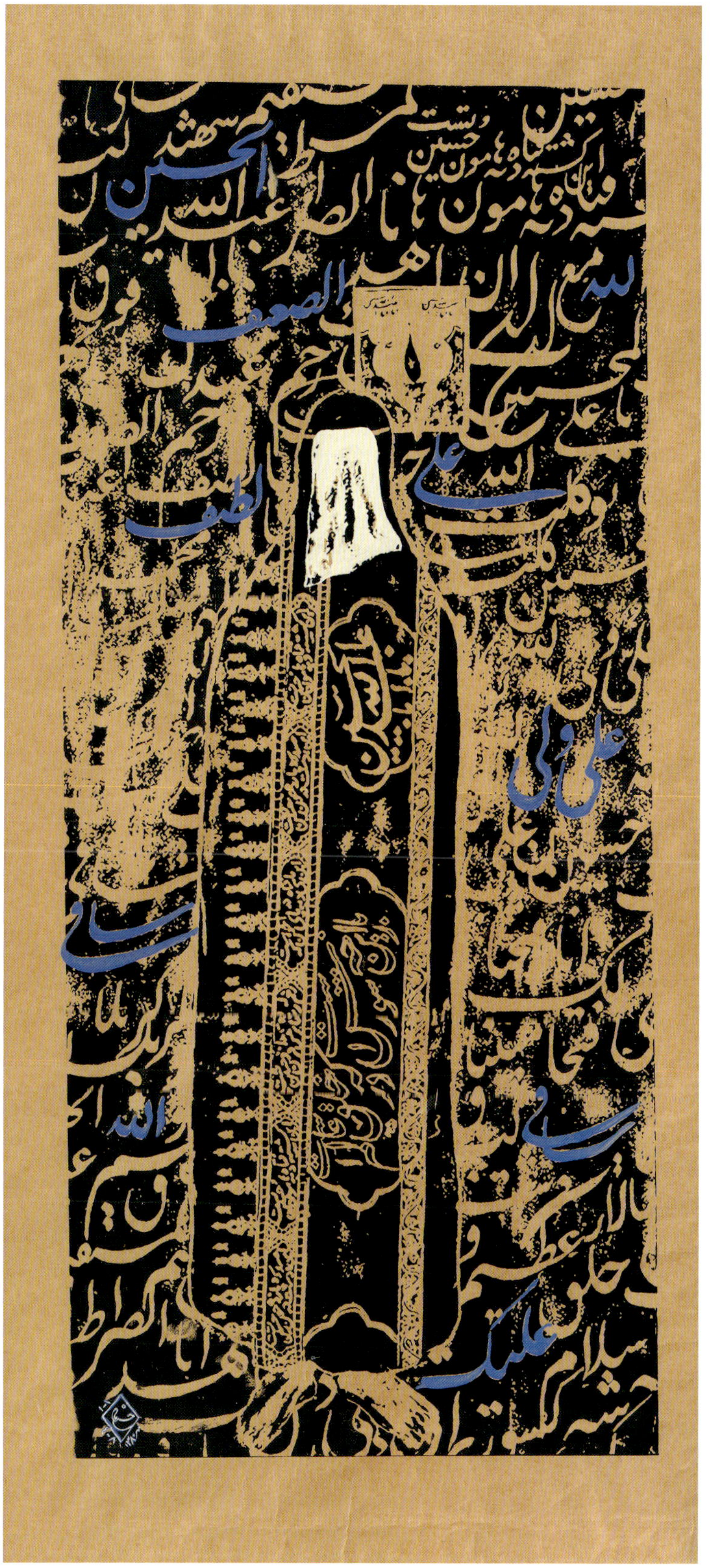

PLATE 84

Khosrow Hassanzadeh
***Untitled*, 2001**

Khosrow Hassanzadeh depicts chador-clad women engulfed by Shi'ite iconography in many of his works on paper. In this version, one of his most effective, the flattened, veiled figure can scarcely be distinguished from the text, which invokes Ali, laments the martyrdom of Husain and his infant son at Karbala, and quotes from the Qur'an. The bright blue paint seems to have been added to balance and enliven the composition rather than to emphasize sections of the text.

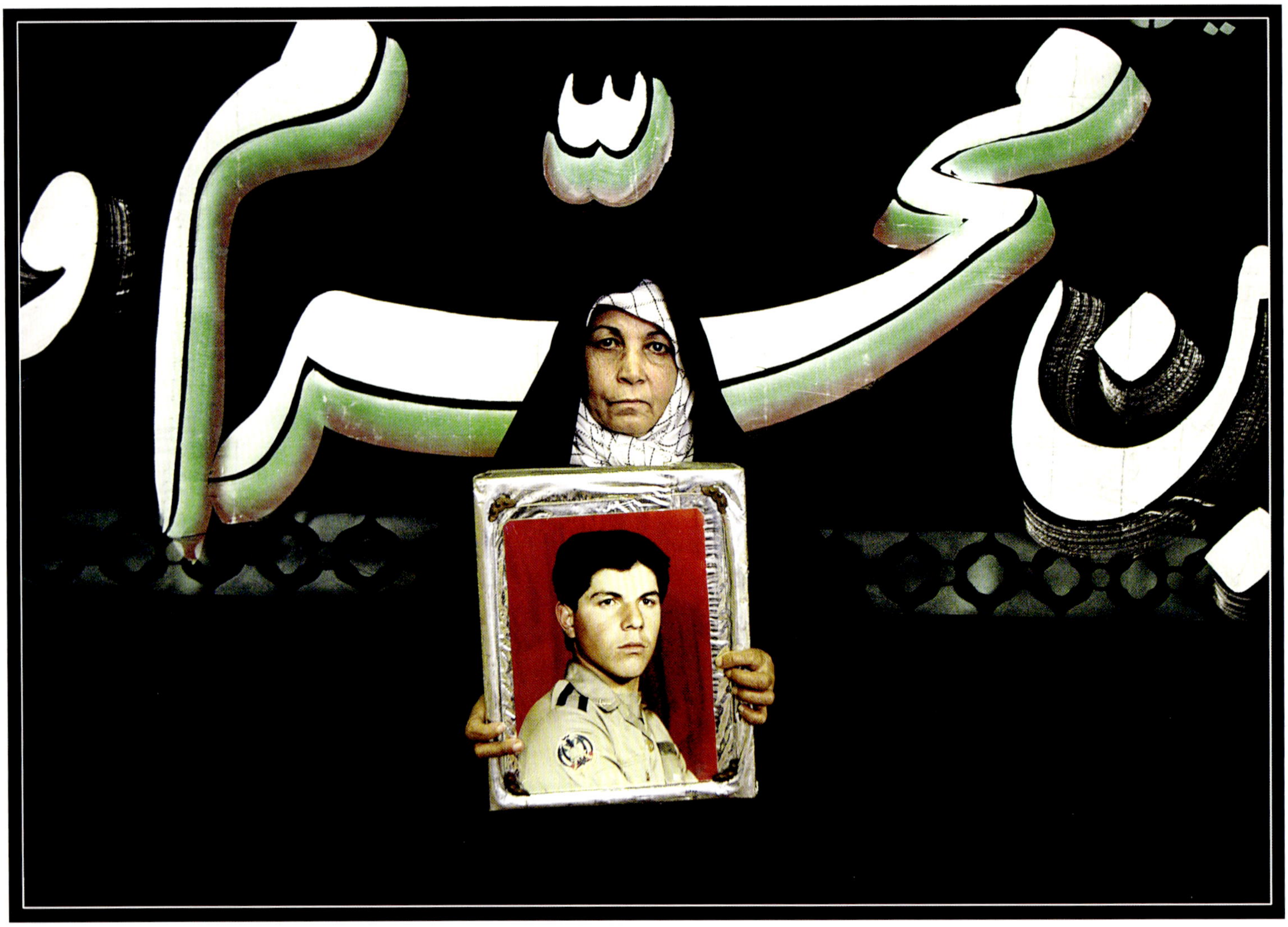

PLATE 85

Newsha Tavakolian
***Mothers of Martyrs*, 2006**
FROM THE SERIES **Mothers of Martyrs**

Part of a younger generation of photographers in Iran, Newsha Tavakolian maintains the documentary tradition of preceding photojournalists, such as Maryam Zandi, Kaveh Golestan, and Abbas. Self-taught, Tavakolian began working for the Iranian press at the age of sixteen and eventually garnered an international reputation, publishing images in the *New York Times*, *Der Spiegel*, and *Le Monde*, among others. Not limited to photojournalism, Tavakolian also produces video works and fine art photography that reflect her documentarian style.

I made the series Mothers of Martyrs trying to find a way to translate into visual terms a relationship that transcends time. The portraits these mothers hold of their dead sons show their faces frozen in the past. If you look closely, you can see the resemblance; just the mothers have lived on, gotten older, their faces transformed by pain.

Newsha Tavakolian

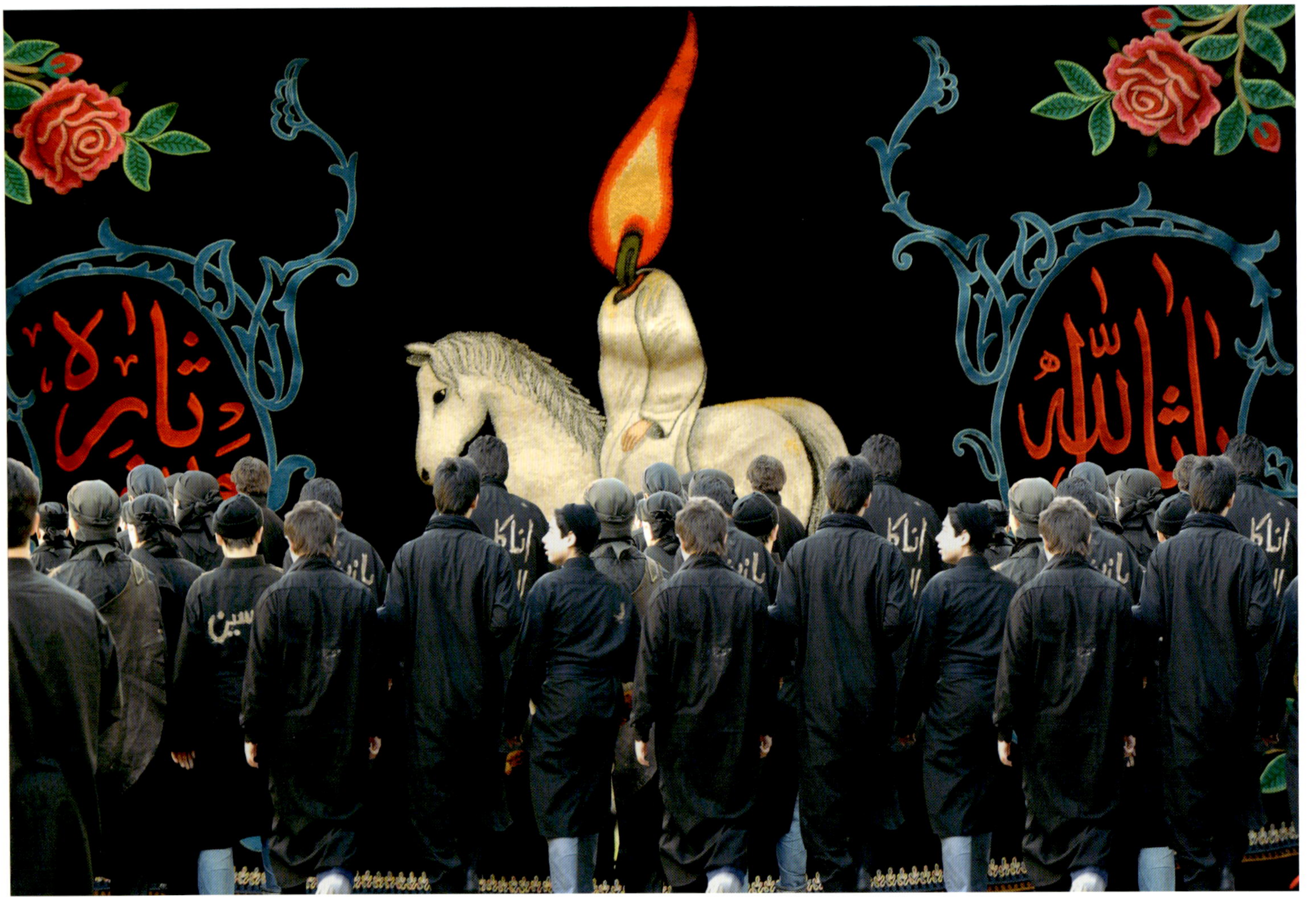

PLATE 86

Sadegh Tirafkan
***Multitude #5*, 2008**
FROM THE SERIES **Multitude**

This print belongs to a series by Sadegh Tirafkan in which multitudes or crowds are united by a singular experience common to Iranians. It captures young men clothed as mourners marching behind a large banner with the image of Imam Husain, whose face is replaced with a flame. The banner references a well-known poem by Muhtasham Kashani (1500–1588) about the Imam's martyrdom at Karbala: "Who is this Husain that the whole world is crazy for him? What a flame he is, that all souls are like butterflies gathered around it."

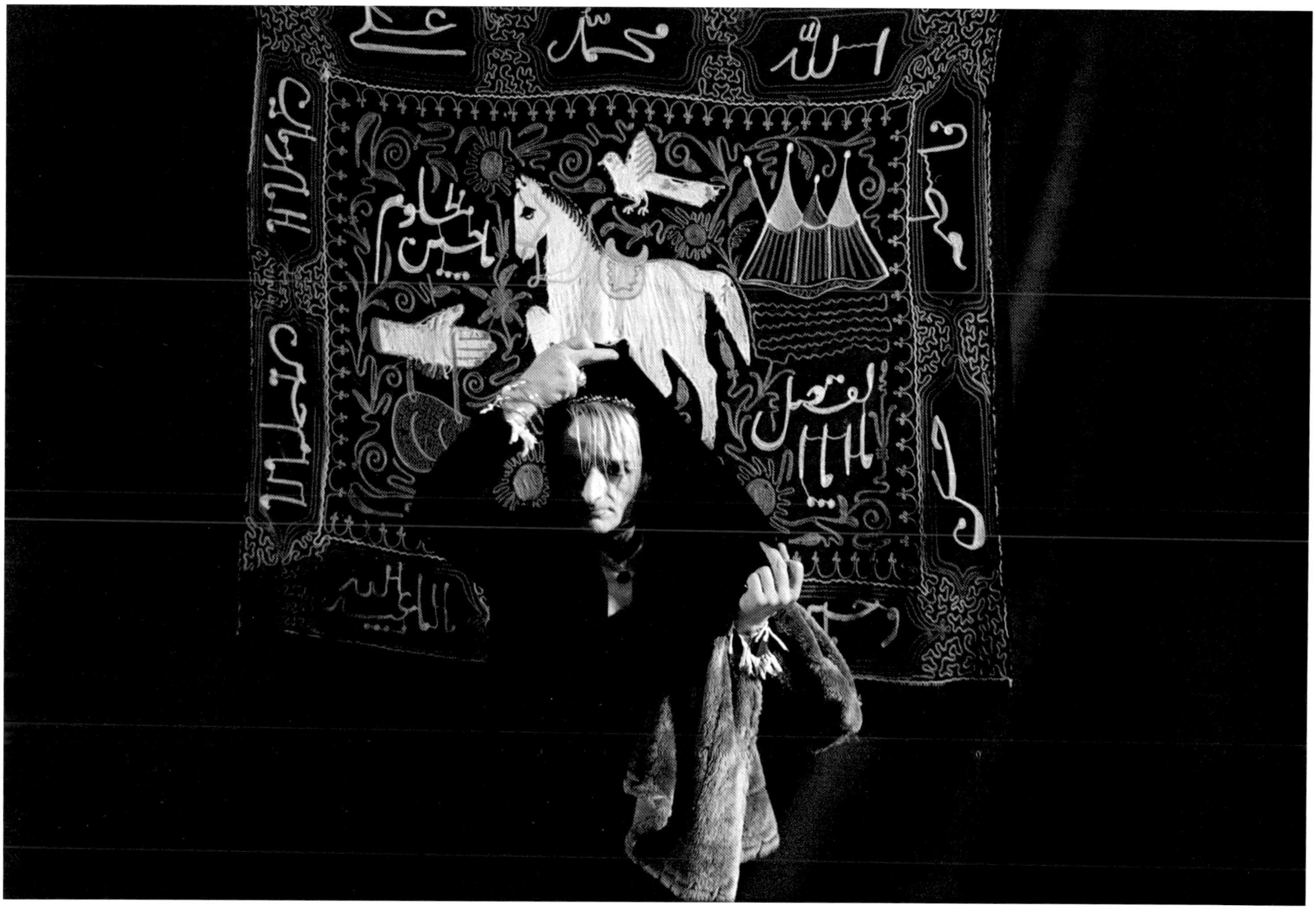

PLATE 87

Tahmineh Monzavi
***Tina*, 2010–12**
FROM THE SERIES Tina

This photograph from the series Tina documents its namesake, a transsexual woman living in Tehran, posed in front of an embroidered banner. The banner is of the type often hung during the months of Muharram and Safar, in which the seventh-century martyrdom of Imam Husain is commemorated. This banner features symbols related to Abbas, Husain's half-brother who was seeking water for the family when his hands were severed by the enemy.

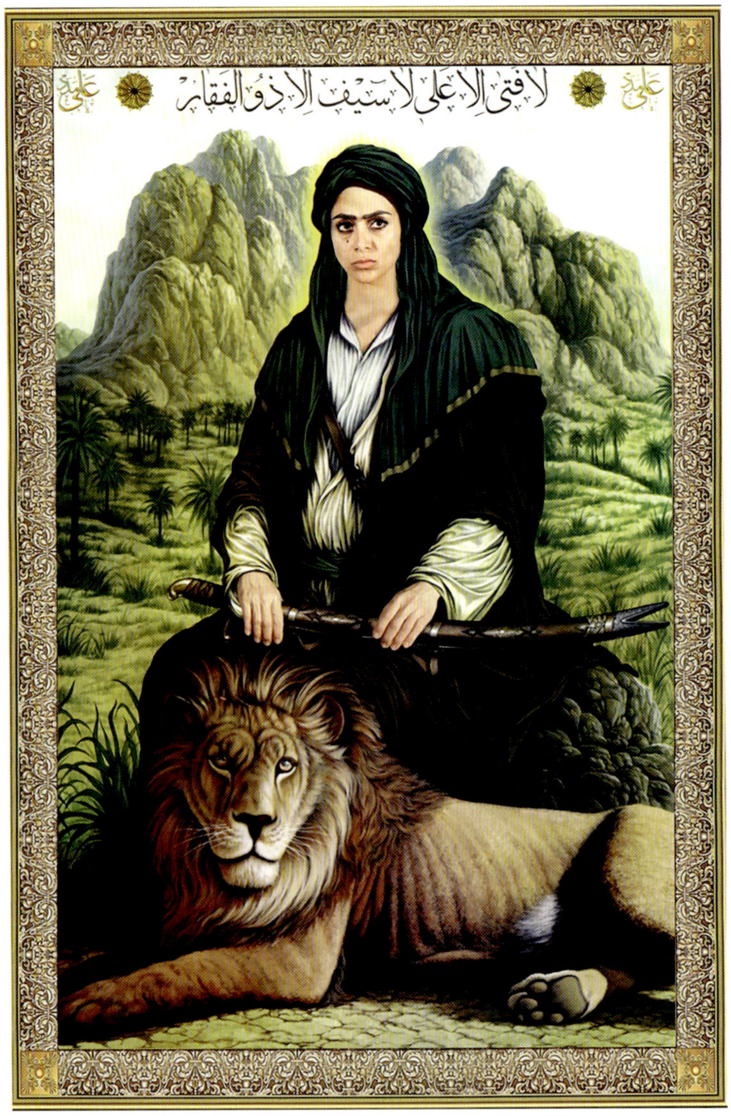

PLATE 88 A

Shoja Azari
***Icon #1*, 2010**
FROM THE SERIES **Icons**

These video portraits are based on a form of poster once popular in Iran (now proscribed) that depicts Shi'ite saints. The men are recognizable by their attributes and inscriptions: the Prophet's son-in-law Ali, with a lion and his famous bifurcated sword; his son Husain, presented by his inscribed name and also with his infant, Ali Asghar, who was killed by an arrow at Karbala; and Abbas, Husain's half-brother, at a river retrieving water. Shoja Azari replaces the men's static visages with videos of women's faces, radically enlivening and transforming the holy figures.

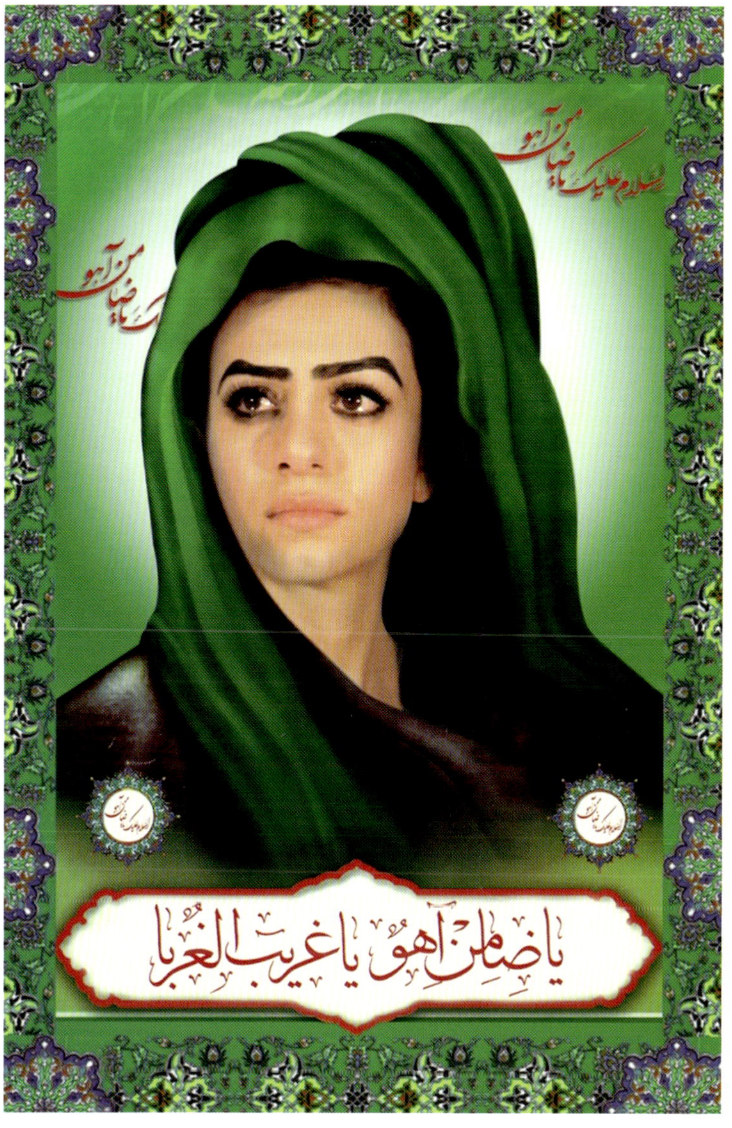

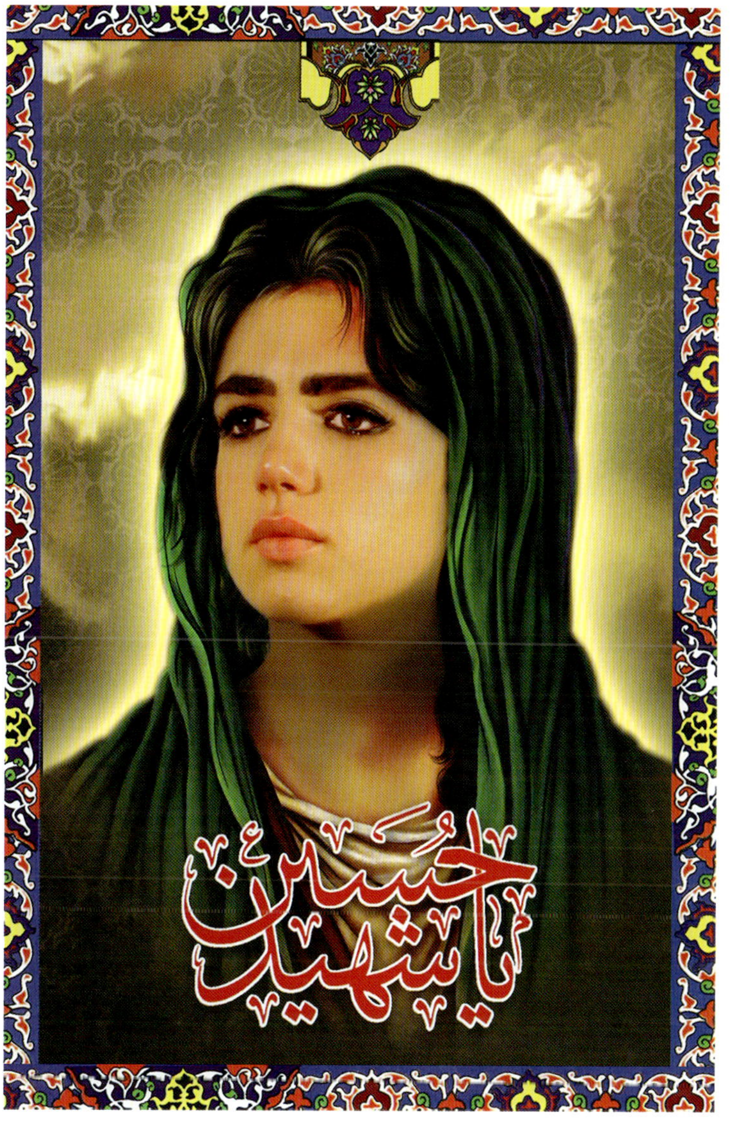

PLATES 88 B–C (RIGHT TO LEFT)

Shoja Azari
***Icon #2*, 2010**
***Icon #3*, 2010**
FROM THE SERIES Icons

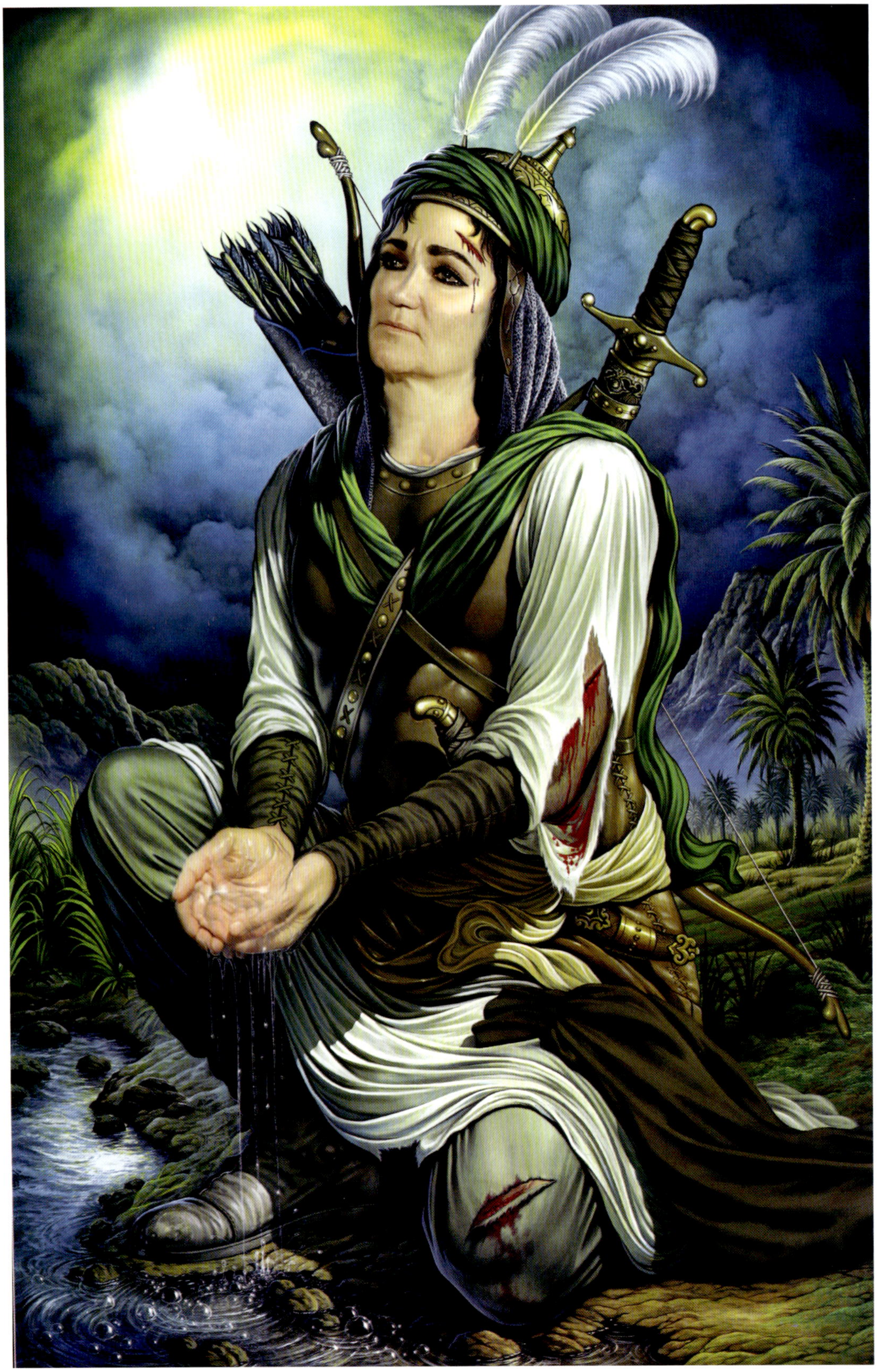

PLATE 88 D

Shoja Azari
***Icon #4*, 2010**
FROM THE SERIES Icons

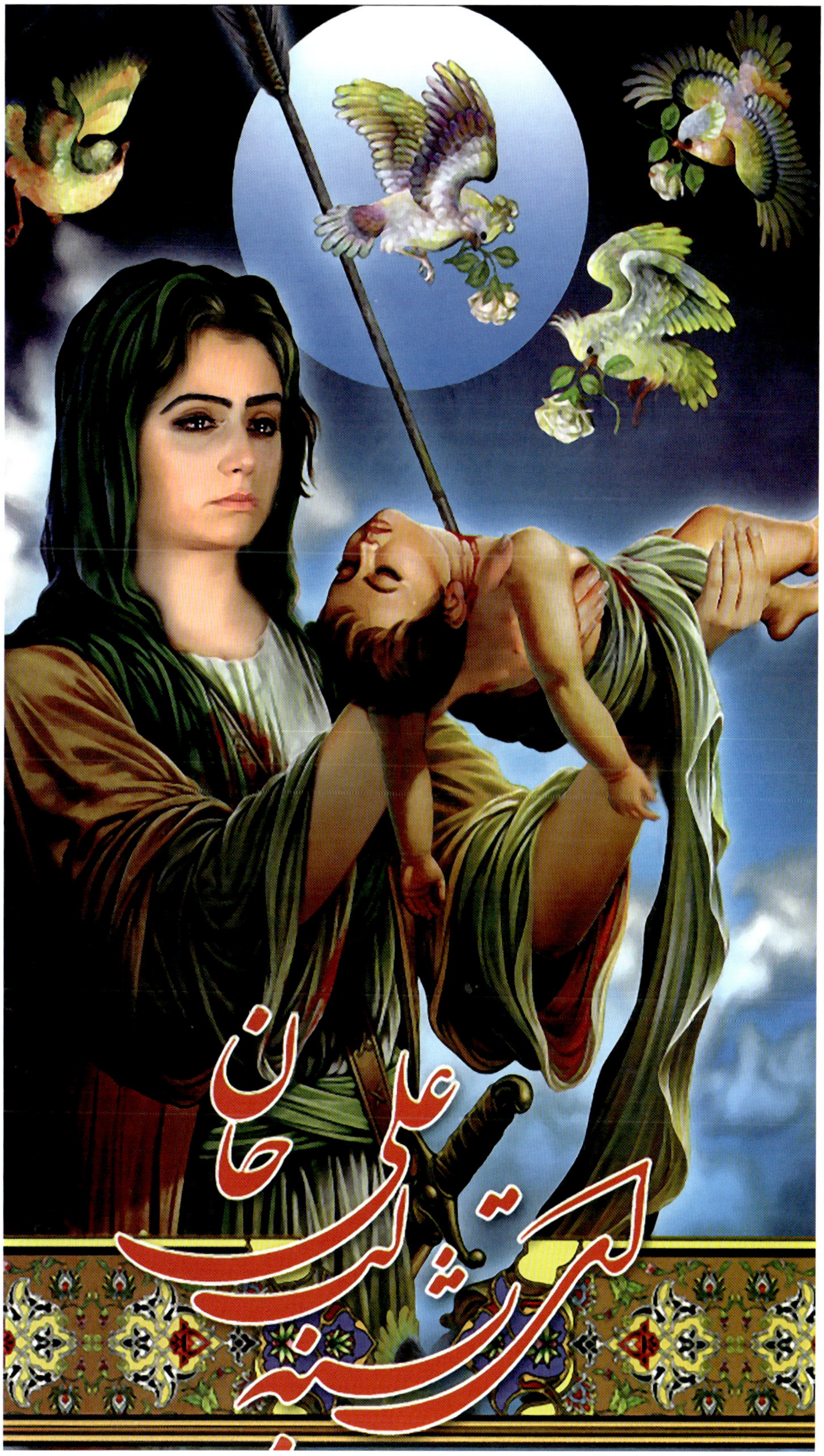

PLATE 88 E

Shoja Azari
Icon #5, 2010
FROM THE SERIES Icons

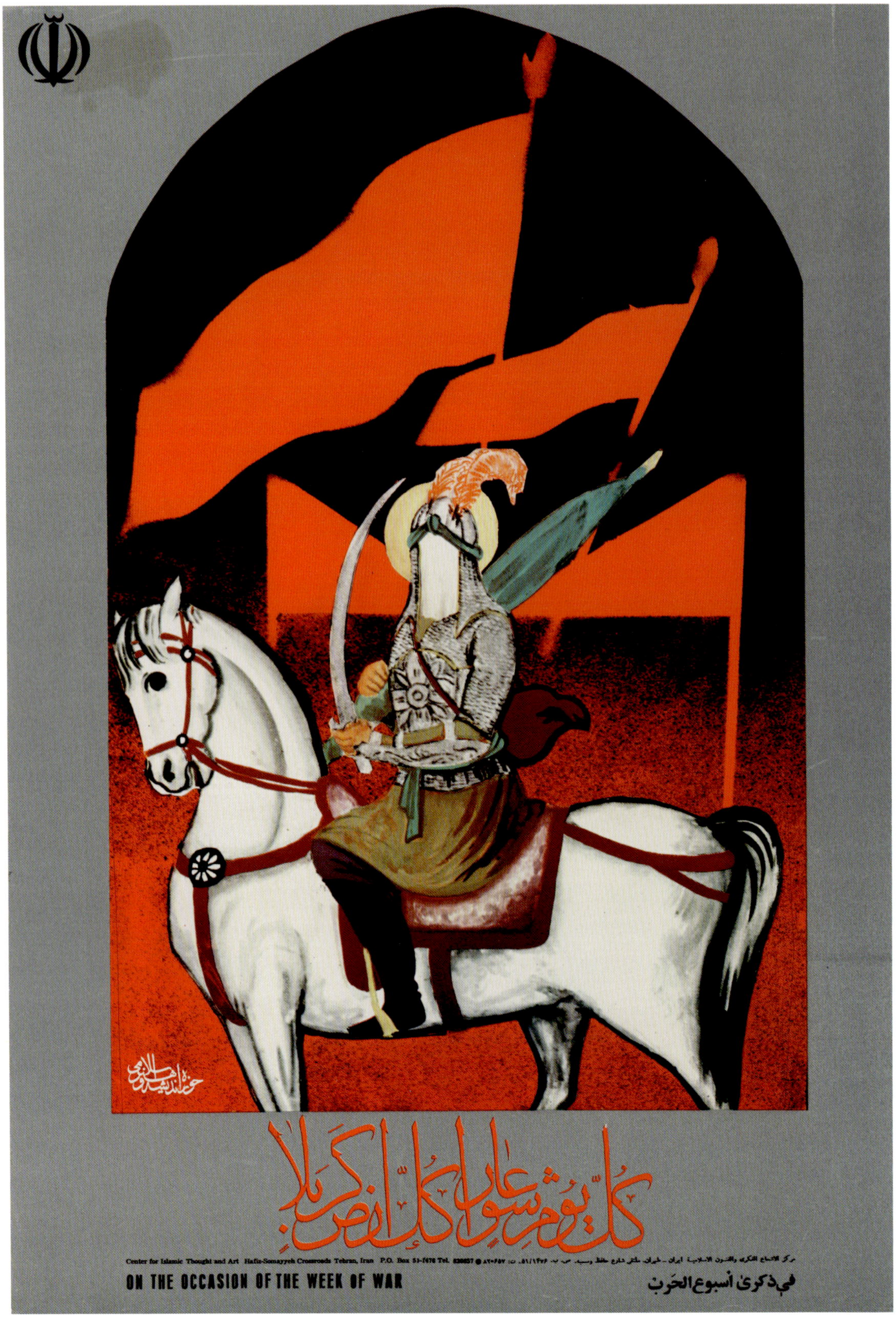

PLATE 89

Kazem Chalipa
***Every Day Is Ashura and Every Land Is Karbala*, 1980s**

This political poster from the 1980s was made to commemorate the Week of War, which is held annually in Iran from August 31 through September 6. It illustrates a core precept of Shi'ism in the never-ending epic of Ashura, through the portrayal of Abbas, Imam Husain's half-brother and standard-bearer, and likewise a martyr of Karbala. Abbas, who was mutilated and killed while in search of water for Husain and his followers, personifies the ideals of loyalty and sacrifice intended here as inspiration for modern-day Iranian soldiers.

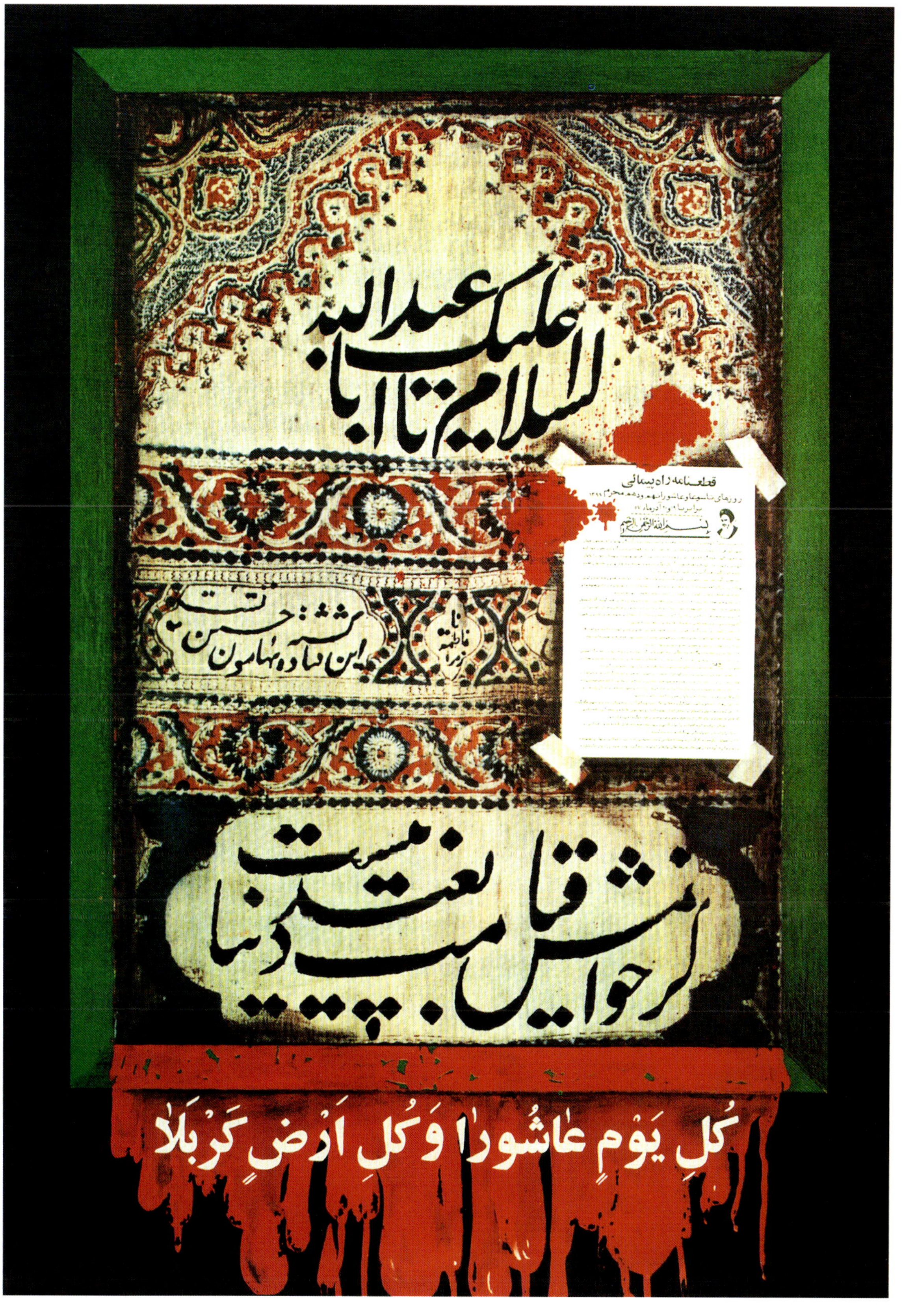

PLATE 90

Habibollah Sadeghi
***Every Day Is Ashura and Every Land Is Karbala*, early 1980s**

Based on the artist's original painting, this poster by Habibollah Sadeghi represents the paradigm of the ongoing battle between the righteous and the wicked, beyond time and place, and epitomized by the massacre of Imam Husain and his family at Karbala. This key event in Shi'ite history occurred on the tenth day of the month of Muharram, or Ashura. At right is a proclamation by Ayatollah Khomeini, issued in the month of Muharram in 1978, in which he drew parallels between Imam Husain's followers and his own followers seeking regime change.

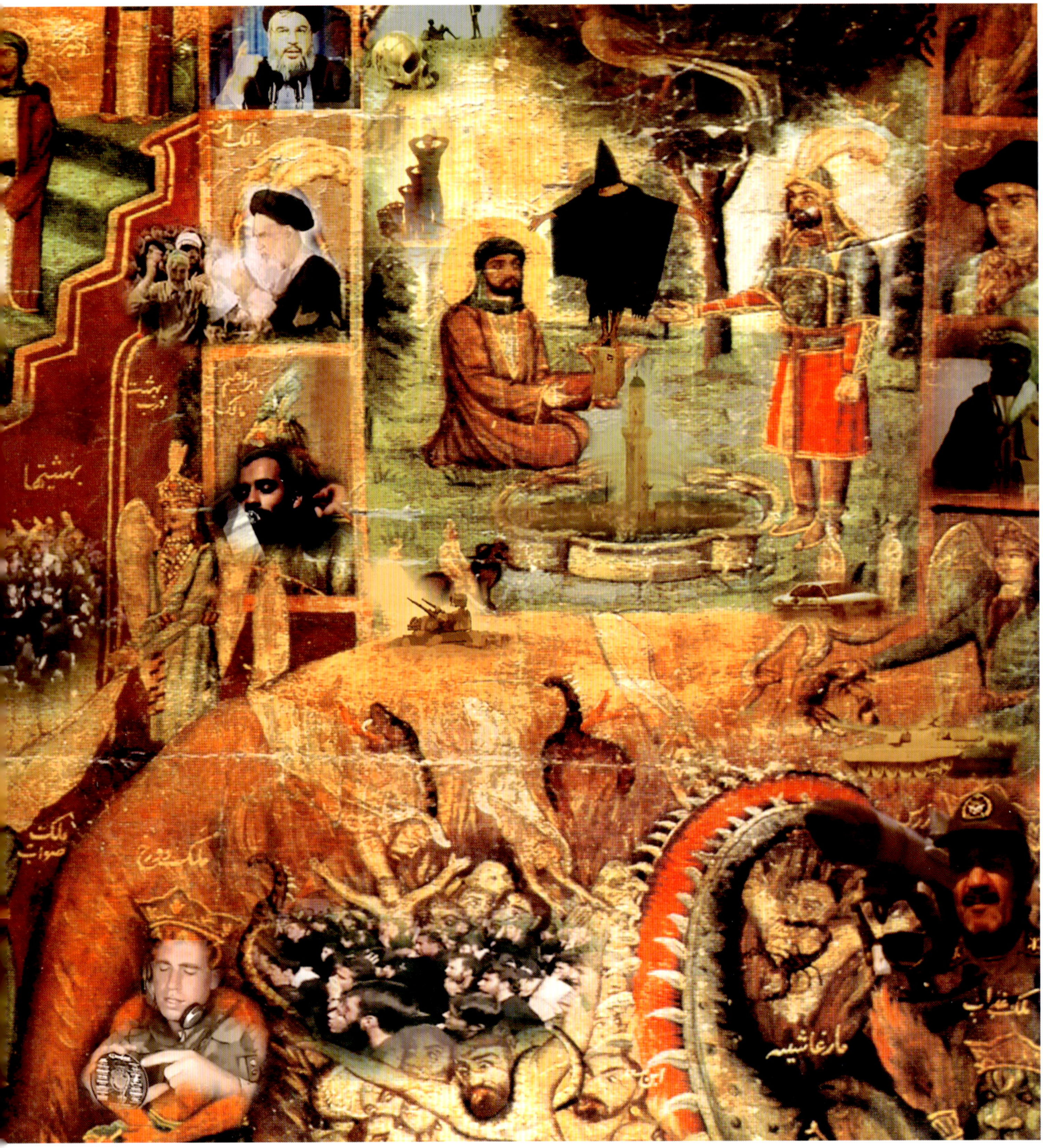

PLATE 91

Shoja Azari
The Day of the Last Judgment (Coffee House Painting), 2009

New York-based Shoja Azari is best known for his video-paintings created from high-definition reproductions of paintings into which he inserts video clips that vastly transform the original works. Here, he takes a typical nineteenth-century so-called coffeehouse painting of martyred Shi'ite imams and the Last Judgment and strategically overlays onto it sequentially timed video clips of battle scenes, religious demonstrations, and modern-day figures such as Ayatollah Khomeini.

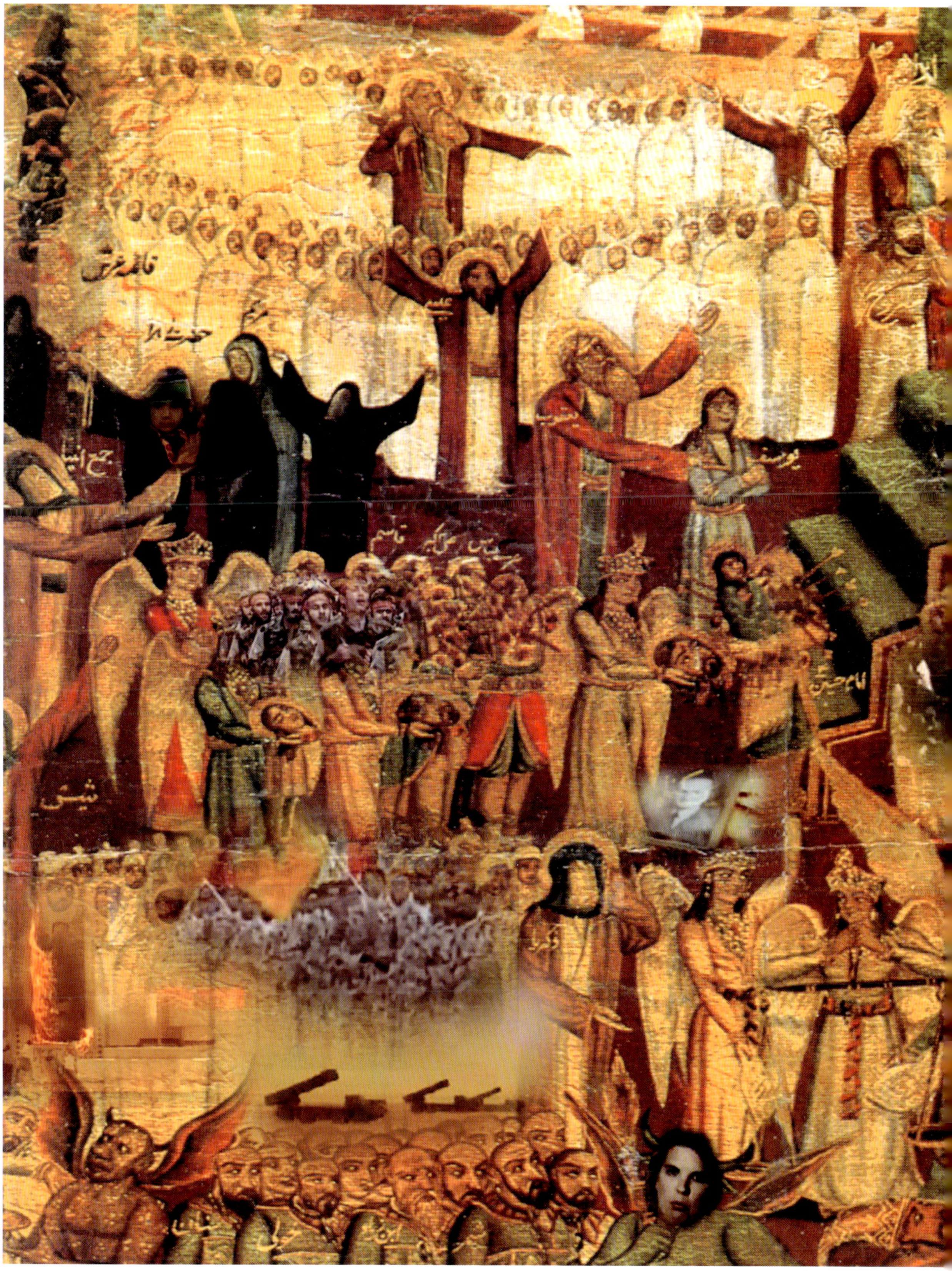

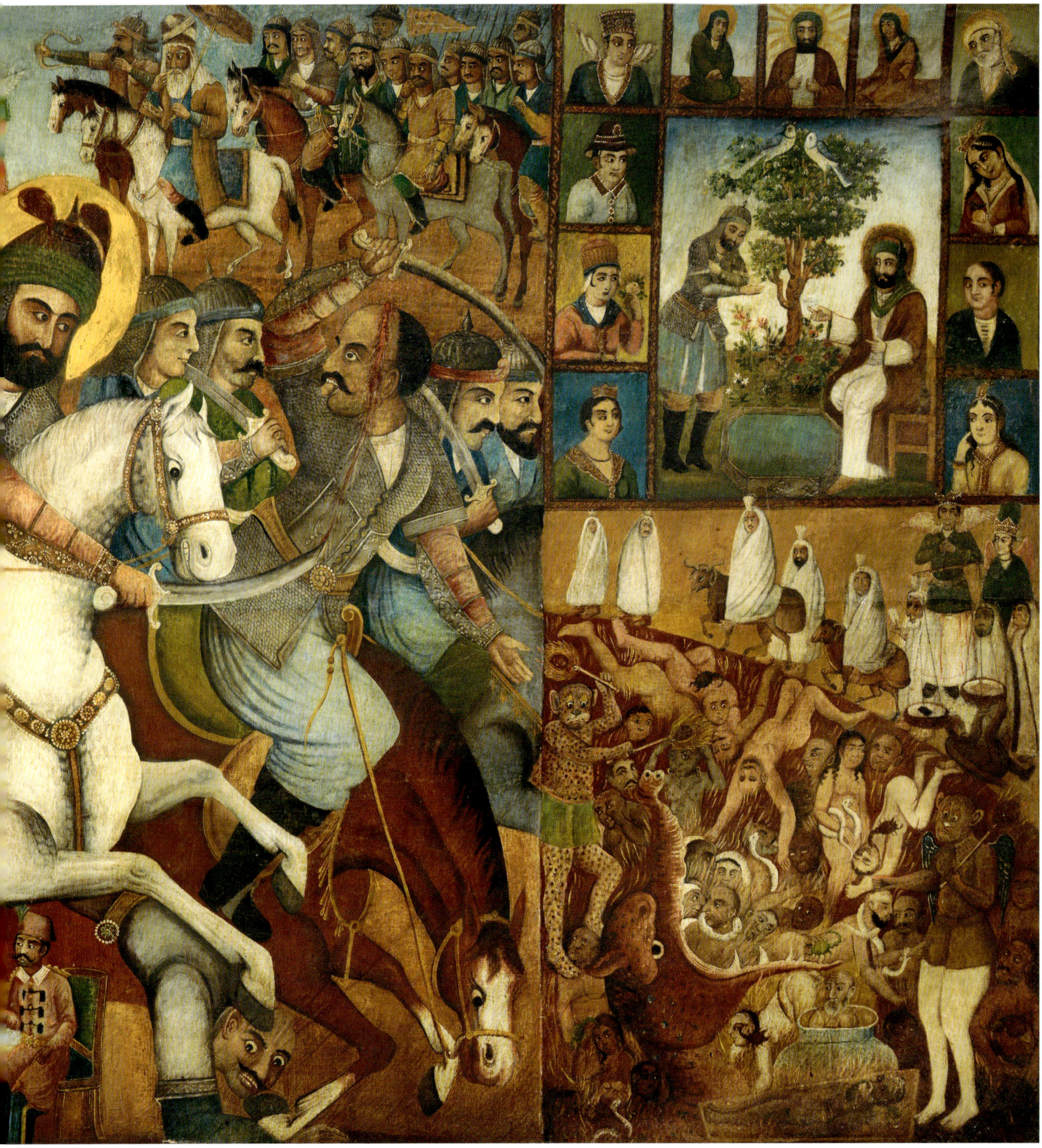

PLATE 92

Abdallah Musavar
***Battle of Karbala*,**
late 19th–early 20th century

Compositions of this type, which belong to a genre often referred to as *parda* paintings, were intended to provide a striking visual form of narration, particularly for Shiʻite subjects such as the massacre of Imam Husain and his companions on the plains of Karbala. Karbala imagery was typically conflated with scenes of the Last Judgment, as depicted here. The central figure mounted on the white horse is Abbas, Husain's half-brother and standard-bearer; in the upper right, the martyred Husain is pictured in Paradise.

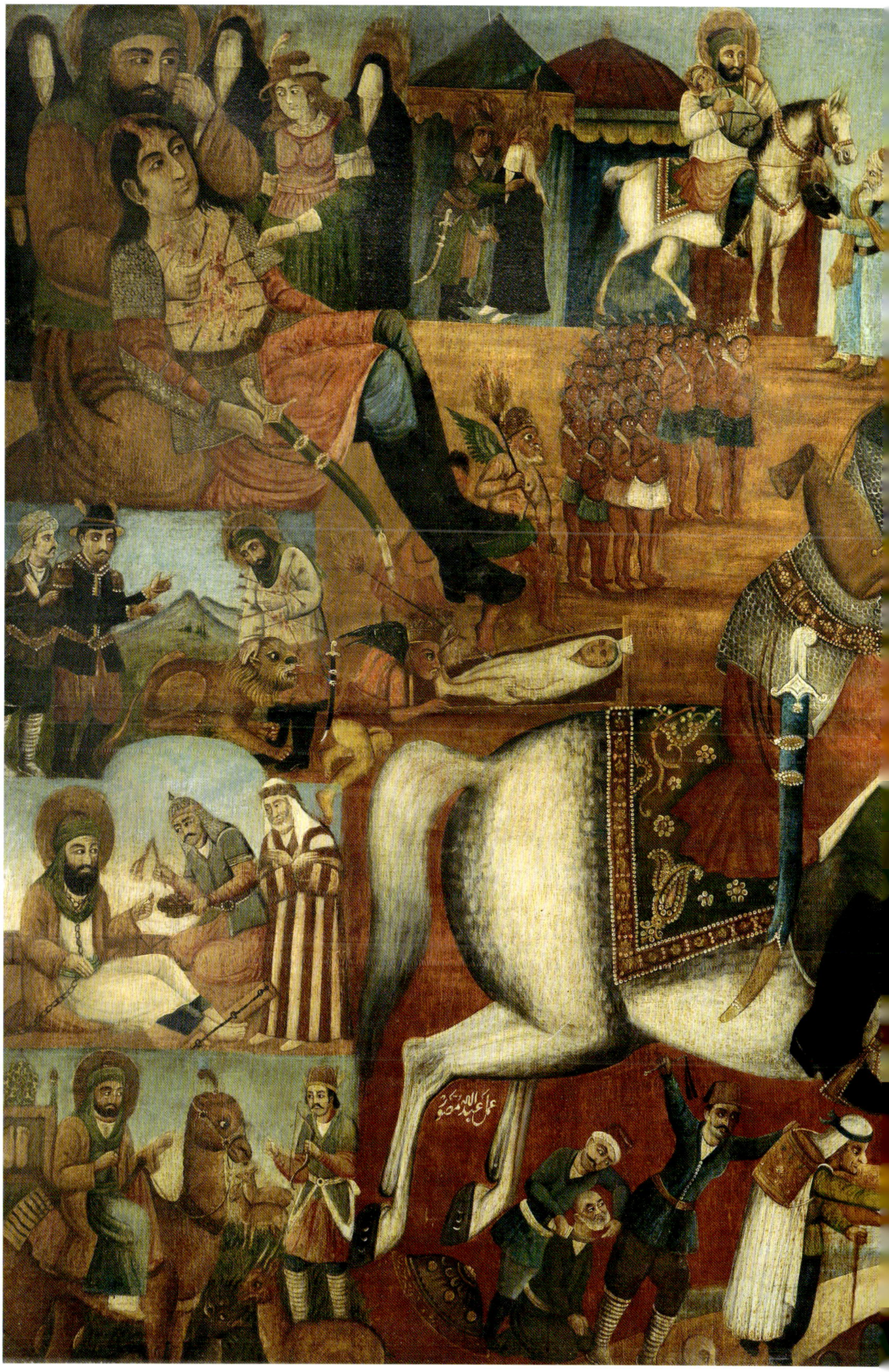

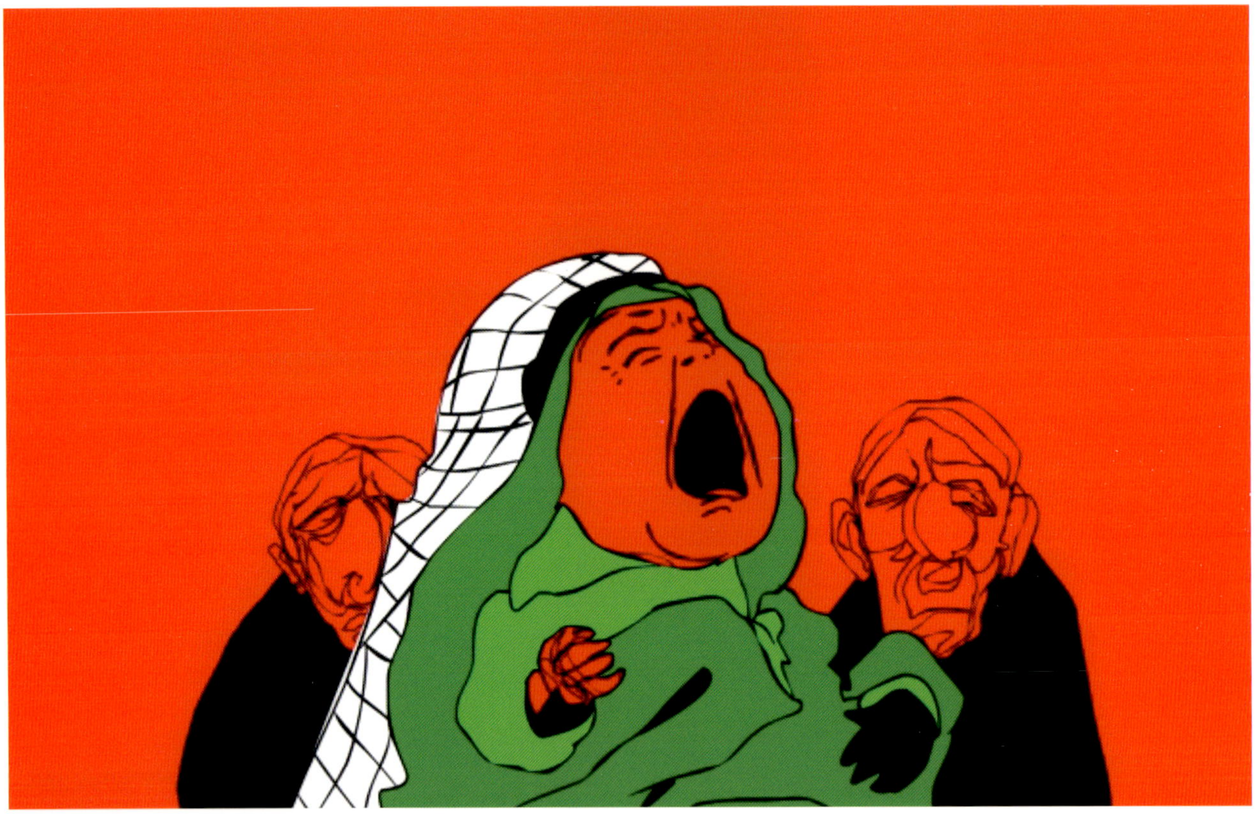

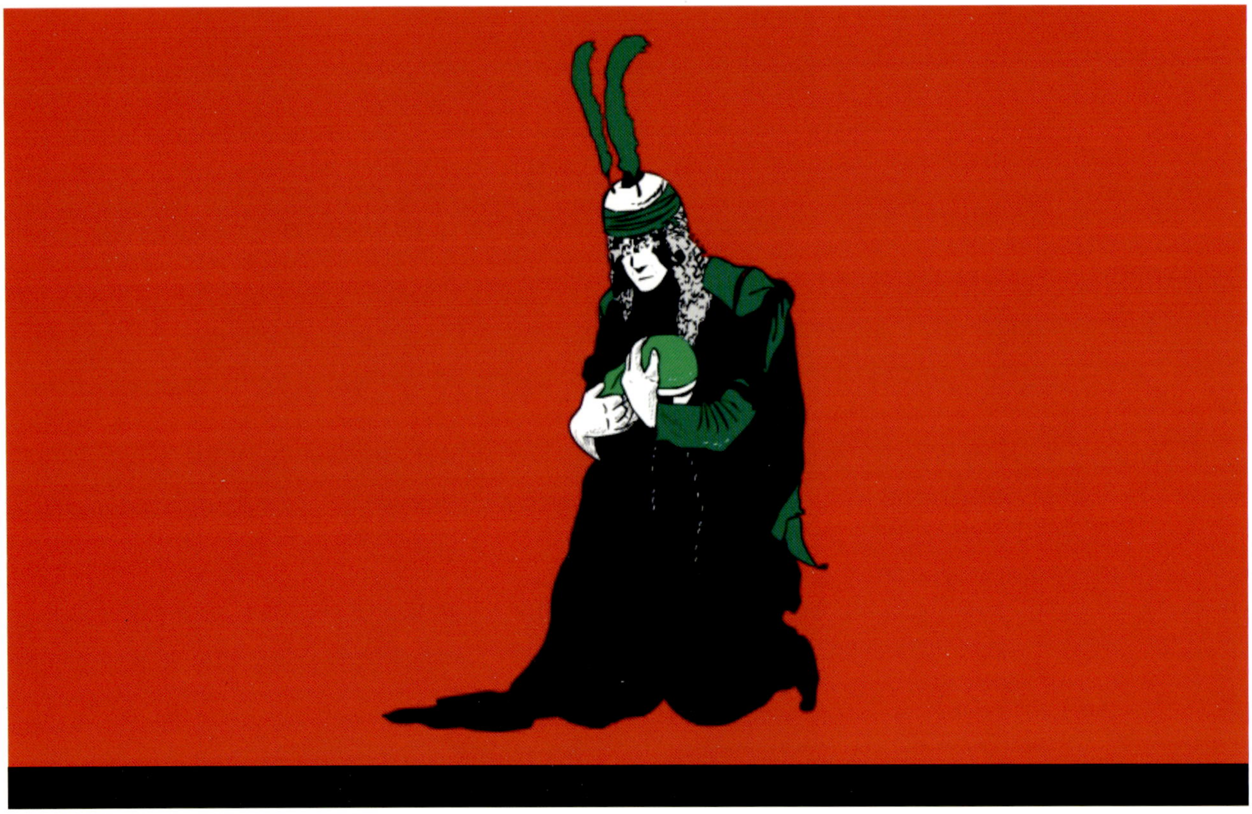

PLATES 93 A–B

Pouya Afshar
***Mourn Baby Mourn*, 2017**

Confronted with the death of a close mentor, Pouya Afshar began a series titled Mourn Baby Mourn that explores *ta'ziya*, a modern form of passion play that re-creates Imam Husain's death. This installation features an animated video with depictions of the historic martyrdom and elements borrowed from the play, such as Ali Asghar, Imam Husain's crying baby, with members of the audience emerging behind him. Afshar seeks to convey both the intense emotional state evoked by ta'ziya and the catharsis of community grieving.

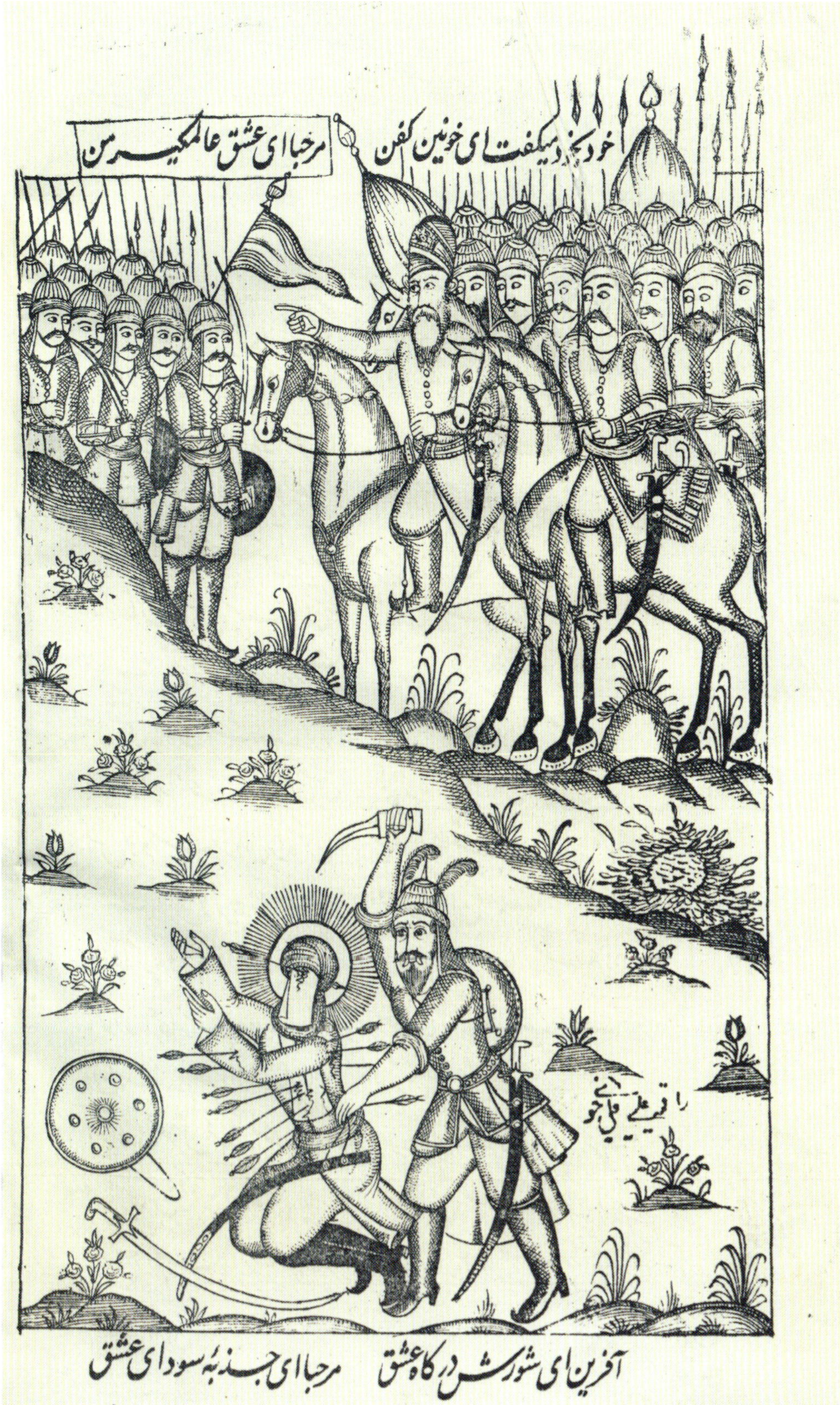

PLATE 94

Ali Quli Khu'i
***Shimr Kills Husain*, AH 1268/1851**
FROM THE *Asrar al-shahada*

The introduction of new technologies from Europe to Iran from the eighteenth century forward often challenged indigenous methods of work. An exception was lithography (introduced in 1821), which perpetuated the same system of manuscript production that had existed for centuries and employed many of the same artists. The pictures, both in terms of which scenes were chosen and the manner in which they were portrayed, often followed the same program of illustration found in traditional manuscripts—as here, in which the scene is similar to depictions from the *Shahnama*.

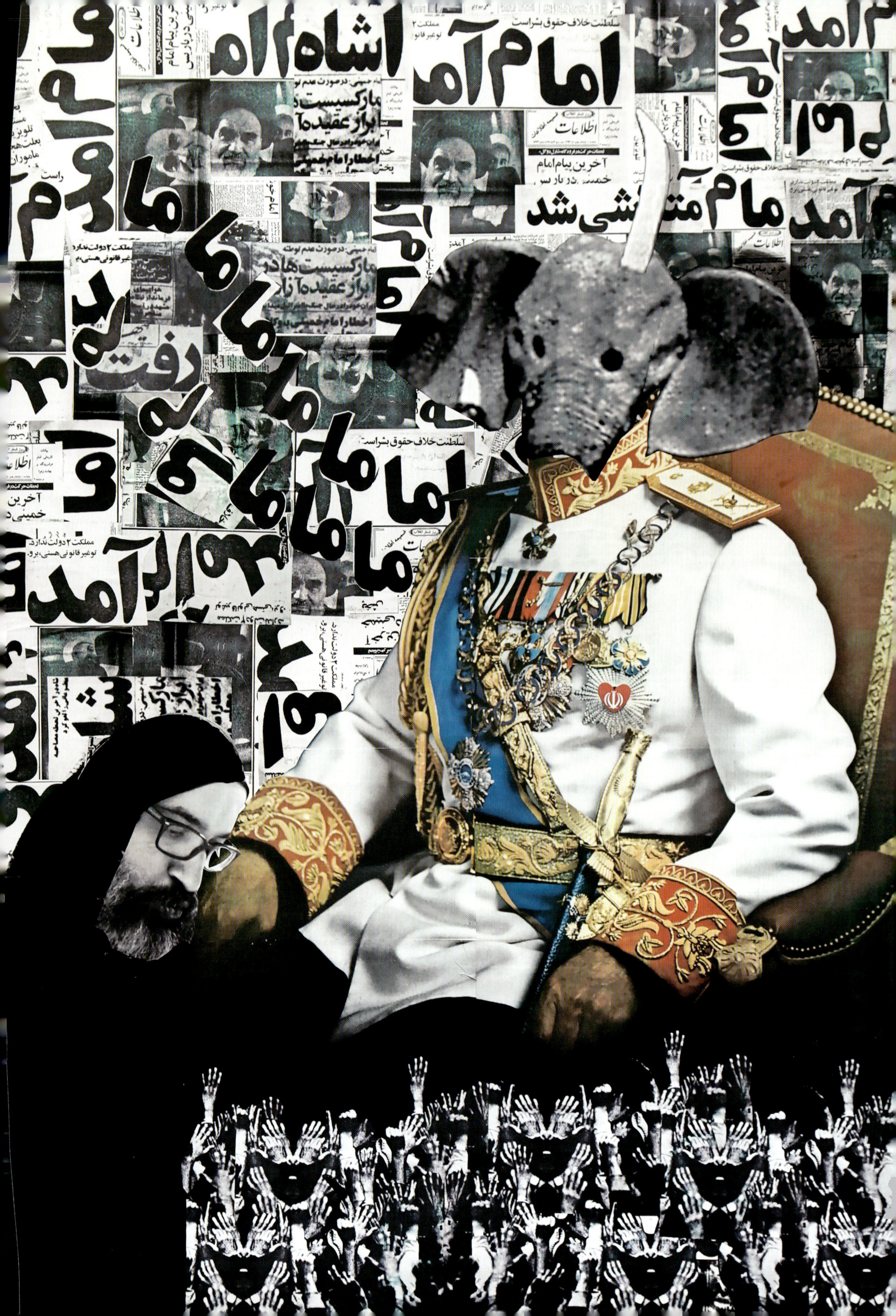

امام آمد
سلطنت خلاف حقوق بشراست
اطلاعات
آخرین پیام امام
رفت
آمد
مملکت ۲ دولت ندارد
توغیر قانونی هستی